Complete
Book of *Ready-to-Use*
Customer
Service
Scripts

MICHAEL C. RAMUNDO

PRENTICE HALL
Paramus, New Jersey 07652

Library of Congress Cataloging-in-Publication Data

Ramundo, Michael C.
    Complete book of ready-to-use customer service scripts / by
Michael Ramundo.
        p.   cm.
    ISBN 0–13–399882–7 (cloth : alk. paper)
    1. Customer services—United States.   2. Business communication—
United States.   I. Title.
HF5415.5.R355   1997
658.8'12—dc21
                                                                        97–10669
                                                                        CIP

Printed in the United States of America

10 9 8 7 6 5 4 3 2 1

ISBN 0-13-399882-7 (c)

Acquisitions Editor: *Tom Power*
Production Editor: *Jackie Roulette*
Formatting/Interior Design: *Dee Coroneos*

ATTENTION: CORPORATIONS AND SCHOOLS

Prentice Hall books are available at quantity discounts with bulk purchase for educational, business, or sales promotional use. For information, please write to: Prentice Hall Career & Personal Development Special Sales, 240 Frisch Court, Paramus, NJ 07652. Please supply: title of book, ISBN, quantity, how the book will be used, date needed.

PRENTICE HALL
Career & Personal Development
Paramus, NJ 07652
A Simon & Schuster Company

On the World Wide Web at http://www.phdirect.com

Prentice Hall International (UK) Limited, *London*
Prentice Hall of Australia Pty. Limited, *Sydney*
Prentice Hall Canada, Inc., *Toronto*
Prentice Hall Hispanoamericana, S.A., *Mexico*
Prentice Hall of India Private Limited, *New Delhi*
Prentice Hall of Japan, Inc., *Tokyo*
Simon & Schuster Asia Pte. Ltd., *Singapore*
Editora Prentice Hall do Brasil, Ltda., *Rio de Janeiro*

Contents

PART TWO
BUILDING YOUR BUSINESS:
CREATING CUSTOMER SATISFACTION—29

Chapter 4
ANSWERING THE QUESTIONS THAT MEAN SALES—31

Chapter 5
CONVINCING THE CUSTOMER OF QUALITY AND
PERFORMANCE CAPABILITY—50

PART THREE
MINDING YOUR BUSINESS:
MAINTAINING CUSTOMER SATISFACTION—67

Chapter 6
TAKING ORDERS, ESTABLISHING RELATIONSHIPS—69

Chapter 7
FOLLOWING UP, BUILDING RELATIONSHIPS—89

Chapter 8
PROFITING FROM COMPLAINTS—113

Chapter 9
TURNING PROBLEM CUSTOMERS INTO YOUR BEST CUSTOMERS—149

Chapter 10
PROFITING FROM DISASTER—158

Chapter 11
CREDIT AND COLLECTIONS—168

Chapter 12
TRAINING CUSTOMERS—192

Chapter 13
ON SITE AND FACE TO FACE—232

PART FOUR
WITHIN YOUR BUSINESS:
SATISFYING THE INTERNAL CUSTOMER—285

Chapter 14
CUSTOMER-ORIENTED LEADERSHIP—287

Chapter 15
A ROCK, A HARD PLACE, AND YOU:
SCENARIOS FOR THE NEW OFFICE POLITICS—339

Why This Book Is for You

This book is a supremely practical guide to doing customer service in ways you may never have thought of doing customer service before. So it is fitting and proper that I begin this book in a way that absolutely no other customer-service book has ever been begun before: in Latin.

De gustibus non est disputandem.

That is what the Roman poet Horace said some 2,000 years ago. It means: *You can't argue about taste.* You like your red Miata. She likes her gray Taurus. She likes dried tomatoes. You don't care a fig for tomatoes, dried or wet. And so it goes. Many of our purchase decisions are based on taste, the one factor in a decision no one can argue about.

You've got a product or service to sell. You can try to anticipate consumer taste. You can even try to cultivate that taste through ads and commercials. You can add certain elements of special quality and value. You can create the most advanced technology. You can even adjust your price downward. However, do what you will, at some point it all hinges on taste. This has been an accepted fact for probably a lot longer than 2,000 years.

But 2,000 years ago there was no such thing as Customer Service, and I'm here to tell you that the time has finally come to rethink this whole *De gustibus* thing. Business is finally waking up to the fact that it does have something in addition to intrinsic quality, value, and technology to balance against the whims of taste. The weight that can tip the scales in your favor is *service*.

Modern techniques of design, manufacture, communication, and media management have leveled the competitive playing field dramatically. Commercial products are increasingly similar, can come from anywhere, and all offer high-quality performance. This will be even more true in the near future, as the world's annual gross domestic product grows from $26 trillion to $48 trillion over the next fifteen years.

Look at the personal-computer industry, for example. You would think that high technology would give one manufacturer the competitive edge over another and drive consumer choice. But the fact is that scores, even thousands of manufacturers—30,000 in the U.S. alone, at last count—are turning out PCs featuring similar degrees of high technology at comparable prices. Moreover, sales price for a given performance capability is plunging and will continue to do so for the foreseeable future. What else plunges? Corporate behemoths that place their faith in brand loyalty rather than dedicate their resources to creating customer loyalty. It is no secret that mighty IBM learned this immutable truth the hard way, flying high with $6.5 billion profits one year, only to augur-in with a $9 billion loss the next. In the PC industry, it has become apparent that the degree and quality of customer service and support offered, more than the degree and quality of technology, confer the competitive edge. Everyone offers high technology at about the same prices, but not everyone offers equal levels of customer service and support. It is no accident that the handful of manufacturers offering the best customer service are the companies who sell the most computers. The rest of the pack? Well, they are left to depend on the whims of taste for the bulk of their sales. And you can't argue about taste.

HARD TO KILL

There are two more important points to make about the example of the PC industry: First, Big Blue wasn't the only company to take a hit. A personal computer is appearing on virtually every desk, yet the lifespan of many computer manufacturers has been measurable in nanoseconds. Neglect customer service, and you don't live long. Second, what is true of the PC industry is true of most other enterprises as well. Neglect customer service, and you don't live long. Consider Pan American Airlines, American Motors, or the thousands of new products that survive less than one year on your grocery shelf.

While businesses and products are distressingly easy to kill, one of the many paradoxes of human nature is that dead paradigms are hard to kill. The traditional paradigm casts customer service into a "support" role as opposed to a "revenue producing" function. In fact, many companies have traditionally seen, and too many continue to see, customer service as nothing more or less than a necessary evil: a cost center you've got to spend money on, because every business needs a "Complaint Department." Well, the paradigms, they are a changin'. Playing on an increasingly level field of technology and access to the media, more and more companies look to customer service not for "support" in the traditional sense, but for revenue production. This book will help these companies drive a stake into the heart of old-paradigm customer service once and for all, and it will provide the practical tools required to perform positive, profitable service in a new business environment. How?

Let's go back to that dead paradigm for just a minute. Not only (according to the outmoded model) did customer service fail to make money, it didn't *make* anything at all. In contrast, other divisions in an enterprise were productive. They actually *made* stuff, and they had the tools to prove it: punch presses, lathes, computers, and so on.

Cast in the new paradigm, customer service is also very much in the business of production. It *makes* customers. It makes better customers, more reliable customers, more loyal customers, and more satisfied customers. We can put this another way: customer service creates satisfaction.

Now, like any other production department, Customer Service requires tools. *The Complete Book of Ready-to-Use Customer Service Scripts* provides these in plenty: It is a comprehensive kit containing precision-crafted and ergonomically designed tools for every customer-service application.

DON'T STOP NOW

I could stop now and go on to the rest of the book. After all, I've given you a new paradigm. What more could you want? The fact is that the shift in thinking about customer service is even more profound than I have suggested. You see, if leading-edge companies have learned to redefine their Customer Service departments, they are also learning to redefine their customer-service concepts. This is happening in two ways.

First, as leading-edge firms have learned, or are in the process of learning, if you intend to remain competitive, you can no longer confine customer service to a Customer Service department. Customer service must become the business of every department and every individual in the company. Modern communications, data-processing, and data-sharing technologies have all helped flatten traditional corporate hierarchies. These days, it is no longer just the sales staff or the customer-service staff that has direct contact with customers. Increasingly, just about everyone in an organization is touching and is touched by the "outside." Accordingly, this book is not restricted reading, for customer-service department eyes only, it is written for everyone in the organization, not because I want everyone in the organization to know about customer service, but because everyone in the organization "does" customer service, at least some of the time. That's a fact. The choice that still remains is whether to do brilliant customer service, lackluster customer service, or terrible customer service.

It is not sufficient to rethink customer service and to liberate it from a single department. You have to rethink the concept of *customer*. This is not just a matter of profiling your customer through tests and market studies. That's important, but it doesn't go far enough. You have to consider that customers are not just those folks out there who purchase your goods and services. You have internal customers, too: colleagues, bosses, subordinates within your organization. The same explosion in data-collection technology that puts practically everyone in direct contact with external customers has put practically everyone in direct contact with internal customers as well. The organizational pyramid is flattening. Power is falling to the front line, and teams are replacing management hierarchies as the corporate norm. Entire levels of supervision are being wiped out, and it is easy to tout any good idea with plentiful support and documentation. Potentially, any individual within the company has access to the information necessary to create a decent argument in support of this or that idea or conclusion.

What determines whose idea will be accepted by the corporate culture? What determines who has the greatest degree of influence and success? And just who are those individuals who realize this potential by creating an internal following?

They are the people who define their *internal* customers and tilt their ideas and agendas to these customers and ensure that they support their specific needs. They sell them their ideas, services, wishes, beliefs, commands, instructions, and conclusions. And then they respond to their customers' needs concerning these "products." By supporting and servicing what they "sell," these individuals create satisfaction among their internal customers.

LET'S STOP NOW

Let's stop for a moment so that you'll be sure to find what you're looking for in this book.

1. If you are called a Customer Service Rep, you'll find the tools you need to create customer satisfaction.

2. If you are called Something Else, you'll find the tools you need to create customer satisfaction.

3. If you want to live long and prosper within your organization, you'll find the tools you need to create satisfaction among your many internal customers: colleagues, subordinates, bosses.

The fifteen chapters that follow treat every aspect of Customer Service and are divided into four main areas, covering communication skills (including telephone techniques and face-to-face tactics), and techniques and strategies for getting new business, for transforming customer dissatisfaction into customer satisfaction, and for building and enhancing current business. The two chapters of Part IV deal specifically with creating satisfaction in the internal customer, and the last chapter in this section of the book explores that mission in terms of the evolving politics of the contemporary business world.

Throughout, my goal has been to provide information that is as specific as possible. Instead of abstract principles and lofty fragments of advice, you will find detailed scripts and scenarios ready to be adapted to your particular situations and circumstances.

One word of caution before we begin. It would be very convenient if you could deal with each and every Customer Service situation by turning to a prepared script or, more realistically, by popping up a script on a computer screen, and simply reading verbatim. Very convenient indeed. But years of experience have demonstrated to me that, unfortunately, such cut-and-dried approaches are doomed to fail. No customer wants his or her "unique" issue or problem answered out of a can. Accordingly, I have worked very hard to make these scripts and scenarios flexible, the basis for imaginative improvisation, ready to be shaped and adapted to fit the myriad special circumstances all Customer Service professionals encounter.

In the preceding paragraph, I used the term "Customer Service professional." Just who is that? Before we get down to business, let me make certain you know who I think you are. Let me tell you who I have written this book for. Everybody.

Because everybody in the company has customers, external and internal. Of course, this includes the staff of the Customer Service Department, but everyone, in every department, who ever speaks, writes, or responds to a customer is, *de facto* (ah, more Latin!), a Customer Service professional. Now: How may I help you?

Acknowledgments

A special thanks to Ellen Coleman, Tom Power, Jacqueline Roulette, Alan Axelrod, Bert Holtje, and all the great folks at Prentice Hall. Without their support and effort this work would never have been completed.

To my lovely wife, Beverly Thomas. I've spent endless hours on airplanes and in lonely hotel rooms just tapping away on a keyboard. It makes no sense without you. Thanks for the endless support and love; thanks for just being there.

To Tara and Jonathan. It is all for you and tomorrow. I can lend a hand and guide, but I cannot touch. You have three lifetimes, I have but one.

One^Part

Off the Hook:
A Telephone
Primer

Chapter

1

The Call-Ownership Concept

WHAT COMES AFTER "HELLO?"

None of the many machines that drive and are driven by contemporary business life is more used, abused, necessary, loved, and hated than the telephone. It is a means of opening doors and windows to the outside, and it is just as surely a means of shutting them tight. The telephone is your customers' lifeline to you, something that is of more than passing importance to your customers, of course, but also critically important to you. "Dead" customers won't keep your business alive. Yet this same instrument is all too often the means by which customers are put off, put down, and driven away. The phone can be the vehicle for delivering personal service in an impersonal world, or it can be just another electronic pigeonhole into which an indifferent "corporate entity" sorts and holds yet another "problem."

If there is a Jekyll and Hyde in this situation, the telephone is neither the good doctor nor the evil villain. It is an instrument and nothing more, an instrument that conveys the will and intention of whomever happens to be operating it. Unfortunately, all too many users of the telephone suffer from one or more of the following destructive attitudes:

1. An unwillingness to communicate.

2. An unwillingness to help.

3. A feeling that the customer is an intrusion.

Invert these ills, and you will have created the three fundamentals of creative telephone usage and, not incidentally, effective customer service:

3

1. Develop not just a willingness to communicate, but a zeal for communication.

2. Develop not just a willingness to help, but a desire to help.

3. Don't merely overcome the conviction that customers are an intrusion into your business; realize that they *are* your business.

What comes after "Hello"? Actually, most telephone difficulties begin *before* hello.

1. The phone rings. You pick it up, and the customer has hung up.
   The fact is that incoming calls should be answered within two or three rings or twenty seconds. You won't find this in any business course. It's just plain common sense. Most customers will hang up after four to five rings, or six tops. That is, unless they are very highly motivated to contact you. Now, when is a customer "highly motivated" to get through to Customer Service? The answer, of course, is when the customer decided to take valuable time and give you a call for some urgent reason. How is that customer going to feel if the urgent problem waits through six, seven, eight telephone rings? You are wasting his or her valuable time. By the time you do pick up the phone, you are going to be talking to one angry, anxious customer, who has already made a negative judgment about your firm's responsiveness, or lack of it.
   And this is the *best* you can hope for, if you don't answer the phone quickly. In many cases, the customer will hang up after four rings. So what? Does that mean that you've avoided hearing a complaint? Maybe. Maybe you also lost an order. Maybe it also means that you've lost a customer. And maybe he or she will also tell others not to call you, and that is the *worst* that can happen.
   The solution: Be fast. Pick up the phone within twenty seconds, preferably on the first ring.

2. In a busy customer-service operation, and on a busy day, you may start to feel like Shiva, that Indian goddess with all those arms. Don't let the rhythm of answering multiple calls trip you up into speaking before you actually pick up the phone.
   Never happen? An insult to your intelligence?
   Just think about how many times you have called the firm of Dewey, Cheatham & Howe, only to be greeted with " . . . and Howe." Pick up the phone, put it to your ear, then greet the caller. If you are wearing a headset, be sure you punch in the call before you start to speak. If your headset is being "beeped"—a call is coming—"dwell" for a second or so before speaking.
   But let's not say "hello" yet. Because, long before you answer the phone, there are certain factors you should address. You need to address these for yourself as well as through coaching and counseling with your team. You may bring to that telephone you are about to answer all of your professional commitment, goodwill, and good intentions, but you also bring to it your personal stresses, anxieties, and

annoyances. Of course, you cannot regulate all of the stress in your life, but you can at least learn to recognize and regulate your flash points. Before you even think about greeting that next call, try to reduce or eliminate some of the factors that make you less than a 100 percent effective telephone communicator:

1. Do you need to get more sleep? Fatigue reduces your patience and tolerance, rendering you vulnerable to angry outbursts. Efficiency is not productivity; efficiency plus effectiveness is productivity. Don't work your team to death.

2. Are you hungry? Given a choice, handle difficult calls after breakfast or after lunch. Hunger makes many people impatient and even irritable. People need control over their own destiny. Allow your team to schedule themselves on the phone log. You focus on the overall performance standards. Let them work out the process.

3. Do you really need another cup of coffee? Caffeine mimics many of the physiological changes of anxiety and rage. The pulse increases. The blood pressure rises. Tolerance and even temper generally diminish.

4. Are you comfortable? Should you turn up the air conditioning or open a window? Heat or a stuffy, stifling atmosphere makes most people more irritable. (Traffic jams are always worse in the dead of a "dogday afternoon.")

5. What about your personal surroundings? Maybe you are blessed with a spacious and comfortable office. Maybe you're stuck in an impersonal cubicle. Whatever your workplace or workstation is like, do whatever you can to make it more comfortable. Bring a personal item or two to decorate your desk. Try to eliminate the dozen little things that annoy you: the fluorescent fixture that buzzes, or the clock that ticks too loudly. Encourage employees to personalize their work spaces as well.

6. Do you like what you do? Some of us enjoy talking to the public. Some of us don't. Really, if you aren't happy with customer-service work, get another job. This work will drive you nuts if you don't like dealing with people. You can't fake it for very long, so even if you need the work, do it as effectively as you can, but go ahead and seek another position elsewhere. As a manager, make sure you select people who truly enjoy working with the public.

Now, at long last, the greeting. "Hello" is an okay way to start a call. But, in the world of business, "okay" rarely puts you at the top. Customer service starts with your greeting. That is, it starts even before the customer has uttered a word. Because you already know what the caller wants. Information.

Whatever else the caller may want, you can be certain that information is at the heart of it. Therefore, pack your greeting with information:

Good morning. This is Utopia Widgets, Jane Smith speaking. How may I help you?

In fourteen words, uttered in the course of perhaps five seconds, this greeting supplies four key pieces of information:

1. The caller is speaking to someone who is pleasant, polite, and civil ("Good morning").

2. The caller has reached a specific place. (Utopia Widgets). This saves the caller the "chore" of asking if he or she has reached the intended target. It also saves a good deal of time and effort in the event that the caller has dialed you by mistake: "Oh! I'm sorry. I was calling my brother-in-law!"

3. The caller has reached a specific person inside the company: you, Jane Smith, a human being with a name. This is absolutely critical! People do not need companies to help them. They need people to help them.

4. The caller learns that you are eager to help, and willing to accept responsibility.

Let's explore that last one: "Good morning. This is Utopia Widgets, Jane Smith speaking. How may I help you?" The question *How* may I help you?" not only conveys a helping attitude, it actually focuses the conversation right from the start. This saves time, reduces frustration, and even makes the "helping" possible in the first place. By contrast, the phrase "May I help you?," certainly a polite enough choice, leaves the caller adrift. "How may I help you?" drives the call to the heart of the matter.

Ultimately, your telephone greeting should convey a commitment to customer satisfaction. Most immediately, it must convey your ownership of the call.

The dread so many customers face when they dial a service number is that they will waste valuable time and emotional energy in a frustrating process of being handed off from one department or individual to another. Picking up the phone to call XYZ Corporation Customer Service, the caller is already resigned to disappointment, anxiety, and frustration. Is this paranoia and delusion? Unfortunately, all too often, it is nothing less than a perception of reality. Customers are routinely given an unwanted tour of many departments before they finally reach someone who can actually help them.

The research done in the area is clear. It is virtually impossible to create customer satisfaction after the customer has been transferred to three or four individuals or departments. Not that you need research to tell you this. How do you feel when this happens to you?

Begin by holding unwaveringly to this principle: *Once you pick up the phone, you own the call.* The call is *yours.* You must handle it. You must take responsibility for it. You own the call until:

☎ the caller's question is answered

☎ the issue is resolved

☎ or until you can "sell" that call to someone else who can answer the question or resolve the issue. "Selling" the call to someone is not the same as "transferring" the call to someone.

The concept of call ownership binds you to the customer. It is your contract pledging to help. Read on for an explanation.

WHAT TO DO WHEN YOU KNOW WHAT TO DO

Not surprisingly, this is easy. The call has come in. You've picked up the phone. You own the call.

SERVICE: Good afternoon. This is Utopia Widgets. Jane Smith speaking. How may I help you?

CALLER: Yes. I wanted to know how to open up a credit account with your company.

SERVICE: I can help you with that. Will this be an individual or a corporate credit account?

And so you continue until the customer has been served and satisfied. Note that your response should assure the customer that he or she has reached the right person: "I can help you with that." It should be a positive, affirmative response, and a pledge of satisfaction.

WHAT TO DO WHEN YOU THINK YOU KNOW WHAT TO DO

Nobody said customer service was easy. But let's put matters into perspective. The vast majority of calls you receive, that is, calls you take ownership of, are straightforward requests for information. Usually, the information requested is basic. Most calls you should be able to handle without difficulty. However, a significant portion of calls will require more effort. Some research is needed before a satisfactory solution can be reached. In an organization with a half-hearted customer-service operation, you would toss the caller to whomever you hoped could handle the question, problem, or issue.

But your organization has chosen commitment to customer satisfaction. Therefore, since you picked up the phone, you own the call. You cannot "abandon" it. You must move it, take a step to somewhere, start research. Following your greeting and "How may I help you?" the caller asks:

CALLER: I placed an order for two dozen Type XYZ widgets on January 23. Can I change that order to Type ABC Widgets and still get delivery by February 1?

Based on your experience, you believe that it is quite possible. But you do not want to commit the folks in Production or in Shipping to a promise they may not be able to keep. If you didn't own the call, you could hand the caller off to somebody in one of these departments. Let's say you sent him to Production. After the phone rang a few times (the people in Production aren't accustomed to handling a lot of calls), somebody answered. So the customer has to ask his question again. The production guy asks around, and someone tells him he will have to check with Shipping. He, in turn, says to the customer: "Uh, I can't really connect you directly. Here's the number." This is called "call runaround."

But you own the call. So this scenario will not occur. Instead:

CALLER: I placed an order for two dozen Type XYZ widgets on January 23. Can I change that order to Type ABC Widgets and still get delivery by February 1?

SERVICE: I can easily get that answer for you. Here's what I need to do: I need to check in with our Production Department and with our Shipping Department. I can do that right now. It should take about three minutes. May I put you on hold for that long? Or would you like me to get the information and call you back?

Take note of the steps involved:

1. Let your customer know that you can and will obtain the needed information.

2. In concise terms, tell the customer what this process involves.

3. Tell the customer how long it will take. Use real time and create a "contract." Don't say "a few moments." Be specific: "about three minutes." Be certain to ask for more time than you think you will need, and always get back to the customer before the alloted time has expired.

4. Give the customer whatever options are available. In this case, being put on hold for a substantial length of time (three minutes is a long time) or to be called back.

Even when obtaining the requested information involves nothing more than calling up and consulting a record on a computer screen, a matter of a few seconds rather than minutes, keep your caller informed by "sharing" your computer screen with him:

SERVICE: I can get the information you need. Let's just call up your record on the computer. Please spell your last name for me. Thank you. You're at 1234 West 23rd Street? Great! Now, what I see are three orders for widgets. They were placed on May 3, July 5, and September 10. Would you like the shipping quantities for all three orders?

CALLER: Yes, please.

SERVICE: Okay. I'm typing in the request for the May 3 numbers. It should be on the screen in just a second. Yes, there it is. That quantity was . . . .

Handling a call when you must perform some task or tasks in order to obtain information is a lot like running a radio program. Your "audience" cannot see the action. In the absence of words, the customer hears nothing but what disc jockeys call "dead air." Now, on a radio show, dead air means that, within a very few seconds, listeners will start turning their dials. On a customer-service call, dead air results in customer anxiety and doubt (he or she may think that you have forgotten about him and are attending to another caller). Providing a "blow-by-blow" narration will avoid such dead air anxiety and frustration and thereby increase customer satisfaction. It also gives you the opportunity to enhance the relationship with the customer.

WHAT TO DO WHEN YOU HAVE NO IDEA WHAT TO DO

Let's face it. Someday someone will call with a problem you have no idea how to handle. Guess what? You still own the call. Given this unalterable fact, you generally have two options:

1. You can attempt to obtain the answer or information.
2. You can "sell" the call to somebody who has the answer or information.

In either case, you may *not* send the *caller* on an expedition to find the answer. You must do the legwork for him. This may mean putting the caller on hold for a length of time, or it may mean promising to call the customer back.

CALLER: Do you have any data on how well Widget XYZ performs when used with Application ABC?

In your experience, this particular question has never been raised.

SERVICE: I don't have an immediate answer to that question. Let me consult our database. I'm typing some information into the terminal. Now I'm waiting for an answer to come up on the screen. It should be just a few seconds. . . . Well, we don't have that information in our database. What I would like to do is consult with our engineers. Let me first be absolutely certain that I understand your question, so that I transmit just the right information to engineering.

CALLER: *Repeats question.* Discuss as necessary to ensure that your notes are clear and that you thoroughly understand the issue.

SERVICE: I will discuss this with our engineers today and get back to you tomorrow afternoon with a status report. I may not have a complete answer, but I will let you know what I have learned. When would be a good time after lunch for me to call? And what is your direct line, where I can most easily reach you? It may be that I will have our engineer call you directly. Would that be all right with you? In either case, we will give you a status report or a solution by (agreed time).

Alternatively, you might judge it most expedient to "sell" the call. Do this only if you believe that someone else in your organization can quickly furnish an answer. Here's what such a "sale" involves:

SERVICE: I don't have an immediate answer to that question. Let me consult our database. I'm typing some information into the terminal. Now I'm waiting for an answer to come up on the screen. It should be just a few seconds. . . . Well, we don't have that information in our database. I think that I can connect you with one of our engineers, who should be able to discuss this issue with you. May I put you on hold while I locate the engineer? This should take about two minutes.

SERVICE dials an engineer.

SERVICE: This is Joe Williams in Customer Service. I have a customer holding on the phone right now who needs to know if we have any data on how well Widget XYZ performs when used with Application ABC. I don't see anything on this in our Customer Service database. Can you discuss this issue with him?

ENGINEER: It is an unusual question. I don't know if I have a positive answer, but, sure, I can discuss the issues.

SERVICE: Great! The customer's name is David Lee. I'll put him in this call with us now.

SERVICE returns to CALLER.

SERVICE: Mr. Lee, thank you for holding. I mentioned your question to Herb Howard, one of our software engineers. He is on the line with us now. He may not have a completely positive answer, but he will help you. Mr. Lee, Herb, I'll hang up now.

Don't handle the tough call as if it were a hot potato, to be tossed to someone else as soon as possible. It is a *valuable commodity* because it represents contact with a customer, and any contact with a customer (the ultimate source of your income) is valuable. Therefore, sell the call carefully and thoughtfully.

EFFECTIVELY TRANSFERRING CALLS TO COLLEAGUES AND OTHER DEPARTMENTS

The effective transfer of a call is really a process of carefully and thoughtfully "selling" the call:

1. Secure permission to place the caller on hold while you identify and brief the colleague to whom you intend to sell the call.

2. If you anticipate that finding and briefing the colleague will take some time, arrange to return the caller's call. Always set a specific time for the return call.

3. Brief the colleague concisely but thoroughly, supplying the name of the caller, the nature of the question, issue, or problem, and just what it is the caller seeks.

Never hand off the call blindly. The caller should not have to repeat information to your colleague.

Your task is not to browbeat your colleague into accepting the call, but to sell him or her on the idea of helping the caller. If the colleague insists that he or she cannot provide the help, ask for advice on who to consult. After obtaining this, return to your caller (if placed on hold) and either ask permission to keep him or her on hold longer or agree on a time for you to call back. Keep it positive:

SERVICE: I've just consulted with Claire Evans, one of our engineers, who recommends that we consult Gary Morris in our Product Development division. It should take me two or three minutes to contact Gary. May I put you on hold for that time, or would you rather I called you back?

Note the positive frame. You don't imply that the first colleague you consulted failed to provide an answer. Instead, she did provide an answer: a recommendation to consult another expert.

RULES FOR PUTTING PEOPLE ON HOLD

There are three reasons why people put incoming calls on hold. Two of the reasons make legitimate sense and do nothing to detract from the ultimate goal of creating high levels of satisfaction. The third reason always detracts from creating high levels of customer satisfaction.

Here are the two legitimate reasons:

1. You must obtain information or consult a colleague
2. You must brief a colleague in order to "sell" the call to him or her.

When it becomes necessary to put a caller on hold in order to handle a request for information or to "sell" the call to a colleague, do the following:

1. Explain what you need to do.
2. Secure permission to put the caller on hold.
3. Tell the caller about how long he or she will be on hold. Create a "contract" with the customer: "I need to pull the service record on that item. May I put you on hold? It will take about two minutes."
4. If the delay unexpectedly becomes longer than the "contracted" time, return to the caller before the contracted time expires and state: "I need another couple of minutes. Will you hold for a bit longer, or should I call you back? Thanks for your patience."

The third reason why people put callers on hold is because another call comes through. Don't do it. People in my seminars everywhere tell me they are trained, or they train their people, to do something like this: Assume you are talking to customer A, and your other line rings. Say to customer A, "Will you hold, please, to let me put my other line on hold?" Then switch to customer B. Say: "Good morning. This is Jane Smith at Acme Widgets, and I'm on my other line. Will you hold, please?" and then return to customer A and say: "Thank you for holding." Then let the conversation continue.

Putting call A on hold in order to capture call B guarantees that you will have two dissatisfied customers. It's a no-win any way you cut it. Caller A is angry because you interrupted her conversation to start a conversation with caller B. Caller B is angry because you did not handle his conversation before returning to caller A. You would have been better off not answering caller B, and just letting her hang up. The only way one person can handle two phones and maintain customer satisfaction is if one of those phones never rings.

So how do you handle more than one phone? If you are the local grocery store, or a "one-person" virtual office operating in the information age, buy yourself a thirty-dollar answering machine for the second line. Program it to say, "This is John Smith, and I'm on the other line. Please leave your name and number and I will call you right back." Allow that recording to pick up the call when you are on the first line.

If you work in an office with nine others, then you need to organize yourselves as a team, not a group of individuals randomly tossed together. A group of ten people, for example, may consist of seven customer-service representatives, one manager, and a couple of support people. However, this office can handle ten incoming customer-service lines. Yes, even the boss can be trained to chip in when the load gets heavy, grab a call and move it somewhere.

HOW TO AVOID MAKING THE CUSTOMER REPEAT INFORMATION

Maybe you remember reading Samuel Taylor Coleridge's poem *The Rime of the Ancient Mariner* in high school. It's about the fella who is condemned to wander the earth, repeating his story to everyone he encounters. Few situations are more frustrating for a caller than being cast unwillingly into the role of the Ancient Mariner, tossed from one person to the next and forced to repeat his story for each.

When you "sell" a call to a colleague, make the sale easy on the caller. Fully but concisely brief your colleague so that the caller need not repeat history. Remember to supply your colleague with the caller's name.

The fundamental rule to follow is that once the customer states a concern to any one person in the company, ownership of the concern passes to the company.

Internal call tracking and internal communication systems should be good enough so that the customer has never had to repeat the concern to any other person in the organization again. The company should maintain ownership of the customer's concern and provide him or her with status reports until the concern is completely resolved.

Chapter

2

Managing Technology

USING VOICE MESSAGING EFFECTIVELY

Put yourself in the caller/customer's position. That doesn't take much imagination, since you've been in that position many times.

You've got a report to print out. You've got to print it out *now*. Trouble is, your brand-new printer doesn't share your sense of urgency. You punch the right keys, turn on the correct switches, and nothing happens. In desperation, you call the tech support line.

> You have reached CompPrint technical support. We are not able to answer your call at the moment, but if you will leave your name, telephone number, and a brief description of your problem, we will call you within one hour.

A machine. This is the last thing you want to hear, right? Wrong. The *last* thing you want to hear is a phone ringing and ringing. If a living, breathing soul cannot always be there to answer the phone, it is far better for a machine to pick up than for the call to go unanswered. However, you should still go the extra mile to make your machine-borne message as personal and as helpful as possible:

1. *Use one message during business hours and another after hours.* During business hours, the message should greet the caller, giving the name of your firm and your name. Effective phrases to start include, "I am away from my desk . . ." or "I am helping other customers . . . ." Avoid such phrases as "not able to answer" or "I am unavailable."

   Following the greeting, ask the caller to leave a message. This should come in the form of a positive, even emphatic request, using the "How may I help you?"

14

phrase: "Please tell me how I may help you. Leave a message after the tone, and please include your phone number and the best time to call. If there is work I can do before I return your call, please include instructions in your message. I will return your call just as soon as possible."

2. *After-hours messages*: These should include a greeting, but it is not necessary to supply your name. The message should state your normal business hours, and it should conclude with an emphatic appeal for a message: "Please leave a message after the tone, and please include your phone number and the best time to call. If there is work we can do before returning your call, please include instructions in your message. We *will* return your call." Do not let your caller go through your automatic voice response pyramid before learning that the office is closed.

3. *Additional after-hours options*: If you have an after-hours number at which you wish to be reached and at which you can dependably be reached, or if you have a beeper or an answering service, your message should provide this information.

4. *Change your daytime message daily.* Even when it is necessary to greet a caller with a machine, you can still let him or her know that there is a human being living and breathing nearby. Begin your greeting by including today's date: "Hello, this is Jane Smith of Acme Widgets. It's Friday, August 25th, and I'm with other customers at the moment. Please tell me how I can help you. Just leave a message after the tone, including your phone number and the best time to call back. I will return your call promptly." Such a message tells callers that you are available *today*, and that you pay attention to recorded messages. It is, of course, critical that this message be changed daily. The message cannot be used after business hours.

5. *Offer an alternative to the machine.* Depending on the size and staffing of your firm, you may be able to offer callers an alternative to the machine. If you have a full-fledged voice-mail system as opposed to a simple answering machine, your recorded greeting might offer a "safety valve," a means by which the caller can speak to someone else if you are unavailable. In this case, your message will probably conclude with an instruction such as this: "If you would like to speak to someone immediately, please press 'zero' on your Touch Tone™ pad or simply remain on the line until the operator answers."

6. *If possible, offer loops.* "I'm currently on the phone. You can hold or press '1' to leave me a message." Be sure to "loop" the message every thirty seconds or so if your technology allows it: "I'm still on the other line. You may continue holding, or press '1' to leave me a message." The customer may choose to hold for a minute or two and then change his mind. By looping, you give him the option to leave a message if he does change his mind.

7. *Keep messages brief: less than 15 seconds long.* A long, rambling message is too hard to remember. Further, the customer can only use his sense of hearing, not sight, to get your message. Concentration is difficult.

USING TIERS AND SORTING CALLS

In recent years, two related devices have come to play significant roles in handling incoming calls for many businesses.

The Automatic Call Distributor (ACD) routes incoming calls and is most useful as an electronic version of the old take-a-number ticket dispenser that still graces many a supermarket bakery or deli department. The ACD is not intended to substitute for a human presence, nor is it intended to reduce the need for humans. It should be used for the following reasons:

☎ To increase the speed with which incoming calls are answered by routing them automatically to the best available person

☎ To ensure that they are answered in the order in which they are received

☎ To reduce the possibility of losing a call because a customer cannot get through on the first try (for example, if the caller wants Bill, the ACD can send the call to John if Bill is talking to another customer.)

ACD messages heard when no one is available to answer the incoming call should emphasize that representatives are "assisting other customers" and that the caller's call will be answered "in the order in which it was received." The better units will tell the customer how many other customers are ahead. The message can also accomplish quite a bit more than this. See the "Creative 'Hold'" section at the conclusion of this chapter.

Another acceptable use of the ACD is in companies that do not supply direct-dial lines for individual employees. In this case, the caller is greeted with a message like this:

> You have reached Acme Widgets. If you are speaking from a Touch-Tone telephone and you know the extension of the person you wish to speak with, you may enter that number now. If you wish to speak to the operator, press "zero" or simply wait on the line. Thank you.

A device related to the ACD is the Automated Response Unit (ARU), which is a customer-assisted routing system. In contrast to ACDs, ARUs always intercept incoming calls. Their purpose is to route these calls and provide information without live intervention.

Many callers dread ARUs. In some cases, this is just a sort of knee-jerk response against automation. In other cases, their dread is justified because ARUS are often grossly misapplied. Intelligently used, the ARU saves the caller time and effort.

However, in other cases, where callers are forced to wade through a catalog of tedious and confusing options the call can indeed seem like torture. Let's face two facts:

1. An ARU does sacrifice the human touch.

2. In a large organization, an ARU is almost an unavoidable necessity.

Intelligent ARU application begins with the design of the initial option menu and the subsequent tiers. If you have only a few options to offer the caller, it may be practical simply to present them all:

> Hello. You have reached the offices of Acme Widgets. If you are calling about a current order, press 1. To place an order, press 2. For account information, press 3. For service, press 4. To speak with an operator, press "zero" or simply remain on the line.

If your choices are all simple, the customer can remember and select among three or four options, maximum.

The ARU message should begin with a greeting and then should be followed immediately by the options. If a few seconds pass without a response to the Touch-Tone options, the caller should be automatically connected with the operator. Note also that time is very important in retention. Present the menu economically. Instead of lumbering through a tedious list like this:

> . . . If you are calling about a current order, press 1. If you are calling to place an order, press 2. If you are calling to obtain account information, press 3. If you are calling for service, press 4. . . .

"Abbreviate" the menu by using the "If you are calling about" phrase only once:

> . . . If you are calling about a current order, press 1. To place an order, press 2. For account information, press 3. For service, press 4. . . .

Brevity is also important for the customer who does not have a Touch-Tone phone. These souls should not have to listen to a several-minute rambling message until they get to an operator. Short messages significantly enhance retention. A properly designed fifteen second message can convey a significant amount of information.

In organizations where you must offer the caller more than three or four options, it is generally best to create a tier design, which presents three or four initial options, then presents additional options as subsets of those first ones. For example:

> . . . If you are calling about a current order, press 1. To place an order, press 2. For account information, press 3. For service, press 4. To speak with an operator, press "zero" or simply remain on the line.

Let's say the caller presses 4. A submenu then kicks in:

For the status of a current service order, press 1. To obtain service on Type A widgets, press 2. Type B widgets, press 3. Type C, press 4. For all other widgets, press 5.

It is true that some callers are annoyed by having to "walk through" more than a single tier. It is also true that the ARU will not be as well received as a human. But it is also true that customers are continuously clamoring for lower prices, and ARUs do help you reduce costs.

To summarize, a few rules:

1. Always keep messages very brief.

2. Do not ask the customer to listen to more than four options before allowing him or her to make a choice.

3. Keep descriptions of the options very short and very specific.

4. You will have a better chance of success if the options available to the customer are very clear and exact. For example, "Press one to pay bills, press two for your credit card balance." or "Press one to place an order. Punch the item number from the catalog into your key pad now."

5. Send out direct-mail flyers to educate your customers on how the ARU works. Add instructions in the form of inserts to standard packaging and invoices. Use catalogs or other methods available as well. Take the time to sell the ARU to your marketplace. Don't just dump the thing on them; sell it to your customers: "Customers receive more flexibility, twenty-four-hour service, less chance for error because only one person is transmitting data into the computer," and so on.

In designing your ARU system, it is important to consider the type of customer you usually deal with. If your customers are normally repeat customers, they will quickly learn the system and get irritated if they continuously have to wade through all the tiers to get to you. The best systems are those that allow the customer to immediately punch in the needed codes in order to get to where he or she wants to go.

Also, think like the local bank. The type of business you run is very important. The local bank is very successful with ARU systems. There are several reasons for this:

☎ The transactions are very specific and exact (pay bills, and so on).

☎ They have spent a fortune educating their customers with direct-mail pieces teaching them how to use the system.

Catalog operations, help desks, parts suppliers, and similar businesses can teach customers to order with the ARU, but they must go through the educational process with the customer.

Beyond the design of an ARU menu and message system, careful thought should be given to the actual voice used to make the recording. Certainly, you want to avoid a bland robotic recording that underscores the presence of automation and the absence of a live human being. Many firms hire professional voice talent to make their recordings. This is a reasonable option, but you should be aware that, in our media-saturated society, people are all too accustomed to hearing smooth, professional voices. In most cases, you are best served by selecting an employee with a lively, pleasant voice and good diction, rather than a professional actor. Better yet, consider using two voices, a man and a woman, who can switch back and forth. This tactic is mildly stimulating and tends to keep the caller more alert.

CREATIVE "HOLD"

Whether incoming calls are handled by a human operator, an ACD, or an ARU, it will from time to time be necessary to put a customer on hold for varying lengths of time. As mentioned previously, "dead air" can be fatal to incoming telephone calls, just as it is to a commercial radio broadcast. Waiting in dead silence, the caller may assume that he or she has been forgotten or accidentally disconnected, and you will either lose the call or prompt the caller to hang up, dial in again, and lose his or her place in line.

Many companies use music to fill the dead air of hold time. While this is preferable to silence for the reasons just stated, some callers find it annoying, especially if the music doesn't happen to be to their taste. If you do choose to play music during the hold time, consider the image you wish to project. Is hard rock really appropriate to your conservative investment firm? In most cases, light classics or contemporary melodic jazz works best.

However, you might consider filling hold time creatively, with *information* your caller can use. Turn this idle time into additional customer contact time, which is, after all, the heart and soul of customer service.

You should not fill hold time with a commercial for your firm. Your caller is probably, to one degree or another, annoyed at having been put on hold in the first place. Being forced to listen to a promotional puff will not make the caller feel any better. Instead, fill the time with information that allows him or her to learn more about your company:

☎ Provide information about how the customer can get better use from the product.

☎ Provide information about hours of operation, location of offices, service centers, and so on.

☎ You might provide a kind of company telephone directory. "While you are waiting, you might want to jot down the numbers of some of our other departments." This also gives the customer an opportunity to learn about the existence of other departments. You may actually save the customer time. For example, the caller has dialed Customer Service, only to realize (while listening to the on-hold company "directory") that he or she really wants Sales.

☎ Tell the customer what information he or she should have on hand for the Customer-Service representative: "To expedite service, please have your account number ready to give your Customer-Service representative."

☎ Provide answers *now*. Perhaps you have a list of Frequently Asked Questions (FAQs). Why not use hold time to provide recorded answers to these? It is just possible that your caller will get an answer before a Customer Service rep is available to pick up the call. For example: "Customers commonly call because they are receiving a system fault code 1345. 1300 series faults are all designed to protect the control from environmental hazards such as lightning or spikes in the line. If you are seeing any system fault code number in the 1300 series, simply press ##1300##. Then hit the enter key. This special command will cause the system to reconfigure itself and your problem may disappear." Or: "If your Superb appliance is not working, just return it to us in the original shipping container, or suitable substitute, and we will repair it or replace it free of charge if it is within the warranty period. Be sure to include proof of purchase and return it to (address). Before returning it to us, be sure to try the appliance in another outlet first, preferably in another room. Often customers return appliances which have no problems. The appliance is fine, the local circuit breaker in their home is tripped."

☎ One of the most effective ways to use hold time is to create more value for your customer. Teach him or her how to use your product more effectively with helpful reminders. For example: "Do you follow our recommended lubricating procedures? Those customers who do get a thirty percent longer lifespan from our wonder widget. Call (phone number) when you hang up and leave your address. We will send you another recommended preventive maintenance list." Or: "If your car was shipped after 1990, it was shipped with our permanent Superfine high-gloss finish. Superfine will give you many years of beauty even in acid-rain conditions. We do not recommend application of any commercial wax as all these waxes will damage the finish and reduce the lifespan of the paint job."

☎ Try getting more involved in your community. These messages during hold always enhance your public image, ultimately leading to higher sales through word-of-mouth. Here are some possible messages to consider: "Do you have a block watch group on your street? Get involved and start one on your block. Call your local police for instructions on what to do. Government statistics suggest that crimes occur less frequently on streets with active block watch groups." Or: "Are you registered to vote? Our democracy works best when we all participate. Get out and vote for the candidate of your choice." Or: "Do you exercise at least three times per week, thirty minutes each session? The results of studies are clear: regular exercise promotes good health."

The one message to avoid during the hold time is a reminder that "your call is important to us." Many companies include just such an announcement. We have all been "treated" to it. How does it make us feel? *"If my $%^#%&* call is so &*$#&% important to you, why am I still on %#&%@* hold?*

THE INTERNET

No section on technology and customer service can be complete today without mentioning the birth of the interactive information age brought to us thanks to the Internet. The Internet, specifically, the World Wide Web, dramatically enhances our ability to communicate at very low cost with tens of millions of customers everywhere. Each year, more customers have at their disposal low-cost net-surfing tools, giving them tremendous power to communicate their every wish to us.

It would be foolish indeed for you to ignore this valuable resource in planning your future customer-service scripts and scenarios.

As you evaluate the power of this emerging technology, consider this one example. Even though Scott Adams had been putting forth his best effort for more than a year, his syndicated comic strip *Dilbert* was being carried by only 100 newspapers or so. In 1993, he launched a determined effort to communicate with his customers and successfully lobbied to publish an Internet e-mail address in the strip. He got the feedback he needed, quickly learning that the business-oriented strips were being cut out and hung on cubicle walls everywhere. He switched the strip's emphasis to 80 percent business and technology and had a booming "Dilbert" business on his hands by mid-1996. His first best-selling collection of cartoons sold 750,000 copies.

To be sure, much of what is currently floating around in cyberspace is nothing but sales-focused puff that is hardly worth clicking at. But this will quickly change as savvy customer-oriented leaders everywhere take over the World Wide Web pages. Customers themselves will drive the movement, as they bypass all the advertising trash and focus on what helps them accomplish their objectives. Federal Express is already getting thousands of hits per day on its webpage. Eager customers are clicking to find the status of packages they have shipped. FedEx's customers love the additional control they have over their shipping, while FedEx saves millions in customer-service costs because its customers are essentially doing the job previously done by customer-service representatives.

Is the Internet for you? Here's a quiz:

1. Do you get recurring questions from your customers? Some examples: Where is my shipment? When will it ship? Is my shipment on schedule? Did you receive the item I shipped in for repair? Do you have these parts in stock? I want to place another order.

2. Are your customers repeat customers?

3. Are your customers computer literate (as are business-to-business customers), or are they becoming computer literate? This question will shortly be obsolete as more and more people acquire user-friendly net-surfing devices and software.

If you answer these questions *yes*, then get with it on the Internet. Start now. FedEx started in 1984!

You do not need to begin with a giant server computer. Rent space from some webserver in town and start getting the specific repeat information customers commonly need out on a webpage. With every call, letter, or outbound promotion, educate your customers about the answers they can find on your web page:

> ". . . Thank you for calling, and we're always glad to help. For your future reference, the same information I just gave you can be found at our website, and you can access it any time you wish. Our address is: *smartcompany@web.com*. You can trace that order any time on the web without having to wait for our 800 line."

A word to the wise. There are many software packages being developed to help you design your own webpage. I recommend you contact a professional educational firm with professional graphic-design expertise to make your webpage as user-friendly as possible. Desktop publishing was born in the eighties and brought publishing tools to the masses. Unfortunately, *tools* and *skills* are not synonymous terms. Just look at the direct-mail pieces in your mailbox and you will surely notice the difference.

Chapter

3

Connected

CREATING RAPPORT

Success in business is the product of many things, ranging from the quality of your product or service, to your competition, to the conditions in your particular marketplace, and so on. But success in business also depends on something that is difficult or impossible to quantify, weigh, or measure. It depends on feelings. It depends on how your customers feel about you and your organization. In short, success in business depends, in part, on the rapport between company and customer.

Now, a positive rapport can be difficult enough to create in face-to-face situations. But, in person, you do have certain rapport builders at your disposal, beginning with a warm handshake, a smile, and the kind of body language that tells your customer that you are concerned about his or her needs, issues, and problems.

On the telephone, all you have is your voice and your words. So, let's begin with the voice. Some folks are lucky enough to have been "born" with what is generally called a "pleasant phone voice." But even if this does not come naturally to you, it is quite possible consciously to cultivate a rhythm and tone that are a pleasure to hear. Really, there's nothing mysterious about developing a good telephone voice. Concentrate on the following:

1. *The pace of your speech.* For the overwhelming majority of people, this can be improved by taking to heart two words: *slow down.* Concentrate on speaking a little more slowly than you normally do. Your pace on the phone should be slower than your ordinary conversational pace.

2. *The pitch of your voice.* Unless you already have a very deep voice, it is usually a good idea to try to lower the pitch of your telephone voice. Lower-pitched voices are usually perceived both as more authoritative and as more pleasing than higher-pitched voices. Remarkably, this applies equally to women and to men. A desirable side effect of self-consciously lowering the pitch of your voice is that you will tend to speak more slowly and distinctly as well. (Try standing when you speak. Standing tends to lower your voice and make it sound more powerful.)

3. *Concentrate on enunciation.* Give each word full value. Make certain that you are understood. This will not only save time and prevent errors, it will create satisfaction in your customer rather than the irritation that arises if the customer has to expend effort on deciphering slurred, mumbled, or garbled speech. Beyond this, careful enunciation tells your listener that you are an intelligent human being. The person on the other end of the line will therefore get the feeling that you are capable of providing the service or help that he or she wants, and he or she will tend to accord you the level of polite respect that makes doing business a pleasure.

The style of greeting discussed in Chapter 1 goes a long way toward creating positive rapport on the telephone. But, after the greeting, you need to make a transition into the business at hand. If a warm and friendly greeting is followed by an abrupt command, such as "What's your telephone number?" "What is your account number?" or "I need your account number?" rapport suffers. Ease the transition by assuring the caller that you can help with the question or problem. *Then* ask for the account or other information that you need:

SERVICE: . . . How may I help you?

CALLER: I can't get my WordMaster software to print with my printer.

SERVICE: I can help you with that. May I have the serial number so that I can pull up your record? You'll find it on the label of the first diskette.

Before you make a demand, assure the caller that you can help. Then do not make a demand. Instead, ask a favor, such as "May I have . . . ." Go on to explain why you want the favor: "so I can pull up your record."

Tip: Purchase one of the excellent "call-management" software packages on the market today. Call-management software lets you organize your customer database any number of ways. The search routines can launch and search for any one of the variables in the database. Most commonly, the engines search off of the person's name or company name. I recommend organizing the database by company name and address. You can have any number of individual customer users at each address. The system works well with the consumer market as well. For example, you can have an entire family identified within one household address.

The databases allow you to track individuals and all information sent to, communicated to, or compiled on individuals. There is an advantage to having groups of individuals grouped by address. For example, say you have XYZ Oil as a customer, and it has ten or more regional offices. You may be communicating with several users at each regional office. If you have difficulty with one customer at one address, perhaps you can build rapport with another at the same address. This new customer may be able to help you fix the problem with the old customer. Further, friends at one location may be able to help you build relationships with those at other locations. Call-management software enables the user to manage this type of information.

Service might say: "Just a moment, let me punch in a few letters of your last name and get your file on my screen." The computer will locate the person, his or her address, phone number, serial number, and other necessary information. Further, others at the same address would immediately be identified as well and all previous communications with this customer and others at this location could also be linked.

The service rep can also build new files as needed:

☎ Is this the first time you called? May I please get some key information for our database? Maintaining a record will simplify all future communications we have together.

☎ What is your company name and address? I would like to add your name to others we are working with at the same location.

☎ You are our first contact at this location. May I get some background information from you? I can load this information in our database and it will simplify all future contacts we have together.

LISTENING EFFECTIVELY

The single most important skill required for delivering great service is the skill of listening, of really hearing what your customer is saying.

1. Concentrate on the call. Don't let another task distract you.

2. Take notes, if necessary. Tell the customer you're taking notes. It's a great way to defuse an angry caller. Quickly jot down the main points of what the caller says.

3. Reflect the caller's message:

CALLER: The unit malfunctions when I try to do X, Y, and Z.

SERVICE: So the unit malfunctions when you attempt X, Y, and Z. When you do A, B, and C, it works properly?

CALLER: That's correct.

4. Reinforce positive progress in the conversation. The caller has just made it clear that the unit malfunctions when he or she tries to do X, Y, and Z, but works satisfactorily for A, B, and C:

SERVICE: Good. Now I understand the extent of the problem. We're making progress. The problem must be with X, Y, and Z.

5. Avoid reacting with language that unintentionally communicates exasperation. For those who have a problem understanding you, you may need to repeat yourself to answer their questions or even to get the information you need to answer their questions. At some point, your natural tendency is to reply with a sentence that begins: "What I'm trying to tell you" or "Look. This is what I'm trying to tell you." The problem with an expression like this is that what it communicates to the caller is your harsh judgment that he or she is none too swift. This will not do you, your company, and your customer any good. Instead of falling back on expressions of exasperation, preface your umpteenth repetition with "Let me see if I can express myself more effectively" or "Let me try to explain this better." Take the burden on yourself.

ACTING DECISIVELY

Once you determine a course of action, whether it is coming up with the answer the caller needs or "selling" the call to a colleague who can answer the question, express yourself decisively:

1. Okay. Here's the answer to your question . . .

2. This is the solution I propose. . . .

3. We can work this out together . . .

Sometimes you need a partial solution: "Let me explain what I have learned. I can call you at (time) with another progress report." Or: "I can do A and B now. I will investigate further about C and D and get back to you around 2:00 P.M. tomorrow. Will I be able to leave a message if you are unavailable?"

Sometimes, you will be unable to give the caller exactly what he or she wants: "The only thing that will satisfy me is a full refund." Trouble is, the caller has owned and has been using the product for more than a year, and your warranty clearly specifies that you will "replace or repair" the product, according to your judgment. You explain this to the customer, who remains inflexible: "Look, I just want my money back."

The natural tendency is to reply with a sentence beginning "All I can do . . ." or "The most I can do . . ." or "The best I can do . . . ." The problem with this is that it sets the caller up for a fall. Your words are "All I can do . . .," but the caller hears "You're not going to get what you want, buddy." Instead of broadcasting such a negative and off-putting message, be firm and straightforward, but ultimately as positive as possible: "I cannot do that. But here is what I can do . . ."

If possible, offer the caller more than one alternative. Most callers will ultimately accept less than they ideally want, provided that they aren't pushed up against a wall with a take-it-or-leave-it proposition. Be aware that you can prompt the caller to take the alternative you prefer by making it the second option you offer: "Would you like to send the widget in for replacement of the part, or would you prefer that we send the part to you, so that you can perform the replacement yourself and be up and running more quickly?" Most customers will go for the option mentioned last, in large part because customers tend to remember the last thing you say or do. There is no guarantee of this, of course, so you must be prepared to act on either option. However, chances are the customer will choose what you would prefer he or she choose, and the customer will have the healthy feeling that he or she is the decision maker.

Be very careful with what you promise, whether that is the "real" promise or the "implied" promise. I spend an inordinate amount of time, and my clients' money, discussing the simple concept of clarifying the promise you make to the customer. Far too often, misstatements are made that everyone regrets later. You cannot create positive rapport unless the promise is clarified before everyone gets off the phone. Here is the most common scenario:

CUSTOMER: I need the widgets by September 4th.

SERVICE: That's great. I got the order for ten dozen widgets. Let me check my inventory for your needed delivery date. Hmmm, things don't look good. Widgets are hot right now. The first availability is October 1st.

CUSTOMER: That's impossible. Get me on a higher priority. I simply can't survive until October 1st. My production lines will be completely shut down by September 9th. You must do something.

SERVICE: This is going to be tough. I don't think I can do anything. Let me use my highest priority.

I was afraid of that. Everyone ahead of you is already on our super-hot priority. I can't move anyone aside. There simply is no additional capacity. We are already running three shifts, seven days. We have even scaled back on preventive maintenance. There is just no more capacity.

CUSTOMER: Look, you just don't understand my problem. My production lines will go down. Thousands will be out of work. I must get something. You have got to try to do something.

SERVICE: I certainly will try. I will do everything I can, but right now September 4th looks completely impossible.

CUSTOMER: Well, see what you can do. Thanks for your effort.

Now, the real question is: What delivery date was promised? Service swears it promised nothing. Yet if the customer loaded September 4th in his MRP (Materials Resources Planning) system, and you accepted the purchase order, then the customer has broadcast to all of his or her production operations that the widgets will arrive on September 4th, and you will be to blame if they do not arrive. This promise must be clarified in order to build proper rapport with the customer:

CUSTOMER: . . . Thousands will be out of work. I must get something . . . .

SERVICE: I certainly will try. I will do everything I can, but right now September 4th looks completely impossible. Please do not put down September 4th as a desired delivery date. If you do, everyone who needs widgets will think we can meet that delivery. Please load in October 1st.

CUSTOMER: They can't live with that date.

SERVICE: If we lie to them, things will only be worse. I will try to find a partial shipment for September 4th. Please note in your system we can only promise October 1st. As bad as it is, it is at least the truth. No one will like it, but at least they can plan for the possibility that nothing will be available on September 4th. In the meantime, I will personally work on this and call you back next week with a status report. Can we agree that you will only load October 1st into your system?

The final phase of the successful call, the call that results in positive, decisive action, is a positive and warm exit. Always make certain that the caller hangs up satisfied. This is accomplished by closing with a question:

☎ Is there anything else I can help you with?

☎ Have I answered your question?

☎ Have I answered all of your questions?

☎ Has this conversation cleared up the issues?

You may also follow this up with an invitation to call if questions or other needs should arise later. Use the caller's name: "Mr. Jones, my name is Mary Hartworth. Please call me if you have any further questions. I'm at extension 1234."

T Part WO

Building Your Business: Creating Customer Satisfaction

Chapter
4

Answering the Questions that Mean Sales

Products and services answer a customer's needs. But first, you must answer the customer's questions. Sometimes the questions are difficult or challenging. More often, they are basic. In either case, how effectively you answer your customer's questions will have impact on the sale:

1. Effective answers remove obstacles. If the customer is unclear about pricing or ordering procedures, for example, he or she may hesitate to place an order. Hesitate long enough, and the moment is lost, inertia triumphs, and the sale doesn't get made.

2. Effective answers communicate your company's commitment to creating satisfaction. Give a shoddy answer to a customer's inquiry, and he or she will start thinking: "If they don't know enough to give me a decent answer about replacement parts, how can they have enough smarts to build a decent widget?"

3. Effective answers build relationships that translate into satisfaction now and continued sales later.

HOW DO I ORDER FROM YOU?

Above all, be certain that you know the procedure. Then do as much of the work for the customer as possible. Get the necessary information such as name, address, phone numbers, credit card information, and so on *now*. If you must hand the customer over to Sales, explain what you are about to do, and ask permission before you do it: "It's easy to order from us. I can connect you right now with one of our sales representatives. May I do that?"

Tip: Always begin by assuring your customer that ordering is easy and that you can help.

CUSTOMER: I am interested in purchasing (product). What do I do?

SERVICE: Ordering from us is easy, and I can help you. If you would like to use a major credit card, I can take the information right now and expedite your order.

Pause for reply. If the customer indicates that he or she wants to use a credit card, take the order. If not, explain the procedure. For example:

SERVICE: All right. You would like (product), model number (number). The total is ($ amount). You can send us a check for that amount, or we can ship (product) to you C.O.D. at an additional ($ amount). Which do you prefer?

Express yourself so that it is clear that the customer has good choices among attractive, convenient alternatives. Once the customer has made a choice, be certain to obtain all necessary information. Then repeat that information to confirm accuracy.

SERVICE: We are mailing (product) to what address? Let me confirm the spelling of your name. And please give me a phone number where we can reach you during the day. Thanks. We are shipping to (name and address) and you can be reached at (phone). Please write this order number on your check: (number). This will help us expedite shipment of your order.

Tip: When you ask the customer to do something, explain how it will benefit the customer.

WHERE CAN I PURCHASE YOUR PRODUCT?

Customer service must have this information available in clear and specific form. Even if your product is widely available, resist the temptation to answer vaguely: "You can purchase (product) in just about any store." A better answer is "Our line is carried in all major hardware stores, including (list chains). If you work through a network of dealers, secure the information that will allow you to supply your customer with the name, address, and phone number of the dealer closest to him or her.

SERVICE: We have a network of fine dealers. Let me locate the one closest to you. You live in what city? (Customer answers.) Yes, we have six dealers in (City). Are you on the north, south, east, or west side? (Customer answers.) On the west side, our dealer is (name) at (address). Is that location convenient for you? (Customer answers yes.) Great! Here's (Name's) phone number. They're open every day except Sunday; hours are (hours).

HOW DO YOU DISTRIBUTE YOUR PRODUCT?

The pace and wide availability of high quality products has tended to dull a competitive edge based on product alone. Increasingly, it is the level of service that hones the competitive edge, and discerning customers often use a company's distribution setup as a barometer of quality and service. When a customer asks you how you distribute your product, emphasize standards and quality over wide availability. For example:

CUSTOMER: How do you distribute your products?

SERVICE: We work through a carefully selected dealer network. Actually, "network" isn't the right word. We think of our dealers as family. We keep in close touch with our dealers, and they also supply us with continual feedback. Our dealers have to meet our high standards, and to tell you the truth, dealer feedback keeps us on our toes. If you, our customers, address questions and concerns to our dealers, you can bet we hear about them. After the dealers are selected, they are required to attend training programs and annual training updates covering additional new features and benefits.

HOW DO YOU SUPPORT YOUR DISTRIBUTORS?

Ultimately, the customer is asking for assurances that he or she will receive your support. You can't stand behind your customer if you don't stand behind your dealers. In answering the question, emphasize communication, product updates, product availability, warranty service, and training.

CUSTOMER: How do you support your distributors?

SERVICE: We consider our distributors our most vital and direct link to you. We support them by maintaining a high level of communication with them, by ensuring that they have complete and up-to-date product information, and by making certain that they have the products our customers want. We back dealers 100 percent on warranty service, so that, if something goes wrong, you can be up and running again as quickly as possible. You should also know about our dealer-training program. We educate our dealers so that they can help you get the most value from our products. Additionally, 80 percent of our dealers are servicing dealers, conveniently located throughout the nation. We also have our direct service force, which supports the dealer network. One of our factory-direct service specialists is available to consult with every ten dealers to ensure that we have sufficient technical support for you, our customer.

WHAT DOES YOUR PRODUCT INCLUDE?

Perhaps your company spends more than a small fortune on sales brochures, advertising, and catalogues, all extolling the features of your products. That doesn't mean that your customer won't ask you to describe accessories and other product benefits. Do not refer your customer to Sales or to a catalogue description. Be comfortable with your own product. Provide an honest, straightforward rundown of included components, emphasizing any extras.

SERVICE: The (product) includes everything you need to get started, including (list). We even include (item), which most other manufacturers require you to buy as an add-on at extra cost.

Tip: If your product does not include "everything," try to put this fact in the best possible light, without being dishonest. For example: "We don't include (item) because most customers prefer to have a choice rather than getting stuck with what we would bundle into the package." Or: "Yes, we charge extra for option D because we have three other versions of that option. Options A, B, and C are also available. While a customer may want A, B, C, or D, no customer needs all four of these versions. That's why we have the options priced as separate items. Could I have your name and address so that I can send you additional information on how the options differ and how you should decide which option is best for your application? I'll also ask our sales representative to follow-up and confirm you have received this information and answer additional questions you may have."

In any case, have some valid reason and never apologize even jokingly with a customer you know well for the customer's having to purchase an additional accessory: "Yes, we charge extra for that. You know, in this business, we've got to nickel and dime you to death!" Bite your tongue.

WHAT DOES YOUR PRODUCT DO?

Again, this information may be available in dozens of forms. But the fact is that this particular customer is asking you for information. If you can supply the information, do so. If you must refer the customer to Sales or if you must send a brochure or spec sheet, be certain that you give your customer the message that you are responding to the question, not just passing the buck.

SERVICE: I can send you complete information on (product). We have several versions. How are you planning to use it? I want to make sure I send information on the right version.

CUSTOMER: (Describes application.)

SERVICE: I can get correct information to you right away. Let me confirm that I have your correct address.

Tip: It is the responsibility of customer service to always close the gap between what the customer is trying to do and what the product can do to help the customer: "Our (product) is really not made for that purpose. There are other similar products out there, and perhaps someone else has a product which will do what you need. I'm not sure, but check with John's Supply. They carry a wide variety of (products), including ours, and they might carry what you need. Hold on. Actually, I do have their number. Here it is . . . ."

The cynic will say I am stupid for suggesting that someone should recommend competitive product in selected cases. Understanding the critical importance of positive customer service in a market-based society as well as the already outlandish cost of sales and marketing in the United States, I have learned from my best clients the critical importance and professional necessity of recommending competitors when necessary.

IS YOUR PRODUCT SAFE?

Safety-related questions must be answered with great care for three reasons:

1. If the customer feels he or she has reason to fear using your product, he or she may not buy it, may not obtain satisfaction from it, or may return it unnecessarily.

2. If you are not crystal clear about safety issues, you expose your company to liability.

3. Most importantly, if you fail to state safety issues clearly, you risk causing harm to your customer.

In responding to safety-related questions, remember: safety sells. Not too long ago, automobile manufacturers resisted including, much less advertising, safety features in their cars because "customers weren't interested in safety." Today, of course, auto makers spend millions on safety and even more millions on promoting these features. What is true in the auto industry is now true for all industry; therefore, be certain to emphasize and highlight all relevant safety features, without minimizing potential hazards or making safety claims that are unauthorized, unwarranted, or otherwise inaccurate.

CUSTOMER: I am considering buying your (product), but I've heard that (products) aren't safe. Can you tell me something about the safety of your (product)?

SERVICE: Let's begin by understanding that no (type of product) is 100 percent safe. If improperly used, our (product), like any other, can cause injury or create other hazard or damage. But we have devoted a great deal of time and effort to make (product) as safe as possible. We have designed it with the following advanced safety features: (list). We have also included a detailed owner's manual with very clear guidelines for operating (product). What you must do is be certain to follow those guidelines. As long as you do, our (product) is safe to operate, and you need not be unduly concerned. Because of our commitment to safety, we maintain a special hotline number to answer any specific questions you may have about safety issues. You'll find this number on the inside front cover of the operator's manual. To help your evaluation of our (product), let me send you the operator's manual. I'll note the pages in the manual that describe safe operation. Could I have your address?

Issues related to the safety of chemical substances are prevalent and important. Above all, be certain that you have authorized, factually accurate information. Do not speculate on your own.

CUSTOMER: I want to use (brand) paint in my child's room. Is it safe?

SERVICE: Once dry, our paint is nontoxic. It contains no lead or other heavy metals, and it cannot be absorbed through the skin. Properly used, it will not flake or chip for many years. However, even if the dry paint were somehow ingested, it is entirely nontoxic. Although the wet paint gives off no toxic fumes, we do recommend that people stay out of the room until the paint has dried thoroughly. We recommend that you allow a 48-hour drying period. The paint will thoroughly cure in about one month.

Tip: Be factual whenever possible. It adds credibility.

CUSTOMER: How do you ensure the quality of your meat products? How do I know the meat is good?

SERVICE: Our quality control checks and balances are very specific and easy for employees to use. One simple example will make the point. Each stainless-steel tank used in our sausage kitchen is washed with 200-degree water after every use. Wash stations are located throughout the kitchen area, as specified by USDA standards. Federal inspectors are on site all day helping us confirm all Federal standards and procedures are followed. Records are maintained on all raw materials used in our products. If, for example, we have a rare case of spoiled meat in the grocery store, we can trace all the ingredients in that particular package all the way back to the farmers who produced the original raw ingredients.

Could I have your address? I would like to send you a brief write-up, which explains how our quality-control procedures function.

IS THE PRODUCT ENVIRONMENTALLY FRIENDLY?

Being environmentally friendly is just good business and means good sales. For example, one popular furniture maker touts in its sales ads that none of its furniture is manufactured with woods that come from endangered rain forests. Have your environmental strategy well documented and spelled out in detail. Drill customer-service representatives on particularly important environmental positions.

Many customers feel a strong moral obligation to protect the environment. Many will only purchase from firms that are bound by legal and regulatory environmental mandates and restrictions. Never dismiss questions about environmental concerns. For a variety of reasons, such questions are serious and may make the difference between creating customer satisfaction and losing a customer. There are also legal and political issues involved.

Arm yourself with a response that goes beyond a simple "yes," but do not embroider on the truth. Be certain that what you claim has basis in fact. Your answer today may be in a national newspaper tomorrow.

CUSTOMER: Is your (product) environmentally friendly?

SERVICE: We at (company) are committed to protecting the environment. Our plant meets or exceeds all current government regulations, both local and federal. We also use biodegradable packaging exclusively. Our packaging materials not only protect the environment, but do a more efficient job of protecting your shipment.

Pitfall: Some customers worry that protecting the environment involves compromises in the quality, value, or effectiveness of the product. Try to emphasize the win-win aspect of your firm's environmental commitment: biodegradable packing material is not only environmentally friendly, it does a great job of protecting fragile merchandise.

Pitfall: Some customers worry that protecting the environment means higher prices. Lay out your company's position in writing and explain your position with confidence. All organizations have the responsibility to keep the public accurately informed.

SERVICE: We have installed state-of-the-art scrubbers on all chimneys to make sure we are not discharging pollutants into the environment. The scrubbers will be paid for over the next ten years. It is true that they are increasing our manufacturing costs slightly. However, our region of the country is under strict government inspection because of past air pollution. If we all don't do our part, government regulations will require very expensive auto-emissions equipment over the next five years.

Know the ingredients of your products and communicate them factually:

SERVICE: Recycling ingredients is a major concern for our company. Our engineers certify that everything consumed in the manufacture of our products is recyclable. All vendors who supply components certify that the components they supply are recyclable as well.

SERVICE: We have the contract to dig up and replace the main street in your community. Recycling the waste material we dig up is, of course, a major concern. Tons of material will be created. We have specified that all of the old concrete will be separated from the old reinforcement steel. The steel will be recycled back to the mill. The concrete will all be crushed and reused as fill here on site or filler at the concrete plant. None of the waste material will be dumped in the local landfill. In fact, our recycling program is one of the main reasons your city officials awarded our company the rebuilding contract.

Socially controversial issues can also be stated positively. Again, most of the information is in your company. It is the responsibility of customer service or consumer affairs to understand what the company is doing and to script out the most positive messages for the consumers:

CUSTOMER: Are any of these foods grown with the use of insecticides?

SERVICE: We, like all growers, must fight against the overwhelming hordes of insects. All insecticides used are approved by our government. We are leaders in the industry in developing innovative ways to grow food without the use of hazardous materials. For example, our production is 20 percent higher than it was five years ago. However, our use of insecticides has declined by 10 percent in the same time period. Our engineers are continually developing new knowledge, and we are always applying what we know to keep our environment healthy. Our company is the leader in our growers association in pushing research into new methods of eliminating use of all insecticides. Currently, our growers association is spending over (millions) per year in developing insect-resistant crops. My company contributes (dollars) to this research effort. Improvements are coming daily.

We are also careful in processing foods. For example, spinach is washed four times before it is packaged for delivery to your grocery. Still, though, we recommend you wash all foods thoroughly before cooking.

ARE YOU RELIABLE?

This question will usually come in the form of something more specific concerning customer support, efficient shipping practices, error-free installation, convenient hours, and so on. Answer the question specifically, but be aware that what the customer ultimately wants to know is *Are you reliable?* Incorporate such words and phrases as *reliable, you can depend on, you can count on, you can rely on*, and so forth into your response.

CUSTOMER: I need that replacement part to show up by (date). I can't afford a delay.

SERVICE: You can rely on us, and you can count on (part) reaching you no later than (date). I'm going to give you a tracking number, which you can use when you call us if you have any questions or concerns. We will also send you a confirmation notice today. I can see on my computer that the parts you need are currently in our inventory.

The impression of reliability is greatly enhanced if you use evidence available. Customer service significantly adds to the selling effort by explaining how the organization supports the concept of reliability. Customer service needs to be aware of the organization's performance statistics:

CUSTOMER: We really do need to ensure the planned shipment schedule is upheld. We carry no reserve inventory.

SERVICE: We understand vendor-managed inventory and have been working hard with many of our customers. For example, one of our main quality-control measurements is our on-time shipment number. Five years ago, we were able to ship on the promised ship date only 70 percent of the time. Since then, we have put forth a major drive to offer additional value to our customers. We have been working very closely with our customers as well to clarify their real delivery requirements. Today, we agree in advance with our customers what the shipping dates will be, and we have been working hard keeping track of critical incidents for the past five years. This past year we have been able to ship on the promised ship date 98 percent of the time. We really want to ship on time 100 percent of the time, enabling our customers to hold no reserve inventory. We are still clarifying our inventory control systems and will likely be able to approach the 100 percent reliability figure within the next year. It's a tough objective, because there are many details involved. But we believe we can attain it.

Reliability is also substantiated by your history:

SERVICE: Yes, you can depend on us to keep our promises. We have been in business for more than a century. Our customer base is worldwide. Many of our customers have used our products for years and years. Our average customer has been with us for more than five years, and these customers would not have stayed with us if we had not reliably worked with them over the years. On average, we receive three letters per week from existing customers, thanking us for helping them out of a jam. Our company newsletter features testimonials from our customers every week. Could I have your address? I would like to send you a few copies.

Explain the total reliability issue and the philosophy your company maintains:

SERVICE: Reliability means more than keeping our delivery promise. Our world is imperfect, and, like it or not, sometimes things go wrong. We understand this, and our contingency planning system is the best in our industry. We have (number) of engineers and technicians on our payroll. In the unlikely event that something goes wrong, we have the depth we need to get things fixed.

Or use finance to support reliability:

SERVICE: We are a publicly held company, and our stockholders understand the critical importance of customer support. That's why we are managed conservatively.

Our debt-to-equity ratio is one of the best in the industry. We have the financial muscle needed to support our customers. In the unlikely event that something does go wrong, we have the financial resources to stand behind our product and our warranty. We can be there, and we will be there. We have a fifty-year reputation to protect.

Even a privately held company can use its history to substantiate reliability. It is up to customer service to understand the leadership values that guide the company:

SERVICE: The Anderson family has been rooted in the community for the past seventy-five years, and the family name is the company name. The family is proud of its service to the community and certainly appreciative of the support the community has given to the business for the past three generations. The company is still run by descendants of the founder. We want to be good citizens, and customer support is absolutely critical to our long-term strategy for success. We don't intend to go anywhere. Any complaint letter is reviewed by the president of the company. Further, our president follows up personally on every customer-service problem that occurs. Our executive leadership is completely involved in service-related issues. As you might guess, not very many service problems occur. Around here, everyone pays attention or they hear from the boss.

HOW ETHICAL ARE YOU?

It is not likely that a customer will come right out and ask you this question, but, as with questions about reliability, this is the message that underlies any number of queries. Customers want the greatest possible value. They also want ethical partners. After all, when firms do business together, their reputations are linked.

CUSTOMER: You bill by the hour. How do I know that your billing is accurate?

SERVICE: We furnish you with a descriptive, itemized accounting of our services. I'll level with you, it *is* easy to inflate hours billed. But we just don't do that. It's unethical and it's not good business. If you feel we've padded the bill you won't come back. We may have made a few extra dollars using an inflated time report once, but we will have lost you as a customer. Besides that, cheating is just plain wrong!

Tip: Your answers to questions concerning ethics will be more convincing if you frame them in terms of good business practices. Suggest to your customer that not only he or she, but *you* benefit from ethical conduct.

You must also know your company's ethical position. Be informed on all relevant policies and procedures. Look for opportunities to sell your ethical position. Sell your business integrity. Here is another exchange:

SERVICE: We have a long-standing ethics policy in our firm as well. It was developed thirty years ago and is reviewed annually. The policy is reworked each year, and all employees are sent to a four-hour workshop to discuss any changes that may have been made. It's really quite specific, spelling out exactly the types of behavior, such as taking gifts, which would be considered unethical.

Candidly, it is possible that some individual employee might take a gift or pad a time sheet. Perhaps even some department head could do it, and maybe even get away with padding for awhile. But the penalties are severe for violating the ethics policy. A violation means immediate dismissal from the company. These harsh penalties make perfect sense and are designed to ensure that our ethics policy is not violated.

SEND ME LITERATURE

The majority of calls to customer service are requests for information. How you respond to these straightforward requests contributes to a climate favorable to making the sale.

CUSTOMER: Do you have any literature on (product)?

SERVICE: I certainly do, a very detailed brochure, complete with specifications and cost projections. I'd also like to send you information on (other related products or options), just to show you your entire range of choices. I want to make sure you get the best product for your application.

Tip: Make the most of any request for information. If your customer is interested in product A, you can help ensure satisfaction by informing him or her of your product and option range. A request for information is an opportunity to promote your business.

Pitfall: Providing more information than the customer asks for is usually an important service for that customer. However, beware of coming on as if you are merely trying to "upsell" the customer, to talk him or her out of a lower-priced product into a higher-priced one. Also, do not bury your customer in such a heap of information that he or she will become overwhelmed and incapable of deciding on a purchase. The best way to avoid this pitfall is to focus on the customer's application. The following illustrates this:

SERVICE: Tell me, what are you planning to do with the product? (*Let the customer explain his or her application.*) Yes, that is the right application. Our (product) will do what you need. I'll get that catalog out to you today. I will also put a paper clip on the pages that discuss your particular application. I'll send you our description of (alternative product) as well, which can also do what you need and has several additional options. They are (list). It carries a higher price, because it provides so many more benefits. Of course, if you have no need for the additional benefits, you should not purchase this higher-priced model. I'll just include the literature so that you are informed of our complete offering.

I'll also staple my business card to the catalog. If you would like to order, just call our 800 number and any of us will be able to help you. Or, if you prefer, you can call me directly.

WHAT ARE THE PRODUCT'S INGREDIENTS?

Food and chemical products must, of course, be clearly labeled. If a current customer is calling you to inquire about product ingredients, refer the customer to the product label, but always offer to review the ingredients with the customer.

CUSTOMER: What does (product) contain?

SERVICE: You'll find a full list of ingredients on the label. I can go over them with you if you like. Do you have (product) nearby? Did you have any specific concerns?

CUSTOMER: Well, yes. Why do you include a number of preservatives, and aren't they harmful?

SERVICE: The preservatives are necessary to ensure that (product) remains stable, retains its full flavor, and does not spoil. When working with perishable ingredients, preservatives are essential. The preservatives we use are not harmful. They have been thoroughly tested and are FDA approved. I should also add that the preservatives we use have stood the test of time; they've been industry standard for many years.

Tip: Have exact data available in writing on all ingredients. Offer to send the customer detailed information.

SERVICE: I have even more detailed information on the preservatives used. May I send it to you? The information I have includes more details on the test results, which were reviewed and approved by the FDA. I can send you these documents along with a coupon for a free (product) sample.

Tip: You can also use questions to sell your product or enable your customer to achieve other greater value.

CUSTOMER: I am using your canned soup as part of a larger recipe. Does it have any additives?

SERVICE: Yes, we do include preservatives to maintain freshness. Those preservatives are all listed on the label. I really don't know how they may interact with other foods and ingredients in your recipe. However, many of our customers use our soups in recipes. In fact we have a series of recipes developed by us and our customers. I would like to send you a recipe booklet we have put together. Perhaps it will give you some ideas for meals. May I have your address?

Tip: Take advantage of these questions to sell your concern for the customer. Here is another exchange concerning preservatives:

CUSTOMER: What kind of preservatives do you use in your products?

SERVICE: We have been using only natural preservatives for the past five years. Annually, we spend three million dollars researching new developments in food preservatives to ensure that they are the best available on the market.

The following is a conversation about a potentially hazardous product.

CUSTOMER: I am concerned that using the cleaning fluid may harm the environment.

SERVICE: All ingredients in our products are biodegradable. We invest $10 million in research annually to ensure that our existing products as well as new products are environmentally friendly. Our tests show that the (product) will be completely decomposed within one year after it is thrown out. It will even decompose in a covered landfill.

Tip: Know the facts about your company, its products, and its position in the community. Saying "we invest $10 million annually to ensure . . ." is far more powerful than saying "we invest millions to ensure . . . ."

Tip: In dealing with any hazardous ingredients, be certain to have specific Material Safety Data Sheets available for the customer. In answering questions concerning these products, insist on communicating in written as well as verbal form.

CUSTOMER: Are there any hazards associated with this cleaning fluid?

SERVICE: Yes. It must be used in strict conformance with the instructions on the label. Is the label on the product you are planning to use?

CUSTOMER: Yes.

SERVICE: Usage instructions are on the back label. The product is an excellent cleaning agent, but it can cause irritation of the eyes, nose, and throat if used incorrectly. We recommend full-body protection. The product should only be used in well-ventilated areas. We recommend that all employees be supervised when using this product. Also, no employee should be working alone with this product. In case of an accident, he or she may need assistance from his or her partner.

May I have your fax number? I would like to fax you a Material Safety Data Sheet, which you should read and keep with the product at all times. Please give me your address as well, and I will send you several copies in the mail. Be certain all employees who work with this product have copies of the Material Safety Sheet.

WHAT ARE MY PURCHASING OPTIONS?

In responding to this question, clearly describe the range of options available. Emphasize that your company offers a range of choices in order to serve its customers optimally. As always when describing a series of options, be careful not to overwhelm the customer into inaction.

SERVICE: You may purchase (product) using any major credit card. We also offer our own financing plan, which features highly competitive interest rates and no money down. You might also consider leasing (product). We offer 36- and 48-month terms. For added flexibility, we offer a buyout option at the end of the lease period. Would you like to hear more about any of these options?

Tip: After listing options, don't just plop the matter in your customer's lap. Be certain to ask if he or she has any questions about the choices. However, you do not need to answer the specific question asked. Take advantage of the opportunity to explain any extra-value arrangements your company has available. The customer may not be aware of all your innovative options; effective customer servicing is effective selling.

CUSTOMER: What are your purchasing options?

SERVICE: You may not wish to *purchase* the product at all. Perhaps one of our partnership programs will work more effectively for you. Let me clarify: You are in the business of manufacturing (products). We are in the business of creating machines that compress air. Compressed air is something you consume during the manufacture of (products). To us, compressing air is a business. To you, it is a necessary part of your manufacturing process. If you buy the compressor, you must purchase, finance, install, learn how to use, and then maintain it. Five years or so down the line, the compressors you buy must be replaced, and the cycle starts all over again. You must worry about compressors as well as the manufacture of (products). This adds more complexity to your core manufacturing business.

Many of our customers prefer our high-value partnership program. It may also be the best program for you. It's simple: You purchase what you need, not what you don't need. To say it another way: You purchase what you use. You do not purchase what you need to *manufacture* what you use. You need air, not compressors. We'll sell you only what you need: air.

CUSTOMER: I don't understand.

SERVICE: Let me outline how this works. With our high-value partnership program, our engineers work closely with your engineers to determine your air requirements. Like your local utility, we become your business partners. Our fee for air is based solely on the compressed air you consume. You do not need to worry about the compressors at all. You do not need to finance, purchase, install, or maintain compressors. You need only worry about the (products) you manufacture. We do everything related to air. This arrangement helps your financing also. Purchasing the compressed air monthly means that it is a simple manufacturing expense. It falls directly to the expense side of your income-and-expense statement. You do not need to fund capital equipment, a compressor, and depreciate it over time.

Dependent upon the criticality of your operations, we can even guarantee the reliability of the air-supply system. For some of our customers in the health-care field, we have built fail-safe air-supply systems. Surgical suites need this type of support, for example.

You have been a good customer for years, and our high-value partnership program is a relatively new development. Could I have our sales representative call on you to discuss this option?

WHAT IS YOUR WARRANTY?

You should be prepared to answer this question concisely, without legalisms and without emphasizing any exceptions. The important thing is to focus on the high quality of the warranty and its positive features and benefits. Promote the warranty as an important product benefit, especially if it is competitive with or superior to warranties from other companies. Stress the following:

1. Term of warranty.
2. Extent of coverage.
3. Add a few words about your firm's long-term reputation.

Also be prepared to answer questions about whether you repair or replace defective merchandise, about turnaround time on warranty repairs/replacement, and about the availability of authorized warranty repair stations.

CUSTOMER: What kind of warranty do you offer?

SERVICE: Our warranty is for three years and covers all parts and labor. You won't find a better warranty in the business. Most others are one year.

CUSTOMER: Do you repair or replace bad merchandise?

SERVICE: If it's a question about a defective part, we generally replace the part rather than the entire unit. But if we have any doubts about the unit, we give you a brand-new one. We also feature a 30-day "no-questions-asked" return policy. If you have any problems within the first 30 days after you take delivery, you may return the unit for exchange or refund.

Note that Service did not mention the 30-day policy when initially describing warranty coverage. You don't want to throw too many time periods at the customer, who might come away from the conversation believing that your warranty is good for 30 days only.

CUSTOMER: I can't be hassled with waiting three and four weeks for a repair. What's your turnaround time on warranty service?

SERVICE: If you walk into one of our authorized service stations, we can usually guarantee a three-day turnaround. If you want to tell me where you live, I'll give you the address of the service station nearest you. They can quote you an exact turn-around, which, of course, is dependant on actual workload at the time.

Tip: If your company offers warranty extensions, now is the time to describe this option. Be careful to offer it as an added product benefit, not as compensation for an inadequate base warranty.

SERVICE: We also offer additional protection with our Priority Service plan. This extends your warranty to five years total, and includes free express courier service of your unit to our service center. Are you interested in this option?

Tip: Ask if the customer is interested *before* you mention cost. Remember, put the emphasis on what you *offer* the customer rather than what *you want from* the customer.

SERVICE: We have been in business for the past thirty years and consider ourselves to be responsible citizens of the community. Our customers know we will stand behind our products and warranties and always place customer satisfaction first.

Tip: This is a subtle way of telling the customer you also will make warranty exceptions and extensions on occasion, without telling the customer exactly what the exceptions are. Be careful here. You want to tell the customer you will stand behind the product and ensure satisfaction, but you do not want arbitrarily to extend the warranty before the product is purchased. Further, you only extend the warranty *some* of the time, not *all* of the time. If you tell the customer you make exceptions now, at this early stage, you are essentially making a verbal contract for a different warranty.

HOW WELL WILL YOU SUPPORT ME?

People don't just buy technology, they buy service and support. Support is seen to be at the heart of a product's total value. The temptation is to answer such a question with vague and general assurances: "We will support you very well!," or "We will provide great service!" Far more effective is a response that proves your point. Try this:

SERVICE: Well, let me give you an example. I'm the first one to tell you that our (product) is terrific, but once in a great while, something does go wrong. Unfortunately, this happened to one of our customers in (city) a few weeks ago, and it happened at a critical time, when the customer was in a major production crunch. You can imagine that we got a call. The customer explained the situation, and we sent a local technician out immediately. He quickly isolated the bad component and called our parts department to reserve a replacement. Problem: a replacement part would not be available for two days. Knowing how desperately our customer needed production, our local field technician called the manager of the main assembly plant and "borrowed" the needed part from our assembly line. The part was hand delivered to our technician who was still on-site, and he had the customer up and running six hours after the initial call came in. Service technicians in the field know they have authority to locate and focus company resources on critical customer needs. We have internal systems that enable the technician to help the organization evaluate the risks it is taking. Essentially, we will even stop a shipment to a new customer in order to keep an existing customer in production. That's the kind of support we aim to give you.

Tip: Many firms have formal escalation systems to ensure that they provide proper support to users of their products. Take the time to explain to the customer any formal systems you have. An example follows.

SERVICE: We in service are well aware of the critical nature of the CAT-scan machine. We know that downtime is totally unacceptable to the hospital. But we aren't naive. The CAT-scanning system is extremely complex technology. It would be silly for us to assume that there would never be any problems. That's why we have instituted automatic escalation procedures to control all service-related issues. Let me explain how our system works.

Our technician is trained in all diagnostic procedures. When she is in the field, she has one hour after arrival on site to diagnose the problem. Specifically, diagnosis means that she knows exactly where the problem is and what is required to get the system back up and running. If she is not certain within an hour where the problem is, she is required to call for assistance. Second-level service then takes automatic command. Two additional specialists will work by computer and telephone hook-up with our technician on site. This three-person team then has an additional two hours to get the problem identified. If a total of three hours goes by without a firm solution, technical management is alerted and allocates additional resources. As I said, we intend to stand behind the products we ship. Our automatic escalation system ensures that our people and organization have the authority and resources to do this.

ARE YOU A SOCIALLY CONSCIENTIOUS COMPANY? PROVE IT.

If your firm supports special charitable programs or, for example, offers internships, it is both easy and a pleasure to answer this customer question. Obviously, you should have at your fingertips specific details covering these fine programs. If, however, your company does not conduct any special programs, you must answer more creatively. Don't make up a story, but do bear in mind that a question of this nature requires a positive answer.

CUSTOMER: I like to do business with companies that have a conscience. Can you give me an idea of just what kind of company you are?

SERVICE: We believe that our greatest resource is not technology or plastic or metal, but *people*. Good people will keep us competitive and keep our nation competitive. Since 19XX, (company) has offered comprehensive summer internships for high-school students. The program has already produced some great employees for us, but, more importantly, the program has given a good many youngsters an opportunity to learn about our industry and business in general.

This is fine. But what if your company offers no such programs? Here's a creative answer:

SERVICE: We feel that by making each and every product we produce the very best we can, we are bringing a measure of quality into the lives of our customers and community. Conscience? Our people couldn't sleep at night if they didn't feel they were giving 110 percent every day.

Or try something like this:

SERVICE: Good companies are organizations of people with a conscience. We have been in business in this community since 19XX. Since then our employees have been involved in (list of socially conscious activities).

We're proud of our heritage and fully recognize that people do not separate business from the community. All of our employees are encouraged to contribute fully in making the complete community a better place for all of us.

Frankly, it helps the company's bottom line. Employees who are proud of themselves and are involved in their community are better employees. They are more productive, and they are more tuned in to the importance of building high-quality, reliable products. We intend to continue our current policy, which encourages and supports high involvement.

WHY SHOULD I DO BUSINESS WITH YOU?

Anybody who answers questions for a living quickly learns that the specific, detailed questions are really the easiest to field. The big, open-ended queries, on the other hand, can catch you off guard and stun you into uncomfortable silence. You should prepare yourself for big, blunt ones that come your way.

CUSTOMER: There are a lot of companies offering your service. Some of them charge less than you do. Why should I do business with you?

SERVICE: I can give you a one-word answer: value. Now, as you know, value doesn't simply mean getting the lowest price. It means getting the most for the money you spend. Cheap (name of product or service) is usually not worth the money you spend on it. High-value (name of product or service) is a real bargain. And that is what we will give you.

If you can give a concise and compelling answer like this one, do so. Another useful strategy is actually to list key product or service benefits and to show how the customer receives value from the benefits.

SERVICE:　What you should know is that our (product or service) offers the following benefits that our competitors *do not* give you at *any* price: (list).

Here is one specific example:

SERVICE:　No one really likes to purchase auto insurance. Even worse, no one even likes to *use* auto insurance. Using the insurance means an accident has occurred. At (name) Insurance, we understand this relationship between our high-value product and our customers and have made the entire process easier. We have developed a national bank of collision repair centers. Hopefully, no one ever needs auto insurance. But if you are unfortunate and are involved in an accident, any of our preapproved centers will repair your car and give you a loaner while your car is being repaired. You do not need to go through the process of getting competitive bids or anything. You only need to contact a preapproved repair center. The towing charge and all other related charges will be handled through our centralized billing operations. Of course, you can still use any other collision repair center, even if they are not on the prior-approval list. We know what insurance means to you, and are finding creative ways to provide the value without all of the hassle.

WHY SHOULD I TELL MY FRIENDS ABOUT YOU?

I recently received a postcard from the realtor who sold me my house. "My survival," the card said, "depends on clean air, clean water, wholesome food, and recommendations from customers like you." Pretty clever, I thought, but not a very effective appeal for word-of-mouth advertising. To paraphrase John F. Kennedy: Ask not what your customer can do for you; tell your customer what you will do for him or her. Instead of pointing out to a customer that your "survival" depends on customer referrals, suggest that the customer will win the gratitude of friends and colleagues if he or she recommends your services. Everyone enjoys having their advice followed.

CUSTOMER:　I'd like to pass your name on to some friends. Should I?

SERVICE:　Well, we'd certainly appreciate it. But, more importantly, your friends will thank you. I don't know anyone who isn't grateful to find good value in a (product or service). You'd be doing your friends a service. As you are well aware, our financial planners managed to help you defer significant funds from your gross taxable income accounts to your retirement accounts, thereby significantly reducing your taxable income this year. You know your friends better than I, and, of course, we are always looking for additional clients. If your friends can benefit from the same type of financial planning, we certainly would appreciate the opportunity to speak with them.

Chapter

5

Convincing the Customer of Quality and Performance Capability

Essential to ensuring customer satisfaction is clarifying the extent of your promise. Make no mistake, satisfaction is directly dependent on how well the product or service actually performs, but Customer Service can do a great deal to create a context that will allow the customer to perceive, to understand, and to appreciate performance, as well as the limitations of product performance. Customer Service can prepare the customer for satisfaction.

This does not mean praising the product or service unconditionally or unrealistically. The last thing you want to do is to create unrealistic expectations that will lead only to disappointment. Your communication goals should include:

1. Conveying specific quality and performance capability.

2. Creating confidence.

3. Assuring the customer that your company stands behind the product/service, and that somebody will be available to help.

4. Educating the customer.

Let's take a closer look at point 4. Educating the customer means assuring the customer that his or her expectations for the product or service are realistic and appropriate. Care must be taken here not to emphasize the negative, but you should not build up unrealistic expectations.

Tip: It is usually helpful to compare performance of your product with that of others. For example, "No widget operates entirely without noise. However, ours is the quietest in its price range."

Tip: Be sure to take every opportunity to educate the customer about how he or she can enhance performance. The customer also has responsibilities. For example, "Lab studies show that our (product) will provide a long life of reliable performance. Reliability is significantly enhanced by recommended regular maintenance. Annual cleaning and lubrication as described in the operator's manual dramatically increases the (product's) reliability.

Explain limitations positively:

SERVICE: Our laboratory tests are quite conclusive: the (product) is designed to operate at a maximum of (units per time period). Our customer-application records are quite clear. A few customers trying to squeeze additional profits, exceed our design recommendations. Over the long run, these customers actually lose profits. The (product) provides long life and long-term profitability when operated as it was designed to operate.

HOW DO YOU ENSURE THE PRODUCT DELIVERED IS WHAT WAS ORDERED?

A common customer complaint is incorrect fulfillment of orders. This is, in fact, a serious problem for customer satisfaction. Customers have the right to expect delivery of what they need when they need it. They should not be obliged to take the time and effort to do what they rightly perceive to be your job. Certainly, customers should not be in the business of repacking and arranging for the return of goods sent in error. But, most of all, your customers do not want to feel that they will be left hanging, having ordered a product, only to be caught short when the wrong item arrives. Begin at the beginning by allaying these anxieties.

CALLER: Look, the one thing I'm not equipped to mess around with is mistakes. I can't be sending back stuff I didn't order. I just don't have the people to deal with that.

SERVICE: I understand. The last thing we want is for our customers to do our job. We are completely networked here. What goes into my computer when I take an order is exactly what our pickers work from. Everything is based on merchandise numbers, so nothing is left to guesswork. You'll get what you ordered and only what you ordered.

Tip: Describe some of the details of how your system works. Detail builds your integrity and helps erase doubts the customer may have. Of course, you must keep yourself informed about how your systems actually do work!

SERVICE: Still, we recognize there is a potential for error. Let me review a few of our checking procedures. First I take the order. We confirm the order back to you. You have the opportunity to check my work to make sure I have described your order correctly. Our computer system automatically assigns merchandise numbers to the items you ordered. Then, your order is picked from our warehouse. All packages in the warehouse are identified with UPC codes. Our warehouse staff prepares shipping documents directly from the picked items. The computer then compares the shipping documents to the entered order. As you see, when we say you get what you ordered and only what you ordered, we mean what we say.

Even with all of this, our system still is not perfect. We track errors and are always upgrading. One of the difficulties in creating perfection is cost. We must only find improvements that do not increase costs to you. Five years ago, 10 percent of all orders left our warehouse with errors. Today, 4 percent have errors. We're still working on it. But we're getting better.

Another customer is anxious not about getting the wrong item, but about items being unavailable:

CALLER: I work on a just-in-time inventory control system. I order only what I need when I need it. I can't afford to stock much inventory. Now, what that means is that I just can't be waiting for back orders.

SERVICE: I can punch up on my computer screen the current inventory status of whatever you order. I can tell you if there is any risk of our not having an item in stock. Look, I can also promise you this: an honest estimate of how long a particular back order will take. We do not want you to be caught short, and we'll work with you to ensure that you have what you need when you need it.

Customer satisfaction comes not just from defining what you promise, but also from delivering on your promise. Make sure the customer understands his or her responsibility in helping you keep your promise. The customer service rep continues:

SERVICE: "Just-in-time" is an idea that requires us to cooperate effectively with each other. Obviously, we must have what you need in inventory when you need it, but excessive inventory only adds costs, which are ultimately paid for by all of our customers. We have very reliable availability arrangements with many of our customers. Our most reliable arrangements are with those customers who involve us in their long-range planning sessions. The more we know about your future needs, the better we can plan and manage our own manufacturing processes. You do not need to be exact with forecasting, no one ever is, including us, but the more closely we work together on forecasting and adjusting to the future, the better our availability system will be.

HOW DO YOU KNOW THAT WHAT WAS DELIVERED PERFORMS AS PROMISED?

This is a more complicated question and concern than may at first be apparent. The customer may be asking for assurances about the product itself, whether it will perform as marketed, and/or the customer may be concerned about quality control.

Depending on the nature of the merchandise, such issues as shelf life and freshness may also be a concern. Be certain you understand just what the customer is asking before you respond.

CALLER: I need this thing to work. How do I know it's going to do what you say it will?

SERVICE: I can promise you that the widget will perform to specification. Do you have another concern?

CALLER: Frankly, yes. I've not had a very happy experience with widgets in the past. Half the time, it seems, there's something that's defective.

SERVICE: Well, you're right to be concerned. A manufacturer can design a great product, but if quality control isn't up to par, even the best design will fail. That's why we focus so much of our effort on quality assurance. Are you familiar with the ISO 9000 program?

CALLER: I've heard something about it.

SERVICE: What this is, specifically, is a set of very high standards for quality assurance. These are standards for managing a business, and, in order to obtain ISO 9000 certification, a company has to meet very rigorous guidelines for documenting and controlling its promises to its customers. We are certified as complying with the ISO 9000 system of process control. That's why we can assure you of the very best quality control. The ISO system obliges us to prove with documentation that we do what we say we are doing. Our system also obliges us to respond to errors in certain and precise ways to ensure the error will not happen again. It obliges us to control all processes in order not just to eliminate the error, but continually to work to eliminate the *potential* for recurrence of the error.

HOW DO YOU KNOW THAT THE PRODUCT IS DESIGNED TO DO WHAT YOU SAY IT WILL DO?

Customers are rightly concerned that you are selling them a product specifically designed to do the job they want it to do. And Customer Service should make it part of its mission to help ensure a good fit between product and application. Few things are more destructive than the frustration caused by a product-application mismatch.

Tip: Don't rush to assure your customer that he or she is making the right choice. Take the time to understand the customer's application (educate yourself) then work with the customer to ensure that he or she selects the appropriate product (educate him or her).

CALLER: Can I be sure that the Model ABC will work with my system?

SERVICE: Let me make certain that I understand what you're working with. You have a (review caller's equipment). Is that correct?

Tip: Make certain that you understand the customer's requirements. Don't put the burden on the caller, however; refer to yourself: "Let me make certain I understand . . . ."

CALLER: Yes, that's my system.

SERVICE: Then the Model ABC is appropriate and will work well. We have, in fact, designed and tested it to work in your specific application. We have proven its performance. I do want to point out that if you would like to add (feature) to your operations, you might take a look at our Model XYZ. It does everything ABC does, but adds (features). Now, the cost is ($ amount) more, but most of our customers find that the added features are worth it.

CALLER: But Model ABC will do the basic job.

SERVICE: Oh, yes. Definitely.

There are many variations to this basic theme. Here is another possible example.

CALLER: Hey look, you guys have been touting this co-operative marketing product to us independent grocers for months. There is a giant community festival that starts on (date), and we're thinking of taking your offer. Before we invest a ton in advertising, we want to make sure you're with us. We want to give away free pizza to all of those coming into the store. How can we be certain you'll keep your part of the bargain and supply the pizza? We don't want to spend a fortune only to find out you don't have product.

SERVICE: I'm glad you called. That's exactly what the co-op marketing program is all about. Let us know what you think you can give away, and we will make sure we build the inventory for you. Include a generous safety margin. We understand how these things work; you can't really know exactly how many customers will come by. Don't worry about the safety margin. Be sure you cover the possible contingencies. If you don't give all the pizza away, you can try to move it at a reduced price. We'll work with you on pricing. If you can't move it on sale, we'll take the excess back, provided they are kept frozen. We intend to work with you to ensure a successful program.

HOW IS MANUFACTURING TOLD HOW TO BUILD THE PRODUCT?

Savvy customers express as much concern for fabrication as well as design. Educate your customer as to the way your company ensures that design specifications are met in fabrication.

CALLER: A lot of widgets look great on paper, but fall short in fabrication. How do you guys stay on top of Manufacturing?

SERVICE: You are absolutely right, and we devote a great deal of effort to making certain that what our engineers design into a product is reflected in the manufactured result. We do this in two principal ways. First, the design team never works in isolation from the factory floor. Our designers design only what is possible to manufacture. We work *with* our fabricators. Second, a member of the design team always oversees fabrication. There is no ivory tower here. Our designers get their hands dirty.

In addition to all this, we inspect and test each widget thoroughly. The mission of quality assurance here is not just to avoid mistakes, but to make certain that what's been designed actually gets made.

There are, of course, always problems, which can and must be solved only when manufacturing of the product actually gets under way. All of our widgets go through an extensive prototyping period before they are offered to the market. In our program we build (number) of prototype widgets completely. These widgets are put into use exactly as our customers would expect to use them. They are tested 24 hours per day, and the results are monitored in our laboratories. Problems are identified. Design and manufacturing details are adjusted to eliminate manufacturing problems before any customer ever gets the product.

Even after all of this, there is more. After the prototype phase, we place several widgets on location with several of our large users. These customers actually use the products in real-world conditions. Again, our engineers and manufacturing experts monitor product performance. They look for manufacturing as well as design problems. Through these extensive testing procedures we are constantly improving our quality in the field.

HOW DO YOU KNOW PURCHASING BUYS WHAT YOUR ENGINEERS SPECIFY?

Many products are assembled from a host of components furnished by various suppliers. It is not always an easy task to ensure that components meet specifications. In many industries, cheap substitutes, even counterfeit components are a problem. It's pretty scary that counterfeit parts do even get into commercial aircraft. A discerning customer may quiz you about how you control and monitor your vendors and suppliers. Be certain you know what steps your company takes to ensure that components meet specs.

CALLER: I don't want any nasty surprises with components. What guarantee do I have that your purchasing people obtain what your engineers tell me they've spec'd?

SERVICE: First of all, we cost out all of our products carefully, and that means that we figure on buying only those components that meet specs. No one here has any vested interest in looking for "bargains." We run internal audits, checking specified component suppliers against invoices. The two have to match. Also, as part of our routine quality-assurance program, we pull assembled units off the line, tear them down, and check components.

You are right to be concerned. Bad components can compromise any design. We have no reported cases of unapproved vendors ever getting their parts in here. Purchasing may, of course, locate alternative suppliers for components. But these alternative suppliers must have their components tested and approved by engineering and research before they can be added to our approved supplier list.

Or try something like this:

SERVICE: Our reputation has been cultivated over the past century. We have no intention of destroying what we took so long to build. We have a premium line of food products for a reason. That reason is that our Purchasing Department buys only what has been specifically approved by our food-processing engineers. Every one of our raw-materials suppliers must be approved in advance. They are inspected by our own people. Further, they must meet all government standards as well. Let me share just a few of our inspection procedures suppliers must go through: (list).

In addition to all of this, every ingredient used in the manufacture of our products is tracked throughout the manufacturing process. Any problem found can be traced back to the original supplier.

I have a small booklet that explains how we ensure nothing but the highest quality ingredients are used in our food-production system. May I send you a copy?

Tip: Never dismiss a customer's concerns. If possible and appropriate, demonstrate that you appreciate the customer's intelligence and prudence. Remember, they are your best salesperson.

HOW IS INVENTORY PROTECTED BEFORE RESALE?
HOW DO YOU KNOW IT IS NOT CONTAMINATED?

Of great concern to buyers of bulk commodities is an assurance of purity. Customers often want to be certain of an unbroken "chain of custody" so that they know who has been responsible for manufacturing and storing raw materials. Your object in answering questions relating to issues of protection from contamination is to make the customer comfortable with your company's accountability for ensuring that the chain of custody is secure.

CALLER: What steps do you take to ensure that (substance) isn't contaminated?

SERVICE: We work only with suppliers we know. We've established long-standing relationships with the major suppliers, and we know them to be reputable. In addition, our buyers and technical specialists make frequent on-site visits. They know the industry standards and practices, and they can tell right away if something's not being done correctly.

Once the substance is at our plant, it is inspected for quality, and it is stored in an environmentally controlled area. The air is filtered, and the temperature controlled. Storage containers are all air-tight stainless steel. We receive shipments weekly, thereby ensuring (substance) has no opportunity to spoil. Stainless-steel tanks are cleaned with 180-degree water before use, which ensures that bacteria cannot accumulate. There just isn't much of a window of opportunity for contamination. We have not had any reported cases of contamination in the past twenty years.

Tip: Know your capabilities well and speak about them. Details help assuage the customer's doubts.

HOW DO YOU KNOW MATERIAL FOR PRODUCT A IS NOT MIXED WITH MATERIAL FOR PRODUCT B?

Another concern for buyers is that their specifications are met without danger of contamination of one product with another. This is a good opportunity to discuss craftsmanship, attention to detail, and state-of-the-art equipment.

CALLER: How do I know I'm getting the grade of (substance) I'm paying for? I mean, you see a lot of (substance). How do you keep somebody else's order from getting mixed in with mine?

SERVICE: Well, I know this is a simplistic answer, but it's true. We care, and we're careful. We don't just shovel out (substance). We dispense it carefully. We also operate state-of-the-art machinery for filling your order. The core of our business is giving you what you want, no more and no less.

Grades are stored in separate containers, of course. Further, a sample is pulled and checked in the lab before every order is filled. Another sample is pulled after the order is filled to confirm quality and purity levels. A written, signed report showing the results of lab tests on the samples taken is shipped with the order. For larger orders, say 100 drums or more, a sample is pulled from every tenth drum to ensure consistency. Again, the lab reports are sent with the shipment, and all reports are signed by the technician who performed the test.

If your business requires batching of materials, you might try something like the following.

SERVICE: There are a number of checking procedures throughout the manufacturing process to confirm that no human errors have occurred that might contaminate the final product. For example, all meat ingredients for all processed sausage products, including all luncheon meats, are carefully moved through our kitchens in stainless containers. The containers are washed each time a batch is emptied.

Specified amounts of the ingredients are then electronically measured into the various mixers, and the mixing operations are automatically timed. The potential for human error is minimized to ensure the consistency of every batch, five samples are pulled and tested in the lab after mixing. Each sample is pulled from a different part of the mixer. After the laboratory confirms the ingredients, the processed meats are then manufactured and cooked. After cooking, the meats are again sampled. The ingredients and quality are confirmed by the laboratory before product is shipped to our customers.

Tip: As is true of so many issues dealing with customer satisfaction, knowing the details of your operations and how you maintain quality for your customers is critical in creating high levels of satisfaction.

HOW DO YOU KNOW THAT YOU ARE BUILDING MY PRODUCT CORRECTLY?

Dealing with issues in this area is an opportunity to sell your customer on your company's critical intangibles. It's not just that your product embodies cutting-edge technology and the finest materials, but that it is also the result of a collective commitment to quality and the sum total of the experience of your people. It is easy to answer questions in this area with the equivalent of "trust us," but you need to go further: "Trust us, because . . . ."

CALLER: This is a complicated job. How do you know you're building (product) correctly?

SERVICE: That is a good question. Let me answer it by reminding you that what you are buying is not just an assembly of parts. You are buying *us.* You are buying what we are. You are buying our knowledge and experience in this field. We've been building (products) for (number) years. (Percent amount) of our engineers have been with us for all that time. You are investing in our experience.

Tip: Knowing some of the details of your manufacturing and building processes is critical in helping the customer understand how you build quality into your product. Customer service must be informed about building and manufacturing methods.

SERVICE: Our search for quality is never ending. All assembly procedures are carefully worked out by manufacturing engineering, design engineering, and the shop assemblers themselves. The final procedures are all developed into written performance standards, which we are all required to follow.

The total (product) is broken into subassemblies. Each subassembly is tested as a discrete unit. By testing and confirming reliability of the many small assemblies, we have a much greater chance of producing reliability with the total (product). For example, the hydraulic subassembly controlling each wing flap can be tested individually before it is mounted to the wing and main hydraulic system.

We have been using assembly teams in manufacturing for the past ten years. Each team is assigned to a particular subassembly and is held accountable for specific written assembly standards and tests. The team must sign off on the quality results they report. They also work with our quality engineers to confirm the test results and every assembly engineer has the power to stop the building process if they detect any problem that might have a negative impact on quality. Further, every assembly engineer receives 40 hours of new training per year to keep him or her completely informed of new developments in quality assurance.

Tip: It is the specifics included in your comments that create satisfaction in your customers.

HOW DO YOU VERIFY THE PRODUCT WILL WORK AS PROMISED BEFORE IT IS SHIPPED?

If you "burn in" products before shipping them, this is the place to explain the process.

CALLER: How do you make sure (product) will perform up to spec before you ship it?

SERVICE: We "burn in" every sub-unit for (number) hours before it is assembled. (Percent amount) of the time, if there is a problem with a sub-unit, it will show up within the first (number) hours of operation. We burn the sub-unit in, monitor it, and then run a full set of diagnostics on it.

In addition to our own rigorous burn-in are the tough quality standards we require of all our component suppliers. Every component manufacturer is required to temperature-test every component before it is shipped to us for use in our (product). Components are cycled in an environmental test chamber between -40°F to +150°F for forty hours before final operational testing at the supplier's site. This very tough environmental test is intended to find weak components before they ever reach our door.

The completed (products) are then cycled for 40 hours before they are shipped. Any failure that occurs during final test must be corrected, documented, and signed-off on. The sign-off requires the testers to confirm that the failure has been isolated and that the specific components have been replaced.

It's important that the 40-hour run test must be restarted at zero with every failure. You, the customer, only receive the product after it has cycled successfully for a total 40 hours without any interruption.

If you don't "burn in," discuss in detail whatever quality assurance procedures you do employ.

HOW DO YOU KNOW THE EQUIPMENT USED TO TEST THE PRODUCT IS OPERATING CORRECTLY?

Customers who inquire about the nature of your test equipment may be satisfied with nothing less than a conversation with your Quality-Assurance department. However, before you pass the caller on to another department, attempt to answer the question simply and directly yourself. Again, know how your company operates.

SERVICE: We use some of the most advanced test equipment in the industry. But advanced equipment alone is not enough. All our test equipment is housed in environmentally controlled rooms, and all (product) testing occurs in these rooms. The atmosphere in these areas is filtered to remove contaminates. General traffic is restricted from these special areas and employees working in these special laboratories are required to wear protective clothing and receive specialized training. Additionally, our test equipment itself is calibrated weekly by our Quality-Assurance department, using specialized calibration equipment dedicated for this purpose. Test results on the test equipment are graphed, analyzed, and maintained over time to help us search for any trends that may indicate wear or other problems. Further, to help us maintain our high-quality leadership position, our calibration equipment is tested annually by the National Bureau of Standards. We send our calibration equipment to the Bureau, and it verifies our settings against known master standards.

Maintaining a quality testing program is difficult and expensive, but it is required to ensure the quality of the products you receive.

HOW DO YOU KNOW THE TESTS EVALUATE WHAT YOU SAY THEY EVALUATE?

This is another area that may require the assistance of a quality-assurance team member. The short answer, however, is a reference to industry standards. If the tests were developed in house, make reference to collective experience and expertise.

Pitfall: Issues such as these can lead to disputes, and it is not in your company's best interest to dispute with a caller. If a dispute seems inevitable, the best thing to do is respond by asking the caller to tell you what further information he or she would find helpful. If necessary, get back to the caller with that information at a later time.

SERVICE: All of our food ingredients are checked, and the purity is confirmed by our Quality-Assurance department. The acceptable method in our industry for controlling quality is gas chromatography. We use this method to test key ingredients for purity. Gas chromatography can measure the amount of impurity in any given sample. The charts produced by our test equipment are then compared to standard charts, which are accepted to represent normative data for a particular impurity in a particular ingredient.

The methodology we use is widely accepted as accurate by governments and food processors around the world. Tests are as correct as current worldwide experience allows them to be. We are measuring impurities down to the parts per billion range; that's somewhat similar to finding a jigger of fluid in a trainload of tanker cars.

Tip: Know something about the specific quality of the tests used in your particular industry.

WHERE ON THE PRODUCT DOES IT SAY THAT IT WAS SUCCESSFULLY TESTED? HOW ARE THE TEST RESULTS RECORDED?

A customer purchases a product and then has concerns about whether it was tested and whether it passed those tests successfully, or the customer needs confirmation of testing for his or her own processes.

CALLER: I don't see any inspection sticker on (product). Where does it say that it has been inspected?

SERVICE: There should be a loose slip of paper in the package. It has an inspector number and date, and it says "passed." There is no sticker on the product itself; most people find those annoying to remove.

CALLER: We use your products as a component of our larger system. Do you maintain the inspection record? I understand that it passed, and I appreciate that. However, I would like to have its exact performance measurements. We need to know how the product is positioned within its tolerance range. May I have the record of actual results?

SERVICE: Yes, we do create a product history file and the final inspection record and all approval signatures is a part of that file. I will need to get over to Quality Assurance and retrieve the record for your particular product from our permanent history files. I can have it mailed to you, and you should receive it within a week or so. Is that okay? Should I permanently change your order to ensure you always get the completed record in the future?

Tip: These scenarios are typically not urgent. The customer just needs the data for future file reference. Even if you can get him the data in a day or so, it is to your advantage to use conventional procedures and to lobby for additional time, as the example suggests. By gaining a bit of extra time for handling non-urgent matters, you create flexibility for yourself. The next call may be much more urgent, and you may be glad to have a few extra days.

WHEN SOMETHING GOES WRONG, WHAT DO I DO?

Increasingly, customer support, which for most people means fixing things when they go bad, is becoming the critical factor that molds a customer's decision to buy from you or from someone else. Now, in addition to offering input about the terms and conditions of your company's warranty policy, you can also do a great deal to convey your company's attitude toward supporting its customers.

Tip: Do not minimize the possibility of something going wrong. Instead, treat your responsiveness as a key product benefit and selling feature.

1. Convey that your company stands behind its product.

2. Convey that customer support is available and is available promptly.

3. Establish a partnership with the customer; you're in this together.

4. Explain the procedure for obtaining customer support and technical help.

5. If your company offers automated options for routine situations or frequently asked questions, explain this option. Stress its function as a time saver for the customer.

CALLER: Just how do you folks respond, anyway? What is the extent of your muscle?

SERVICE: Obviously, we hope nothing ever goes wrong. But we aren't naive, either. We know the system is complex. We have different support levels for different types of product users. Our blood-diagnostic units are used in hospital emergency rooms as well as businesses, such as blood banks. There is a giant difference in how these two groups operate. A hospital emergency room needs very advanced back-up. A blood bank typically has more than one unit in-house and is working on less urgent problems. That is why we have developed several different levels of support.

Our most advanced support level guarantees we're always right behind you. You call our 800 number any time any day, and our service technician will be attached to your system via a telephone modem within fifteen minutes. For less critical installations, we recommend our standard 24-hour response. For your application, we recommend the standard 24-hour service.

Overall, we have 2,000 service technicians in the field to ensure we're there when you need us.

WHEN SOMETHING GOES WRONG, WHAT ENSURES THE SAME THING WILL NOT GO WRONG AGAIN?

Making things right when things go wrong eliminates a source of considerable dissatisfaction, but it does little to create satisfaction. After all, the thing should never have gone wrong in the first place. To create satisfaction, you must assure the customer that his or her confidence in you is still valid, even though the error did occur.

SERVICE: (After a discussion of the problem and whatever remedy is required.) A shipment of new parts will be expedited to you today. I will confirm this to you by fax later this afternoon. The fax will include the shipper number, which will enable both of us to track this situation overnight to make sure the parts arrive for your production people tomorrow morning.

Again, I'm terribly sorry some of the parts shipped were out of tolerance. Certainly, we make errors in production, especially at startup or at shift change, but I really don't understand how those inaccurate parts made it through to you.

Admit error when it is necessary to admit error, and then move to rebuild the confidence.

SERVICE: Candidly, there was a breakdown in our quality-assurance system, or this simply couldn't have happened. In fact, our quality-control procedures are reviewed continuously to ensure this type of thing never happens. Our production and engineering people are required to work together in development of procedures to stop such problems. But it did happen.

What I will do now is develop an error report on this incident. The error-report procedure is our system to ensure we continuously improve our quality control. The report will be studied by the specific individuals who were responsible for building quality into your shipment in the first place. They will be required to develop checks and balances, if possible, which do not add cost, but which minimize the possibility of this type of mistake occurring again. We will never be perfect, but we are always improving.

IS THE PRODUCT PACKED AND STORED SO THAT DAMAGE CANNOT OCCUR?

Business partnerships are blooming everywhere. Vendor-managed inventory (VMI), just-in-time (JIT) deliveries, even sequenced JIT deliveries, "outsourcing" and other creative shared-responsibility relationships are realities in today's world. Customers need information that assures them that their production processes, now totally dependent upon your abilities, will not be disrupted.

CUSTOMER: Look, with this new contract, we're totally dependent on you people. You are making deliveries to us twice per day, and my entire operation is completely dependent upon your warehouse. How do I know damage cannot occur?

SERVICE: You have every right to be concerned. Frankly, I do not blame you one bit.

Express empathy for this position. Who wouldn't be concerned? The customer needs assurance that you can perform as planned.

SERVICE: We are well aware of your special contract requirements and our new, unique relationship. Believe me, when our respective companies were initially discussing this relationship, support teams were developed to review all of the details. We have had extensive reviews and have developed methods and procedures to ensure damage cannot occur. Shipping damaged product to you is certainly not in our best interest. We both want this partnership to work. Here are a few key concepts in our new procedures:

1.   All warehouse employees have received extensive training in the new procedures. Their knowledge has been tested and they understand our special partnership.

2.   Every employee is held directly responsible for his or her portion of the total operation. Each also has the authority to act. For example, any employee has the authority to stop the pack-and-store operation if he or she perceives the potential for damage can occur. There are multiple check points.

3.   Weekly meetings are held by those directly responsible for the pack-and-store. Management is involved in these meetings to support employees with problem solving.

4.   Engineers check our warehouse operations monthly to ensure structural integrity of the warehouse and all equipment.

There is no perfect system. But there are very good systems, which can continuously improve themselves. We have similar arrangements with other customers. Our quality-assurance program does work. We make mistakes, but no customer has received a damaged product in the past five years.

SHOW ME A RECORD OF THE PRODUCT'S PERFORMANCE

Customers commonly need copies of your product's performance to complete their own quality-control procedures. Customer Service must be integrally involved in operations, so that questions in this regard can be effectively answered.

CUSTOMER: We need to warrant our product to the end user, and you are an integral part of the process.

SERVICE: Yes, we are. We will be shipping you (ingredient) on a daily basis. Every shipment is sampled before shipping. All samples are tested in our laboratories, and the results are permanently recorded. Records on the samples are maintained for three years. By then, the (ingredient) would be beyond its useful life. What we normally do is automatically ship you test results with each shipment. I can arrange for such a system. It would be better if the test results were shipped to a particular person. Would that person be you? If you give me your address, I can put a system in place that ensures you start receiving all test results tomorrow.

For a different type of product, try something like the following.

SERVICE: We, of course, cannot check every radio. That would be too costly and would drive the selling price of the radio out of reasonable range. But, all components currently used in manufacturing have been tested extensively during a three-month prototyping stage. Now that the product is in full manufacture, we constantly sample the finished products. Our labs are always life-testing products rolling off of our production lines. Samples are pulled daily. Would you like me to send you a few sampling charts?

HOW DO YOU ENSURE YOU ARE OPERATING AS YOU THINK YOU ARE OPERATING?

It is not unreasonable for the customer to want assurances that what you *say* you do you *actually do*. As noted earlier, customer service must be informed on operational processes to be able to answer these questions intelligently.

SERVICE: Indeed, assurance of quality operations is a major concern here at (company). Workers throughout our manufacturing operations are involved in the development of operational procedures as well as development of the quality-control test systems that ensure that agreed-upon procedures are correctly executed. But we recognize that human error is inevitable. We realize the war for perfect quality is never won. Only individual battles can be won. In fact, fully 5 percent of our total direct-manufacturing budget is devoted to checking for and continuously improving quality systems. Employees meet daily to discuss problems. Engineers are continuously reviewing the best new manufacturing systems available, always looking for new ways to guarantee quality in the process. Finished goods are continuously monitored, not just to ensure they perform within acceptable tolerances, but to ensure that gradual changes are not occurring. We want to catch quality shifts before they become quality problems.

HOW DO YOU KNOW THE PEOPLE WHO BUILT THE PRODUCT ARE ADEQUATELY TRAINED? DO YOU DO CONTINUOUS TRAINING? DO YOU HAVE A CERTIFICATION SYSTEM?

SERVICE: Training is continuous here. First, new employees receive eight weeks of basic training in fundamental operations, systems, and processes. They are tested and must pass those basic tests before they are assigned to your manufacturing sector. If they do not pass all necessary tests, they must stay in training until they do, or until we determine they are not suited for our type of work. Once fundamental training is completed, they are then assigned as support apprentices for an additional six months. During this period, they work on simpler systems and are close-ly monitored by more experienced employees. Experienced employees are part of the supervisory and evaluation team for new hires and participate in the coaching, counseling, and certification process. Employees are certified as competent by their supervisors and other team members before being assigned to a manufacturing team.

Still, though, training is never complete. Each team meets weekly to discuss issues and problems that occur. They are responsible for maintaining and improving qual-ity. If a problem occurs, the team members assign someone to research the problem and to create a solution. That individual then has the responsibility to build that knowledge in other team members. Training is never ending. Certification for an employee is reviewed on his or her anniversary date, and employees are recertified. We have the best quality record in the industry, and we are certain that it is direct-ly caused by our very highly trained workforce.

Part
Three

Minding Your Business:
Maintaining Customer Satisfaction

Chapter
6

Taking Orders, Establishing Relationships

Please linger a moment over the title of this chapter. It's not meant to cover two processes, but a single one. You see, taking an order should not stop with a simple exchange of information. It should establish a relationship between your firm and the customer; one that's a positive, business-growing one. This does not mean that you should use the caller's time to explain the virtues of your company. Above all, take the order quickly and efficiently. But in doing so, communicate an attitude of helpfulness, service, pride, and accountability.

Tip: Never forget that the key to taking an order is accurate information. Build a double-check and review into the order-taking exchange. Confirm the order in writing.

Tip: Set up the order-taking process so that you, not the customer, does the work. Request, never demand, information from the customer.

Tip: These days, most companies enter customer information into a computer database. (If you are not maintaining a database, you should be; but that's another book.) Ensure that you accurately record all information. Explain to your caller that you are entering a "customer profile" into your database in order to serve him or her most efficiently in the future. If you are taking an order from a repeat customer, be certain to review and update key database information.

TAKING A SIMPLE ORDER

CALLER: I want to order (quantity) widgets.

SERVICE: I can help you with that.

Inform the caller that he or she has come to the right place. The words *help* or *assist* or the phrase "I can do that for you" convey a willingness to serve.

SERVICE: We will need some information. May I have your name?

Transition the exchange from "I" and "you" to "we" as quickly as possible. This simple pronoun in and of itself goes a long way toward building a relationship and creating rapport. Also, never *demand* information from your caller. Request it politely: "May I have . . ."

SERVICE: Mr. (name) What we're doing is creating a customer profile for our database. This will help us to serve you most efficiently in the future. So if I may just get some more information from you. Your shipping address? (Record response.) And is that the same as your billing address? (Record response.) May I have a daytime phone number? (Record response.) We generally ship via (carrier) with a (number of days) turnaround time. Do you have any other preference? (Record response.)

Now, let's get to the order. You want (quantity) widgets, correct?

As soon as you have obtained the caller's name, use it. However, do not presume to use the customer's first name. Courtesy dictates *Mr.* or *Ms.* If the caller corrects, preferring *Miss* or *Mrs.,* immediately acknowledge this and use this form of address. No apology is necessary. Make an appropriate note on the record for your colleagues, who may answer inquiries from this customer in the future.

CALLER: Yes.

SERVICE: Those are available in red or black (or whatever specifications must be clarified). Do you have a color preference?

CALLER: Oh, yes. All black.

SERVICE: Great. So we are shipping to you at (repeats shipping address) (quantity) black widgets. Is that correct?

CALLER: Right.

SERVICE: The total cost, with shipping, is ($ amount) if you use a major credit card. For an added charge of ($ amount), we will ship C.O.D. Which would you prefer?

CALLER: I'll use my (name) credit card.

SERVICE: May I have the number?

CALLER: (Gives number.)

SERVICE: And that card expires . . . ?

CALLER: (Provides expiration date.)

SERVICE: We are just about finished, but let me just make certain I've gotten that credit-card number right. (Repeats number and expiration.)

As you reach the end of the call, inform your caller of your progress: "We're almost finished."

CALLER: That's right.

SERVICE: Mr. (name), may I help you with anything else today?

Always offer to help with more. Be certain to offer it as help, not "Is there anything else you want?"

CALLER: No, that'll be it.

SERVICE: It's a pleasure doing business with you. Your shipment should arrive within (number) days. Please call me, (service rep name) at 555-5555 if you have any questions. To expedite handling of any questions you might have, I'll give you an order confirmation number: (number). Have a good day.

Giving your personal name tends to create greater bonding. Some will say, "but we don't want customers calling for particular individuals. It slows everything down." Give the personal name anyway. If the customer calls back, the team can easily be trained to offer something like: "John is on another call. May I help with this? I can access all of John's notes in my computer. What did you need to check . . ." and so on.

TAKING A COMPLEX ORDER OR MULTIPLE ORDERS

Taking a complex order or multiple orders need not differ radically from taking a simple one, except that you need to take extra care to confirm each item, and you need to ensure that neither you nor your customer gets confused.

Tip: Gently take control of the situation. Don't let your caller rattle off a list of items, with you running behind, trying to catch up.

CALLER: I have a long list of items I need to order from you.

SERVICE: Sounds good to me. I can help you with that. (Rep begins by obtaining name and address information, as for a simple order. Then proceeds to get the merchandise information.) Let's just begin at the beginning, one item at a time. I need to make sure I get all the details loaded correctly.

Subtly but unmistakably suggest a method of proceeding one item at a time. Usually, this will be sufficient to make the ordering process reasonable and rational. If, however, the caller insists on pulling ahead of you, apply the brakes gently.

SERVICE: You're getting a little ahead of me. Let's just take this one item at a time. I want to make absolutely certain that I don't leave anything out or ship you the wrong item.

Resist the temptation to ask for a favor: "Slow down! I can't keep up!" Instead, make it clear that you have the customer's interest uppermost in mind: "I don't want to leave anything out."

Demanding as it may be, both on you and your caller, be certain to review the entire order before concluding the call. Acknowledge gratitude for your caller's patience.

SERVICE: You've been very patient. I would like to ask for just a few more moments of your time so that we can review your order. I wouldn't want to ship you anything you didn't order, or leave out anything you need. I'm going to read back the order to you, all right?

After acknowledging that the caller has made a commitment of time and patience, Service asks for a modest amount of time to review the order. This is not for the company's benefit, but to ensure that the customer will get all that he or she has ordered. Service explains the procedure ("I'm going to read. . .") and then asks for permission (". . . all right?") to read the order back. The object is not only to ensure an error-free and efficient transaction, but to communicate your commitment to a high degree of quality service.

People communicate with their eyes as well as with their mouths and ears. A written confirmation is always a good idea, especially for the more complex order. These days, written confirmations can be transmitted electronically or, if time permits, by mail.

SERVICE: Okay, we're in agreement on the order. Getting all the numbers correct is always difficult. Do you have a fax, or perhaps e-mail capability? I would like to give you a written or electronic copy of this order to look over one more time before I send it to our warehouse. I know you are in a hurry. I could fax or e-mail this to you, receive your final okay on the order within the hour, and still get your requirements to the warehouse today. Using express carriers, we will get this shipment to you within 48 hours.

TAKING ORDER AND CREDIT INFORMATION

As every first-year physics student knows, inertia is the tendency of a body to resist acceleration or to remain at rest unless acted upon by an outside force. And as every sales professional knows, the major obstacle to closing a sale is inertia: getting your customer to *move*. Overcoming inertia takes more than a persuasive sales approach. You need to provide a clear and direct course of action for the customer. Get the caller's attention, arouse desire, develop interest, then instruct him or her in what to do.

If ordering and paying for merchandise seems to the caller a difficult or obscure process, inertia may win out and the sale may well evaporate. Even some purchasing professionals find it difficult. Credit usually provides the biggest push for overcoming inertia.

If you use major credit cards, obtaining the necessary credit information is a simple and straightforward process of obtaining a card number and expiration date, then double checking to make certain that you've gotten the information right. If, however, you need to set up a line of credit directly between your caller and the company, your task is more challenging.

1. You must obtain more information.

2. You must obtain the information while maintaining the momentum of the sale.

3. You must obtain the information in such a way that the caller feels you are trying to help him or her obtain what's desired, not throw obstacles in the path.

Tip: Anyone in the position of managing credit must learn to wear two very different hats. Credit management makes business possible. It enables transactions. On the other hand, credit management also involves assessing risks and excluding some business. As a customer-service professional making a sale, your objective is to emphasize the first hat and hide the second.

In the following scripts, the order has been taken. The customer-service rep now addresses the manner of payment. Depending on your firm's policies, you may wish to emphasize prepayment, C.O.D., or invoicing over credit. However, many companies make it a goal to develop as many credit customers as possible.

Tip: Credit customers are typically repeat customers. Remember this when you are obtaining credit information. Doing this job effectively means that you are making more than a single sale. You are cultivating a customer, a long-term relationship. You are enabling ongoing business. Convey to the customer that the time he or she is investing with you now will pay off in making it easier to do business with your firm in the future; time invested now will also pay off in increased flexibility and buying power.

Depending on a number of factors, such as the type of business you are engaged in, the type of customers you are dealing with, and the amount of money involved in the purchase, you may be able to make a credit decision during the course of the phone call, or you may have to take the order, obtain the credit information, and then submit it for processing. In the latter case, inform the caller of the procedure, but also let him or her know that the order is being processed simultaneously and will be shipped just as soon as credit is cleared: "It will take three days to process your credit information."

For a case in which credit is processed immediately:

SERVICE: I can set up a credit account for you. It will not only expedite this order, but, once it's set up, it will make ordering from us very easy in the future. Would you like me to set up an account?

Note the emphasis on what "I" can do. Convey your willingness to take ownership and perform a service.

CALLER: Yes, I'd like to open up an account.

SERVICE: This won't take long. May I have your full name? (Response.) And your address, Ms. (name)?

Once you have obtained the caller's name, use it (unless the caller expresses another preference). Also, make each of your information requests a full sentence or phrase, not a one-word command ("Address?"). Make certain that you put your questions in the form of requests, rather than demands. After the caller has responded with her address, continue.

SERVICE: And you have lived at (reads back address) how long? (Response.)

Take opportunities to review and confirm key information, in this case, the caller's address.

SERVICE: And may I have a daytime telephone number? (Response.)

The questions necessary for completing a credit application vary, of course, from firm to firm. Service continues through the remaining questions. End by explaining the next step. In this case, the credit information is being transmitted to a reporting agency, which will issue an immediate approval.

SERVICE: I am now transmitting your credit information to our reporting agency. The information is going through now. Bear with me just a moment. And here comes the approval.

Whenever you are performing a task or waiting for information, narrate the action. Remember, using the telephone effectively is a little like being a radio DJ. Avoid "dead air," that is, silence. Your caller cannot see what you are doing. Tell him or her what you are doing.

SERVICE: So we are shipping you (quantity) (merchandise) to (address), and we are charging this to your brand-new account with us. You will receive your new account information at the end of the month. Is there anything else I can help you with today?

CALLER: No, that will be all.

SERVICE: Well, I thank you for your patience, and it's been a pleasure doing business with you, Ms. (name).

In cases where lead time is required to complete the credit check, the following script should be helpful.

SERVICE: (The merchandise has been ordered and the credit information obtained.) We need to take two steps before your credit approval goes through. First, I will run this by our credit-approval department. In most cases, I can have approval within three business days.

Explain why three business days are needed. You do not want to leave the impression that the customer is not trusted.

SERVICE: We do the credit check to protect the interests of our reliable and honest customers. You and I both know that, unfortunately, a very few folks simply abuse credit privileges and refuse to pay their bills. This destroys the system and raises prices for all of us who use the system correctly and honestly. To protect all of our valuable customers and avoid unnecessary cost increases, we check references on everyone.

CALLER: I really would like to get my order expedited.

SERVICE: And we want to get it out to you as fast as possible. While we're doing the credit work, your order will be picked and packed, so that we can ship it out just as soon as the approval comes through. As I said, we expect your order to ship within three business days. Would you like me to fax or e-mail a shipment confirmation to you?

Give your caller a realistic estimate of the turnaround time involved. Emphasize that the process will not hold up delivery to any significant degree; the order will be prepared simultaneously with credit processing. Focus on the positive aspects of what you can do.

TAKING ORDER AND SHIPPING INFORMATION

Usually, shipping information is taken with an order. If you have the caller's shipping address on record or in a computer database, be certain to confirm the address. The customer may have relocated or may simply want this particular shipment sent to someplace other than the shipping address of record. Also obtain any other shipping instructions, such as desired arrival date, carrier, and so on.

SERVICE: (Merchandise has been ordered and payment terms arranged.) Now, where would you like us to ship your order?

CALLER: To my office (Gives address.)

SERVICE: Are we shipping to you, or do you want another name on the shipping label?

CALLER: My name is fine.

SERVICE: Our standard method of shipment is via (carrier), which takes (number) days. However, we can offer expedited service at an additional cost. Would you like me to tell you about this service?

CALLER: Yes. I want to get the shipment as soon as possible.

SERVICE: Using (carrier), we can get the shipment to you the day after tomorrow, by (time) o'clock in the morning. The charge is ($ amount). How does that sound to you?

CALLER: Fine. Yes. I want the expedited service.

SERVICE: I'll set that up for you right now and add the ($ amount) to your invoice statement. Is there anything else I can help you with this afternoon, Ms. (name)?

CALLER: No, that's it.

SERVICE: Your expedited shipment will arrive by (time and day). If you have any questions, please call me at 555-5555. It's been a pleasure doing business with you, Ms. (name).

Be aware of special considerations or instructions that may be relevant to your product. This is the time to start clarifying the customer's responsibility, if any. Further, the individual taking the order and receiving the shipment may not be the person who actually performs the site preparation. Clarify these special situations at this time.

SERVICE: (After ordering is completed.) The computer requires a dedicated circuit. Do you have this availability in your home office?

CALLER: What do you mean by a dedicated circuit?

SERVICE: A dedicated 15-amp circuit is necessary for the computer to operate correctly. When running on full power, the computer will need nearly 15 amps of power. Even several room lights added into the circuit may cause the circuit breaker to trip. This could cause you to lose any work on the computer that has not been saved. Many home offices do not have sufficient circuits. Do you know if yours has the power available?

CALLER: No, I don't know.

SERVICE: I will fax you information about electrical requirements today and go ahead with your expedited shipment. Your electrician can tell you if you have the necessary electrical wiring and should be able to offer any needed solutions for your specific application, if any are needed. What is your fax number?

TAKING ORDERS WHEN ADVANCE PAYMENT IS NEEDED AND EXPLAINING WHY

Most customers will readily understand and cooperate in situations where advance payment is required; however, you can grease the wheels of the transaction by briefly explaining why the arrangement is necessary.

Pitfall: It is never a good idea to say something to the effect of "It's company policy to get payment in advance." Your objective is to focus on the customer and what the customer needs. Alluding to "company policy" immediately shifts the focus from customer to company; even worse, it suggests that you care more about a bunch of rules and regulations than you do about human beings. It is generally best to avoid the phrase "company policy" entirely when dealing with customers or clients.

Good explanations for requiring advance payment include:

1. Customer has not established credit.
2. At present, your company offers no credit program.

3. To keep prices down, it is necessary to request payment in advance.

4. The merchandise item is custom made on order only; therefore, advance payment is required.

CALLER: I want to order (quantity) (item).

SERVICE: I can help you with that. May I have your full name? (Responds.) And now, Mr. (name), your shipping address? (Responds.) A telephone number, please, where you may be reached during the day. (Responds.) Mr. (name), (item) is custom made for each application. For that reason, it cannot be returned, and we will need payment in advance. The total charge, including shipping, comes to ($ amount).

CALLER: You can't start the process until you receive payment?

SERVICE: That's correct. However, I will put your order through immediately, which will reserve fabrication time for you and we will expedite delivery. You can expect (item) (number) days after we receive your payment.

Asking for payment in advance and holding production until payment is received are major demands on the customer. Take the time to explain them and put them in their best light. Look for ways to emphasize services you are performing: The order doesn't just sit on a stack, but a positive action is taken, reserving production time, pending arrival of the payment.

SERVICE: You may mail a check or money order directly to (address). If it is important to you to move things along as quickly as possible, you may transmit the payment by wire. Would you like that information?

It is critically important that you give explicit instructions for making payment. Leave nothing to guesswork. If possible, offer choices and alternative methods of payment. Especially when *you* are making a demand, giving your customer choices empowers him or her and creates a more positive transaction.

It is possible that you may encounter some resistance to the request for payment in advance. Resist the temptation to refer to "company policy." Remember, the essence of any business transaction is an exchange of value for value. Try to show how the request for advance payment is such an exchange.

CALLER: I think it's a little unreasonable to ask for payment in advance, before I receive the product.

SERVICE: Mr. (name), our objective is to give you the best price possible. This means cutting our overhead expenses to the bare bones. This is a custom order. We have special setups on our machines and special fabricating instructions for our workers. All this adds considerable overhead expenses. Eliminating credit and C.O.D. apparatus helps us do just that. Your advance payment ensures that you are getting the lowest possible price.

Then there is the matter of trust:

CALLER: How do I know that you will ship on time, and that once you have my money, I won't have to wait for months. For that matter, how do I know that you'll send me what I ordered at all?

SERVICE: I can appreciate your concern, Ms. (name). We've been in business for (number) years. We've stayed in business by delivering great products and first-rate service. Our aim is to create lasting business relationships, and we couldn't do that if we delivered shoddy service. The usual turnaround time on orders is (number) days. You can expect to receive your (item) by that time. Fifty percent of our total business volume of over $100 million annually is custom orders like the one you are requesting now.

TAKING ORDERS WHEN PROGRESS PAYMENTS ARE NEEDED AND EXPLAINING WHY

For projects or products that involve multiple steps or multistage fabrication over a long period of time, or in the case of certain subscription-type products or services, a series of progress payments may be required. In these cases, the objective of Customer Service is not only to explain the procedure to the customer, but to enlist him or her as a partner in the transaction. A progress-payment relationship should be a collaborative relationship rather than an antagonistic one. Progress payments ultimately reduce costs for the customer. Without progress payments, your company would need to borrow money to support manufacturing. The interest would ultimately be paid by the customer.

SERVICE: (The order has been taken, and the basic information exchanged.) You will receive your set of custom-created reports in four installments, beginning on (date). Payment for the first installment is due when you receive the first installment of the report. The second payment is due with the second report, and so on. The pay-as-you-go option is easier on your cash flow and ours. Of course, you also have the option of paying the entire balance due in a single payment. Some customers prefer that, since it simplifies their accounts payable. It's up to you.

For most customers, of course, progress payments are preferable to a single payment in full. However, present payment in full as an option and show how it may be useful to the customer. Perhaps your company may even discount the total price if payment is made in full. Note, too, how the progress payment is presented as a win-win plan: a boon to the seller's and the buyer's cash flow.

Progress payments linked to the shipment of installments of a project or product are usually easy for a customer to understand and accept. In some situations, it may take more elaborate explanation to make your customer comfortable with progress payment for projects that are not delivered in installments or that are not useful to the customer until completed. In these cases, it is important to link payments to explicit project/product milestones rather than arbitrary dates.

SERVICE: The machinery will be fabricated in five stages: (list the stages). In order to make payment convenient for you, we will break down the payments stage by stage. ($ amount) will be due after we have completed and you have inspected stage 1 of fabrication. And equal ($ amount) payments will be due at stages 2 through 4. The final payment of ($ amount) is payable on delivery, installation, and successful start-up of the unit at your site. This payment option gives you maximum control at each stage of production.

Underscore how progress payment benefits the customer. Remember, that is what he or she cares about. Your company's needs and policy requirements are of no concern. The customer still may resist. Use a persuasive argument.

CUSTOMER: Our policy dictates that payment can only be made in full after the machinery is delivered.

Discuss the partnership arrangement for the capital expense.

SERVICE: We ask for progress payments to support our manufacturing overhead costs as the (product) is being manufactured. On a special design of this type, we will be incurring considerable costs throughout the manufacturing period, which is planned to be six months. If we must borrow cash to support our costs through manufacturing, the total price must be increased to cover bank interest charges. Your finances are already arranged to support this equipment or you would not be purchasing it at all. It just makes good sense for both of us to use the cash that is already available to build this machinery. Bringing in new financing will only increase costs for no gain.

TAKING ORDERS AND EXPLAINING PAYMENT OPTIONS

Let's face it, no customer likes to hear how much something is going to cost. Talking about product benefits and value is fun. Pondering payment isn't. In presenting payment options to a customer, put the emphasis on *options* rather than *payment*. Payment is an obligation; option is a choice. It empowers your customer rather than obligates him or her.

SERVICE: (The basic ordering information has been exchanged.) Three payment options are available to you. You may use a major credit card, and I can take that information over the phone now. That option will expedite your order. You may choose to send ($ amount) by check or money order in advance of shipment. Or you may choose our C.O.D. service option, which carries a charge of ($ amount). Which option would you prefer?

Quantify the available options. If you offer three, say "three" rather than the more vague "several." Emphasize the option your company prefers, in this case, a credit card transaction, but do not slight the other available options.

Tip: Some customer-service professionals prefer to put the company-preferred option at the end of the list rather than the beginning (in this script, credit card payment would be mentioned last). The rationale is that, offered a series of choices, most customers tend to take the last one mentioned. This is a useful strategy to try. Just make certain that you are able to get through all of the options. If a caller interrupts you at option two, stating "Yes, I prefer C.O.D.," say something like: "I can set that up for you. You know, you also have the option of credit card payment. I can take that information now, and it will expedite your order." If the caller still prefers C.O.D., simply acknowledge the preference and proceed: "All right. I'll set that C.O.D. delivery up for you."

EXPLAINING DISCOUNTS AVAILABLE AND HOW TO GET THEM

When taking orders by telephone, discounts are less an inducement to making a sale than they are incentives to purchase greater quantities, additional accessories, and so on. At the very least, informing your caller about discounts available adds to the perceived value of the merchandise. The key words to use are "offer," "special," and "savings," all powerful terms in a sales situation.

CALLER: I would like to order (quantity 1) of (item).

SERVICE: I can help you with that. Are you aware of our special volume discount program on (item)?

CALLER: No. Tell me about it.

If you leap into a quantity discount, your customer may feel that you are simply pressing him or her to up the order. It is a better strategy to *ask* if the caller is aware of a "special discount program." By doing this, you prompt the caller to ask you for information, which you willingly provide. Rather than angling for more cash from the caller, you are now in the position of *giving* the caller information.

SERVICE: On quantities of (quantity B) or more, you get a (percent amount) discount across the board. (Quantity 1) of (item) will cost you ($ amount 1 total), ($ amount 2) per item. (Quantity B) will cost ($ amount 3 total), ($ amount 4) per item.

Compare and contrast quantity versus price. Make the savings crystal clear.

CALLER: Gee, I hadn't planned on buying so many. Can't you give me a break on a smaller amount?

SERVICE: We believe our prices already represent great value. The additional discount is available only on quantity purchases, as our mailing and processing costs are reduced. The quantity discount is available using the same payment terms as (item) purchased at the regular price.

Put the special discount in context. If the caller wants more, persuade him or her that he or she is already getting exceptional value. Note that the service representative here points out that it is not necessary to sacrifice liberal payment terms in order to get the quantity discount.

Another discount situation is the special offer:

CALLER: I'd like to order (item).

SERVICE: I can take that order for you. Are you aware of our special offer for purchasers of (item)?

CALLER: No, I am not.

Again, steer the transaction away from a selling situation and toward providing information.

SERVICE: Many of our customers purchase the following accessories for their (item): (list.) We are offering substantial discounts on these items when they are purchased as a package with (item).

Set a precedent for the offer: "Many customers choose the option I am about to offer you."

CALLER: I can't get the discount later?

SERVICE: That's right. The discount is available only when the accessories are purchased with (item) as a package. Because so many customers were purchasing these accessories anyway, we have arranged a number of special kits. Would you like more information about the accessories?

Again, an offer of information. Put the caller in the position of asking *you* for the information.

CALLER: Well I am interested in (lists some accessories) . . .

SERVICE: Yeah. That's great. These accessories extend the usefulness of (item) by (describe benefits.) If you order the kit with the total accessory package now, they will cost only ($ amount 1). That saves you ($ amount 2).

CALLER: Yes, I'd like to go ahead and order that.

SERVICE: That total, then, will come to ($ amount). We offer three options for payment . . .

MAKING THE CUSTOMER FEEL COMFORTABLE WITH THE ORDER-ENTRY PROCESS

Perhaps confrontation with a complex order form is the only thing worse than the prospect of a lengthy and tedious phone call. Customers who place orders by telephone fear three things:

1. They will be tied up on the phone for an excessive length of time.

2. Errors will be made.

3. They will be bombarded by a sales pitch and pressured to buy merchandise they do not need or want.

Recognize that these fears exist and try to put them to rest from the very outset of the call:

CALLER: I am calling to order (item).

SERVICE: I'll be happy to help you with that. This should take us about (number) minutes. That will give us plenty of time to make sure that I get the order right, the first time! May I have your name? (And the order process continues.)

Giving the caller a time estimate is a very effective way of reducing anxiety by eliminating fear of the unknown. Note also that the caller is assured that enough time will be taken in order to avoid errors. Then, by going directly into the process, you suggest that you will not "waste" the caller's time with additional sales pitches.

Occasionally, you may be challenged by an anxious customer:

CALLER: You're not going to bust my chops with a lot of sales hype, are you?

SERVICE: No, sir. Your time is valuable, and you obviously know what you want. Let's get right to the order.

Tip: Often, it is quite appropriate to inform the caller about additional merchandise. Just be certain that you present the information as something useful to the caller, not a sales pitch, which is perceived as beneficial only to *your* bottom line. As you repeat the essentials of a caller's order, you might ask permission to provide more information. For example: "We're shipping (quantity) (item) to you at (address). Have you considered (accessory) for (item)? It (concisely describe accessory benefits). Would you like any information on (accessory)?

If the caller expresses interest, continue. If the caller does not want additional information, conclude the transaction and book the order as is. Do not press the issue or comment on the caller's choice.

FAILURE-PROOFING ORDERS TO PREVENT CUSTOMER ERRORS

Few things are more damaging to customer satisfaction than shipping the wrong order or an order that contains errors. It does not matter if the error is yours or the customer's, your company will be blamed. Even if the customer agrees that he or she actually ordered such-and-such, you may well be blamed for not knowing enough to question his or her choice ("Are you certain you want those D.C. motors for an A.C. system?"). Take steps to failure-proof all orders.

1. The first and most important step is to repeat information the customer gives you.

Tip: Repeating information can be quite tedious and time consuming. Use lists: "I have noted four items . . . ." Another technique is to repeat aloud any information you are given while you type it. To avoid monotony both for you and the caller, try varying this technique: repeating aloud some information and reading back other information.

2. If something doesn't seem right, question it. You are not merely a passive order taker. You are part of a Customer Service operation, and your function is to guide the customer to satisfaction.

Pitfall: Question anything that doesn't sound right, but do not challenge the caller. Watch your tone of voice. "Are you *sure* you want that?" can sound awfully close to "You're an idiot, aren't you?" A better approach is to say, "I just want to confirm that you want such-and-such. Usually, so-and-so is better suited to the application you intend." You might also begin your questioning with, "May I make a suggestion . . ." or "Have you considered . . ." or "You may not be aware . . ." or "May I give you some just-released information on this item? . . ."

3. If you *know* the caller is making a mistake, intervene.

Tip: Know your products. If you are unaware that Widget A will not work with Framiss B, you will not be able to respond when your customer tells you that he or she wants a dozen Widget As to go with his Framiss Bs. When these type of errors occur, the customer always blames you. If, however, you are familiar with your product line, you will be able to assist and advise your customers effectively.

4. Don't guess. If you need more information in order to help a caller order the correct item, obtain the information even if it means interrupting the call.

Tip: If you must look something up, ask permission to put the caller on hold. Tell the caller what you are doing in order to help. Tell the caller approximately how long he or she will be on hold. If absolutely necessary, arrange to call the customer back when you have the appropriate information.

Tip: Compile, index, religiously update, and use a list of FAQs, or frequently asked questions. This will save time when you are dealing with callers. You might also start a list of FMEs, or frequently made errors: mistakes callers commonly make. Review these FAQs and FMEs often during departmental meetings.

Pitfall: Never correct an error silently. Always confirm any corrections with the caller. Do not silently assume that the caller has made an error.

Pitfall: The customer's always right? Not exactly. But you do have to make some concessions. Avoid disputing with callers over matters of preference and opinion. Know the difference between a customer about to order something in error and a customer whose preferences happen to differ from yours.

5. Get help. If you discover that you don't have (and cannot readily obtain) the information (or expertise) your caller needs in order to make the appropriate choices, get help. If at all possible, transfer the call to the appropriate depart-

ment or person (an engineer, for example). Remember the call-ownership principle discussed in Chapter 1: If you answered the call, you *own* it, and cannot simply pass it off on someone else. You must *sell* the call. First, determine the appropriate person or department to supply the help that the caller needs. Second, with the caller on hold, call that person or department. Third, introduce the caller's problem. Fourth, after your referral "buys" the call, return to your caller and tell him or her that you are transferring the call to "Joe Smith in Engineering. He's equipped to advise you on what parts to order for such-and-such. I'm transferring you now. Once you've had the discussion, he'll send you back to me, and we can complete the order."

CALLER: I need to order (accessory 1) for my (item).

SERVICE: I can help you with that. But first let me confirm that it is (accessory 1) that you want. You see, while (accessory 1) will work with (item), the fit is not optimal. We offer (accessory 2), which is expressly designed to work with (item). Would you like me to tell you more about (accessory 2)?

The correction is made in a nonchallenging manner, as an offer of information. As in an upselling situation, it is always best to prompt the caller to ask *you* for more information.

CALLER: Well, are you telling me that (accessory 1) won't work?

SERVICE: No. It *will* work, but the following features will not be available: (list). With (accessory 2), all features are available. These include: (list).

Tip: If the caller doesn't quite get it, don't lose your patience. Your mission is to educate. Try a different pathway.

CALLER: Will (accessory 2) cost me more?

SERVICE: The great thing is that the cost is *almost* the same. The difference is only ($ amount). I think you'll agree that that is a small price to pay for the added value.

CALLER: Yes. Thanks. I'll go ahead and order (accessory 2), then.

Engage the caller. Ask questions or make statements that prompt a positive response, and most important of all promote agreement.

Another caller is not about to make an error, but may be unaware of a new model of the accessory he or she is ordering:

CALLER: I need to order (accessory 1) for my (item).

SERVICE: I can help you with that. But may I give you some late-breaking news about our line of accessories for (item)?

CALLER: Yeah, sure. What?

SERVICE: We now offer an enhanced version of (accessory 1). It is (accessory 2), which offers such additional benefits as (list). Let me tell you up-front that it costs

($ amount 1), that's ($ amount 2) more than (accessory 1), and (accessory 1) is still available. However, a great many users of (item) are buying (accessory 2). The response to it has been tremendous. Most of our customers recognize that it represents better value.

CALLER: So (accessory 1) is obsolete.

SERVICE: Not at all, but it does not represent the latest in technology and benefits that we have to offer. (Accessory 2) does.

Another common error is signaled by the inconsistency of the caller's request. Be on the alert for this. Inconsistencies are easiest to detect if you take down information as it is given to you:

CALLER: I want three gross of (item.)

SERVICE: I'll put you down for three gross of (item) right now. (The call continues with a number of other items ordered.)

CALLER: Okay, let's see. What else did I need? I've ordered (quantity item), (quantity item), and two gross of (item) . . .

SERVICE: Oh, Mr. (name), *two* gross of (item)? I've put you down for *three*. Did I hear you incorrectly?

Always offer to shoulder the blame. Do not accuse the caller of inconsistency. Do not ask if the caller has changed his or her mind. Do not say: "Oh, so *now* you want . . . ." Just point out the inconsistency by assuming that you have heard wrong, even if you know you haven't.

CALLER: No. You're right. I do want three gross.

SERVICE: Great. I've got you down, then, for (reviews order). And that is being shipped out to you at (reviews address). Is there anything else I can help you with this morning?

SHARING THE PROCESS: WHAT WILL SHIP FIRST, SECOND, AND SO ON

There is one product that is easier to sell than any other and that everyone wants. It is *information.* Almost every customer needs or wants to know when to expect a shipment. In the case of complex, multipart shipments, it may be critically important to know which parts are coming first, second, third, and so on. Your customer may need to coordinate other aspects of operation or installation with the time of arrival. Lay the information out clearly.

SERVICE: As you know, this will be a multipart shipment. I can lay out the schedule for you now, if you like.

CALLER: Yes, please.

SERVICE: The first part of the shipment, which includes (list items), will leave our warehouse on (date) and arrive at your site on (date). This shipment includes everything you need for phase 1 of the installation, so you can have your installer available at that time. All installation and assembly instructions will be included. The second shipment will leave us on (date) and arrive on (date). That includes all of phase 2, which does not require professional installation. Finally, shipment number three is all of your supplies. That will leave us on (date) and arrive at your site by (date). Be prepared to store the material in a dry place. Now, this is a lot of information. Should I fax or mail this to you? You will want to schedule this now with your support staff.

Tip: Provide written copy of even fairly simple shipping schedules.

TELLING THE CUSTOMER HOW TO PREPARE TO RECEIVE THE ORDER

Large, complex equipment, major bulk orders, hazardous materials, or perishable deliveries may require the customer to make special preparations for accepting shipment. Even a complete set of new kitchen cabinets being shipped to an enterprising do-it-yourself home owner can create major havoc throughout the house. Depending on the delivery schedule, Customer Service might give receiving instructions at the time the order is taken or might make a separate follow-up call prior to shipment. In either case, faxing or mailing a set of instructions is always necessary. There is simply too much opportunity for confusion.

Pitfall: Be certain to secure confirmed professional advice in writing on how to advise customers appropriately in the case of hazardous shipments or shipments whose improper handling or storage could cause injury, damage to property, or damage to the shipment itself. All of these situations require specialized training. Always supply these instructions to your customer in writing. Failure to instruct your customer appropriately may expose your company to serious liability.

Here is a follow-up call:

SERVICE: Mr. (name), this is (name) at (company). I am calling to advise you that your order will be shipping on (date) and will arrive at your site by (time) that afternoon. We have sent you by mail very important instructions for handling the shipment, and, if I may have a moment, I would like to review those instructions briefly. May I? So do you have those instructions currently available?

Announce the purpose of your call, emphasizing the importance of the issue. Then ask permission to continue. Make the customer get the documents. If the customer tells you that now is not a good time to call, arrange a suitable time. If the customer cannot grant you time, repeat that the information is critically important. If necessary, tell the customer that you may have to hold shipment until you have had an opportunity to advise him or her of how to receive and handle the material.

CUSTOMER: Sure. Now's a good time. Go ahead.

SERVICE: Fine. As I mentioned, your order will arrive on the afternoon of (date). Many of the electronic components of the (item) are highly sensitive to excessive heat, cold, and moisture. When you take delivery, please store the equipment indoors at a temperature above 45 degrees F but below 95 degrees F, and avoid direct sunlight. Do you see these instructions on (page number)? Relative humidity should not exceed 60 percent. You also need to keep (item) at least six feet away from any strong magnetic field, away from large motors, television or video imaging equipment (continue with list).

Tip: If the customer does not have the previously mailed instructions, get his or her fax number and fax an additional set now. Then call the customer back and go through the review.

CUSTOMER: No, I don't know where those instructions are. They must be around here someplace.

SERVICE: I can fax you a copy of the instructions now if you don't have the set previously sent. Your fax number is . . .?

CUSTOMER: Look, we really don't have to go through all of this. I'm sure those instructions are around here someplace. Just ship the equipment.

SERVICE: This equipment is extremely sensitive. To protect both our companies, I must review the special handling instructions. This is essential for success, and we really can't ship until we are certain that the critical nature of this merchandise is completely understood. This won't take long. I can fax you another set of instructions now and call later if you like.

You may wish to emphasize in your call that your firm has taken all necessary steps to protect the order in transit, but that now it is up to the customer to carry the ball.

SERVICE: (Item) is highly temperature-sensitive. We ship it in a specially insulated container, but it is still critically important that the unopened shipping carton *not* be stored at temperatures lower than (temperature 1) or exceeding (temperature 2) for more than (time period). And please don't expose the unopened carton to direct sunlight.

WHERE DID YOU HEAR ABOUT US?

This question is not just a pleasant way to conclude the order-taking process. Systematically recorded, the answers to this question can tell you a great deal about how effective or ineffective your overall marketing program is, and about how you might better make your presence known.

Tip: Always reserve this question for the end of the call. Asked at any earlier time, the question will be perceived (quite rightly) as an interruption of the business that is of most concern to the customer.

SERVICE: It's been a pleasure doing business with you. I hope I might ask you just one more question, which will help us to serve you and other customers better. How did you hear about us?

CUSTOMER: I saw an ad.

SERVICE: Was that in *The Post?*

Tip: Motivate an answer not by asking the customer to do *you* a favor, but by suggesting that the answer will ultimately benefit the customer. Also, you may ask *one* additional follow-up question, if necessary, in order to make the answer more useful to you. (For example, which ad is working?) But don't go beyond this single question. Beware of turning an order call into a customer survey that your busy customer does not want.

Tip: The question "Where did you hear about us?" is an idle one if you do not have a system (however informal) for keeping track of the answers. You might prepare a checklist, including such items as "newspaper ad," "customer referral," "trade magazine," "trade show," and so on, that you tick off for each caller. Or use a simple spreadsheet on your computer. A spreadsheet makes tabulation and analysis significantly easier.

Chapter

7

Following Up, Building Relationships

A customer's initial contact with your company is, of course, critically important. Not only does the customer form his or her first impression of the company, an impression that may promote or defeat satisfaction with your product or service, but it is quite possible that the initial phone call may be the only contact you have with the customer. You may not hear from this customer again, and it may not be necessary for you to call him or her in the future.

Yet, when they occur, follow-up calls confirming an order, advising a customer of the status of an order, or responding to a customer request also serve a vital function. How many times have you heard someone praise a firm for its follow-up? "They have really great customer support. You know, they had somebody call me to tell me that my order was going to be two days late. They didn't *have* to do that."

This is precisely the impression you wish to create: service that goes the extra mile, that prompts your customer to say, "They didn't have to do that." If you achieve that response, you have truly built a relationship with the customer that is likely to result in repeat business and in the kind of advertising that even the most powerful mogul can't buy: word-of-mouth.

There are many kinds of follow-up calls you might make, but they all have one element in common if they are to be effective. You must convey to the customer:

1. That you know who he or she is.

2. That you know what he or she ordered.

3. That you know when he or she ordered it.

4. That you know on what terms the order was made.

5. That you know what he or she wants.

6. That you are on top of the situation.

7. That you care about his or her satisfaction.

CONFIRMING THE MAILED-IN ORDER

Various mail-order scenarios such as ordering a high-ticket item, ordering an unusually large amount of an item, cases where the ordering instructions are incomplete, ambiguous, or otherwise unclear, or where there are problems with a credit card or credit card account number, may require a telephone call follow-up.

SERVICE: Good morning. This is (name) calling from (company). May I speak to (full name)?

CUSTOMER: That's me.

Begin with a polite greeting and quickly identify yourself and your company. Ask for the customer by his or her full name. If that person is unavailable, you have three alternatives:

1. Ask for a good time to call back; find out when the customer will be available.

2. Ask permission to leave a message. After leaving a clear message, underscoring its importance, leaving your number and a good time for a callback, thank the party with whom you've spoken, and conclude the conversation. *Note:* If the delivery cannot be made without a response from the customer, make this clear in your message. If you don't hear from the customer promptly, call back. Leave the message on voice mail if it is available. This ensures that your message will be delivered the way you want it delivered.

3. Combine both options: leave a clear message and ask for a good time to call back.

SERVICE: Hello, Mr. (name). We've just received your order for (item). Unfortunately, the shipping address has been left blank. We've got a billing address, but we don't want to make an error by assuming that the two are the same. Do you want us to ship to (reads off billing address)?

Don't fix blame. Why is the shipping address blank? Probably because the person you're talking to made a mistake and failed to fill it in. Keep pronouns out of it: not "*You* forgot to fill in the shipping address," but "Unfortunately, the shipping address *has been left* blank." This is one occasion where it is good to use that bane of English teachers everywhere, the passive voice. There should be no "actor" present in the sentence. It's the situation, not the people involved, that counts.

Tip: If possible, don't ask for brand-new information. Instead, start with what you've got and try to confirm it. In this example, Service has a billing address. Playing a hunch that this will also serve as the shipping address, the service rep reads it off.

CUSTOMER: Yes . . . that would be okay.

SERVICE: No other address is more convenient for you?

The service rep *listens* to the customer. He or she detects hesitation in the customer's voice and decides to take an extra step to ensure satisfaction by offering convenience. Listening skills cannot be taught, but they can be learned through practice. Learn to pick up on what your customer really wants, and you will deliver truly first-class service.

CUSTOMER: Well, if it's okay, I'd rather take delivery at our main office.

SERVICE: It's no trouble at all. May I have the address?

Tip: Do what you can to turn a "routine" follow-up call into an example of how your company goes the extra mile to accommodate its customers. Make the call an opportunity for service.

CUSTOMER: (Furnishes address.)

SERVICE: We are shipping to (repeats shipping address), and we are still billing to (repeats billing address). Do I have it right?

"Do I have it right?" means taking responsibility for accuracy. This phrase communicates your assumption that the customer is intelligent and accurate, especially important in a call that was made to correct his or her error.

CUSTOMER: Yes. Thanks.

SERVICE: Well, thank you. This will go right out to you. Expect delivery in (gives time frame). Is there anything else I can help you with today?

CUSTOMER: No.

SERVICE: My phone number is 555-5555, if you have any questions. Have a good day, and thank you for the order.

ADVISING OF ORDER STATUS

You may want to make a follow-up call even when one is not absolutely required to advise a customer of the status of his or her order. The purpose of such calls is to:

1. Communicate a caring attitude to the customer.

2. Pave the way for an ongoing relationship by affirming your commitment to the customer.

3. Communicating that you and your company are "on top of" the situation.

Such follow-up calls are especially useful if there is considerable lead time between the order and the delivery.

SERVICE: Good morning. This is (name) calling from (company). May I speak to (full name)?

CUSTOMER: That's me.

SERVICE: I'm calling just to let you know that your order for (item) is on track, and we expect to ship by (date). That means it should be at your site by (date). Did you have any questions about (item) or the delivery?

CUSTOMER: No. We have been waiting quite a while for it, though.

SERVICE: We realize the lead time we quoted is long. As you know, each (item) is custom-assembled to your specifications. And then we burn the unit in, so that any kinks or bugs become our problem rather than yours. I just wanted to let you know that we are about finished with testing and ready to ship. We appreciate your patience and are planning to ship on (date).

CUSTOMER: Okay, thanks.

It may be necessary to remind a customer as to why long lead time is required and that he or she was informed of the long lead time. Make this a very subtle reminder. Emphasize that, during this time, the customer's needs are being served, even though he or she has yet to receive merchandise.

ADVISING OF LATE DELIVERY: ITEM NOT IN STOCK

It is always better to call a customer as early as possible to advise of lateness. No customer likes to be told that an item he or she ordered will be shipped late, but, as is true of most adverse circumstances, late delivery is an opportunity to communicate the level of concern that goes with top-notch service. In calling a customer to advise of late delivery, communicate the following:

1.   The fact that the shipment will be late.

2.   The reason why it will be late, stated in terms that benefit the customer.

3.   Your apology for its being late.

4.   Revised delivery date.

5.   Any help or alternatives you can offer.

Tip: Put the situation in the most positive light possible. In the case of an item out of stock, emphasize its popularity and the difficulty in increasing production without sacrificing quality. This helps assure the customer that he or she has made a good choice in ordering it.

SERVICE: This is (name) calling from (company). May I speak to (full name)?

CUSTOMER: That's me.

SERVICE: Ms. (name), I'm calling about your recent order for (item). (Item) is an excellent choice, and has proven extraordinarily popular. For that reason, we're temporarily out of stock, and I'm sorry to have to tell you that your shipment will be delayed. I expect to be restocked no later than (date), we've put a rush request into our production facility, and I will expedite your shipment. But we can't sacrifice quality standards. You can expect to receive (item) by (date).

CUSTOMER: I was really counting on getting it by (earlier date). We need the production!

SERVICE: I will do everything I can to expedite shipment to you. If it will help, I can arrange to lease you an earlier model of (item), which I can have at your site by (date). You could get started on programming, and all programs are upwardly compatible with the new (product).

ADVISING OF LATE DELIVERY: PRODUCTION DELAYS

Put production delays in their best possible light by emphasizing such factors as unusual demand, extra care required in fabricating the customer's merchandise, added quality control steps, and so on. Do not imply that your firm is overwhelmed or that your company has somehow goofed. Your customer does not want to hear you bad-mouth your company.

SERVICE: This is (name) calling from (company). May I speak to (full name)?

CUSTOMER: That's me.

SERVICE: Mr. (name), I'm calling about your recent order for (item). Production is taking longer than we had originally anticipated. As you know, (item) is manufactured to mission-critical specs, and, because of that, we have deliberately slowed the line and have introduced additional quality-control procedures. The minor delay you experience now should pay off in added confidence when it comes to quality performance. I expect to ship to you no later than (date), and I am very sorry for the delay. I wish there were more I could do.

CUSTOMER: Yeah, there is. Kick butt and get me my shipment on time!

SERVICE: I wish I could meet the original schedule, Mr. (name). As I mentioned, we're evaluating quality issues. It just makes good business sense to get this right now. We certainly don't want any problems, but we can't ignore them, either. The extra time we're investing now will pay off. I will do everything I can to minimize the delay and expedite shipment to you. I'm tracking progress daily. What I can do is give you progress reports several times per week.

ADVISING OF LATE DELIVERY: SUPPLIER PROBLEMS

When you attribute the source of a delay to a third party, you risk looking as if you are simply passing the buck. Avoid fixing blame: "My supplier screwed up." Instead, express the problem in neutral terms: "My supplier has experienced delays." Beware of putting yourself across as a passive victim of a third party. What are you doing about your supplier's failure?

Tip: You should not lay the source of a delay at the doorstep of a third party. Just remember that, ultimately, your customer is dealing with you, no matter what the source of the delay.

SERVICE: This is (name) calling from (company). May I speak to (full name)?

CUSTOMER: That's me.

SERVICE: Mrs. (name), I'm calling about your recent order for (item). Our production facility has been delayed by a supply problem. Until we can get (raw material), I'm afraid we're in a holding pattern. We're working with our supplier now, and it looks like he'll be able to get us what we need by (date). That means production on your units will be completed by (date), we'll expedite shipment, and have the units to you by (date). Now, Mrs. (name), I realize that's (number) days later than we had estimated for delivery. I'm sorry for the delay, we're doing what we can to shorten it, and I hope you can help us with flexibility.

CUSTOMER: Well, what are you doing to get things moving?

SERVICE: We are very limited in our ability to influence suppliers right now. Unfortunately, the worldwide availability of (raw material) is scarce at the present time. It's not like we can threaten to take our business elsewhere. However, we do have a good relationship with our supplier, and we are one of his key customers. I am confident that he is doing his best to turn out product. We'll do our best to expedite production and shipping for you. But I do have to ask for your patience. Our supplier is rationing raw material to us and others, and, unfortunately, we are forced to do the same with our customers. Additional capacity for (raw materials) will not be available for another six months. It's just tough for all of us.

ADVISING OF LATE DELIVERY: UNANTICIPATED ORDER VOLUME

This can be a delicate situation. Advise a customer that his or her order is being delayed because of high volume, and he or she may well conclude that that "volume" is going to every other customer first.

1. Make it clear that customers are served chronologically, not in order of importance.

2. Accent the positive: high order volume is solid evidence of a sound product that is in great demand.

3. Provide closure by estimating a new delivery time.

Tip: What do you do if you have no clear idea of when you will be able to deliver? Explain as much as you possibly can anyway, even if that only amounts to why you cannot give an accurate estimate. Then, at the very least, supply a time range or promise to give status reports. If you present a hopeless case, your customer will likely cancel the order if he or she possibly can.

SERVICE: This is (name) calling from (company). May I speak to (full name)?

CUSTOMER: That's me.

SERVICE: Mr. (name), I'm calling about your recent order for (item). We have been hit with an extraordinarily high volume of orders, much higher than we anticipated. We knew (item) was a great product, but we did not expect demand to exceed our manufacturing capability. You are, of course, a high-priority customer, but we have to be fair and fill orders on a first-come, first-served basis. With demand running as high as it is, I'm afraid we're not going to make the (date) target for shipping (item). I apologize. We've put an extra shift on here at the plant, and I expect to be able to ship your order no later than (date). I will try to better that, but I'll at least make that date.

Tip: Highlight any active, proactive, positive steps you are taking to serve the customer. Make conservative promises that you can keep; however, if you see the possibility that you may do better than your promise, point out the possibility cautiously. Do not quote the delivery date, and then miss it again. Missing the second promise date will dramatically increase dissatisfaction. If you aren't sure you can make a new date, promise status reports, not actual dates.

SERVICE: (Assume the conversation starts as noted above): . . . With demand running as high as it is, I'm afraid we're not going to make the (date) target for shipping (item). I apologize. We've put an extra shift on here at the plant, and I am doing everything possible to get shipments out the door.

CUSTOMER: When *is* my (item) going to ship?

SERVICE: Right now, I can't quote a firm date. We're comparing the current backlog to our increasing production capacity and should be finished with our analysis near the end of next week. I really don't want to guess a date and miss again. What I would like to do is call you next week with another status report. I want to give you a date we will be able to meet. I'll call you on Friday and let you know our status then. At minimum, I will keep you apprised of our status.

ADVISING OF LATE DELIVERY: SPECIAL PRODUCT

It is, of course, best to anticipate any delays that may be associated with special products, especially merchandise that must be custom built, but when you can't advise the customer in advance of possible delay, the next best thing is to advise him or her as soon as possible. To the degree that it is possible to do so, emphasize the positive implications of the delay: for example, the product is special, and we are developing special quality-assurance steps.

SERVICE: This is (name) calling from (company). May I speak to (full name)?

CUSTOMER: That's me.

SERVICE: Mr. (name), I'm calling about your recent order for (item). As you know, (item) is a special product and, as such, is manufactured on a custom basis. This has the advantage of pretty intensive quality control, a great plus for you, but the downside is that we can't always be absolutely certain about delivery schedules. Any number of small manufacturing problems can cause delays. Right now, it looks like we are not going to meet the ship date we originally discussed. To be frank, I'm not sure exactly when (item) will be shipped, but I am confident that it will be before (date). If I had to guess now, I'd say that you'll get it between (date) and (date).

CUSTOMER: You're sure you cannot make the original target?

SERVICE: We've just completed our manufacturing review, and it looks like we're going to miss it. And I did not want to wait until the last minute to drop a bombshell on you. I thought you would want to know as soon as possible.

Even delivering negative news is a positive customer service. Underscore that fact when you have the opportunity to do so.

CUSTOMER: Well, look, I just can't handle it. You have got to take care of business and get me my shipment. You're going to mess up my whole schedule. I'm going to hold you to the original date. I just don't want to hear any of your excuses. Just get it here.

Customers can be tough. You can be tough back and still be professional.

SERVICE: The lateness does not help us, either. We're already on overtime. As I said, we just completed our manufacturing review. At the moment, we have an intermittent problem that is baffling our engineers and assembly staff. Candidly, we just don't know where it is, and its intermittent nature makes everything worse. We have everything here we need to test, locate, and fix the problem. We just need time. As bad as this is, it is better for it to show up here rather than in your plant.

Look, this does not serve our objectives either. We just want to tell you now so that you can activate your contingency plans. Be certain that I will stay on top of this.

CUSTOMER: But I can't accept the lateness.

SERVICE: Neither can we. We're both forced to. We have to accept lateness or have a poor product. Quality problems on your site would be much worse.

Continue to paraphrase and reflect this general thought. The customer is not perfect, and he also has had quality issues to deal with in the past.

REVIEWING CONTINGENCY PLANS TO MEET A CUSTOMER'S SPECIAL NEED

Delivering quality "routine" service means making your standard treatment special, so that the individual customer perceives that he or she is being given tailored attention. But there are many occasions when special or "extra-special" handling is required. It is how Customer Service handles these instances that defines the essence of value-added service, service that is not merely a routine or rote corporate function, but service that produces exceptionally valuable returns for you and your customer.

In special-need situations, it is most helpful to think of yourself as your customer's partner. This partnership is most effectively established by working with your customer to develop a plan of action for whatever situation presents itself.

1. Get information first. Find out what the customer needs. Determine concerns.

2. Determine what you can offer to address these needs and concerns.

3. Formulate a plan.

CUSTOMER: (The basic order has been taken.) Now, I have one big problem. It is possible that I will need an additional (quantity) (item) almost immediately after the main shipment is scheduled to arrive. But I won't know this until (date), which doesn't give us any real lead time. I can't afford to order enough to cover the surplus; I just can't carry the inventory.

SERVICE: So you're talking about only (number) days lead time, correct?

CUSTOMER: Yes.

SERVICE: Are you certain that you will know whether the additional units are a go or no-go by (date)?

Confirm critical information.

CUSTOMER: Yes.

SERVICE: Okay. I think we can help. I'll put an additional (quantity) units on hold from (date) to (date). We'll hold the inventory for you. As long as you can get the word to me by (date), I'm able to guarantee delivery by (date). If I don't hear from you by (date), I'll release the units into our generally available stock. Does that seem workable to you?

Obtain approval and agreement.

CUSTOMER: Yes. That would be great.

SERVICE: Than let's go ahead.

Note that the basic structure of a contingency plan is *if-then*. *If* such and such happens, *then* such and such action will be taken. A contingency plan unites you and your customer. Together, both of you gain some control over future events. It is a powerful service alternative.

Tip: If-then plans can get complex, especially if there are a number of if-then scenarios and subscenarios. In the case of complex plans, follow up your telephone conversation with a faxed memo outlining the plan of action agreed to. This memo is important because it will serve as a contractual agreement. Always invite the customer to call you with any questions he or she may have.

Here is another special circumstance:

CUSTOMER: Yeah, you have the order down pat. But we need some special consideration. You are going to be shipping us 35 versions of (item). The problem is in our manufacturing. Each item is individually packed, and all of your (items) will arrive in identical packages. We know the part number is stamped on each item, but, people do make mistakes. People will make errors with the numbers and, therefore, errors in production. We need a different system. We need some way to differentiate all of these parts other than by comparing part numbers.

SERVICE: I understand. I can see that identical shipping cartons would cause problems on the shop floor. We could consider a special circumstance. What I can do is evaluate the possibility of shipping the different (items) in color-coded boxes. This should greatly enhance your internal tracking and inventory control ability. There would be a cost increase, because we would have to purchase and store all the different boxes, but the additional cost may well be worth it.

CUSTOMER: I don't want the unit price to go up.

SERVICE: The total unit cost should not go up. Part of the total unit cost must be your internal tracking, inventory control, and error correction. Let me suggest this: I'll investigate how much our price must increase to support different shipping containers. Meanwhile, you investigate the value in increased accuracy you will achieve with the color-coded containers. I'll call you back next week, and we can discuss further whether this option is mutually beneficial.

RESPONDING TO CUSTOMER-REQUESTED CHANGES: INCREASE QUANTITY

How flexibly, efficiently, and courteously you respond to customer-requested changes in orders says a lot about your company. The key to effective response is two-fold:

1. Demonstrate flexibility. By demonstrating flexibility you signal the customer that his needs are more important than "company policy" or SOP (standard operating procedure).

2. Do not get rattled. Your unflappability communicates volumes about your company. Even if you have to turn down your customer's request, by not getting rattled and upset, you still communicate concern.

Pitfall: How flexible can you afford to be? Being flexible does not mean bending over so far that you cost your company its profit on a transaction. It is up to you and other management staff to set limits on the requests you can and cannot accommodate. Plan ahead: 1) Determine how flexible you can afford to be. 2) Offer to be that flexible, and be certain to follow through.

CALLER: I need your help. I need to change my order for 60 of (item) to 90. I realize this is the last minute, but we're really in a bind.

SERVICE: I understand, and I will do everything I can to accommodate you. May I put you on hold while I check our inventory situation? This will take about two minutes.

CALLER: Sure.

Avoid making a knee-jerk response one way or the other. Acknowledge the customer's issue ("I understand"), and promise that you will do whatever you can. Then take the steps necessary to determine what you *can* do. Explain to the caller the steps you must take to help. Ask permission to put the caller on hold, if necessary.

SERVICE: Unfortunately, I don't have 90 of (item) immediately available. However, I do have 60 now, with the additional quantity available by (date). Will it help you if I shipped 60 immediately?

CALLER: It would help, yes. I think I can work things out with my customer. It would help a lot.

SERVICE: And then will you need the additional shipment when it is available on (date)?

CALLER: Yes.

SERVICE: Okay. Let's review the revised order, then. We are increasing your order to 90. We are delivering what we can, that's 60 now, before the original promise date of (date). We will ship an additional 30 when they are available, on (date). We're shipping to (confirms address) via (confirms carrier). Have I got it right?

CALLER: Yes.

SERVICE: Let me update your billing. This brings your revised total to ($ amount). There is no additional charge for the change of order. There will be additional shipping charges.

Make it clear whether or not the order change carries any cost and what that cost is.

CALLER: Great. Thank you.

SERVICE: I'm glad I could help, and I appreciate you're working with us on accommodating the later delivery for the additional quantity.

Don't just accept thanks. Also acknowledge any compromise the customer may have had to make.

RESPONDING TO CUSTOMER-REQUESTED CHANGES: DECREASE QUANTITY

Usually, this request presents fewer difficulties than the request for an increase in quantity, except that you may have to inform the customer of an increased per-unit cost, which may be met with resistance.

Pitfall: Avoid betraying any disappointment because of a request to reduce a quantity. Do whatever is necessary and possible to accommodate the customer, without editorializing of any kind.

CALLER: Hi. I'm calling regarding the order I placed on (date). I had ordered 90 of (item), and what I need to do is cut that down to 45.

SERVICE: I can help you with that. I'm just calling up your order on my screen now. Just a moment. Yes, here it comes.

Remember, the telephone is like radio and unlike television. Your "audience" can hear, but not see you. Tell your caller what you are doing.

SERVICE: I can bring that quantity down for you; however, your unit price will go up from ($ amount 1) to ($ amount 2). That will bring your revised total to ($ amount 3).

CALLER: But I was counting on the ($ amount 1) unit cost.

SERVICE: Yes, Mr. (name), I understand. But that unit cost was quoted on the basis of your purchase of nine cases. If you order 60, that's only 15 items more than what you want to change your order to, that will bring your unit cost back down to ($ amount 1), for a total of ($ amount 4).

CALLER: How much time do I have to think about it?

SERVICE: You mean before we ship an order to hold the promise date of (date)?

CALLER: Yes.

SERVICE: I'd need to know no later than tomorrow morning, by (time) o'clock. Would you like those comparative figures again?

Anticipate the information the customer needs.

CALLER: Yes.

SERVICE: Your original per-unit cost was ($ amount 1) for 90. That's a total order price of ($ amount 2). If you reduce your order to 45, your unit cost goes up to ($ amount 3), for a total order price of ($ amount 4). If, however, you order 60, your unit cost stays at ($ amount 1), for a total order price of ($ amount 5). I'll fax you these figures to make sure we both agree.

Always put the complex stuff in writing.

CALLER: Okay. I'll call you back by this afternoon with my revised order.

SERVICE: Great. I'll be here until (time) o'clock. You can direct dial me at 555-5555, extension 555. I'll talk to you later.

RESPONDING TO CUSTOMER-REQUESTED CHANGES: EXPEDITE DELIVERY

One of the most common customer-requested order changes is for expedited delivery, a request to push up a delivery target date. This can be a demanding Customer Service situation.

1. The caller is often anxious, even desperate.
2. You will be pressured into making unrealistic promises.
3. You will be tempted to make unrealistic promises just to reduce the pressure on you.
4. You will be tempted to deny the feasibility of the request out of hand.
5. Quick footwork is often required to determine just what is possible.

Approach this call with the understanding that the customer is anxious. Here is an opportunity to render truly meaningful value-added service, which will greatly influence the customer's perception of your company and of the purchase made. Yet this call is also a challenge to formulate a *realistic* plan and to set *realistic* limits.

Tip: Your customer is pressed for time. But you need not be. Quite often, step one in handling this call is simply to slow down. Proceed methodically, even when the caller is not in a methodical mood:

1. Determine the caller's needs.
2. Gather whatever information you need from your people (Production, Shipping, and so on) in order to respond accurately, realistically, and helpfully.
3. Lay out a plan.

CALLER: Hi. I called on (day) with an order for (quantity) (item). You said delivery would be on (date). I need delivery on (earlier date).

SERVICE: All right, sir. Let's see what can be done. First of all, may I have your name?

The fact that the caller failed to announce her- or himself suggests a degree of anxiety. Be sensitive to this, but don't get caught up in it.

CALLER: (Provides name.) I'm really in a bind here . . .

SERVICE: I understand, and I am going to do whatever can be done to expedite delivery. What I need to do in order to help you is lobby with my production and shipping folks to see what they can realistically do. I can call you back by (time) today. Will you be available?

CALLER: Can't you get back to me any sooner?

SERVICE: Mr. (name), you obviously have an important situation here, and I don't want to make any promises I can't keep, or overlook any possibilities that might be of help. I need the time to make certain I come back with the optimum plan.

Explain *your* needs in terms of the *customer's* needs.

SERVICE: (Calling back after coordinating with other departments.) Mr. (name), this is (name) at (company) Customer Service. We can expedite delivery of your order. However, there is no way to accelerate production to the point that we can make the (earlier date) you mentioned. Your (item) simply cannot be produced that quickly *and* meet our quality standards. We can get it to you by (revised date), however. That's through a combination of high-priority overtime production and expedited delivery. You need to know, however, that this will add cost. Both the overtime and expedited shipping will add ($ amount) to your cost. Do you want to implement this plan?

CUSTOMER: It's better. But I really, *really* need it by (earlier date). Isn't there any way to cut corners on production?

SERVICE: Even if we did, I doubt we'd make that target. But we can't cut corners and risk producing a unit that will fail you or your customer at a critical time. Ultimately, that kind of gamble won't improve the situation or help either of us.

Avoid scolding your customer. Reason with him or her, always framing your responses in terms of the customer's needs.

CUSTOMER: Well, I suppose we'll have to go with it. But can't you give me a break on the cost?

SERVICE: We are doing what we can on that, Mr. (name). We are fast-tracking production and absorbing those costs ourselves. However, we cannot take shipping and overtime out-of-pocket. We have to pass that added cost on to you. I think you'll agree that that's fair.

Underscore the benefits you are providing.

RESPONDING TO CUSTOMER-REQUESTED CHANGES: DEFER DELIVERY

From time to time, customers find it necessary to defer taking delivery of merchandise ordered. This can present problems if:

1. Payment is C.O.D. or the equivalent.
2. Your firm is compelled to bear warehousing or inventory-holding costs.

To the extent possible, respond efficiently and positively to a request for deferred delivery. However, as with responding to requests for expedited delivery, don't put your firm in a losing position by rushing to oblige. Take the time you need to investigate all billing and warehousing implications.

CALLER: This is (name) at (company). I ordered (quantity) (item) and scheduled a delivery date of (date). I need to defer that delivery to (later date).

SERVICE: I can help you with that, but I first need to gather some information about the status of your order. May I put you on hold for approximately two minutes?

CALLER: Yes.

SERVICE: Thanks. I'll be back.

SERVICE: (Returns.) Ms. (name), this is a very large order. We were planning on shipping it out by (date), and to send it out later is going to cause an acute shortage of warehouse space for us. We don't have facilities for holding such a shipment. I do not want to charge you a warehousing fee, so let me propose an alternative. Can you take (percent) amount of the shipment by (date) and then let us ship the balance to you at (later date)?

CALLER: That way I'll avoid any extra cost?

SERVICE: Absolutely.

CALLER: Okay, yes. I can do that.

SERVICE: Great. I'll set it up. We'll ship (percent) amount for delivery on (date), and the balance for delivery on (later date). We're agreed, then?

CALLER: Yes.

SERVICE: Well, I appreciate your willingness to work with us on this.

Or your response might be something like this:

SERVICE: Ms. (name), I have investigated this matter. Unfortunately, this is a very large order, and we simply can't hold the shipment. First, we just don't have the warehouse space available. Secondly, this is the end of our reporting quarter. We have significant manufacturing and materials expenses already locked into your order. We must ship it before the quarter ends, so that we can record an account receivable. If we hold this order as inventory, it is large enough to seriously disrupt our cash flow for the quarter.

CUSTOMER: But, I simply can't accept the order now. I have to delay receipt by two weeks.

SERVICE: Let me suggest an alternative. I can investigate the possibility of shipping to a third-party warehouse. We can transfer the title to you, and then put it in storage for you. That way we can keep it off of your shop floor while listing it as a receivable on our books. You will have some modest cost increases to cover shipping to the site, storage, and insurance. Other than those costs, this plan should work.

CUSTOMER: I don't understand why I should have to absorb any additional costs.

SERVICE: I don't like passing along costs either. But, in this situation, there will be additional costs. I'm trying to come up with the best alternative for both of us.

Usually some compromise such as this is possible, with a bit of creative thought and a cooperative customer. If you explain your business concerns positively, the customer should not become intransigent.

RESPONDING TO CUSTOMER-REQUESTED CHANGES: DIFFERENT ITEM

Generally, this common change-order should not present a problem, provided that the item requested is available and that special manufacturing is not involved. The manner in which Customer Service responds to the request speaks volumes about your company's willingness to serve the needs of the customer. Even a simple change order is an opportunity to demonstrate stellar service.

Pitfall: Be absolutely certain that your company has the internal mechanisms in place to receive and carry out change orders quickly, efficiently, and accurately. The only service affront a customer will perceive as more serious than your unwillingness to accept a change-order is your assurance that the change will be made, and then not be taken care of.

CALLER: Hello, this is (name). I ordered (item 1), and I would like to change my order to (item 2).

SERVICE: I can help you with that, Mr. (name). What I need to do first is punch your order up on my screen. It's coming up now. Yes: (item 1) ordered on (date). Let's change it now, and we'll still be able to hold the original delivery date. Do you want Model 123 or Model 124?

CALLER: What's the difference?

SERVICE: (Describes features of each.)

CALLER: I'll go with Model 123.

SERVICE: Now, (item 2) costs a bit less than (item 1). I see that you paid by (major credit card). I will credit your account for the difference, ($ amount). Your new total is ($ amount). Just to confirm, are we shipping to (address)?

CALLER: That's right.

SERVICE: Okay. You can expect your (item 2) by (date). Is there anything else I can help you with this morning?

CALLER: No. That's it.

SERVICE: It's been a pleasure. Have a good day, Mr. (name).

Sometimes the change-order does not go so smoothly. Here is a customer who has changed her mind *after* the original item was shipped:

SERVICE: Ms. (name), (item 1) was shipped out to you yesterday. It will arrive tomorrow or the day after. If you are certain that you would like to change your order, I can put that through now, and I'll give you instructions for returning (item 1). Do you want to go ahead and change that order to (item 2)?

CALLER: Well, yes. But what's involved? I don't want to get charged for both items.

SERVICE: Don't worry, you won't. (Item 1) will arrive via (carrier) in (color) box with our name on it. Don't open the box. Accept delivery, affix ($ amount) postage to it, and return it via first-class mail. There is no charge for the change-order, but we do ask that you pay for the return postage for (item 1).

CALLER: Sounds fair.

SERVICE: Now, Ms. (name), we also ask that you return (item 1) within (number) days to credit your account properly. If we do not receive (item 1) within (number) days, you will be automatically invoiced for it.

CALLER: I understand.

SERVICE: Okay. I'm going to go ahead and ship out (item 2) now. You should receive it in about (number) days. Is there anything else I can help you with today?

CALLER: No, that is it.

SERVICE: It's been a pleasure doing business with you, Ms. (name). Have a good day.

RESPONDING TO CUSTOMER-REQUESTED CHANGES: SAYING YES, AND COLLECTING ADDITIONAL CHARGES

Besides price adjustments for different items ordered, some change-order requests carry additional charges. The key to handling these situations is to present the charges to the customer as fair exchange for additional value added, rather than a penalty or a "hidden cost." Customers do not resist paying for value received.

CALLER: This is (name). I talked to you the other day, when I placed an order for (quantity) (item). Would it be possible for me to split that shipment, and have (quantity 1) delivered to (location 1) and (quantity 2) to (location 2)? Is it too late to do that?

SERVICE: I can tell you right away what the status of your order is, and if it hasn't left our warehouse, we can make the change. Please give me a moment while I punch up your order on my computer. It's coming up on the screen now. I'm checking the status. Yes. It has not shipped yet. So, if we act now, I can make that split for you.

CALLER: Great.

SERVICE: Now, before I take the information we need to make the split, let me tell you that there is a cost, since this is two shipments. There's no charge for the change in the order, but we do have to charge for two deliveries. I'll get you that figure as soon as you give me the delivery information. Shall we proceed?

Tell the customer up front that there will be additional cost before the both of you invest time in exchanging information. Customers resent having additional charges "sprung" on them unawares, especially after spending time on the phone. Ask for permission to proceed.

CALLER: Yes, I understand. Go ahead.

SERVICE: Okay. (Quantity 1) is going to (location 1). May I have the address? *CALLER responds.* And (quantity 2) is shipping to what address? *CALLER responds.* So I have (quantity 1) going to (repeats address), and (quantity 2) going to (repeats address). Do I have that right?

CALLER: Yes.

SERVICE: May I put you on hold for about thirty seconds while I get you delivery costs?

CALLER: Yes.

SERVICE: (Returns promptly.) The total delivery charge for both shipments is ($ amount). There is no charge for changing the order.

Underscore the fact that the customer is not being charged for the help you are giving, but for the service your company is performing.

CALLER: That's fine.

SERVICE: Then you can expect delivery at both locations by (date). Is there anything else I can help you with today?

CALLER: No, that will be it. Thank you.

SERVICE: Thank you. It's been a pleasure. Have a good day.

Tip: If you meet resistance to additional charges, do not argue and do not offer ultimatums: "If you don't pay, we can't do it." Instead, explain what the customer is receiving for the additional charge. Sell the charge as value for value.

CUSTOMER: I still need the 1000 units. However, I want to change the delivery schedule. I would like 500 shipped this month and 500 shipped in two months.

SERVICE: Yes, let me pull your order. I can do it, but there will be charges. As I read the production planning sheet, we planned to run this order in one setup of 1000 units. That is the lowest-cost method. If you split the order, I will need to send two production sets through the shop. With your needed change, the price will go up as the setup charges will be incurred twice. Do you still want me to split the order?

CUSTOMER: Just run the whole lot. Ship half now and half in two months.

SERVICE: There still will be additional charges, because your parts will show up in our inventory for an additional two months. There will also be additional warehouse charges levied against your order, which will show up in the selling price.

CUSTOMER: I think you're just gouging me for extra bucks just because I need an extra break.

Don't respond to the negative talk. Keep the discussion on a constructive plane.

SERVICE: The costs are real. When we quote special jobs, we make sure we keep the selling price as low as possible. We really don't have a lot of maneuverability. Let me suggest that we investigate this. I will price out the additional charges both ways. I will price this job assuming we split the lot and also assuming we store the parts for you. Meanwhile, you price the cost of storage on your end. How about if I call you tomorrow? We can discuss this further and come up with the lowest cost solution for you.

Continue the dialogue in this manner. You do not need to accept unplanned costs, and a rational customer will understand this. If the customer does not want to be rational, then you have a business decision to make: Is the order still worth it to you under the terms and conditions dictated by the customer?

RESPONDING TO CUSTOMER-REQUESTED CHANGES: SAYING NO

If it were always possible to meet customer demands and do everything a customer requests, Customer Service would not be a very challenging operation. Unfortunately, reality often intervenes. Sometimes we must say no.

Pitfall: Beware of the knee-jerk "no." For the moment, it is almost always easier to say no than yes. "No" ends a conversation, and you get out faster. But you are not in business to get out of the conversation fast. You are in business to create business, and that means saying yes more often than no. That means you must maintain customer satisfaction even if you must say no.

Tip: Practice reluctance to say no. Investigate the alternatives before you say no. When you must say no, try to accompany the response with an alternative proposal.

Pitfall: Practice reluctance to say no, but know when to say it. Do not give a customer false hope, and do not make promises you can't keep.

CALLER: This is (name) from (company). I need to change my order for (item 1) to (item 2).

SERVICE: Ms. (name), I will need just a moment to check on the status of that order. I'm calling it up on my computer now. Ms. (name), I'm showing here that the order has already been shipped. Now, if you give me another moment, I can call down to confirm that.

CALLER: Yeah, sure.

SERVICE: (Returns.) Ms. (name), that order has been shipped. What that means, of course, is that it's too late to change the order. I do have an alternative suggestion, however.

CALLER: What's that?

SERVICE: Place a new order for (item 2) now, and return (item 1) immediately on receipt. I can process the new order immediately. I don't have to wait for the return. However, you won't be credited for the returned (item 1) until we receive it.

CALLER: How do I know that you'll credit me properly?

SERVICE: We'll send you written confirmation, and, if you like, I'll flag your account and call you to confirm that we've received the return and have entered the credit. If, however, you are uncomfortable with having two charges outstanding even for a little while, I can take your order for (item 2) now, but hold it until I've received and credited your return. This will delay shipping (item 2), but you won't have two charges outstanding.

Give your customer a range of options, but beware of overwhelming him or her with confusing choices.

CALLER: No. I'd rather expedite the order. Go ahead and take my order for (item 2). . . .

Some situations require a *no* plain and simple. Deliver it without editorializing or moralizing, but do provide an explanation.

CALLER: Is it possible to get (item) without (safety feature)? That (safety feature) really reduces its efficiency, and I bet everybody gets it removed after installation anyway. Why should I spend the money?

SERVICE: Mr. (name), we cannot sell you (item) without (safety feature). The (item) would be dangerous to operate. I also urge you not to have (safety feature) circumvented later. Here's why: (briefly explains safety hazards). Also, your warranty will no longer be valid. You are right about the efficiency reduction, but this is a very modest trade-off to protect your operators. For that you are assured of a product that operates safely and that greatly reduces your risk of injury or liability.

Pitfall: "It's against company policy" is never a valid reason for saying no. Always provide an explanation. Don't moralize, but do explain. Where safety issues are involved, be certain that you are in compliance with the requirements of all applicable laws and regulatory provisions.

CUSTOMER: I would like to cancel my order for the special item.

SERVICE: Okay, let me pull that up. Yes, I see it here. This order was placed thirty days ago. I see it is a complete special and required a 50-percent-advance payment. Let me check with production control. Could you hold for two minutes or so?

(Service returns.) I don't have good news. Unfortunately, that (item) has already been produced. It's in final assembly and testing right now and will be shipping in two days. I can't cancel the order, because it had special features added to it.

CUSTOMER: You can sell it to someone else.

Accept personal responsibility, and do your best to explain the reality to this customer.

SERVICE: I can't resell it as it is currently assembled. It is not a standard product any longer. I would need to find a special application exactly like yours, which would be a very difficult undertaking. That unit could sit around here for months before we found another exact application.

CUSTOMER: But, I really don't want the thing.

SERVICE: I can cancel your order out. Unfortunately, though, I cannot refund your deposit. As I said, the (item) is not salable as it is currently configured. We would need to completely disassemble the unit and rebuild it as a standard unit. Perhaps you can reconsider. Perhaps your business conditions will change in the next few months and you can make use of this unit.

CUSTOMER: No, things are not going to change that quickly. I think it is unfair of you to keep my deposit.

SERVICE: I'm sorry. I really wish there were more I could do. We have already invested considerable sums in the manufacture of your (unit). We are both going to incur losses on this transaction.

Just state it and get on with it. Be as friendly as you can be. But, no matter what you say, this customer will just want his or her money back. For the benefit of future sales, you may decide to do just that. Many companies will return the money and absorb the loss just to create positive public relations.

RESPONDING TO CUSTOMER-REQUESTED CHANGES: ADVISING CUSTOMER OF RISKS

Sometimes the customer makes requests that you can satisfy, but involve risks. It is your responsibility to advise the customer of these risks.

Pitfall: Be certain to distinguish between risks to equipment and risks to people. Make certain that you fully understand your company's advisories, safety literature, and safety position. Make certain that you understand your obligations under the law or areas of potential liability. Never mislead a customer in matters of safety. Never minimize or dismiss official safety advisories ("Oh, *that*. We just print that label because of our lawyers.")

Presenting risks can be a delicate matter. In general, your responsibility begins and ends with giving the customer a clear picture of any risks involved in a choice he or she proposes to make. If you are pressed for more than this, for advice, follow these guidelines:

1. Advise the customer of any official company positions and recommendations.

2. If you feel strongly about an issue and you have the required expertise, give the advice solicited.

3. Err on the side of caution.

4. If you do not feel qualified to give advice, but you can consult another resource, propose this to the customer.

5. If you do not feel qualified to give advice and you cannot think of an appropriate resource, be honest. Tell the customer that you cannot give advice.

Pitfall: Option 5 is a last resort. It is preferable to fabricating expertise you do not possess. But it still is not a satisfactory response. You should make it your business to become familiar with resources on which you can draw or to whom you can refer your customer. You should include resources and expertise beyond your company. Consider hiring consultants or referring customers to consultants or other resources.

CALLER: I would like to order (item 1), which I want to use to upgrade the (item 2) I already own.

SERVICE: I can certainly sell you (item 1), but it is not what we recommend as an upgrade to (item 2) . . .

CALLER: (Interrupts.) I know. I know that you recommend (item 3), which happens to cost ($ amount) more.

SERVICE: You're certainly correct that (item 3) is more expensive. This is because it includes (list features), which ensure compatibility with (item 2). I am not going to tell you that (item 1) won't function with (item 2). It will. However, you are putting yourself at risk for (list risks). I think you'll agree that any of these risks involves expense well in excess of what (item 3) costs.

Avoid a dispute. Present the facts. Keep your tone neutral. Use the language of accord, "I think you'll agree . . .," not argument: "You're mistaken . . ."

CALLER: Well, it is really important to me that I save money.

SERVICE: I understand. And it is certainly possible that the combination of (item 1) and (item 2) will work well for you. But there is a significant risk of a system failure, that it will cost you in down time, not to mention what it might cost for new equipment. You certainly wouldn't be alone in using (item 1) and (item 2) together, and I will sell you whatever you choose. However, I do want you to be fully aware of the risks. As I said, you could cause significant damage to the system.

Here is another situation that requires Customer Service to help the customer weigh risks against benefits:

CALLER: Can I use (product) to remove stains from (fabric)?

SERVICE: Let me consult our database. The information is coming up on my screen now. (Product) is generally safe for use with (fabric), but, if it is rubbed vigorously, it may damage the fabric. There is also a chance that it will fail to remove the stain entirely.

CALLER: Well, this has me worried.

SERVICE: I wish I could give you a more solid and reassuring answer. What I can tell you is that my database shows nothing that will work more effectively or more safely on the stain. I can't offer any additional recommendations. We just don't have further knowledge on the subject. I want to emphasize that we cannot guarantee the fabric won't be damaged, and we cannot guarantee the stain will come out. However, it looks to me like your best shot. The choice, of course, is yours.

Here is a customer who is making a last-minute change order:

CALLER: I want the shipment diverted to (address).

SERVICE: At this point, the shipment has already left the warehouse. I can send a message to our dispatcher, who will attempt to divert the shipment, but I have to tell you there is a chance we won't reach the carrier in time to prevent a delay of (number) days. That's the risk involved in diverting a shipment at this late date. Do you want me to give the order?

CALLER: Well, now I'm not sure. How much chance is there that the shipment will be delayed?

SERVICE: I can't be too accurate on that, but I'd say there is a pretty good chance you will experience a (number) day delay.

CALLER: Any danger of a longer delay?

SERVICE: Barring some unforeseen accident, no. The worst-case scenario is arrival on (date). More than likely, we'll do better than that. Maybe we'll even meet the original target, though, as I say, I wouldn't count on that.

CALLER: Well, I can live with the worst case. Go ahead and make the change.

SERVICE: I'll call it in right away. Is there anything else I can help you with today?

Here is another possibility for that last-minute request for a change in shipping destination:

CUSTOMER: I want the shipment diverted to (address).

SERVICE: Let me check. . . . Sorry, that package has already been transferred to your preferred shipper. I can call immediately and try to divert it, but I can't guarantee the outcome. They would most likely phone their driver, and your shipment may even get lost.

CUSTOMER: What are the odds of that happening?

SERVICE: I really can't quote odds. But I know things like that have happened, because we have been involved in the search effort. Your preferred carrier is a huge operation, and this is only one parcel. It happens to be an important parcel, nevertheless, it is still only one box.

CUSTOMER: I really don't know what to do. I simply have to divert the shipment.

SERVICE: I understand. I only wish I could do more. I can call and divert it for you. I could also give you the tracking number, and you can start tracking the shipment from your end. Maybe working together we can minimize the possibility of its getting lost. But again, I can't guarantee what might happen. We do not have control over your carrier.

CUSTOMER: I really have no choice. We have to try it. Go ahead and ship to the new address.

SERVICE: Let's hope for the best. Okay, I'm going to call immediately and ask them to divert the shipment to (repeat address). Is that the correct address?

CUSTOMER: Yes.

SERVICE: Okay. The current tracking number is (number). I'm going to call them now and switch the address. I will also get a specific name, if I can, and a problem number, if the carrier uses problem tracking numbers. I will then call you back with any information I get from them.

CUSTOMER: Let's try.

SERVICE: (After doing all of the above.) Well, we tried it, and the carrier sent the information out to the driver. I spoke with Bill Jones, and he gave me a problem tracking number, which is 12345. That's the best we can do from here. Bill suggested that we give this some time, say four hours. I recommend you call him at 555-555-5555 later this afternoon and see if he has a confirmation that the delivery address has been changed. The specific problem is that the driver had to be called. He had to stop the delivery and bring the parcel back to the warehouse. Then the warehouse dispatcher had to change the address label and ship to another warehouse for final shipment to your new destination. That's a lot, and I sure hope they get it right for you. Good luck.

CUSTOMER: Thanks. I appreciate everything you've tried to do.

SERVICE: Glad to help. As I suggested, I recommend you start tracking in about four or five hours.

Chapter

8

Profiting from Complaints

You would be crazy to *want* things to go wrong. But go wrong they do, and you might as well make the best of it. In fact, you might as well *welcome* being told about those situations. Once again, you've stumbled upon an opportunity to give exceptional service, and that means satisfying a customer.

Sure, when the widget your company sold to Joe Smith crashes and burns, Mr. Smith is furious. Think how much more enraged he will get if he calls your company and finds no help. So you've got to be there for him. But responding to complaints is more than an obligatory function. It's more than damage control. It's even more than living up to the letter of a warranty agreement. There's no denying it: When a product or service fails, fails to work or fails to satisfy, it's bad for your customer, and its bad for your company. Everyone is striving for perfection. However, if Joe Smith calls you on it, and you are forthcoming with a helpful response, if you freely demonstrate your company's willingness to stand behind the product or service and make things right again, Joe Smith may still be able to like his widget. Certainly, at minimum, he will feel a whole lot better about your company.

Tip: Responding to complaints is an opportunity to build and strengthen a positive relationship with your customer. It is an opportunity to turn a negative into a positive.

Understand that your customer is calling with a freight of anxiety and anger. Address these intense feelings not with condescending assurances that "everything will be all right," but by communicating two key items:

1. That you are committed to help.
2. That you are competent to help.

It will help you to convey this twin message if you approach the call with a plan. Effective customer service requires flexibility and the ability to improvise, but you don't have to reinvent the wheel with each caller.

1. Begin by listening to the complaint, gathering as much information as you can.

2. Acknowledge the complaint.

3. Express empathy, understanding, and concern: "We're sorry that this has happened."

4. If you know you can fix the problem, tell the caller what you propose to do.

5. Tell the caller what he or she must do, to make the repair, replacement, or adjustment possible (for example, take the product to the nearest authorized dealer).

6. Explain all necessary procedures, not only what you are asking the customer to do, but what you (and your company) will do.

7. Provide all of the information the customer needs, such as a list of authorized repair facilities in his or her area. Follow up by mailing this list.

8. Provide closure to the call by apologizing. This does not mean abject wailing and protestations of guilt. In fact, do not dwell on the negatives, and certainly do not underscore your company's culpability. Instead, use your apology as a springboard to ending the call on an upbeat note, emphasize your gratitude for the customer's patience and understanding. Saying "I sure am sorry this has occurred" is not the same as saying "This is our fault, and we're terrible."

But what do you do when there is no quick fix? The worst thing you can do is abandon the caller, leaving him or her high and dry. Instead, provide the best you can:

1. A plan of further action.

2. A set of alternatives.

3. A temporary fix.

The customer, says the old saw, *is always right.* Well, of course that isn't true, and never was. Nevertheless, your goal should be never to let the customer feel that he or she was wrong in having chosen to do business with your company. The customer may not be right, but you do have to live with him or her. The fact is, callers will come to you not only with valid complaints, but with *unfounded* ones as well. Your goal in handling such calls is not to argue the customer into admitting that he or she is wrong, but to educate. Demonstrate that the complaint is without basis, and, furthermore, do this without alienating the caller. Ideally, the caller should hang up pleased that what he or she thought was a problem has been solved, painlessly and efficiently.

Once you determine that a caller's complaint is unfounded, do the following:

1. Make clear that you appreciate your customer's concern.

2. Explain why the complaint is not valid.

Pitfall: Never address subjective issues such as taste or judgment. Avoid addressing personalities. ("Maybe you're just not the right person for an Acme Widget!") Keep the focus sharply on the product or service issue at hand.

3. Offer appropriate alternatives, including (for example): advice on using the product more effectively, sources of additional information or alternative products and accessories designed to make the product perform more closely to the customer's expectations.

Tip: If the caller is making a claim, for example, demanding a refund, offer the most positive alternative possible: "I can't make a refund in this case, but I can offer you a 15 percent discount on a replacement part . . . ."

4. No apology is called for here, since you do not want to be in the position of offending your customer by saying, in effect, "I'm sorry I'm right and you're wrong." But effective, positive closure is provided by expressing your regret that the customer experienced a problem, thought he or she experienced a problem, or has been less than fully satisfied.

5. As a final remark, it is helpful to express your hope that the alternative(s) you propose will be of help to the caller.

Tip: Customer service is, ultimately, a marketing function. Many suppliers will go right ahead and resolve the problem, even taking the product back and refunding the customer's money, when the customer is absolutely wrong. This is done purely for marketing reasons. These companies, of course, know the customer is taking advantage of them. It's just that they would rather be abused by the customer than have the customer bad-mouth the company to friends and relatives. It's cheaper to give away the product than to overcome the negative advertising. For example, many consumer-product companies will go ahead and routinely give coupons for additional free product, even though they know there is nothing wrong with the product the customer has purchased:

CUSTOMER: Your detergent is not cleaning my dishes. There must be something wrong with this batch.

SERVICE: Do you have the UPC number? It's right on the back of the container. I would like to record your concern. (Customer gives number.) Well, thanks for the call. This is very strange, since we have not had other calls of this type. Anyway, let me send you a coupon, which is good for another free container of (detergent) or any number of other products. We're sorry about the inconvenience.

Obviously, if there were really something wrong with the detergent, service would be receiving thousands of calls. The prudent customer-driven company tracks these individuals and their complaints. If the abuse becomes a pattern, the company has no choice but to end the relationship:

SERVICE: I'm really sorry, but this is the tenth time you have called complaining about our detergent. I would suggest you try another brand, which may work more effectively with your dishes. As for the container you have, I suggest you ship it to our laboratory at (address). Include a letter describing your concern. If the lab determines that, somehow, the detergent is faulty, we will certainly refund your total purchase price by check.

WRONG PRODUCT SHIPPED

One common customer complaint is that the wrong product was shipped. Often the error may be traced to the customer, not to your Shipping department. But it is not your job to assign blame or even to trace the source of the error. Assume the customer is right. Apologize, get the right information, give the customer instructions for returning the unwanted merchandise, and confirm the corrected order.

Pitfall: Avoid an accusatory tone of voice. Avoid talking down to the caller when you confirm the corrected order. Maintain a positive, cheerful, businesslike tone.

Tip: Focus on correcting the error. Ignore personalities.

CALLER: Hi. This is (name) at (company). Listen, you guys shipped me the wrong merchandise. I ordered (item 1) and received (item 2).

SERVICE: I'm very sorry. We'll get that corrected right away.

CALLER: I should hope so. We really need (item 2) without further delay.

SERVICE: Well, I'll arrange for it to be cross-shipped. We don't have to wait for the return of (item 1). Let me check some information with you, and then I'll give you instructions for returning (item 1). First, we are still delivering to (address), correct?

CALLER: Yes.

SERVICE: Now, when we deliver on the morning of (date), will there be somebody in your receiving department to accept the delivery?

CALLER: Yes, sure.

SERVICE: Good. That makes it all the easier. What I would like to do is have our driver pick up (item 1) when he delivers (item 2). That will save you trouble and expense. Is that good for you?

CALLER: Fine.

SERVICE: We do ask that you repack (item 1) carefully prior to pickup on (date).

CALLER: No problem.

SERVICE: Mr. (name), I am very sorry the error occurred. I'm putting in the corrected order immediately. Is there anything else I can help you with today?

CALLER: No.

SERVICE: Well, thank you very much for your patience and understanding.

Tip: Always acknowledge your customer's courtesy in a trying situation. Note that Customer Service expressed *empathy* for the situation without accepting *responsibility.*

DAMAGED PRODUCT

Careful attention to packing and shipping will reduce the volume of complaints about damaged goods, but when a customer does receive damaged merchandise, act quickly to correct the situation. Depending on the product, it may be appropriate to replace the entire unit or only the damaged parts. It may also be necessary to dispatch a technical representative to inspect the shipment. In all cases, be certain to explain the customer's options fully.

Tip: Whenever possible, give the customer a choice of remedies. Don't overwhelm him or her with a demand for decisions, but, remember, offering a choice is empowering. The customer becomes the focal point of your attention, which is what he or she wants.

CALLER: Hello. This is (name) at (company). Listen, we've got a major problem here. Our (item) arrived, we unpacked it, and found a number of components damaged.

SERVICE: I'm very sorry to hear that. Is it absolutely clear which parts have been damaged? Or would you like us to send a technician to your site to inspect the unit?

CALLER: No, it's clear what's wrong.

SERVICE: What parts do you need, then?

CALLER: (Lists them.)

SERVICE: We can ship those to you overnight, or we can have an installer come out with them the day after tomorrow.

CALLER: I have no problem installing the parts.

SERVICE: Okay. What we'll do is send the parts to you in reusable packaging. Once you've unpacked the replacements, just pack the damaged parts in the boxes. You'll find shipping labels filled out. We do ask that you return the parts within (number) days, or we will have to invoice you for the new parts.

CALLER: I understand.

SERVICE: Mr. (name), I'm very sorry for the inconvenience. Now, let me just confirm the shipping information I have. (Confirms information.) I appreciate your patience and understanding. Is there anything else I can help you with today?

PRODUCT DEFECTIVE

Selling a defective product is a black eye for your company; there's no getting around that. But this minor disaster also affords an opportunity to stand by your product and your customer and demonstrate your commitment to providing satisfaction.

The first rule in handling a call reporting a defective product is not necessarily to assume that the product is defective, but that, for whatever reason, it has failed to satisfy the customer. Focus on that.

1. The customer claims the product is defective. Do not dispute the claim.

2. Ask questions to discover reasons for the product's failure to provide satisfaction.

3. Based on the customer's answers, respond appropriately. If the product does indeed appear to be defective, repair or replace it. If the product is functioning properly, further explore the reasons for the customer's lack of satisfaction. Is he using the product correctly? Does he need training? Are his expectations unrealistic? Consider the alternatives available, such as exchanging this product for one that is more appropriate to the customer's needs.

CALLER: My name is (name). I recently purchased (item) from you. I just can't get it to work right.

SERVICE: I'm sorry you are having difficulty with it. Can you describe the problem?

CALLER: (Describes problem. Service concludes that the unit is defective.)

SERVICE: Well, the problem isn't you. It's the unit, specifically (part name). There are two ways I can work with you to resolve the situation and get you up and running as quickly as possible. I can send you a replacement (part name), with complete directions for installing. This option should correct the problem most quickly. However, if you prefer, you may return the entire unit to us, and we will replace the defective part, thoroughly test the unit, and return it to you, together with reimbursement for your shipping costs. That's a bit more time consuming, I'd estimate turnaround at (time period), but we'd be the ones doing the work.

CALLER: I'd really rather have you folks do the work.

SERVICE: We'll get right on it. If you would, please, Mr. (name), pack the unit in its original carton with all of the original shipping material and ship it to us via (carrier); this will ensure that the unit reaches us safely. The carton and the shipping material are specially designed to prevent damage. We will mail you a reimbursement check for shipping charges.

CALLER: What if the new part doesn't resolve the problem?

SERVICE: I am confident that it will. But, Mr. (name), we'll thoroughly test the unit before we ship it back. If there's another problem, we'll make it right. Let me give you a service reference number you can use to expedite any inquiries you may want to make: (number). Is there anything else I can help you with today?

CALLER: No.

SERVICE: Mr. (name), I am very sorry for the inconvenience. We'll get you up and running again just as soon as possible. Thank you for your understanding and patience. Have a good day, sir.

There is no certain way to avoid disputes over products that fail to satisfy. Especially sensitive is the area of warranty coverage.

1. Customers sometimes dispute whether a failure or part is covered.

2. Customers sometimes fail to recognize the difference between "wearable" (or consumable) and "nonwearable" parts.

3. Customers sometimes object to noncovered labor charges.

4. Customers sometimes object to voiding of warranties due to their unauthorized action (for example, an unauthorized product modification by a third-party vendor).

5. Customers often plead for unauthorized extension of expired warranties.

The most effective way of dealing with these areas of dispute is to:

1. Provide full explanations.

2. Offer alternatives.

Pitfall: The key here is to avoid making the customer feel abandoned. Second only to this is avoiding the creation of a parent-child scolding scenario: "You wouldn't be in trouble if you had purchased a warranty extension!"

CALLER: (Having been told that her warranty doesn't cover a wearable part.) But I don't understand. Your warranty says *all* parts and labor are covered.

SERVICE: All *durable* parts. Wearable parts are like any other consumable product, such as gasoline or oil in your car. A wearable part gets used up. That's normal. It's part of its function. That's why we can't guarantee it. In fact, the only thing we can guarantee is that it won't last forever. We do offer our customers (part) at a highly competitive cost, and you are assured that it is expressly designed for your unit. Replacement is simple, and the part includes full installation instructions.

Emphasize the value of what you *can* offer. Do not apologize for what you cannot offer.

CALLER: It doesn't seem right that I have to pay for (part) and then do the work of replacing it, too.

SERVICE: Ms. (name), (part) is specifically designed to be replaced by the customer. In the unlikely event that you have any trouble replacing it, we are available here at 555-555-5555 to talk you through the procedure. But we sell a lot of (product) and, sooner or later, every user has to replace (part). I don't anticipate your having any difficulty whatsoever.

Educate the customer. In this case, education requires assurance and confidence building. Here is an exchange with a customer whose unauthorized third-party product modifications have voided her warranty.

SERVICE: Hello, may I speak to (full name)?

CUSTOMER: Speaking.

SERVICE: Ms. (name), we received your (product), which you returned to us for warranty repair. That unit has a (third-party modification), which, unfortunately, voids your warranty.

CUSTOMER: (Interrupting.) What? How can that be?

Do not accuse the customer of having made the modification. Just point out that the modification was made. Address the issue, not the customer.

SERVICE: Yes, a (third-party modification) was added, which (explain how the modification caused premature failure of the product). That's why the addition of the modification voids the warranty. However . . .

CUSTOMER: (Interrupts.) Well, I didn't know that. I don't think it's right, not honoring the warranty. I didn't know adding this voided the warranty. Nobody told me that.

SERVICE: We try to be explicit about it, both in the Owner's Manual and in the warranty literature provided with the unit. But, look, what's done is done. Let me make a suggestion as to how we can help you in this situation.

Shift the conversation quickly from dispute to cooperation. Rush to help, however you can.

SERVICE: We do offer out-of-warranty repair, even on modified units. Now, the bad news is that we do have to charge for the repair: ($ amount). The good news is that this repair will reinstate your warranty for the balance of the time left on it, which, in your case, is (time period). I do need to point out that the repair will remove the (third-party modification), which you must not reinstall, or the warranty will again be voided. This modification just does not work with the unit. Is this option helpful to you?

CUSTOMER: Well . . . the warranty will be reactivated?

SERVICE: Yes.

CUSTOMER: Okay, go ahead.

SERVICE: I will need a major credit card to charge the ($ amount) repair cost to.

Offering the customer a way out of a difficult situation, especially a situation which he or she has created, goes a long way toward restoring satisfaction with the product.

Responding to a customer whose warranty has expired presents the Customer Service representative with two temptations:

1. Simply to deny service.

2. To "give the caller a break" through unauthorized warranty extension.

Neither alternative is a good one. Instead, respond this way:

1. Inform the caller that warranty has lapsed.

2. Provide the caller with alternatives, usually out-of-warranty service for a fee.

CALLER: This is (name). My (item) is on the fritz. I have a warranty.

SERVICE: I'm sorry you're experiencing a problem. Let me begin by getting your purchase record on my screen. Just a moment, please. Yes. Here it is. Ms. (name), your warranty on (item) expired on (date).

Pitfall: Avoid breaking the bad news with the phrase "Are you aware that . . ." ("Are you aware that your warranty expired on (date)?") At the very least, the question is irrelevant. If the caller had been aware, why would he or she be calling for warranty service? At worst, the question implies your belief that the caller is trying to cheat your company by asking for warranty service when he or she knows that the warranty has expired. Just deliver a factual declarative statement.

CALLER: My warranty has *expired?* Well, can't you make an exception? I'm a very good customer and have been doing business with you for (number) years.

SERVICE: You are a valued customer, Ms. (name), and we can help you. Our out-of-warranty service is fast and reasonably priced. It is the same high level of service you enjoy during the warranty period.

Respond with a positive offer rather than an apology. Always look for ways to emphasize what you *can* do, not apologize for what you cannot do.

CALLER: You know, I'm really irritated. You people design these products to fail the day after the warranty expires.

SERVICE: We design for long life; but products are mechanical, and they do eventually require service.

CALLER: Why can't you stand behind them for life?

SERVICE: That would be an unrealistic warranty for a product like (item). If we offered perpetual service, we would have to price (item) so high that most of us simply couldn't afford it.

CALLER: Well, how do I know that (item) is even worth repairing?

SERVICE: Ms. (name), if you like, we will give you an estimate before any work is done. We'll also offer you a frank assessment of the situation, whether your (item) is worth repairing. The charge for the estimate is nominal, ($ amount).

CALLER: Okay, what do I do next?

SERVICE: You have two options. You can either ship the unit to our main service center, or you can take it into one of our authorized dealers for repair service. Taking it to a dealer generally saves some time. Would you like me to look up the dealer nearest you?

CALLER: Yes, go ahead.

SERVICE: Your address is still (address)?

CALLER: Yes.

SERVICE: Now, let me get the information up on the screen. Yes, here it is. You have two dealers in your area. Are you ready for name and address?

CALLER: Go ahead.

SERVICE: (Supplies information.)

CALLER: Okay. Thank you.

SERVICE: Ms. (name), I'm sorry you've had a problem. Our dealer will get you up and running again quickly. Is there anything else I can help you with today?

CALLER: No.

SERVICE: Have a good day, then.

POOR-QUALITY MERCHANDISE

Few issues demand more diplomatic restraint from Customer Service than customer complaints about the quality of a product or service. Not only do they offend the service rep's sense of pride, they are usually subjective evaluations that invite fruitless dispute. Often, customers complain about quality as if it were an absolute, unrelated to cost. All other things being equal, a given product costing $1,000 is probably of higher quality than the same-function product costing $500. Yet customers often fail to take this into account, totally ignoring the relative value of the product, that is, its quality relative to its price.

In handling quality-related complaints, your primary mission is threefold:

1. Apologize, *not* for the product or service, but only because the customer is not experiencing satisfaction.

2. Gather as much information as possible. This may help other departments, including design, manufacturing, marketing, and so on, especially if this complaint is revealed as part of a trend.

3. Ask the customer what he or she would like you to do.

Your secondary mission is to discuss the issue further. If necessary, educate the customer by comparing your product/service to others and by talking about the product/service in terms of value (cost vs. quality).

CALLER: My name is (name), and you're not going to like this call. I am really unhappy with (product).

SERVICE: I'm sorry to hear that. Can you tell me something about why (item) doesn't meet your expectations?

Apologize, not for the product, but for the customer's lack of satisfaction. Do not demand an explanation. Instead, invite one.

CALLER: Well, it's just garbage! It's junky, and not made well.

SERVICE: What in particular don't you like?

CALLER: You use plastic instead of metal throughout. You are using glue rather than screws to hold this thing together. General construction is lousy!

SERVICE: Is (item) not performing up to your expectation?

CALLER: Oh, it works all right. But it's just not made well.

SERVICE: So (item) is working satisfactorily, but you don't like the way it's built?

CALLER: That's it.

SERVICE: I understand. Mr. (name), I am reporting your comments to our design and manufacturing departments. Now, is there anything you would like us to do about your particular situation?

CALLER: No. I'd just like to see you put a little more care into what you make in the future. Why can't your product be more like (item from another manufacturer)?

SERVICE: To answer your question, (item) could be more like (item from another manufacturer). But then we would have to price it where the other manufacturer does, at about ($ amount). Our (item) is meant to give good value for the money. It's meant to be affordable. And, as I'm sure you'll agree, that takes a certain amount of compromise. Mr. (name), we've poured a lot of resources into researching and designing an (item) that will work well with economical materials. That's what you've purchased.

CALLER: Well, maybe.

SERVICE: Mr. (name), I will pass your comments along . . .

CALLER: (Interrupts.) Oh, I *bet* you will.

SERVICE: Sir, I'm sincere. Part of my job is to find out what customers like and don't like about our products. We evaluate each and every comment, especially when the customer obviously feels strongly about an issue. Your comments are very helpful to us.

Empower the caller by explaining that his or her opinion is taken very seriously.

CALLER: Well, I'm glad to be able to help.

SERVICE: Now, is there anything I can do to help you feel better about (item)?

CALLER: No, not really.

SERVICE: Is there anything else I can help you with?

CALLER: No. Thanks for listening to me.

SERVICE: Thank you for taking the time to call.

Ideally, the call ends on a note of thanks and cooperation, not rancor and dissatisfaction.

If your company offers a satisfaction guarantee, you may have to administer it. While you should not attempt to argue the caller out of exercising the guarantee amd obtaining an exchange or refund, neither should you suggest it as a first alternative. In general, allow the customer to raise the issue first. Of course, if the customer asks you to review his or her options, you must list all of them, including any "no-questions-asked" return and refund policies.

Tip: A refund is not the end of the world if given ungrudgingly and accompanied by a sincere expression of hope that your company will be able to satisfy the customer in the future. Even this revenue-loss situation can help build (or help rebuild) a positive relationship between the customer and the company.

CALLER: This is (name). I just bought (item), and I really hate it. The quality is just not there. I want to get a refund. You have a thirty-day "no-questions-asked" policy, yes?

SERVICE: That is correct, and I am very sorry to hear that you are not satisfied with your (item). Of course, we will take it back and refund your money. It would be very helpful to us if you could tell me a little more about what you don't like . . .

Just because you have a no-questions-asked return policy, it doesn't mean that you can't try to gather some useful information. Before you ask anything, however, assure your caller that he or she will get the refund sought.

CALLER: (Interrupts.) I thought your policy was no-questions-asked!

SERVICE: Mrs. (name), it is. You don't have to give me a reason for returning (item). However, the more information I have, the better chance we have to satisfy you in the future and to serve our other customers more successfully with improved-quality products.

CALLER: I see. (Describes quality problems.)

SERVICE: Thank you for taking the time to explain that to me. Your comments will be reported to our design and manufacturing departments. Now, here's what you do to obtain your refund. . . .

POOR CUSTOMER SERVICE

Customer complaints about "service" may be directed against tech support, against sales personnel, or against Customer Service itself. Responding to service complaints is often even a more demanding and delicate task than responding to product complaints. It is difficult to avoid taking sides, especially if the complaint is directed against you, your department, or your friends and colleagues. The most effective way to avoid taking sides is to refuse to focus on personalities and character. Determine your caller's specific issues, focus on them, and try to resolve them.

Tip: But what if the issue is personality? "Your salesperson was awfully rude to me!" In this case, obtain all the information you can, without comment. Accept neutral phrases like "I see" and "please continue," then assure your caller that you will look into the matter and that you will speak to the salesperson involved. Close by apologizing for having failed to satisfy the customer. Do not admit wrongdoing. Do not imply that the employee will be disciplined. Close by thanking the customer for taking the time to call, with assurances that your company will try harder in the future to ensure satisfaction.

In general, responding effectively to most service complaints may take this form:

1. Acknowledge the complaint and hear the customer out, gathering as much information as possible.

2. Express your understanding, concern, and commitment to resolve the situation.

3. If there is a quick and ready fix for the problem, propose it.

4. If the situation requires investigation, explain how you propose to go about that.

5. If appropriate, apologize.

Pitfall: Do not focus on company shortcomings or errors. Instead, apologize for not having delivered absolute satisfaction, then emphasize your gratitude for the customer's patience and understanding.

6. If you conclude that the customer's complaint is not justified, you should still express regret over your customer's absence of satisfaction.

Tip: In cases where there is no ready solution to a problem, provide the customer with the best alternatives available. Usually, this means a promise to follow up on the complaint. Be certain that you keep your promise.

CALLER: My name is (name), and I want to complain about the absolutely terrible service I got from your Tech Support people.

SERVICE: I'm sorry that you had a less-than-satisfying experience. Perhaps you could tell me what happened.

CALLER: I was treated like a number, not a person. I was put on hold immediately, and nobody got back to me for at least ten minutes. When a Tech Support guy did get on the line, he asked me a few questions, told me what to do, and then told me to call back if the problem persisted. Well, it did persist, and I had to go through the whole holding pattern again.

SERVICE: Was the problem finally resolved?

CALLER: Yes, it was.

SERVICE: Well, I'm happy to hear that. Ms. (name), we pride ourselves on the high quality of our technical support staff, and we take any negative reports very seriously. I will speak with the technician who took your call, and I will get back to you. Can you still be reached at 555-5555?

CALLER: Yes.

SERVICE: When is the best time to call?

CALLER: (Responds.)

SERVICE: I'll be back to you in a few days, then. Now, is there anything else I can help you with today?

CALLER: No. That's it.

SERVICE: Well, thank you very much for taking the time to call me about this matter. We will do everything in our power to see to it that you are more effectively satisfied in the future.

Follow-up Call:

SERVICE: Ms. (name), this is (name) from (company) Customer Service. We spoke a few days ago.

CUSTOMER: Yes, sure.

SERVICE: I followed up with Bill Smith. He is the representative who took your call, and he is here in the office with me listening on another extension. We don't want to offer excuses. We just want to apologize for our less-than-professional performance. Bill's department had a particularly high volume of calls on the day you spoke with him. Making matters worse, the department was also short-handed. Too many people were out ill, which is why you were put on hold for what we admit is too long a time. Candidly, we just had a very bad day, and we're sorry we did not do a better job for you. Bill, is there anything you want to add?

BILL: Only to say, like you, that I'm sorry about our inability to perform.

CUSTOMER: Well, thank you.

SERVICE: We appreciate your understanding and patience. Have a good day.

Notice that the follow-up call did very little beyond simply following up. A brief explanation was offered, and an apology was made. Keep it simple. The fact that you followed up is enough to satisfy most customers. Also notice that the follow-up call included the responsible person. We didn't talk about Bill Smith. He was part of the solution.

SERVICE TAKES TOO LONG

What is "too long?" Often, the customer's perception differs from that of the service department. Generally, this is a subjective issue, unless your service department has promised to repair an item by a certain date and then slips that date. When that happens, the task of Customer Service is to apologize to the customer, with assurances that you will investigate and get back to him or her, and then proceed with whatever internal inquiries are required to find out the status of the repair. If no date was promised, the task of Customer Service is usually one of assurance. The point is that the customer is not so much complaining about a delay as he or she is concerned about being neglected. The cure for this condition? Short of getting the repair out the door, simply pay attention.

CALLER: This is (name) at (company). Look, I'm calling you because I can't seem to get any action out of your repair department. On (date), I sent in (item) for repair. It is still in the shop.

SERVICE: I understand. Have you spoken to anybody in our service department?

CALLER: I'm talking to you. As I said, I sent the (item) in and have heard nothing. I'm trying to find out what's going on.

SERVICE: I will need to look into this and call you back. Can you still be reached at 555-555-5555?

CALLER: Yes.

SERVICE (calling back after investigation): Mr. (name), I have investigated this. We have a very high volume of repair work right now and are running long on turnaround time. I'm sorry we did not notify you with a time estimate. We're on maximum overtime until we catch up on the workload, but we still must meet our high-quality standards on every repair. I located your job and you're in line for the bench. Your job hits in two days and should be shipped by the end of next week. That's our best current estimate.

CALLER: Well, do you think they'll make it?

SERVICE: Our technician is confident, based on what she thinks is currently wrong. However, she still has not disassembled the unit and checked it out. In the worst case, she might find more problems.

CUSTOMER: What might happen then?

SERVICE: I don't know. Depends on what she finds. Let me suggest this. At this moment, we're assuming everything should go okay and that we should have this unit repaired in (days). I think, though, you should assume the worst case, that we encounter another problem and that the repair takes longer. Put contingency plans in place on your end. You have nothing to lose and everything to gain.

CALLER: My schedules are getting tight. I'm getting nervous.

SERVICE: I'll note your concern on the call sheet and check personally with the bench technician. I can give you another call in two days after she disassembles the unit. We'll know a lot more then.

CALLER: Okay, I guess that will have to do.

SERVICE: Sir, as I mentioned, though, to be safe, look into a contingency plan.

CALLER: Thanks, I'll do that.

SERVICE: I'll go ahead and set things up right now on my end. Mr. (name), I'm sorry you got caught in our short-term crunch. You can be assured that the job we do will be careful and thorough and that I will call you as promised. Is there anything else I can help you with today?

Close on a positive note. Assure the customer that he or she is getting something in return for his or her time: quality. Waiting, therefore, becomes a good investment rather than a waste of time.

CALLER: No. That's it.

SERVICE: Then have a good day, sir.

PRODUCT DOES NOT PERFORM AS EXPECTED

The chief issue in these calls is disappointment. The caller is usually convinced (or at least strongly suspects) that the product he or she has purchased doesn't live up to what it's advertised to do or that your company has shipped a defective unit. Sometimes, though rather rarely, the caller will express doubt about the way he or she is using the product ("Maybe I'm doing something wrong"). Any of these things, misleading product advertising/package labeling, defective unit, customer's failure to use the product correctly, may contribute to lack of customer satisfaction. However, before you and your caller can begin to address these issues and make these determinations, the two of you must establish two things:

1. What, exactly, are the caller's expectations for the product?

2. Are these expectations realistic?

If the expectations are realistic, your next task is to ascertain exactly how the product fails to meet them. Based on this, suggest a solution. If, however, the caller's expectations are not realistic, adjust your response accordingly. This may include:

1. Suggesting other products more appropriate to the caller's desired application.

2. Explaining the limitations of this type of product, so that the caller can adjust his or her expectations.

3. Suggesting workarounds that the caller may find helpful.

CALLER: This is (name) calling from (place). I recently purchased a (product) from you, and, I have to say, I'm disappointed with it. (Pauses.)

SERVICE: I'm sorry to hear that, Ms. (name). Can you tell me in what ways you are disappointed?

Use probing questions to help your caller focus and explain.

CALLER: Well, I use (product) to (perform task 1), and it just doesn't do a very adequate job.

The conversation can go in three different directions at this point, depending on the following:

1. You understand the nature of (task 1) and know that (product) is not designed to perform the task or not designed to perform it in the way that the caller expects.

2. You understand what (task 1) is, and you know that (product) is designed to perform the task.

3. You understand what (task 1) is, the product is not designed to perform the task, but there is a work around.

Here is a script for situation #1:

SERVICE: Ms. (name), (product) is not designed to perform (task 1). For that you need (product 2). (Product) is intended for light-duty applications such as, (task 2, 3, and so on). If you're going to perform (task 1), you need a heavier piece of equipment, and that's (product 2).

CALLER: You mean I bought the wrong item?

SERVICE: If you want to perform (task 1), (product) will disappoint you, I'm afraid. May I have just a moment to call up your records on my computer screen?

CALLER: Sure.

SERVICE: You bought (product) on (date), correct?

CALLER: Sounds right.

SERVICE: We can give you full exchange value for (product) toward the purchase of (product 2). (Product 2) will allow you to (perform task 1), as well as (list other tasks). It's an excellent value at ($ amount). With (product) in exchange, you'll pay ($ amount).

CALLER: I hate to shell out another ($ amount).

SERVICE: Well, unfortunately, (product) is just not designed for what you want to accomplish. (Product 2) has these features, which are not included in (product): (list). You are getting a good deal of value for your money. But, of course, it depends just how important (task 1) is to you.

CALLER: Oh, I guess I'd better order (product 2) . . .

Here is the continuation of the script for direction #2:

SERVICE: (Product) should perform satisfactorily for that application. Can you tell me a little more about what you mean by an "adequate job?" In what ways is (product) falling short of what you expect?

Find out precisely how the product is failing to satisfy. Perhaps the caller has unrealistic expectations.

CALLER: Well, I expected (product) to work much faster. I mean, it takes me (number) minutes to perform (task 1).

SERVICE: I understand, and I think I understand the reason for your disappointment. While (product) is designed to perform (task 1), it cannot do it as quickly as you seem to expect. Cycle time is at least (number) minutes. That means (task 1) should take you at least (number) minutes. Now, if you like, I can tell you about an accessory we sell that should cut that time down to about (number) minutes. Are you interested?

Avoid denigrating, or putting down the product. Stress the positive: the product does what it is designed to do. Ask the caller's permission before you attempt to sell her on an additional product or accessory.

CALLER: Yes, I'm interested, but what's the cost?

SERVICE: I think you'll find the price attractive, but let me get to that in a moment. (Describes accessory.) The price is ($ amount). For that, you save (number) minutes each time you perform (task 1).

Emphasize value over price. Spend X amount and get X benefit. Don't quote a price without connecting it to value.

CALLER: I'd like to order . . .

A continuation for situation #3:

SERVICE: I'm not surprised that you aren't pleased with performance on (task). (Product) was not designed for that application. However, you can get that job done if you follow an alternative procedure. Do you want me to go over the details with you now?

CALLER: Yes, but is it complicated?

SERVICE: No. And, if you prefer, we have a one-sheet outline of the workaround. I can fax it to you.

For any instructions relating to process, it is always a good idea to have printed material available. Make certain that the print is highly legible and suitable for faxing.

CALLER: I don't have a fax machine. Could you go over the procedure on the phone?

SERVICE: Certainly. Are you ready to take some notes?

CALLER: Yes.

SERVICE: Okay. Step one. (Explains step one.) Is that clear? (Service goes through each step, frequently pausing to ensure that the caller has taken in the information. After the procedure has been explained, Service continues:) Now, this workaround does involve these extra steps, but it will get the job done. We are currently working on new software (or accessories, and so on) that will get (task) done in a more direct manner. Would you like me to put you on our notification list for an announcement to be sent to you when the new (software, accessory) is available?

CALLER: Yes, sure.

SERVICE: Let me just confirm your address, and I'll send you a copy of those procedures we have just discussed.

It is imperative to back up this script with written information. Remember, we mostly learn through our sense of sight.

CUSTOMER RECEIVED WRONG INFORMATION

Let's face it: When your company's product fails to meet your customer's expectations, your firm's credibility takes a hit. But, as Al Jolson used to tell his audiences, "You ain't seen nothin' yet." For there is worse. The one thing that will torpedo credibility with greater explosive power than a bad product is bad information. A faulty product involves materials, a slip-up, an item that "got by" somebody. Faulty information suggests to the customer that something is wrong with a company's *people*. And that is a far more serious blow to corporate credibility than a bad widget that somehow slipped through the cracks.

You need serious damage control in this situation. Rush in to reestablish the customer's confidence.

Tip: It is, of course, perfectly possible that the customer misunderstood, failed to understand, or somehow simply failed to hear information that was given. However, you should not suggest this as a possibility. Do not accuse the customer of stupidity. Do not blame the customer. There is no point to it. Your task is not to investigate the cause of an incident of miscommunication, but to correct the miscommunication and to heal a wounded relationship. Your task is to avoid loss of business. Proceed on the assumption that the customer was misinformed. However, read on. You will want to end your conversation with the customer by asking for his or her help.

No matter what the substance of the bad information the customer received, or of his or her failure to comprehend good information, this complaint is about miscommunication. Do not compound the problem by allowing communication to break down now. Begin by listening to the caller. Get the details. Avoid defensive responses that tend to cut the customer off or provoke more anger.

Once you have heard the customer out, do not use his or her time to explain or excuse the error, at least not right away. That's probably not the main reason for his call.

Tip: But what if the caller begins by asking for (or even demanding) an explanation? If you can, if you know why the error occurred, go ahead and explain it. If you do not know, say the following: "At this point, I don't know why there was a breakdown in communication. I don't want to give you more bad information by guessing at the problem. I will look into it. We certainly don't want this happening again."

You should assume that what the customer wants is the correct information, not a series of excuses. Begin your response with a short, simple, sincere apology. Then, after you have given the caller what he or she wants and needs, you should conclude with an apology and, if the caller's time permits, one or both of the following:

1. An explanation of why bad information was given, but only if the explanation is brief, simple, and *accurate* (that is, you know that this is what really happened): "We just revised those specs, and I'm afraid your customer service rep hadn't been updated yet."

2. A request for the customer's help. "Is there anything you might suggest to help us avoid such miscommunication in the future?"

Tip: Should you ask the customer for help? Yes, if circumstances permit. Few gestures create a bond more effectively than rendering help. If you can get the customer to help you, you empower him or her, you make the customer feel valued, and you turn a negative situation into a bonding situation. Not incidentally, you might also get a good idea or two.

Pitfall: Don't demand help. Be sure to ask the customer if he or she has time to stay on the line for another moment or two: "I appreciate your understanding and patience. Do you have the time to stay on the line with me a moment or two longer? (Answer: yes.) Is there anything you might suggest to help us avoid such miscommunication in the future?"

After hearing the customer out, act to correct the problem.

1. Supply the correct information.

Pitfall: Don't panic. Don't rush. Take the time you need to ensure that, this time, the information is correct. Ask whatever questions you need to be certain that you understand what the customer wants or wants to know. If you don't have the information at your fingertips, find it. If you can get the information in a matter of a minute or two, tell the customer that you need a moment to retrieve the information. Ask his permission to put the customer on hold. If retrieving the correct information will take longer, explain this to the caller and offer to call back with the information. Be certain to get a phone number for the callback. Establish a time for the callback, a time that is convenient for the customer and that will give you sufficient opportunity to obtain the information. If you are unable to get the information by the callback time, you must call back to explain to the customer that providing the information will require more time. Set a new callback time.

2. If the bad information resulted in inconvenience for the customer or another error (for example, because of bad information, the customer ordered the wrong product), do whatever you can to remedy the situation.

Pitfall: Beware of legal liability situations. If your caller says something like "You people cost me a million dollars. It's your fault! What are you going to do about it?," make no promises beyond supplying the correct information, replacing a product, refunding the purchase price, and so on. You do not want to make any statement implying that you accept responsibility for consequential damages. If the customer persists, do not get into a legalistic argument. Instead, twist the conversation back to what you can do. Do not suggest that the caller consult an attorney, and do not volunteer the name and phone number of your firm's legal counsel. If the caller demands the name and address of your firm's attorney, furnish it, or tell the caller that you will obtain that information. Obtain the information, and call back. In all such cases, do not allow your legal counsel or CEO to be sandbagged. Be certain to supply them all necessary details of the disaster before the customer calls them.

CALLER: You know, I'm really annoyed at you guys. I called two weeks ago asking if (accessory) was available for (product 1) and was told that it isn't. I was told that I had to get (product 2) if I wanted function). So I went out and spent ($ amount) on (product 2). And now I just found out that for (lesser $ amount), I could have gotten (accessory) after all! What am I supposed to do? I'm out ($ amount)!

Note that Customer Service has let the caller talk without interruption and without offering any excuse or defense. Above all, Customer Service has refrained from using such words and phrases as "calm down" or "relax," which are certain to have the opposite of the intended effect.

SERVICE: I think I understand. Sir, I sure am sorry this has happened. One of our customer reps informed you that (accessory) was not available. Do I understand that correctly?

Confirm your understanding of the situation. Empathize with the situation, if you can do so without accepting responsibility for it. You are about to put into motion an adjustment and extend an apology. Note that your language should put the burden of understanding on yourself: "Do *I* understand correctly?" It is your job to understand.

CALLER: That's right! What's wrong with you people? Doesn't the left hand know what the right hand's doing out there? If I ran my business this way, I'd go broke.

A lot of fuel here for anger, plenty for both the caller and the rep. Don't take the bait. Run with skill and personality, not emotion. Deal with the issue.

SERVICE: I understand that you've been put in a very irritating position, and I will help you. Can I have your name? (Caller gives name.) Mr. (name), my name is (name). I believe I have a quick and easy solution. I will give you a return authorization number. Please write it down, and then return (product 2) to (dealer), who will exchange it for (accessory) and refund the difference to you. Will that work for you?

Get a name as soon as possible. Then use it. Give the caller your name as well. It's easy to be angry at a nameless person; staying angry is harder once names are exchanged.

CALLER: Well, it's better than nothing, I suppose. But that still means I have to take time out of my job here to return this thing and hassle with the dealer.

SERVICE: If it is more convenient for you, we can handle it another way. Pack (product) in its original shipping material, and return it to us. We will ship (accessory) to you, along with a refund check that includes reimbursement for your shipping expenses. The bottom line is, we want to make this right and see you satisfied. Would you prefer the shipping alternative?

CALLER: Well, how long will it take?

SERVICE: If you ship via (express carrier) today, we'll get the unit tomorrow. I'll give you an address, and it will be marked to me personally, so that I can ensure that it is turned around immediately. That means you'll have your (accessory) by (date).

CALLER: Okay. That sounds good.

SERVICE: Great! Here's where to send it (gives instructions). Now, Mr. (name), you've been very patient, and I appreciate it. Do you have just another moment or two to stay on the line with me?

CALLER: Yeah, I guess.

SERVICE: I just want to make certain that I understand how you were misinformed. Is it that our service representative was unaware that (accessory) was available? You see, I want to prevent such a miscommunication from happening again.

CALLER: Well, maybe I didn't explain myself fully enough to him, but he should have understood what I meant.

SERVICE: Perhaps he should have asked you more questions about what you needed?

CALLER: That's right. He was very abrupt.

SERVICE: Probably a high volume of calls. But that's no excuse. Mr. (name), I'll advise our service representatives to be certain to take enough time to ask all the right questions, and save all of us trouble. You've been very helpful. I appreciate your comments. Is there anything else I can help you with today?

Gather data from the caller. If possible, at least hint at ways in which you will prevent future problems. Offer no excuses, and resist last-minute blame. (Note that Customer Service does not pounce on the caller for saying that he might not have explained himself clearly. Also note that Customer Service does not pounce on the service rep, either.) Thank the caller for his comments. Always close by offering further assistance.

CALLER: No. That's all.

SERVICE: Okay. I'm sorry for the miscommunication. We'll be expecting your package, and we'll turn your exchange around as quickly as possible. Have a good day.

YOUR COMPANY IS DIFFICULT TO DEAL WITH; CUSTOMER IS FRUSTRATED

You have choices in handling calls from customers frustrated by their experience with your company. You can be "loyal" to the firm and defend it at any cost. You can be "sympathetic" to the caller, taking the customer's side against the firm. ("I know what you mean. Our manager is a real jughead, isn't he?") Or you can listen to what the caller is saying to you, discover the nature of the frustration, and respond to it in a manner intended to reduce it, while you also learn something that may help your company serve customers more effectively and satisfyingly.

The first two choices are likely to lose your firm business. An us-against-them scenario may satisfy some emotional craving, either in yourself or your customer, but it is not likely to generate good business. Defending the company will ultimately produce little more than additional frustration, perhaps even anger, while putting your firm down will very probably drive the customer away. As usual, the best choice is the one that offers the greatest opportunity for communication, for your learning something that may enable you to improve service.

Approach this caller by addressing his or her frustration first and foremost. Don't try to convince the caller not to feel frustrated. Indeed, it is highly probable that, from your point of view, these emotions are unreasonable. But that is entirely beside the point in this situation. Your job is not to talk the caller out of his or her feelings, but to accept the feelings and address them. Find out why he or she feels this way. Once you have determined the causes of the feelings, you can begin to deal with the causes rather than with the feelings. You will have moved the discussion away from personalities and toward issues, always the most productive direction.

CALLER: Hi. My name is (name). Now, I don't want you to switch me to another department, okay?

SERVICE: You're not going anywhere. Ms. (name), I'm here to listen. Go ahead.

Engage the caller. If he or she is concerned about being bounced from department to department, make it clear that *you own the call* and will take responsibility for it.

CALLER: Okay. Because I have found you people very frustrating. I have called six times to ask a question about (product). Each time I've called, I've gotten bounced from one person to another. Usually, I'm finally able to get an answer to my question, but each time I have another question, I'm put through the same runaround.

SERVICE: I understand. Perhaps if you ask me your current question, I can give you the help you need directly.

CALLER: I hope so. (Asks question or presents problem.)

If you can give the caller a quick and direct answer, do so. If you cannot, then remember the call-ownership principle. It is not the caller's responsibility to wander from department to department in search of an answer. As owner of the call, it is your job to bring the answer to the caller, or to send him or her to someone who definitely can help. If you do transfer the call, be certain that you provide the caller an "escort" by first briefing your colleague on the caller's issue. The balance of this script assumes that you can answer the necessary questions directly.

SERVICE: I need to call up the manual for (product) on my screen and then search the topic. This should take about a minute. Can you stay with me?

CALLER: Sure, yes. Just don't send me on a wild goose chase.

SERVICE: I'm pretty confident that I can answer your question with the resources I have right here. Now, the manual is on my screen, and I'm looking up (topic). Yes, here it comes. And here is your answer. Let me read it to you. (Reads.) Is that clear? Are you clear on the procedure? First (explains). Second (explains). And then (explains).

CALLER: Yes, I understand.

SERVICE: Well I appreciate your patience, especially after being frustrated with us. Our Customer Service department has regular meetings to discuss procedures. I will discuss what you've gone through. We will improve our procedures to ensure that customers aren't bounced around. However, may I also make a suggestion to you that will get you even faster answers to most of your questions?

CALLER: Sure.

SERVICE: Use your manual as your first information resource. It's been put together with quite a bit of thought and is the result of long experience with (product). Most questions you are likely to have are answered in the manual. I know it can be a real pain to plow through a manual, but ours has a good index and a very effective troubleshooting guide. Look, we love to hear from you anytime. But you've obviously got better things to do with your time than spend it on the phone with us. Now, is there anything else I can help you with today?

This conversation closes with an acknowledgment that it can serve as a learning experience for both the company and the caller. This is a very positive way to end the call.

CANNOT GET A "STRAIGHT ANSWER"; CUSTOMER IS FRUSTRATED

If there is one thing that will frustrate a customer even more than getting the runaround from department to department, it is the feeling that, ultimately, he or she is not getting a straight answer. Obviously, you and your firm should do your best to prevent this situation from arising. Endeavor to provide direct answers. It is obvious that the basis for any enduring business relationship is confidence. Once you are perceived as evasive, whether deliberately or because of a failure of competence, that confidence disintegrates, and the business relationship falls apart. But what do you do when, despite your best efforts, the customer still feels that he or she is not getting a straight answer? The most effective approach is to avoid defensiveness and, instead, start to work in an effort to understand just what it is the customer wants but is not getting.

CALLER: This is (name) at (company). You guys are going to have to forgive me, but I'm getting more than a little steamed. I own a (product), and I've been trying to find out when the next upgrade will be available. I've called several times, and all I get is a vague answer, something like "It will be ready in the near future." Look, I have to decide whether to purchase (new product) or wait for the upgrade to (product). I really can't afford to be put off with nonanswers.

SERVICE: Mr. (name), I understand your frustration, especially when you are faced with an important buying decision. However, I honestly don't know how satisfying an answer I can give, because the upgrade is still in development. I don't have a final release date for it at this time. Let me do my best to give a ballpark estimate of when you might expect the upgrade. Based on our usual development time, I'd anticipate release about (month). Possibly, the release will be somewhat later, depending on what happens during testing. We don't want to release a product upgrade prematurely and create quality problems for our customers. Does this answer help?

CALLER: Yes, but I wish I could get more accurate information.

SERVICE: I wish I had it here to give you. I would be happy to put your name and address in my notification file, and I'll send a notice as soon as the upgrade release date is officially announced. That's usually a good (number) weeks before the actual release. So you won't have to call us again. Would you like me to do that?

CALLER: Will I be certain to receive the notice?

SERVICE: Yes, I can promise that. . . .

CUSTOMER FEELS "LIKE A NUMBER": IMPERSONAL SERVICE

Business is not about taking money from customers. It's not even about making this or that product or supplying this or that service. Business is about making customers.

An essential ingredient in making a customer is satisfaction. In part, of course, satisfaction is created by product or service performance and perceived value. But it is also created by the relationship or bond the customer feels with the company. If a customer calls complaining that he or she is being treated as something less than a person, as a number, you've got a serious relationship crisis to address. The customer is telling you that he or she feels used, cheated, and is not receiving good value for money invested. And that perception, sooner or later, will affect the customer's perception of whatever product or service your company offers.

Pitfall: Beware of trying to make the alienated customer feel good by "laying it on with a trowel." Phony attempts at making a customer feel "special" usually backfire. The customer quickly sees through the smoke. There are no shortcuts. Give the customer an opportunity to express and to define what he or she needs. Then do your best to address these needs. Even if you cannot address them all, the very fact that you have made an effort to determine them, and that you have *heard* them, will establish or repair your bond with the customer.

CALLER: This is the umpteenth call I've made trying to check on the status of my (repair order). I'm told that it's still "in process" and to call back the next day. I'm really getting frustrated. You are totally impersonal and treat your customers like numbers, not like people.

SERVICE: I understand your frustration, and I'm sorry this has happened. My name is (name). Yours is?

CALLER: (Gives name.)

If the caller is telling you, either outright or in so many words, that he or she is being treated like a number, the faster you get a name, the better. Give the customer your name, too.

SERVICE: Mr. (name), please give me a moment to get your order up on my computer screen. I'm searching . . . it's coming up now. Yes. Okay. Your unit is still in testing, and I am afraid that I don't have a shipping date here yet. Obviously, we're still determining what's wrong with the unit. Here's what I can do right now. I can make a call to our technical department and speak directly to the technician who is working on your unit. I'll get as full a report as I can, and I'll call you back. Would that be of help to you, Mr. (name)?

Particularly when dealing with an alienated caller, be sure to "narrate" your actions, so that, in effect, the person on the other end of the line can look over your shoulder.

But you are still facing a hazardous situation. Your attempt to get your customer the kind of concrete, definitive information he or she wants has failed. The information on your computer screen is not very helpful. Offer something else, in this case, a "friend" in the company, an inside track.

CALLER: What would be of help is getting my (product) repaired!

Sometimes what you can offer is not perceived as enough.

SERVICE: I understand, and we'll work as fast as we can to get the unit repaired. But, obviously, you want the unit to work properly and dependably. We want to ensure that we find and correct the problem, so that you're not stuck in the repair shop again. If you will give me an hour or so, I will get you what additional information I can at present. Can I call you back about (time)?

CALLER: Yes, I guess so.

SERVICE: All right, Mr. (name). Let me see what I can pin down.

CUSTOMER IS SHIPPED THE WRONG PRODUCT MORE THAN ONCE

We have repeatedly observed that problems can be opportunities. Sure, no one wants a product to malfunction or a part to go bad, but, when this happens, you can actually strengthen the bond between customer and company by handling the adjustment, repair, or replacement effectively.

But what happens when lightning strikes twice? What happens when you make a mistake, then "correct" it, only to be called by an irritated customer who tells you that, once again, your company has screwed up? The proper response is threefold:

1. Express genuine concern, and apologize.

2. Make the adjustment.

3. Assure the caller that the error will not occur a third time. If possible, explain briefly what steps you are taking to prevent a future recurrence of the error. In all cases, this will require some personal intervention.

CALLER: My name is (name). I am (title) at (company). Not once, but *twice* you people have messed up my order. This is costing me money. Now, what do I have to do to get what I ordered and *only* what I ordered? Is there anything that keeps you folks from screwing up?

SERVICE: Mr. (name), this is bad news, and I apologize. Please give me a moment to get your order up on my screen, and bear with me another moment or two, please, so that we can review the order and get it corrected right away.

CALLER: Look, I haven't got a lot of time. I just want you to get me the right order.

SERVICE: I want to get you the right order. This situation does not serve either of our objectives. Obviously, if we've made a mistake twice, something in the system has gone wrong. If we spend just a few minutes now, I can get the problem cleared up and not have to put you through this again.

CALLER: Okay, okay. Let's go.

SERVICE: Thank you. (Reviews order and determines problem.) Mr. (name), we will ship the balance of your order (list items) immediately by overnight courier. I will key in the corrected order just as soon as we're finished talking. Now, to ensure proper credit for the items you don't want, I ask that you pack them in the carton they came in, and return them to us at the address you'll find on the label. Please mark the following on the box (gives code number). This will ensure that you are also credited for the cost of shipping the merchandise back to us. We ask that you return the merchandise within ten days. Is there anything else I can help you with today?

CALLER: So I'll get the rest of my order tomorrow.

SERVICE: Yes, Mr. (name), and I am very sorry for this inconvenience. We will look into whatever it was that caused the breakdown in communication. I know it doesn't help much to hear this, but such an error is very rare. Just to make sure, I'm going to personally carry this documentation to the warehouse and check the order package with our people. We certainly don't want this happening again. If there is nothing else, then, have a good day.

CUSTOMER IS SHIPPED A BAD REPLACEMENT PRODUCT OR PART

This situation is similar to shipping a wrong order twice. It creates significant anxiety in the customer, who is made to feel as if he or she will be unable to get the support needed. Maybe he or she has invested personal or company money in the wrong product and the wrong firm.

Your task is damage control, an effort to restore the customer's faith in your product and your company. But you must also make certain that your company can, in fact, come through. Does the fact that the customer received a bad part indicate a problem with a particular lot? Or is it merely an isolated error? After you take care of your customer, be certain to follow up with the parts department.

CALLER: My name is (name), and I recently purchased (product). It was bad enough when it failed after only (number) days. But when you shipped me a (replacement part), which arrived yesterday, that turned out to be bad, too. Level with me: Is there a problem with (product)?

SERVICE: Mr. (name), I am very sorry to hear that you have been inconvenienced like this. No, there is no problem with (product), and I have not had other customers who have experienced problems with the replacement part you've been shipped, so I see no reason to believe that we've got a bad lot of these parts. Unfortunately, I think this is just a case, a rare case, of a bad part that slipped by us. Now this is what I propose to do.

Give a straight answer, backed up by a solid reason for that answer. As soon as you've answered the caller's question, proceed directly to a remedy for the situation.

SERVICE: (Continues.) I am calling down to Parts as soon as I get off the phone with you. I will explain this situation and have them pull another (replacement part), and I will ask the parts manager to open the sealed carton and visually inspect the part and confirm quality before shipping it to you. We will send it by (express courier), so that you will have it by 10:30 tomorrow morning. A prepaid shipping label will be enclosed, so that you can just pop the bad part into the same box, slap on the label, and send it back to us. This should limit your downtime pretty much to the balance of today and an hour or two tomorrow.

CALLER: But what if this part is bad?

SERVICE: That is highly unlikely. As I said, we will inspect it carefully before shipping it, and the chances of your getting two bad replacement parts in a row are remote. However, if the "unthinkable" does occur, we will do a complete quality audit here and send someone to your site to install the part and inspect it in operation. But I really don't think we're going to get to that point, Mr. (name).

TECHNICIAN IS UNABLE TO DIAGNOSE PROBLEM

We live in a society that takes quick fixes for granted. When something goes wrong, we expect that somebody will show up at our doorstep to make the problem go away. Unfortunately, it doesn't always happen like this. Sometimes, a perfectly competent technician is dispatched to a customer's site, works for hours on the idle widget, and comes up with nothing. The customer is steamed. The customer is panicked. The customer hates you and your company.

Approach this scenario proactively. You should never make the customer's mistake of taking a quick fix for granted. Have a contingency plan ready for those occasions when, for whatever reason, your technical staff is unable to effect a quick repair. The objective of such a plan is twofold:

1. It should give the customer the feeling that you are in control of the situation.

2. It should focus on getting the customer up and running as soon as possible.

Contingency plans may include:

1. Dispatching a technician-advisor to the scene.

2. Installing a "loaner" widget while the customer's device is down.

3. If the warranty terms allow, replacing rather than repairing the unit.

Pitfall: In handling complaints that involve failure to diagnose a problem, neither make excuses nor denigrate the product. Address the problem. Focus on the objective, which is, one way or another, to get the customer back in business.

Tip: Many great pieces of music are characterized by a leading theme. The theme may go through many variations in the course of the piece, but it is always there. In this situation, the leading theme is "Stand by Your Customer." Your customer should always be made to feel that you will help correct this glitch and that, whatever happens, you will work until the problem is solved.

CUSTOMER: You've been here for more than two hours, trying to figure out what's wrong with my (product). Now you've got to call in your supervisor. Look, is this *normal?* I mean, what's wrong here? You just get out of technical school or something?

SERVICE: Ms. (name), I'm sorry the service call is taking more time than either of us would like. In most cases, I'm equipped to handle diagnosis and repair on my own. However, each situation is different, and diagnosis is not always a cut-and-dried matter. Rather than waste more of your time or, even worse, make inappropriate repairs, I'm calling in somebody from the senior technical staff. This is our standard procedure.

Customer Service addresses the issue, assuring the customer that the situation, while not usual, is still routine. Customer Service also ignores the customer's sarcastic remark about technical school. You do not need to respond to everything said. There is nothing to be gained by getting bogged down in personalities and losing focus on the issues.

CUSTOMER: Well, how long is this likely to take? I mean, first you spend two hours here. Then we wait for a supervisor. I need this machine up and running!

SERVICE: I understand. If my advanced technical support and I cannot diagnose the problem by the end of your workday today, we will drive out with a "loaner" unit tomorrow and have it installed and operational by (time). So, in the very worst case, you'll be up and running by (time) tomorrow.

CUSTOMER: Well, that's just fine for tomorrow. But I'm losing time today. Wouldn't it be more appropriate for you to compensate me for time lost? I mean, I do a lot of business with you.

SERVICE: We appreciate that business, and we hate to see you have any down time. We can and we *will* get you up and running as soon as possible. If we can't get you diagnosed and repaired today, you'll have another unit in here tomorrow.

Pitfall: Notice that the customer asks for compensation for downtime, and service dodges the issue. The issue is important enough to merit a warning: Don't be trapped into negotiating compensation for down time. Just tilt the conversation away from the subject. It is a bottomless pit that will not only expose your company to expense, but may well open the door to a liability suit. On the other hand, do not make reference to a "company policy" prohibiting such compensation. "Company policy" is a nonexplanation. It's an arbitrary phrase that, quite rightly, will trigger strong negative emotion in your customer. He or she, after all, is a human being and does not relish being sacrificed to an arbitrary phrase.

REPAIRS DO NOT WORK

A repair is made, and fails. The customer calls and is angry. Now, what is he or she angry about?

The question is not as stupid as it sounds, because the answer is not as self-evident as it seems. You see, your customer is not just angry, but also anxious, and afraid. Why angry? The $200,000 widget busted. Time was lost during repair, and arranged around the technician's schedule. If the repair was out of warranty, perhaps a lot of money has already been spent. Maybe, and this is perhaps the most potentially damaging aspect of the customer's anger, as far as your business relationship goes, maybe he or she is angry about having bought a second-rate widget from a second-rate firm.

But the customer is also scared. About wasted money, about being cheated, about a downtime that will have no end. He or she fears that, having pocketed the money, you will walk away and leave behind a malfunctioning pile of circuit boards. The customer fears that he or she has made a bad business decision.

Whatever other issues you will have to deal with, issues of time, money, questions about competence, the driving force behind both anger and fear must be addressed first. And there is a single key that may be used in dealing with both: Communicate your assurance that you will stand by the customer. This is not his or her problem. It is a problem you both share. You are partners in this problem. Together, you will resolve it.

CALLER: I just had my (product) repaired by you about two weeks ago, and now I've got the same exact problem.

SERVICE: I'm sorry to hear that, Mr. . . .

CALLER: (Interrupts) I mean this is *costing* me downtime. I really can't be messing with this stuff. I need it to be right the first time.

SERVICE: I understand, and I will help you and work with you to get you up and running as quickly as possible. Look, my name is (name), and you are?

CALLER: (Gives name.)

SERVICE: Okay, Mr. (name). Give me just a moment to get your service record up on my screen. I'm typing in the search request now, and it's coming up. You have a (product) at (address), and we dispatched a technician on (date) who (briefly describe procedure). The notation I have here says that the problem you called about was (describes problem). Is that all correct?

CALLER: Yes. And I've got the same problem now. (Describes.)

SERVICE: Did the unit function properly up until now, in other words, for about two weeks?

CALLER: Yes.

SERVICE: Okay. That suggests we're on the right track, but sometimes there's just no way to test a repair except to run the device. If it fails, we learn something. Here's what I propose to do: I'm sending our technician back tomorrow, who will rediagnose the unit, based on what this failure tells us.

Without deception, put the failure in as positive a light as possible. If you can, suggest that the work performed previously was not in vain.

CALLER: What guarantee do I have that I won't get the same failure?

SERVICE: Of course, there is no charge for our return visit. And we'll keep working until the unit is operating to your satisfaction. But I won't deceive you: although highly unlikely, it *is* possible that we'll have to return. I hope that won't be the case. The bottom line is, we'll make it right.

You can't guarantee the unknown, but you can promise to stand by the customer.

TECHNICIAN IS SENT TO FIX PROBLEM A; CUSTOMER WANTS TECHNICIAN TO STAY TO FIX PROBLEM B

Customers have an uncanny knack for taking possession of technicians dispatched to their site. Sometimes this presents no problem. However, if a work order is put in for problem A, and the technician's time is scheduled accordingly, being shanghaied into working on problem B as well can really torpedo a work schedule. You may please the first customer, but you will let down any others who are waiting for the arrival of the technician. It is important, then, to be able to say no to a demanding customer without alienating him or her, and the best way to do this is to explain, to share, briefly, with your customer the system under which you operate. Let the customer know that you are a specialist whose time must be scheduled precisely so that you can serve other customers. Always conclude with an offer to schedule the additional work.

Pitfall: Recognize that your customer may not so much resent your scheduling an additional visit as he or she does being *billed* for an additional repair call. Consider allowing some flexibility in billing policy.

CUSTOMER: I'm glad you solved (problem A) and got the machine back up and running. Now, while you are here, take a look at (problem B). It just cropped up over in (system B) after you were scheduled in here. Now that you are here, you might as well get it fixed too.

SERVICE: I can take a quick look, a very quick look, because I have to move on. I'm scheduled to see customer B. (Service takes a quick look at the new problem.) Mr. (name), this is more serious than it looks. We're going to have to get into this heavily. I can't just ignore my previous commitments. I will need to reschedule myself or someone else in to take care of (problem B).

CUSTOMER: But you are here now. I really don't want to have to pay you for another service call.

SERVICE: Let me call into dispatch and see what is happening. Perhaps we can reshuffle the schedule. Sometimes we get lucky. (After checking the schedule) Mr. (name), some days are not as good as others. I really do have to leave. There is no one else available to back me up here or handle customer B. The situation is a little bleak over there. They are in a "hard-down" situation. I really can't put them off. I will need to reschedule myself back over here to work on (problem B) later.

CUSTOMER: Look, it doesn't make any sense. I don't want another travel charge. You are already here.

SERVICE: And if I could, I would stay. However, customer B is completely down. If you were in a similar situation, and you had a committed schedule with us, certainly you would want me to keep the schedule and show up as promised. We must be fair to everyone.

CUSTOMER: I don't care about (customer B). I don't want to incur additional expenses.

SERVICE: No offense intended, but I'll bet you would care for customer B if he were you. Look, the travel should not be that much. Customer B is just across town. I'll call dispatch and ask them to schedule me or someone else in here tomorrow. For now, I must go. As I said, (customer B) is in a critical situation, and I must respond as scheduled. I need to go now. I'll call you, or have our dispatch office call you and confirm who will be here tomorrow.

TECHNICIAN DID NOT GET THE PROBLEM TOTALLY RESOLVED IN THE TIME ALLOTTED; CUSTOMER WANTS GUARANTEE THAT YOU WILL RETURN TOMORROW

Another scheduling demand! If it can be accommodated, fine. But if not, it is important to make the customer understand the following:

1. That the work has taken longer than anticipated.
2. That you are locked into appointments.
3. That you will take action and move mountains to get yourself or another technician on site as soon as possible, which is such-and-such time and date.

SERVICE: We're getting into this pretty deeply here. I can't get this finished today.

CUSTOMER: Fine, but I will need you here for certain tomorrow, first thing. I want this done.

SERVICE: I can't guarantee that right now, but I can check with dispatch and see what has happened today. We never know what sort of critical things may have occurred during the day.

CUSTOMER: Call your dispatcher if you must, but I want you here tomorrow.

SERVICE (after talking to supervisor and dispatcher): I've got good news. Tomorrow I am scheduled to handle one emergency call about five miles from here, and then I can get right back here.

CUSTOMER: No way. I want you here first thing.

SERVICE: And I want to be here first thing. I checked with the office, and I think the emergency stop is going to be very minor. I'm pretty sure I already know what it is, bad load tape. If it is, it should only take me a few minutes to reload. After running some diagnostic tests, I will be right over.

CUSTOMER: Let them send someone else. As I said, I want you here tomorrow.

SERVICE: She is totally shut down, and she is in desperate need for production. I understand your position, but she is desperate and will only take an hour or so of my time. You would want me to help you if the situation were reversed. I'm the only person close by. No one can get there as quickly as I can.

CUSTOMER: I'm not running, either.

SERVICE: But you are cycling production around me and the problem. You can at least survive without us. She can't. I have things going pretty well here, and I feel confident that I will still get you up and running tomorrow before the day ends. It's just a small emergency over there, and I should be here by ten. I'm planning to get an early start tomorrow and will make sure I'm at my other call first thing, before 8:00 A.M., even. We've got to take care of all of our customers, including you, and I intend to do just that. Tomorrow, if necessary, I'll work through lunch, and even stay late. Here I have already found the problem and only need to complete the rebuild and test. Again, I appreciate your consideration and understanding. As I said, if you were desperate, you would want us to pull you out of a tight spot, too. I promise, I'll get back here quickly.

Tip: Always conclude the conversation with a firm and specific appointment.

TECHNICIAN KNOWS HOW TO FIX THE PROBLEM; CUSTOMER DOES NOT TRUST THIS

From time to time, your skills will be challenged. The customer will have a crisis of confidence concerning a repair job under way. Try to see the situation from the customer's perspective: expensive machinery, perhaps vital to his or her business, lies in a million pieces. The customer's emotions are akin to someone who faces the prospect of putting a loved one under the surgeon's knife.

The task of Customer Service in these situations is to persuade the customer that you are competent to effect the repair. Of course, this assumes that you believe you are competent. If there are any doubts, staffing and training practices should be reviewed.

CUSTOMER: Look, you're telling me that my (product) needs a complete strip-down. I called in the repair order because of a strange noise I was hearing. You are saying that this major procedure is required. And I'm really nervous. I can't afford downtime.

SERVICE: Mr. (name), can you live with my time estimates for completing this job?

CUSTOMER: Yes.

Your objective is to get the customer back to reality. This may require addressing one issue at a time. In this case, the "downtime" issue.

CUSTOMER: But that's not my point. I'm not sure. How do I know you can do this?

SERVICE: Perhaps you can tell me what gives you concern about me and my estimates.

Don't start off with a speech about how great you and your colleagues are. Listen to what the customer has to say. Try to get him or her to define feelings and doubts. Then address these.

CUSTOMER: Oh, I know you're not supposed to say things like this. But you're so young!

SERVICE: Well, Mr. (name), I'm fully trained. Like all of our technical staff, I've gone through the full factory course on (product). In fact, I was at the top of my class. I know that machine, Mr. (name). You can have confidence in what I say. Strip-down is prescribed periodic maintenance. The noise you heard is a warning. Getting this work done now will prevent a major and costly failure down the road.

CUSTOMER: I'm still concerned.

SERVICE: Mr. (name), we will stand by you. Should an unforeseen problem develop, we can get a loaner unit to you on very short notice. You'll be insulated from downtime, even in the worst-case scenario. That's a belt-and-suspenders approach.

Chapter
9

Turning Problem Customers into Your Best Customers

Good customers are made, not born. First and foremost, your company is in the business of making loyal customers. Some customers are easier to make than others, but, sometimes, those that were most difficult to create turn out to be among your very best.

Strong emotion is the cement that binds the most enduring relationships, and this can include business relationships. It is the business of advertising and sales to attract new customers, but it is the business of customer service to create and nurture the bonds that keep present customers loyal. This is a powerful mission, since, in terms of generating new business, your best resources are your present customers. Obviously, you want to avoid alienating and losing these valuable assets. And such preventive action is an important customer-service function. But you can and should set the bar even higher.

It is not enough for customer service merely to intervene in a difficult situation to prevent losing a customer. The goal should be to turn the "problem" customer into a distinctly positive asset: a loyal customer, a satisfied customer. Make no mistake, it is a very pleasant feeling for both you and your customer when everything goes well in a transaction: the product performs to expectation, the service is satisfactory, the customer feels he or she has gotten good value. Yet the feelings generated by these positive "routine" experiences are not nearly as powerful as those created when things go wrong: the product breaks down at a critical time, the Billing Department repeatedly makes errors, the service technician is unable to solve a problem. If you can intervene effectively in such situations and turn those strong negative emotions into positive feelings, you will have created an especially strong bond.

Tip: You've heard the theme here before, that adverse situations are not problems; they are opportunities. They are your chance to show how your firm feels about the customer and just how far it will go to satisfy the customer.

Of course, as with so many worthwhile undertakings, all of this is easier said than done. Difficult customers are, well, difficult. What they say and do can provoke strong negative emotions in you. They challenge your integrity and that of the company. Your natural response may be to defend yourself and your firm, or it may be to spurn the customer. In either case, you'll probably lose business. Telling a customer off may be emotionally satisfying in the short term, but how pleased will you be when you lose his or her business? And the business of the next person who ticks you off? And the next?

Tip: Always approach difficult calls with a firm objective in mind. It is not to prove the customer wrong. It is not to claim victory over the caller. It is to create satisfaction. It is to move the situation from a negative to a positive.

CUSTOMER RETURNS "FAULTY" PRODUCT; NOTHING WRONG WITH IT

This call may be initiated by Customer Service in response to the customer's return of a product he or she believes is faulty, or it may be a response to a customer's call, after he or she receives the package you've returned.

Now, the information that there is nothing amiss with the customer's product may come as good news. The customer will be pleased. On the other hand, it may cause perplexity or even anger and disbelief.

1. *Perplexity:* The customer believes your assessment, but still cannot understand why the product fails to perform adequately. In a case like this, your task is to explore the issues with the customer in an effort to determine why he or she is not deriving satisfaction. Perhaps the customer is not using the product correctly, or is using it with applications for which it is not intended. Perhaps he or she has unrealistic expectations concerning performance. Determine the source of dissatisfaction, and work with the customer to educate him or her appropriately.

2. *Anger and disbelief:* Some customers are convinced that they know how to operate/use the product and that their lack of satisfaction with it is due to a defect. They become angry if you deny this "truth."

Approach this situation by recognizing that it is not entirely unreasonable. Technicians do make mistakes, and unscrupulous manufacturers and dealers do try to palm off defective goods. Not to pick on any particular industry, but who among us has not had the experience of bringing a car in for repair, pealing off a sheaf of bills, and driving off, only to feel that same shake, rattle, and roll that brought us into the shop in the first place? We hang a u-turn and march back into the garage, where we are told that the car is "much better now," and that what we are experiencing is "perfectly normal."

Your task is fourfold:

1. Begin by acknowledging the caller's lack of satisfaction with assurances that your goal is to help him or her obtain satisfaction.

2. Only after you have made this acknowledgment should you persuade the caller that your firm's evaluation of the product is objectively accurate. This involves explaining how the evaluation was made.

3. Next, explore the sources of dissatisfaction. How is the caller using the product? For what applications? In what environment? And so on.

4. Finally, educate the caller. This may require "selling" the call to a technical support specialist, or it may be a task you are equipped to handle.

CALLER: I just got back a box from you. I had sent in (product) for repair. It does not work right! And I just got it back from you, with a letter saying that there is nothing wrong with it. Now, look, I'm not stupid. This thing just hasn't been working right. I don't want a runaround, and I certainly don't want to be stuck with a faulty (product).

SERVICE: Ma'am, I want to work with you on this. My name is (name). Yours is? (Caller gives name). Ms. (name), please give me just a moment to get your service record up on my screen. Okay. I'm keying in your name, and here it comes. You sent in a (product), and you reported that (describes problem). Our Technical Service Department performed a complete inspection. Now, that includes (briefly list). They found that the unit is performing within specifications. But, Ms. (name), you and I both know that doesn't mean you aren't having a problem with it. May I ask you a few questions that may help you get the full benefit of (product)?

CALLER: Yes, sure. If you think that will help.

SERVICE: First, have you used (product) since it was returned to you?

CALLER: No.

SERVICE: Has (product) ever performed to your satisfaction?

CALLER: Yes.

SERVICE: When did it stop performing adequately? What were you doing?

CALLER: It wouldn't (perform certain function) when I tried to (do something).

SERVICE: When you use (product) to (perform certain function), do you (describes a set of conditions)?

CALLER: Yes, I do.

SERVICE: Bingo! I believe we've found the cause of the problem. (Explains, and advises how to avoid the problem.)

Note the use of the plural pronoun. Avoid references to *your* problem versus *my* solution. Use "we" and its variants consistently throughout the conversation. Persuade your caller that the two of you are in this enterprise together.

CALLER: Ah! I see. But, you know, your manual isn't clear on this at all.

The caller is grateful for having the problem solved, but then returns to anger and irritation. Be careful not to throw away a victory. Keep listening. Show how much you value the caller's views.

SERVICE: I see. So you found the manual unclear on this point?

CALLER: Yes. And that caused me a lot of trouble.

SERVICE: Ms. (name), I understand, and I'm sorry you were inconvenienced. I am making a note of this issue, and I will discuss it with our documentation staff. Perhaps we can improve the manual so that this kind of problem doesn't occur again. Ms. (name), go ahead and try (product) in light of what we've just talked about. If you have any questions at all, please call me at this number. You may ask for (name). For now, is there anything else I can help you with?

CALLER: No. Thanks a lot.

PRODUCT RETURNED, DAMAGED BY CUSTOMER

Customers are not above abusing warranty terms, even when they realize that damage they have caused to a product voids a warranty or is not covered as an in-warranty repair/replacement. Not that customers are out to perpetrate wholesale fraud, but, typically, the attitude is "all donations cheerfully accepted." When a product damaged by the customer has been returned for in-warranty repair or replacement, and you must inform the customer that the warranty does not apply, you may encounter the following:

1. *Acquiescence*: Great! Your customer agrees that he must pay for the repair. You're home free, right? Not quite. Acquiescence may mask a smoldering resentment that could result in loss of business down the road. It is a good idea to ensure that the customer does not feel abandoned and that, in paying for the repair, he or she is getting good value.

2. *Defensive argument*: While the customer doesn't deny the intent of the letter of the warranty terms, he or she attacks the principle: "Well, your warranty really should cover a circumstance like this. It's only fair." Or: "The unit shouldn't be built so that you can damage it so easily. It's a defective design, and it should be covered."

It is best not to argue with the caller, nor to defend the product. Instead, you might reply that, while you've not received reports of a problem before this, you will note the customer's comments and pass them on to design (engineering, quality control, and so on). Then proceed by underscoring your company's intention to provide great repair service at a price that offers significant value.

3. *Offensive argument, with threats*: Fortunately, this response is rare. But there are customers who will vent rage over what they feel is unjust treatment. Characteristically, these tirades end with a threat or a promise never to do business with the firm again. You will be tempted to give up on this customer. Instead, hear the customer out. Demonstrate that you value his or her opinions. If that proves calming, proceed with a discussion of repair or replacement.

Tip: If a customer is actually abusive, you should not be obliged simply to take it. See "Dealing with the Customer Who Is Personally Abusive" later in this chapter.

Here is a script that may be applied to the first situation, the customer who acquiesces. Note that this is a call Customer Service initiates:

SERVICE: Mr. (name), this is (name) from Customer Service at (company). We received your (product), which you returned with a request for warranty service. Mr. (name), because of the nature of the damage to the unit, we cannot service the unit under the warranty. We *can* offer you nonwarranty service.

Note the phrase "request for warranty service." Define the situation as a request, not a right.

CUSTOMER: The damage voids the warranty?

SERVICE: Yes, it does. The warranty covers ordinary wear-and-tear. Your unit is severely damaged. However, we do offer the same level of expert service, in or out of warranty. I have an estimate prepared for you.

It is a good idea to prepare for the call by having all the necessary information, especially cost, at your fingertips.

CUSTOMER: What will it cost me?

SERVICE: (Gives $ amount.) I think you'll agree that this represents an excellent value. And the repaired (product) is guaranteed for (warranty period).

CUSTOMER: I guess I have no choice.

SERVICE: Well, it's a good choice. The cost of the repair is a good value, and you should get many years of use from (product).

The following is a variation representing the defensive argument:

SERVICE: Mr. (name), this is (name) from Customer Service at (company). We received your (product), which you returned with a request for warranty service. Mr. (name), because of the nature of the damage to the unit, we cannot service the unit under the warranty. We *can* offer you nonwarranty service.

CUSTOMER: You know, that really isn't fair. I agree that the unit is damaged, but it's damaged because it's poorly designed. And that is just my point. It's a defective design. Inferior materials. When I dropped it, it just fell apart.

SERVICE: Mr. (name), I can't say that we've ever had a report of the unit sustaining damage so readily. I'd like to take some notes, which our design and production staff might find helpful. From how high did you drop the unit?

CUSTOMER: Maybe three feet.

SERVICE: And did it hit a hard surface?

CUSTOMER: Yes.

SERVICE: Well, I'll certainly pass this information along. However, the damage is such that the warranty does not cover it. We do offer the same high degree of expertise on our out-of-warranty repair service, and, once repaired, the unit is again under warranty for a period of (period). I have an estimate prepared. . . .

Finally, for the customer who takes the offensive:

SERVICE: Mr. (name), this is (name) from Customer Service at (company). We received your (product), which you returned with a request for warranty service. Mr. (name), because of the nature of the damage to the unit, we cannot service the unit under the warranty. We *can* offer you nonwarranty service.

CUSTOMER: You know, this is ridiculous! You have to honor the warranty. I used the unit. It failed. Period.

SERVICE: The nature of the damage is not consistent with ordinary wear and tear . . .

CUSTOMER: You're just trying to evade your agreement, your responsibility.

Don't argue with the customer.

SERVICE: Mr. (name), we won't evade anything. I promise you that we can offer the same level of service that you would get with in-warranty repair. I think you'll also agree that the service represents very good value.

CUSTOMER: I bought (product) in large part because of the warranty. Your manual should make it clear that you cannot do (function) with the unit. If I had known that, I wouldn't have used it that way. You can't put out a product with an inadequate manual and then charge the customer when the thing breaks. Look, I don't have much of a choice. I've got to get this thing repaired. But I intend never to buy another (product) from you people again. And I'll tell my associates.

SERVICE: I am very sorry that you feel that way, and I appreciate your feelings. However, I have an estimate prepared, and I believe that you'll agree that the repair service we offer is an excellent value.

Listen to the customer. Let him or her vent. Then do your best to offer good value for the money the customer must, against his or her will, spend on the repair.

PRODUCT RETURNED, MODIFIED BY CUSTOMER

This situation is similar to the case of a customer who returns a damaged product for in-warranty repair. However, in the instance of unauthorized modifications, make clear that you are not punishing the customer, but that your firm cannot take responsibility for the performance and durability of a product it did not design and manufacture. That would neither be reasonable nor fair, and your firm must be reasonable to more than one customer.

SERVICE: Mr. (name), this is (name) at (company) customer service. We received your (product), which you returned for warranty service. Unfortunately, Mr. (name), an unauthorized modification has been made to the unit, which voids the warranty.

Avoid the second-person pronoun, *you*. There is no point in accusing the customer of personally making the modification. The point is not who did the deed, but that the deed was done.

CUSTOMER: Oh. I didn't realize. Where does that leave me?

SERVICE: Unfortunately, it means that our warranty does not cover the repair that is needed. Once a modification is made, we can no longer vouch for the integrity of our original design. However, the good news is that our technician reports that the unit can be repaired. We will give it the same high level of expert attention we give to regular warranty repairs. The estimated cost to you is ($ amount), and that includes shipping. If you authorize the repair, we can have the unit back to you within (time period). That charge is inclusive of all labor and carries a warranty of (time period). Of course, we will remove the modification as part of the repair.

CUSTOMER: But I paid to have that modification made.

SERVICE: I understand, but we cannot guarantee the continued reliable operation of the unit as modified. It was not designed to accept that modification. There would be no point in repairing it unless we removed the modification.

CUSTOMER: Could I have the unit repaired elsewhere, with the modification?

SERVICE: You are certainly free to seek other repair. However, I believe you will find this costly, and, of course, you won't have the benefit of our factory-qualified technicians. But the bottom line is that the modification renders your unit unreliable. I strongly advise against taking it elsewhere. We can't support the modification for a reason: Our product simply is not designed to work as modified. But the final decision is yours.

DEALING WITH CUSTOMERS WHO ARE WRONG

There is a certain class of venerable sayings that ring with great authority, but are dead wrong. "Lightning never strikes twice," for example. And practically everyone knows this old saw: "The customer's always right."

Just as the last thing a manager or employer needs is a yes-person who mindlessly agrees with everything the boss says, so "yes-ing" an errant customer is also ineffective. Perpetuating an error will not create satisfaction. On the other hand, rubbing your customer's nose in his or her mistakes will not win loyalty to the company or its products. Yet again, the best course is to remember that you are in a position to educate your customers, and you should not hesitate to do so when necessary, while avoiding mindless agreement, patronizing, or scolding.

Tip: Avoid telling a customer that he or she is "wrong" or "mistaken." Instead, make the issue the subject of the sentence. Not: "You are wrong about such and such." But: "That is not the case with such and such" or "There is a more effective way to approach such and such."

CALLER: Why are you telling me to do it (that way)? I know that (product) works best when it is used (this way).

SERVICE: Ms. (name), I wouldn't presume to tell you how to use (product). I would like to suggest you try using it as the manual suggests. This is how (product) was designed to work best. It's not a question of right and wrong. It's a matter of getting the maximum value from (product).

DEALING WITH THE CUSTOMER WHO IS PERSONALLY ABUSIVE

You should never feel obliged to accept insults, threats, or other abuse from a caller. Nor should you return the abuse in kind. Defuse the situation by advising, and not threatening the caller that you will end the conversation if he or she continues to shout or use abusive or inappropriate language.

CALLER: Look, you (expletive) . . .

SERVICE: Mr. (name), I cannot continue our conversation if you persist in using offensive language.

Tip: If possible, use the caller's name. The caller is less likely to continue to be abusive if he or she is not anonymous.

CALLER: Tough. You are going to listen to me, (expletive)!

SERVICE: Mr. (name), I'm going to have to leave this conversation. Please call back when you feel you can speak in a manner appropriate to business. (Hangs up.)

Tip: Invite the caller to call back after he or she has cooled off. Use terms such as *appropriate* and *business*.

Fortunately, few callers are genuinely abusive, and in the case of those few who do cross the line, a warning that you will terminate the conversation is generally enough to bring an end to the unpleasantness. After all, the one thing an irate caller does not want is to be deprived of the satisfaction of venting.

Pitfall: It is very difficult to control your temper in these situations, especially if the caller makes painful references. If your calmly delivered warning that you will terminate the conversation fails, it is better to hang up than to risk returning the caller's anger.

Chapter
10

Profiting from Disaster

Your most difficult customer has the potential to become your best customer. The same can be said for difficult situations. Handled correctly, they are opportunities that create a positive bond between your company and a customer. When a product goes bad, your customer, unfortunately, identifies that problem with your company. "Oh, Acme. They produce widgets that last about fifteen minutes." If, however, you intervene to put a bad situation right, and you do so efficiently and with demonstrated concern for the customer, your company will more than likely be identified with the solution rather than the problem. That is, the product will be seen as a rotten apple accidentally produced by a fine orchard. It will be seen as separate from what you are and what you do, rather than as a metaphor representing what you are and what you do.

Your customer is usually willing to tolerate a mistake if you not only correct it, but, in the process, demonstrate how much you value the customer.

STATUS REPORTS ON PROBLEMS

It is bad enough when something goes wrong, but nothing will turn a situation from bad to worse more certainly than keeping your customer in the dark. Rome wasn't built in a day, it's true, but you can be sure that plenty of status reports were issued during the long construction process. Your customer will welcome any and all evidence of progress.

Pitfall: Issuing such progress reports is not always easy. You may be reluctant to open up a can of worms, to invite the customer to pipe in with: "Yes. I'm glad you're making progress. But when will it be done?" Always try to have a reasonable estimate of a completion date in hand. If this is not possible, explain why: "I wish

I could give you a firm completion date, but that will depend on (factor). As soon as we have resolved (factor), I can get you a firm delivery date."

SERVICE: Mr. (name), this is (name) at (company) Customer Service. I am calling to update you on repair of your (product). I am aware that we've had (product) in our shop for (number) days, and I wanted to give you a status report. Is this a good time?

CUSTOMER: You're darn right it's a good time. I'd about given up on you.

SERVICE: Well, we haven't been idle. Our technicians have broken the unit down and have diagnosed the problem. It is (problem). Repair will involve rebuilding (part). We have (part) in our shop now. It should be ready by (date 1), which means repair on the unit should be complete by (date 2). We'll expedite return shipping, so you should have the unit by (date 3).

CUSTOMER: I can live with this, but will you let me know if any of these dates slip?

SERVICE: Mr. (name), I don't anticipate that happening, but, of course, I will keep you informed. Is there anything else I can help you with today?

Tip: If you are called by a customer requesting a status report, do your best to find the information immediately. However, do not fabricate information, and do avoid vague answers, such as "It will be ready shortly." If you know that you cannot find reliable status information quickly, avoid saying things like, "Now, where did I put that folder?" Or, "I'll have to hunt down that information." Instead, report to the customer that you "need to retrieve that information from another department," and ask permission to call back. Establish a specific time for making the return call.

CALLER: This is (name) at (company). I'm calling to check on the status of my order.

SERVICE: I can help you with that, Ms. (name). I am keying your name into the system. Waiting for the information to come up on the screen. Yes. Here it is. We have back-ordered (product) because we are out of stock. Generally, back orders take from (number) to (number) days to fill. If you like, I can try to get you some more specific information.

CALLER: I *really* need (product). Can you please get me more information?

SERVICE: Certainly. I will have to retrieve that information from another department. I want to be sure that what I tell you is accurate and up to date. Can I fax you that information later today?

CALLER: Yes.

SERVICE: Should I fax you at (phone number)?

If you have a number recorded on your system, do not ask the customer for a phone number. Instead, verify the number you have.

CALLER: Yes.

SERVICE: You'll hear from me then.

ERRORS IN SHIPPING: WRONG PRODUCT SHIPPED

Your task is twofold: apologize for the error, and ensure that the error is corrected. Be aware that your customer is not interested in hearing an abject apology, but in getting the mistake fixed quickly and simply. Use words like *speed, rush,* and *expedite,* and phrases like *special attention.* The message you want to give is that you are on top of the situation and in control of events.

Tip: If you have any control over how returns are handled, it is best to allow either for transshipping you ship the replacement simultaneously with the customer's return of the erroneous shipment, or for a variation on transshipping, you send the correct item and the customer reuses that shipping carton to return the incorrect item. Enclose a preaddressed, prepaid shipping label. Also include an invoice that explains that the customer will be billed the amount of the original item if it is not returned within ten days. Your principal objective is to create the least amount of work for the customer, and secondarily, to ensure the safe return of the product erroneously shipped.

CALLER: This is (name) at (address). I ordered (product 1), and you just shipped me (product 2)! I unwrapped it, and there is cardboard and paper all over the place, and it's the wrong piece of merchandise!

SERVICE: Mr. (name) I am very sorry for the mistake. I will work with you to get that corrected immediately. Let me just recap while I get your order up on my screen. You ordered (product 1), but you received (product 2)?

CALLER: Correct.

SERVICE: Yes. I see your order on the screen. It was entered correctly, but, obviously, shipped incorrectly. This is what I can do about it: I will expedite shipment of (product 1) via (carrier). You'll have it on (date). In the meantime, I ask that you repack (product 2) in its original . . .

CALLER: (Interrupts.) Look, the packing stuff is spread out all over the place. I don't see how I can get this thing back in its box. I mean, I wasn't expecting to have to return it.

SERVICE: Of course you weren't. Here's another alternative. When you receive (product 1), open the shipping container carefully. Then reuse the shipping container to return (product 2). I'll include a preaddressed and prepaid shipping label. Please return (product 2) within ten days.

CALLER: That sounds more like it.

SERVICE: Mr. (name), again, I apologize for the error. Is there anything else I can help you with today?

Tip: This kind of error may offer an opportunity for extra-mile service. If practical, you may offer to send a driver to the customer's location to deliver the correct merchandise and pick up the merchandise that had been sent by mistake.

ERRORS IN SHIPPING: WRONG QUANTITY SHIPPED

Depending on the type of merchandise and the quantities involved, this can be a relatively minor or a major problem. A customer who ordered a large quantity and has received less may be in a tight spot. How will the customer fill his or her orders? A customer who has ordered a small quantity of bulk goods and suddenly finds him- or herself burdened with a bunch of heavy sacks of stuff he or she didn't order is faced with considerable inconvenience.

In handling these calls, begin by determining the cause of the error. If the customer has been shorted, might this be because of a stocking shortage? If so, it's no error, but you will have to explain the situation to the customer. Be prepared to answer questions about when he or she can expect the balance of the shipment.

If the customer is desperate for additional quantities, be inventive. Can you call other stores, other suppliers, or other customers? This is an extra-mile opportunity. If, on the other hand, the customer is annoyed because he or she is buried in unwanted merchandise, let him or her know that you will expedite removal of the merchandise. If it is up to the customer to return the unwanted items, be certain to give full instructions, especially how to obtain reimbursement for shipping costs.

CALLER: Hey. This is (name) at (company). I ordered (quantity) (product), and you guys just shipped me (lesser quantity). What gives? I've got a real problem here. I need (quantity) to fill a major order, and now I'm stuck.

SERVICE: Mr. (name), I am keying in your information right now, so that I can tell you the status of your order and why you received less than you expected. Yes. Here it comes on my screen. You ordered (quantity), and because of limited quantities on hand, we shipped (lesser quantity). I expect to be able to ship the balance of your order by (date).

CALLER: That's not good enough. I have a (date) deadline.

SERVICE: I can certainly appreciate the problem. It is possible that I might be able to track down additional (product) in one of our other warehouses and have them ship it. I will need (amount of time) to check around. Would (time) o'clock be convenient for me to call you back?

Note the phrase "the problem." Avoid "your problem." You must share the problem with the caller. However, do not pin blame on your company: "I can appreciate the problem we've caused."

CALLER: Yes.

SERVICE: I can reach you at 555-555-5555?

CALLER: Yes.

SERVICE: Okay. I can't promise anything, but I will try my best to get you what you need. I'll talk to you at (time) o'clock.

Here's a script for a case in which the customer received too much of a good thing:

CALLER: This is (name). I just got home and found (number) sacks of (product) dumped on my front porch. I could hardly get in the door. What in the world is going on? I ordered (quantity), and you sent me (greater quantity)? What am I supposed to do?

SERVICE: I am very sorry. Please give me one moment to get you up on my screen and look at the order. Yes, Ms. (name), we have you down for (greater quantity). I have to assume that your order was taken incorrectly. I'm very sorry for that. Here's what we'll do. First, we'll adjust your bill, so that you're paying for (quantity), not (greater quantity). Then I can dispatch one of our delivery trucks to your door to pick up the extra bags. May I put you on hold for a couple of minutes, while I call down to shipping to see how quickly I can get a truck out to you?

CALLER: Yes.

SERVICE: (Back from hold.) We can be out at the end of the day today. Just go ahead and take the (quantity) you ordered. Leave the rest out on your porch, and we'll be there. The driver won't even knock on your door. He'll just cart the stuff off. Sound good?

CALLER: Just fine.

SERVICE: Again, I apologize. Is there anything else I can help you with today?

ERRORS IN SHIPPING: DELIVERED TO WRONG ADDRESS

These calls may come from a person who has received a shipment meant for another; a customer who has gotten a call from someone who has received his or her shipment by mistake; or a customer who has received a shipment at an incorrect address, for example, delivered to a billing rather than a mailing address. In all of these cases, your usual task will be to pick up at one address and deliver to another or to ask the person who has received a shipment in error to return it to you. This involves persuasion, instruction, and assurance of rapid reimbursement.

CALLER: My name is (name), and I am calling from (company 1). I just received a large box from you with my address on it, but not my name. The box is addressed to (name). Can you get somebody to pick this thing up and get it to whoever it belongs to?

SERVICE: Ms. (name), I'm sorry you have been inconvenienced. I can help you right away. I am keyboarding the name on my computer: (name) at (company 2). Well, that's certainly not your company. We've made a mistake. The fastest way to fix it would be for you to hold the package, and we will have (courier) come out to pick it up. Is that all right with you?

CALLER: Sure. Yes.

SERVICE: Okay. Please fill out a shipping label or just a plain label of any kind with this address: (gives address). Now, where should the courier pick up? What's best for you? (Answers.)

And when is the most convenient time? (Answers.)

Okay. We'll expedite this, and I am very sorry for the error. Thanks so much for calling. Is there anything else I can help you with today?

Another scenario, from a customer who has just learned that someone else has received his shipment:

CALLER: My name is (name 1), and I'm at (address). I just got a phone call from a Mr. (name 2), telling me that he received a shipment intended for me (describes shipment). How do we handle this?

SERVICE: Ms. (name 1), I am sorry to hear that you were inconvenienced. Let me get your file up on my computer. I'm keying in your name, and your order has come up on my screen. We shipped (product) to (address).

CALLER: Well that's my name, but it's not my address.

SERVICE: Well now, that wasn't supposed to happen. Let's begin by getting your correct address.

CALLER: (Gives address.)

SERVICE: To expedite delivery of your order, Ms. (name 1), I'm calling down to our Shipping Department and I'm having them send you (product) via (courier). You'll have it at (repeats address) by (date). I don't want you to have to go through the trouble of dealing with Mr. (name 2) to get your shipment. Let me take care of getting (product) back from him. Did he give you a phone number?

CALLER: Yes. It is 555-555-5555.

SERVICE: Thank you very much. I'll take care of that. Ms. (name), I want to thank you for your patience and understanding, and I am very sorry for our mistake. We've got your correct address, and it won't happen again. Is there anything else I can help you with today?

A common error is shipping to a billing address rather than a mailing address or, in cases where a customer has multiple locations, shipping to the wrong one.

Pitfall: Having a customer address on file is a great benefit and conveys to the customer that you are not only efficient, but that you value his or her business. However, always confirm your on-file address before shipping an item. This is especially important for customers with more than one address, or in cases where the billing address differs from the mailing address.

CALLER: I'm annoyed. Look, this is (name) at (company). I specifically told the guy who took my order for (product) that I wanted it *shipped* to (address 1) and *billed-* to (address 2). So what happens? I get these big boxes at my doorstep here at (address 2). What am I supposed to do, load them in the car and take them down to the plant myself?

SERVICE: Mr. (name), I am very sorry for the misunderstanding. Of course, we don't want you doing our job. We will dispatch a courier to (address 2), who'll load the boxes onto a truck promptly, and take them down to (address 1), where they should have gone. I'll set that up right away. However, if you could stay with me just another minute, I want to get your file up on my computer so that I can see what went wrong and make certain it does not happen again. Do you have a minute?

CALLER: Yes, I guess so.

SERVICE: All right. I've got the information here. We do have a separate shipping and billing address listed. (Address 1) is shipping, and (address 2) is billing. That's correct, isn't it?

CALLER: Right.

SERVICE: Well, somehow that got lost in the translation here. I'll flag your account to ensure that it doesn't happen again. In the meantime, I'll get a courier to you at (address 2). Let me confirm your telephone number. Is it 555-555-5555?

CALLER: Yes.

SERVICE: Mr. (name), the courier will call you at that number to confirm a convenient pick-up and delivery time. Is there a good time that I should suggest to our courier?

CALLER: Tell them any time between three and five is okay.

SERVICE: Of course. Is there anything else I can do?

CALLER: No.

SERVICE: Then have a good day. I apologize once again for our error, and I appreciate your understanding and patience.

CUSTOMER'S ORDER FOR PRODUCT IS LOST

From a customer service point of view, this is potentially a very damaging situation. Misplacing an order conveys two messages:

1. You're careless.
2. You couldn't care less about your customer.

These are not the messages you want to convey. In handling a call that reveals a misplaced order, emphasize two elements and two elements only:

1. Your apologies.
2. Your intention to expedite processing and shipment of the order.

Be certain to walk the customer through the ordering process. Take as much of the burden from the customer as possible.

Pitfall: Do not occupy the customer's time with speculation or investigation about what went wrong. Don't take time to search for the order. Do not put the caller on hold in order to locate the order. Simply assume that it is lost, and reprocess the order. If your system allows you to cancel any previous order for the item, cancel, just to ensure that a duplicate order doesn't find its way into the system.

CALLER: This is (name) at (company). (Number) weeks ago, I ordered (product) from your company. My order hasn't arrived yet, and I'm calling to check on its status.

SERVICE: I can help you with that. Let me just get your order up on my screen. It should just be a moment; the system is searching. Okay. I see the problem. We don't have a record of your order.

CALLER: But I called it in on (date)!

SERVICE: I am sorry, Ms. (name), but it didn't get into the system. Let's go ahead and put that order in now, and I will expedite processing and delivery for you. Let me walk you through this, so that we don't have to use up your time. This should take just about (number) minutes. Shall we proceed?

CALLER: Yes, sure.

SERVICE: (Obtains order information and confirms all addresses.) Ms. (name), I can now say with 100 percent certainty that the order is in the system. I have flagged it as a rush, and I will personally call down to Shipping to ensure that it gets to you as soon as possible. Expect delivery by (date). In order to get you a quick update on the status of the order, if you require one, I'm going to give you your order number. Are you ready for it?

CALLER: Yes.

SERVICE: It is (number). If your (product) does not arrive by (date), please call me at 555-555-5555. If you have that number handy, it will help me get you a quick answer. Is there anything else I can help you with today?

CALLER: No.

SERVICE: Okay. This got lost once, so, after I talk to shipping, I'll send you a confirmation fax. Your number is . . . ?

CUSTOMER'S PAYMENT LOST

Another customer-service disaster. Added to the negatives above, perception of carelessness and a suggestion that you don't care about your customers is the customer's anxiety that he or she will be cheated or will be bogged down in a morass of billing problems, double charges, failure to credit, and so on. Your objective in handling this type of call is to apologize and to assure the caller that you are intervening *right now* to correct the problem and that the customer will *not* suffer inconvenience or any financial problems as a result of the mishap. Do not use the caller's time to investigate the problem. Get the information, and assure the caller that the problem will be fixed.

CALLER: My name is (name), and my account number is (number). I just received a bill for (product), which I ordered and paid for on (date). What's going on here?

SERVICE: Mr. (name), let's take a look at your order. I'm bringing it up on my computer now. It should take just a second or two. Okay. Here it is. We don't show payment with the order, so here's what we'll do. Just ignore the bill you received, and we'll put a trace on the payment. Did you pay by check?

CALLER: Yes.

SERVICE: Do you happen to have the check number handy?

CALLER: Yes, I do, It is (number).

SERVICE: Thank you very much. That will help us find out what's going on.

Never demand information from the caller. Request it in a nondemanding manner, emphasizing convenience to the Customer: *"Do you have so-and-so handy?"*

SERVICE: (Continues.) Mr. (name), have you called your bank to see if that check was deposited?

CUSTOMER: No, I haven't.

SERVICE: My suggestion is that you do so, and it would be helpful to get that information from you.

Pitfall: Don't tell the customer what he or she *must* do. Suggest what he or she can do in order to resolve the situation. Do not frame your request as a demand for proof of payment.

SERVICE: (Continues.) We'll get this resolved quickly. In the worst-case scenario, we'll assume the check is lost. I'll ask you to stop payment on it and issue a new check to us. Of course, we'll reimburse you for any stop-payment fees. For now, though, if you can obtain that information from your bank and call me at 555-555-5555 with it, that would be a great help in resolving this. I am very sorry for the inconvenience, and I really appreciate your patience and understanding.

CUSTOMER BILLED INCORRECTLY

Only slightly less anxiety-provoking than the situation in which a payment is lost is the scenario in which a customer is billed incorrectly. Added to the customer's anxiety is a dose of annoyance as well. Leap in to convey your assurance that the error will be corrected fully and without delay, and that the customer will not be put to any further bother.

CALLER: This is (name) at (company). There is a problem with my bill.

SERVICE: I can help you with that, Mr. (name). I'm bringing up your file on my computer. What's the problem?

CALLER: I just got an invoice for (product A), (product B), and (product C). Trouble is, I ordered and received only (product A) and (product B).

SERVICE: I'll take care of this right away. Mr. (name), please disregard your current invoice. I will reprocess the bill and send out a corrected invoice. I'll look into the cause of this error, and I'll see to it that we don't make the same mistake again. I'm very sorry for the inconvenience, and I greatly appreciate your patience and understanding. Is there anything else I can help you with?

Tip: Acknowledge and affirm the customer by thanking him or her. End on a positive note by offering additional help. This conveys to the customer that your relationship is based on positive business, not just correcting mistakes.

Chapter
11

Credit and Collections

At the very least, credit is the oil that lubricates business and keeps it running. In many cases, it is not merely a lubricant, but a fuel: the very element that makes doing business possible. Gathering credit information is an opportunity to serve your customers and to serve your company, to keep both moving ahead productively.

But of course, credit alone is not sufficient to run a business. At some point, your customers have to maintain their credit with cash. Sometimes, it is customer service that is called on to resolve payment problems. When this is the case, ask yourself what your primary function as a customer service rep is. Is it to get the money?

Well that would be nice, and it is one object of the particular call you are making. But the fact is that it is not your primary function. Even in the case of collection calls, your main purpose is to retain the customer and create satisfaction. However, this does not mean giving up on payment due.

Quite a dilemma! How can you avoid alienating a customer, let alone create satisfaction, *and* get the money due your company?

Seize on this remarkable truth: Your customer wants to pay. Put another way: It would satisfy your customer to pay you.

Even the deadest deadbeat wants to settle an account. He or she may not want to part with money, or may not have the money to part with. But no one wants the open account hanging over his or her head. The customer does not so much want to *pay* you as he or she does not want to *owe* you. Looked at from this perspective, the most effective customer-service calls regarding collections create a "win-win" situation, in which you work out a plan to get your money, and your customer is relieved from the burden of debt.

MOTIVATING PROMPT PAYMENT

If the introduction to this chapter seems optimistic, it is. Not unrealistic, but certainly optimistic. There is a better way to handle collections, and that is to avoid letting your customer get into a late-payment situation in the first place.

You may believe your business specializes in this product or that service, but, actually, one of your hottest items is cash flow. That's right. You are selling your own cash flow. More precisely, you need to sell your customers and clients on the desire to pay you on time, even before the bill is due.

As with any other sales situation, you have to offer your customer something of value. Commonly, this "something" is tangible incentive for prompt payment, such as a modest discount or waiver of an established finance/service charge. (In the scripts that follow, I've used 3 percent for payment within 10 days as an example. You should substitute whatever terms are appropriate in your case.) Often, all other things being equal for the customer, such offers provide sufficient incentive to secure prompt payment. Even when this tactic fails, however, the incentive can be renegotiated with a follow-up call in order to secure the next best thing to prompt payment, timely payment. This does require a modest investment of time and effort, although the ready-to-use models in this section will make the task much easier.

Tip: All calls regarding dollar amounts and payment terms should be followed up with written confirmations.

Tip: How proactive can you get? You might introduce prompt-payment incentives even before submitting a formal bid on a project. Then, with the bid itself, include a cover letter stating the incentive terms. After this, enclose a reminder with the first invoice.

Early-payment Incentive During an Update Call

SERVICE: Hello, (name). This is (name) at (company). I know how important it is for you to get prices on (product), so I thought I'd give you a call to let you know that we'll have the bid prepared early this afternoon and fax it to you. We've cut the numbers as close to the bone as we can, but I might point out to you that you can take an additional 3 percent off the top if you pay the invoice total within 10 days of our invoice date.

CUSTOMER: Already you're trying to get your money!

SERVICE: No, no, (name). Our normal terms are 30 days net, and that's a great price. But we could both enjoy an advantage if you pay within ten days: You will save a few dollars, and we keep our cash flow in high gear. And that will benefit you too, by allowing us to offer you the very best prices in the first place.

Anyway, (name), don't go for your checkbook just yet. But do keep in mind the benefit of prompt payment: an extra discount to you. Please call me at (number) if you have any questions. And that bid will be in your hands this afternoon.

In Advance of Submitting a Proposal

SERVICE: Hello, (name). This is (name) at (company). I am calling to let you know that our proposal for (project) was sent out to you this morning. I think you'll be very pleased with the numbers, and you might want to bear in mind that, good as the prices are, they're based on payment within 30 days. We'll knock off an additional 3 percent for payment made within 10 days of our invoice date.

CUSTOMER: So I should take off 3 percent from the bid you submit?

SERVICE: Yes, with today's payment. We spell it out in the proposal. You'll see two bottom-line prices.

CUSTOMER: Okay. I'll look for it.

SERVICE: Do give me a call it you have any questions. My direct line is (number).

A variation on this script follows:

SERVICE: Hello, (name). This is (name) at (company). I'm calling to let you know that the proposal for the (project) will be sent by courier later today. I know you're under pressure to get started, and I'm happy to say that I'm confident you'll be pleased with the figures.

CUSTOMER: Well, let's hope so.

SERVICE: To give you some extra value, we've built in an additional incentive discount for 10-day turnaround on our invoice. This is something you might want to think about when you're comparing our bid to others. We like to make it simple for the two of us to cooperate in order to achieve mutual benefits: lowering costs on your side and easing cash flow on ours.

CUSTOMER: What's the deal?

SERVICE: You can take an additional 3 percent discount off the bottom-line price for payment within ten days of our invoice date. You'll see this spelled out in the proposal.

Handling a Negative Response

What if your customer reacts negatively to your incentive? Try this:

SERVICE: You'll notice that we've invited you to take an additional 3 percent off the total for making payment within ten days.

CUSTOMER: What you really mean is that you tack on 3 percent for invoices that go past ten days. You just inflate the offering price. Now, don't try to kid a kidder.

SERVICE: No, (name). That's really not the case at all. We are interested in getting your business, so we're not about to inflate our prices and let some other guy undercut us. We give you our best shot for our standard 30-day terms. And as you'll see from the proposal, after 30 days, we do charge 1.5 percent per month, up to 90 days. After that, we consider the account delinquent. But we believe you should get a benefit from paying earlier than the standard 30 days. The 3 percent discount for prompt payment is a genuine discount off our best net price. It's not a hidden charge. It is, quite frankly, an incentive. We're a small company, and it's worth 3 percent to us to keep as much cash coming just as quickly as we can get it in here. That's the whole truth and nothing but the truth.

CUSTOMER: Well . . . I don't know . . . What about *my* cash flow?

SERVICE: (name), don't feel pressured. We're also very happy to do business on the basis of 30 days net. The choice is yours and yours alone.

COLLECTIONS

Preventive Medicine

The trouble with most collection calls is that they come too late, *after* a problem develops. In this era of skyrocketing health-care costs, insurance companies, health-care providers, and health-care consumers have all come to recognize the importance of preventive medicine. Preventing disease and injury is always more cost-effective than treating problems after they occur.

Take a lesson when it comes to collections. Anticipate and prevent poor payment performance. Even when the kind of incentives suggested in the preceding section fail to elicit prompt payment, they can still serve you. You may take the customer's failure to respond to the incentive as an early warning sign of potential poor performance. Sure, the customer may have many reasons for not acting on your offer. The incentive may be too insignificant. The cash-flow benefit of withholding payment until the last minute may outweigh the benefit of a small discount. Even more likely, despite your phone call, the customer may simply have failed to take note of the incentive or may have forgotten about it. But it is also quite possible that the customer is financially unwilling or unable to act on the incentive offer. For this reason, when a customer does not respond, it is time to practice preventive medicine.

This does not mean that you have the right to go after your customer because your invoice is now a big two weeks old. Preventive action should be a service to your customer, not a clumsy attempt to collect a bill before it is reasonably due. Try making a call informing the customer that it is not too late to take advantage of an incentive offer, or that there is still time to avoid service/finance charges.

Tip: Ideally, the "preventive medicine" call should come across as your way of saving the customer money. Reassure the customer that his or her account is in good standing, but that you believe he or she will be grateful for a money-saving reminder.

Regardless of whether or not you have offered a prompt-payment incentive, you need to be aware of marginally late accounts, especially those that are frequently a few days past due. Do not wait for such accounts to become collection problems, but communicate with them early. If you have a stepped scale of service charges (so much at 30 days, so much more at 60 days, and so on), remind the customer whose account has passed 30 days that she can avoid an additional service charge by paying before 60 days.

For an Account at Fifteen Days After Invoice Date

Assuming 30-day net terms, this account is *not* past due. Practice preventive medicine, always positioning it as a service for the customer, not an attempt to rush payment to yourself.

SERVICE: Hi, this is (name) from (company). I was just looking over our customer list and noticed that your order of (date) is the first order you've placed with us. I wanted to ask if you are aware of our 3-percent discount offer for accounts paid within 10 days of our invoice date.

CUSTOMER: No. What's the gimmick?

SERVICE: No gimmick, (name). Just an opportunity to obtain additional value. We included a note about it with the invoice, but we don't make very much noise about it. However, it is our regular policy, and you might want to keep it in mind for future orders. In the future, if you pay your account within 10 days of our invoice date, you can take 3-percent off that invoice. I'll tell you what. If you can get the current payment out to us today, I'll give you the 3 percent anyway. If you can't bend a rule to make a new customer happy, what good is a rule?

CUSTOMER: So, if I mail you a check today, I should take 3 percent off the invoice?

SERVICE: That's right.

CUSTOMER: Okay. I'll do it.

SERVICE: So that will bring the amount due to ($ amount).

Here's a variation of the 15-day incentive script:

SERVICE: Hi, this is (name) from (company). I was just looking over our customer list and noticed that your order of (date) is the first order you've placed with us. I also noticed that you haven't taken advantage of our 3-percent discount offer for accounts paid within 10 days of our invoice date. Were you aware of that offer?

CUSTOMER: Oh, yes, but I'm afraid I just haven't been able to get around to that invoice yet.

SERVICE: Well, it's no problem, of course. Your account is on 30-day net terms. But I did want to alert you to our offer, just in case it had slipped by you. Maybe you'll want to take advantage of it on the next order.

CUSTOMER: Well, yes, maybe.

SERVICE: Good talking with you.

For an Account Nearing Thirty Days

The customer's unpaid account is nearing the 30-day mark. Time for a mild dose of preventive medicine.

SERVICE: Hello, this is (name) from (company). I thought I'd give you a friendly call to remind you that your account is approaching the 30-day mark, which means that we'll be tacking on a percentage finance charge beginning (date). There's no problem with the account, of course, but it seemed to me that you might want to avoid paying even a few extra dollars. If you can get payment to us by (date), we'll bill the account at net.

A variant follows.

SERVICE: Hello, (name). This is (name), calling from (company). I had written a note to myself to give you a call before your account with us went beyond 30 days. So here I am, giving you a call.

CUSTOMER: What's the problem?

SERVICE: There's absolutely no problem with the account, but I did want to remind you that a (percentage) finance charge kicks in after (date). I thought you might want to be reminded in order to save yourself some money.

CUSTOMER: So, if I get a check to you by (date), I'll avoid a surcharge?

SERVICE: A finance charge. Yes.

CUSTOMER: I can swing it. I'll put it in the mail right away.

SERVICE: Great! Thanks!

COLLECTIONS: DID YOU FORGET?

Accounts that are only slightly late warrant a reminder call before they become seriously late. Present this as a service to the customer, never as a threat. Stress the positive benefits of paying on time.

Marginally Late Payment(s) on a Monthly Payment Schedule

SERVICE: Hello, (name). This is (name) from (company). I've just received your (month) payment on your account and wanted to thank you for it. I also wanted to make you aware that, since we received the payment after the due date, it's subject to a ($ amount) service charge. Not a big deal, of course, but my point is that the payment was only (days) behind the due date, and it seems a shame to incur service charges unnecessarily. (Name), if you can get us your next payment by (date), you'll avoid a service charge on that one.

GETTING MORE AGGRESSIVE

Even if you have faithfully practiced preventive medicine, advising your customer of incentives from the beginning and providing a timely reminder, it is inevitable that some receivables will remain in the Never-Never Land of 30, 60, or 90 days beyond the invoice date. Playing the cash-flow game of delaying payment has become a numbingly regular feature of business, and some managers are content to take this as par for the course. *Everyone,* they say, *pays late.* These folks play by the old rules, faithfully grinding out the second, third, and fourth statement before sending a semithreatening letter. Then they turn the mess over to a collection agency, who eats up the all-but-forgotten profits.

It is a far better customer-service policy to base actions on anticipation rather than response and to regard an account that has gone beyond its 30-day net period as a serious matter. Neither panic nor anger is called for, and the object is not to punish a "delinquent" account. Rather, it is to enable that account to pay you.

Tip: In collections, the goal is money, not revenge.

When a customer or client lets a bill slip 30, 60, or 90 days, it is not only the account that is in peril, but, more critically, your relationship with the customer. It is an immutable law of nature that debtor avoids creditor. Through a persistent but nonthreatening program of communication, especially by telephone, you need to overcome this natural tendency and talk with your client in order to maintain the relationship. You literally cannot afford to alienate a person who owes you money or to let the person feel that he or she has alienated you.

This does not mean that you should let your customer know that it is "all right" to owe you money. It's not all right at all. However, it is in your best interest never to threaten, never to scold, never to dare him to pay. The most effective approach is to help your client or customer pay you. Believe it or not, that is what your customer really wants to do. Out of feelings of guilt, the customer may avoid your phone calls, but, really, he or she does not want to avoid paying you, and wants to settle the debt.

Following are some scripts aimed at helping your client or customer pay you.

☎ If the account is just past due, you may want to renegotiate original incentives to prompt payment. Done correctly, this strategy does not make you seem like a wimp. What it may do is keep your customer on your team.

☎ For older accounts, negative incentives may be called for, reminders that service charges are accruing, for example.

Tip: If possible, stress that you are in a position to help your customer avoid extra charges or that you are very willing to discuss alternative payment plans.

☎ For accounts very seriously overdue, you may point out that suspension of credit or even legal action is impending. Be firm, but avoid threats.

Keeping the Customer on Your Team: Scripts for Accounts That Have Slipped Past Thirty-day Net Terms

Deft "minor surgery" is called for when an account eases past your deadline for net terms (typically, this is 30 days) or when a customer calls to advise you of a payment problem, a service charge is due but unpaid, a single installment payment is missed, or a check bounces.

Sending a cover letter or insert with a second copy of an account statement or invoice is far more productive than simply sending the statement or invoice alone. Including a letter with an invoice lets your customer know that he or she is dealing with a human being, not just a company, and most of us are more responsive to people than to corporate entities. If you originally offered an incentive to encourage prompt payment, use the cover letter to renegotiate the incentive. (You will find such letters, ready to use, in my *Complete Customer Service Model Letter and Memo Book* [Prentice Hall].) Follow up with a phone call. Let your customer know that paying today will not only earn him or her the gratitude of a fellow human being, but will, even now, earn something more: a small discount, perhaps, or the waiver of a finance or service charge.

An alternative to letters and telephone calls that renegotiate positive incentives are those that help the customer avoid negative incentives. A 30-day invoice insert may remind the customer that the enclosed statement includes a service charge, but that he or she will avoid paying an additional service charge by sending a check before a certain date. A follow-up phone call may do the same thing.

A very special situation arises when a customer calls you to advise you of a payment problem. Although such a call is hardly an occasion for celebration, it is nevertheless an opportunity: to cultivate, nurture, and strengthen your relationship with the customer. There are many ways to handle such calls, but two overriding principles should always guide you:

1. Be sure to tell your customer how much you appreciate the call, letting him or her know that you realize such a call is not pleasant to make.

2. Announce your willingness to "work with" your customer to resolve the debt. Note that *work with* is a better phrase than *help* or *assist*. It avoids patronizing

the client, but, even more importantly, it implies a team effort, and it does not obligate you to make undue compromises and concessions. *Work with* conveys your willingness to cooperate and your eagerness to continue the business relationship over the long term.

Here is a casual, friendly approach to the account that has slipped past the net period:

SERVICE: Hello, (name). This is (name) from (company). I was just going over some accounts and noticed that yours has passed the 30-day net mark, which means that we're about to send you a new invoice with a ($ amount) service charge tacked on. To tell you the truth, it's easier for me to make this phone call than to process and mail a new invoice. If you can settle your account now, and get the check into the mail today, I won't have to create another invoice, and you'll save ($ amount).

Here's a variation on the casual call, which puts the emphasis on performing a service for the customer:

SERVICE: (Name), this is (name) from (company). I'm calling to save you some money. Your account with us has just gone beyond the 30-day net terms, which means that it is subject to a service charge of ($ amount). Let me level with you: I'd much rather have that account paid in full at the present time than collect an additional ($ amount) on it later. If you can get payment to me by (date), I will waive the service charge.

You may meet with resistance or other problems:

SERVICE: . . . In looking over our accounts, I noticed that yours has passed the 30-day net mark. Normally we'd assess a service charge at this point, but, to tell you the truth, I'd rather have the cash at this time, and I'm willing to waive the service charge if you can get a check into the mail right away.

CUSTOMER: I'd love to, but our cash-flow position isn't the greatest just now. I'm going to have to let the bill go for another couple of weeks and just pay the service charge.

SERVICE: Well, that's not the end of the world, of course. And, obviously, I know what it's like to try to manage cash flow these days. Before we leave the matter, is there anything I can do to help? I'm thinking that if you can send me a check for (percentage) of the current invoice now and pay the balance by (date), I'd still have the authority to waive the service charge. We like to make things as flexible as possible for our customers.

A Customer Calls You to Advise You of a Payment Problem

CUSTOMER: I'm calling to let you know that I'm going to be a little late paying your latest invoice. We're in the middle of a cash-flow crunch, and I was wondering if

I could ask you for a favor? Can you hold off another 30 days on finance charges?

SERVICE: First, let me tell you that I appreciate your call. Your name is . . . ? (Customer responds.) (Name), many people don't like to talk to people they owe money to, so I appreciate the call. Now, unfortunately, I don't have the authority to waive the finance charges entirely, but I certainly would like to work with you on this. Together, let's see what can be done. Can you settle a portion of the outstanding balance at this time?

Service seizes on the customer's gesture of making the call. The representative defines the limit of his or her authority, but emphasizes what can be done and works to establish a partnership with the customer.

CUSTOMER: Well, I guess I could send you ($ amount) now.

SERVICE: ($ amount)? Congratulations! You've just bought thirty more days without a finance charge. The balance will be due on (date). Now, after that, I will have to begin collecting interest on any unpaid balance. I hope this arrangement will help you and be useful for you. I appreciate your willingness to work with us on this matter.

CUSTOMER: Well, thank you, too.

SERVICE: I'll send a revised statement out to you today, and I'll be looking for your check for ($ amount) by (date). Is there anything else I can help you with today?

Missed Installment Payment

A missed installment payment should be handled promptly. There is no reason to wait for the client or customer to miss two payments. One option is to send a letter after one payment is past due and include a self-addressed return envelope. Keep your letter brief and nonaccusatory. Do not say, "You have not paid" but, rather, "We have not received" or "Your payment has not arrived." (See the *Complete Customer Service Model Letter and Memo Book* [Prentice Hall].) If you telephone rather than write, include as part of your conversation a definite date on which payment is to be made.

SERVICE: Hello, (name). I'm (name) from (company). Your payment of ($ amount), which was due on (date), hasn't arrived in our offices, and I was calling to check on it. When can we expect it?

You may prefer to begin this way:

SERVICE: . . . Your payment of ($ amount), which was due on (date), hasn't arrived in our office. When did you send that out?

This implies your expectation (and confidence) that the customer has (of course!) sent the money.

CUSTOMER: Uh. Well. I was planning on sending it out later in the week.

SERVICE: It was due on (date). Can you get it into the mail today?

CUSTOMER: I'm not sure.

SERVICE: Since this is an installment contract, I need to assign a date to the payment. That's a requirement of the contract.

Use terms such as "contract" and "requirement" to emphasize the seriousness of the commitment.

CUSTOMER: Okay. I see. Can I check with my husband on this?

SERVICE: Sure. When would be a good time for me to call you back later today?

Responding to a Bounced Check

Another situation that calls for quick attention, and little discussion with the customer, is the bounced check. The only real choice you have here is one of tone. You can keep your phone call businesslike and completely nonjudgmental: *"Your check was returned. Should we redeposit it or are you sending a replacement?"* Or, if your relationship with the customer warrants it, you can adopt a lighter tone, which conveys the absence of hard feelings even as it communicates the same practical message.

SERVICE: Hello, (name). This is (name) from (company). We had an unwelcome surprise in the mail this morning. Your check number (number) was returned by the bank. I can go ahead and redeposit it, if everything's all clear on your end.

CUSTOMER: I'm really sorry. Yes, go ahead and redeposit it.

SERVICE: I understand. Accidents happen. I do have to ask you for a check for an additional ($ amount) to cover what the bank charges us and our own handling costs. We'll invoice you for that.

Here's a script that takes a more casual tone:

SERVICE: . . . You know that check you wrote us for the last order, check number (number)? I'm afraid the bank bounced it.

CUSTOMER: Yes, I was about to call you. We had a major screw-up here. I'm very sorry. You can just go ahead and redeposit it. It's good now. I really feel bad about it.

SERVICE: It's hardly the end of the world. And we won't stop doing business with you or anything like that. In fact, you can make up for the whole thing by placing another order as soon as possible, and by sending us a check for ($ amount) to cover our handling costs and what the bank charges us.

CUSTOMER: We're very embarrassed.

SERVICE: Don't worry about it, (name). Just one of the bumps in the road.

MORE SERIOUS DELINQUENCY:
SIXTY DAYS AFTER INVOICE DATE

Once an unpaid account reaches 60 days beyond a 30-day-net invoice, it is time to get serious about helping your customer pay. This does not mean loaning cash, but, if possible, continuing to use positive and negative incentives and steady communication to create the emotional as well as business climate in which the errant customer will positively entertain thoughts of paying you.

How do you convince someone to pay? You can try bullying and threatening, which may, in fact, work. Once. (After that, you will probably have lost a customer.) A much better approach is to help your customer make the payment decision by demonstrating how it will benefit him or her. If you have a schedule of service/finance charges in place, you can make a phone call to tell the customer how much is owed now and how much more will be due after a given date. You can also build on your relationship with the customer. Explain that prompt, personal service at the best prices requires the cooperation of the customer in the form of prompt payment, which keeps costs down. It can also be helpful to point out that prices quoted were based on net terms. In ordering from you, not only did your customer promise to pay promptly, but he or she received in return for that promise the added value of the best possible prices. This appeal to justice and fair play can be quite effective, if it is handled gently.

It is quite likely that you will encounter vague or evasive customers. Remember that it is important to ask questions that can be answered. If the customer tells you that now is a bad time to talk, remind him or her that "we" are running short of time and ask when it would be a good time to call back. Get a definite time. If the customer is vague about when he or she can pay, ask the customer to think it over and explain that you will call back at a specific time to get a response. If the customer passes the buck to "accounting people," ask if you should be talking to the accounting person.

If, on the other hand, the customer is willing to negotiate, do so now. Once you have an agreement in principle, it is absolutely necessary that you follow up with a memo summarizing your new understanding.

SERVICE: . . . I'm calling to talk to you about your account with us. As you know, the prices we originally quoted were based on 30-day net terms. We're approaching 60 days, which means that you will be paying us a ($ amount) carrying charge on the account. Frankly, I'd rather have the account settled now than collect the ($ amount). Can you get us a check by (date)?

CUSTOMER: I'll have to talk to my accounting people.

SERVICE: Is there someone in your accounting department that I should be talking to? I'll give him or her an opportunity to save you some money.

Here is another approach:

SERVICE: . . . I'm calling to talk to you about your account with us. It's almost 60 days beyond the invoice date. Payment is overdue, and I'd like to ask you when we can expect your check for ($ amount).

CUSTOMER: Well, I'll have to look into it.

SERVICE: You know, (name), the prices we gave you were based on 30-day net terms. We're a small company, and, frankly, it's very difficult for us to carry open accounts for any length of time. It would help us a great deal if you could pay the account in full.

CUSTOMER: I'll look into it.

SERVICE: May I call you at this time tomorrow to get a status report from you and, if necessary, to work out a payment plan together?

CUSTOMER: Tomorrow is a bad time.

SERVICE: The problem I have is that we are running short on time. After (date) the account is subject to a ($ amount) carrying charge, and I'd much rather work with you on a payment strategy that will save you that fee. When is a good time to call?

CUSTOMER: I'll have my accounting person call you.

SERVICE: What is this person's name? (Customer gives name.) And is there a number where I can reach (name), to save him or her the trouble of remembering to call? . . .

Another evasive customer:

SERVICE: . . . I'm calling to talk to you about your account with us.

CUSTOMER: I really can't talk to you now. It's a bad time.

SERVICE: Okay. The problem is that we're running short of time on this account. After (date), your account will be assessed a service charge of ($ amount), and I'd like to talk to you about how you might avoid the extra expense. When would be a better time to talk before we get to (date)?

The advantage of contacting customers now is that there is still time to work with the customer, to help him or her pay:

SERVICE: . . . I'm calling to talk to you about your account with us. As you know, the prices we originally quoted were based on 30-day net terms. We're approaching 60 days, which means that you will be paying us a ($ amount) carrying charge on the account. Frankly, I'd rather have the account settled now than collect the ($ amount). Can you get us a check by (date)?

CUSTOMER: I'm in a real cash-flow bind just now. You know how it is.

SERVICE: Unfortunately, I do. That's why I'd like to work with you on this, to help us both out. We need to come up with a plan that we can both live with. The balance due is ($ amount). If I can get partial payment on this by (date), I'd be in a position to waive the carrying charges on the entire balance due, provided the account is completely settled by (date). How does that sound?

CUSTOMER: Yes, that sounds doable.

SERVICE: Terrific! I'll write up a revised invoice and send it off to you this afternoon.

Another option follows.

SERVICE: . . . I'm calling to talk to you about your account with us. As you know, the prices we originally quoted were based on 30-day net terms. We're approaching 60 days, which means that you will be paying us a ($ amount) service charge. The best thing for me is to have the account settled now rather than collect the extra ($ amount) from you, and I'm sure you don't want to spend extra cash.

CUSTOMER: You got that right.

SERVICE: You can avoid the service charge if you get us a check by (date).

CUSTOMER: I'm in a real cash-flow bind just now. You know how it is.

SERVICE: Unfortunately, I do. That's why I'd like to work with you on this, to help us both out. We need to come up with a plan that we can both live with. The balance due is ($ amount). If I can get (partial $ amount) by (date), I'd have the authority to waive the carrying charges on the entire balance due, provided, of course, that the entire balance is paid off by (date). How does that sound?

CUSTOMER: I just can't manage it at this time. I'll have to pay you later and just absorb the finance charges.

SERVICE: Well, before we give up, can you tell me if I'm in the ball park with that (partial $ amount)?

CUSTOMER: You really want to get some money, don't you?

SERVICE: I told you that I know what it's like to have to manage cash flow carefully. What if we tried something else? What if we set up (number) payments and spread them out?

If this new approach meets with resistance, assess the service charge. Don't push to the point that you alienate the customer.

THE SERIOUSLY DELINQUENT ACCOUNT

As an unpaid account approaches 90 days, there is still room for positive incentives (usually renegotiation of original incentives) and negative incentives (usually timely reminders of mounting service charges). Additionally, telephone conversations at this point should direct the customer to ask him-or herself two questions:

1. Why has the bill gone unpaid?

2. What will further delay cost, in terms of service charges as well as impact on credit history?

Strange as it may seem, at 90 days, the creditor is in a strong position. If a program of finance/service charges is in place, the creditor has more negotiating power at his or her command. Even if no external incentives are available, the customer is usually more anxious to settle now than he or she was earlier, provided, of course, that the lines of communication have been kept open. Now is not the time for threats, panic, or anger, but for powerful reasoning. This is your account's final opportunity to remain in good standing, and it is you who are giving him or her that opportunity.

The following scripts are governed by essentially the same principles that apply to accounts nearing 60 days. However, and this is critical, at this point, your communications should begin to separate yourself from such entities as "company policy" (or Accounting, or the Legal Department) and the passage of time itself. You would like to grant infinite extensions, but "company policy" won't let you because "time" is running out. This rhetorical strategy is not meant to make things emotionally easier on you, although it is true that few people are comfortable playing the heavy. Rather, it is intended to strengthen the cooperative bond between two people who have to work within certain rules. The subtle separation of the voice behind the letters or on the phone and The Company, The Rules, or Our Policy serves another compelling persuasive purpose by hinting that the two of you are in control of the situation now, but soon, if positive action is not taken, other forces will take over. The result: Credit will be suspended. Lawyers will send letters. Things will get ugly. Choices will be few.

Tip: Note that in most customer-service situations, references to "company policy" are counterproductive and should be avoided. In this case, however, such an abstraction may be used to define a third-party menace that you and your delinquent account can ally against.

This approach is not a threat, and it should not be expressed as a threat. But unresolved debt is a serious matter, and it is time to let your customer become aware of this fact.

SERVICE: Good morning, (name). This is (name) at (company). I am calling to alert you to the next invoice you'll be getting from us. By the time you receive the statement, your account with us will have gone past 90 days from the invoice date, that's 60 days beyond our net-terms period. And what that means to you is an additional ($ amount) in service charges.

CUSTOMER: Oh, I didn't realize I'd let that bill slip so far . . .

SERVICE: (Name), we don't make any money on these service charges, and, to tell you the truth, I'd rather have your payment as soon as possible than charge you more money. Look, I am authorized to waive not only the 90-day charge, but the 60-day charge, which you, at this point, also owe. This means that if you get a check into the mail today, you'll pay ($ amount) instead of (greater $ amount), which is what you would pay if you wait until you receive our latest invoice.

Another slant on a similar incentive-based script:

SERVICE: . . . I just put into the mail a statement of your account with us. You already have two statements from us, sent at 30 and at 60 days. I've sent this one a little early because I wanted to give you the opportunity to beat the 90-day deadline and avoid paying a service charge of ($ amount). Tell me, (name), are you interested in saving some more money?

CUSTOMER: Well, yes, I guess I am.

The question will seize the customer's attention, especially under the circumstances. The customer is late with a payment to you, and you are offering him or her a way to save money!

SERVICE: It's strictly your option, but if you can get a check into the mail today, you'll not only beat the 90-day service charge, I'll also waive the 60-day charge. That means that you'll pay (lesser $ amount) instead of (greater $ amount). How does that sound to you?

CUSTOMER: It sounds reasonable.

SERVICE: Then I should be looking for your check in the next day or two?

CUSTOMER: Yes. I'll send it out today.

Here is another version. Assume it started as noted in the preceding script:

SERVICE: It's your decision. If you can get a check into the mail today, you'll not only beat the 90-day service charge, I'll also waive the 60-day charge. That means that you'll pay ($ amount) instead of (greater $ amount). How does that sound to you?

CUSTOMER: It sounds fair enough, but I'm short on cash just now. I know you want to get paid, but with my cash flow, I'm afraid it will be another couple of weeks.

SERVICE: True enough. I'd like to collect on this invoice. And I'd like to save you some money as well. Let's try something else: If you could manage to pay half now and the balance by (date), I'd still be able to waive the 90-day charge. You would pay only the 60-day service charge.

You may still encounter resistance and reasons for nonpayment:

SERVICE: . . . I just put an invoice for your account with us into the mail. You already have two invoices from us, sent at 30 and at 60 days. I've sent this one a little early, because I wanted to give you the opportunity to beat the 90-day deadline and avoid paying a service charge of ($ amount). Are you interested in saving some more money?

CUSTOMER: I'd be crazy if I told you I wasn't. But I don't have the cash on hand to lay out on your bill for the next couple of weeks. I'm sorry. But that's a fact.

SERVICE: (Name), I'd like to work with you on this. Are you in a position to make a partial payment at this time?

CUSTOMER: Not really.

SERVICE: I'd still be willing to waive half the service charge if you could manage, say, one-third now, another third by (date), and the balance before 120 days, which will be by (date).

CUSTOMER: Well, let me think about it.

SERVICE: Obviously, I'd like to give you some time to think this over. But the fact is, we don't have much time. My accounting department is asking me to initiate collection action on your account. Because of the negative impact on your credit history, I don't want to do that. I'd like to find another way. Would it be all right with you if I followed up on this conversation with a call at about this time tomorrow?

CUSTOMER: Sure.

SERVICE: I'll need your answer, your definitive answer, at that time.

A customer may respond quite honestly that he or she doesn't have the cash:

SERVICE: . . . (Name), your account is about to go 90 days past the invoice date, and that's 60 days past our net terms. Now, that's not a disaster, and I'm certainly not calling to give you a hard time, but I did want to alert you to the fact that the account is about to slip through another month unpaid. And what that means to you is an additional service charge of ($ amount). If you want to avoid that charge, and pay us only (lesser $ amount), might I suggest that you send out a check today?

CUSTOMER: I just don't have the cash on hand right now. Can you give me a grace period on that service charge?

SERVICE: When would you be paying?

CUSTOMER: In about two to three weeks.

SERVICE: Well, that's going to start getting close to 120 days. I'd like to accommodate you, but we can't afford to carry an account that long without a service charge. It's not fair to you or our other customers, since we'd soon be unable to offer competitive prices and best values.

CUSTOMER: Well, I just don't know what to do. I mean, you can't get blood from a turnip.

SERVICE: Let's try to work together on this. If you can get me ($ amount) by (date), we can at least avoid letting the account slip into delinquency. Then, together, we can work out a schedule for the balance. How does that sound?

CUSTOMER: Well, I could handle the ($ amount).

SERVICE: Great! I'll send you a memo of understanding.

Response to Repeated Late Payments

The customer is a good one, but, lately, he or she has been paying his bills later and later. It's time for a friendly, nonalienating call:

SERVICE: . . . (Name), I've been meaning to give you a call to discuss your account. First, let me tell you that I'm not here to pester you. We've been doing business together too long for that. I *know* I'm getting paid, and I'm not worried about that.

But what is beginning to concern me is a pattern that has developed over the past (period of time). You've paid your last (number) invoices well beyond 90 days after the invoice date. Frankly, (name), I'm just not set up to sell on those extended terms, at least, not at the high-value prices I offer. Our company prides itself on being efficient, cutting everything to the bone *except* for service. We deliberately do not build in "fat" to manage late payments. I don't think our customers should have to pay inflated prices to maintain our cash flow. But it's not fair or reasonable to expect us to carry you, either.

Well, I don't want to lecture. I just wanted to point out a problem before it gets out of hand. What I'd like to do is to collect on the current invoice right away; it's gone past 90 days. And, in the future, I'd like to see payments within our 30-day net period. Look, (name), if you are finding that you need more flexibility, why not let us set up a line of credit for you? In the meantime, though, we really do price 30-day invoices on the assumption that we can collect on them within 30 days.

COLLECTIONS: CREDIT SUSPENSION

This, sadly, is where many traditional books about "collections" start: just when it is about to be too late. Once an unpaid account has passed 120 days, that is, 90 days beyond the net-terms period, you have some important choices to make. Should you suspend the customer's credit? (The answer is, almost without reservation, yes.) Should you turn the account over to a collection agency or an attorney? (That depends on the amount involved and your relationship with the client or customer.) More important are the questions, "What more do I have to give?," and "What do I have left to gain?"

You can still give your help, your offer to work with your customer to resolve his or her debt to you. This may seem difficult or impossible as you drift toward what neither of you can avoid perceiving as an adversarial relationship, perhaps even legal action. But this is where the tone and rhetoric of your communications play so important a role. At the 90-day mark, you began to separate yourself from the force of the inevitable and unmovable: "Company Policy," "Our Attorney," "Our Accounting Department," and the like. Now that separation should be made more dramatic. Hold yourself apart from the necessary steps that are impending. But remain available for discussion and negotiation.

Often, the first issue to address is lack of response. Accounts that have drifted this far tend not to reply to letters or take phone calls. Be persistent. Once the lines of communication are open, it is your job to outline your customer's choices. And do make it clear that the choices are his or hers. As for yourself, make it clear that you are running out of choices: In X number of days you will "have no choice" but to suspend the customer's credit unless he or she "chooses" to pay X amount by such-and-such a date.

Understand that your customer feels that he or she has little power, that he or she, in fact, is wrong, and you are right. You can take away his or her credit. You can take the customer to court. The problem is that none of this presumed "power" will help you resolve the situation quickly. What your communications need to do now is empower your customer, not make him or her feel smaller, weaker, and more guilty. The customer can choose to settle, choose to help him- or herself, choose to preserve credit with you, and to protect his or her credit history in general. But the customer has to choose now: by working with you.

Informal Warning of Credit Suspension

This phone call is designed as a prelude to a letter formally suspending a customer's credit. You should not actually suspend credit verbally. A contractual relationship exists, and the relationship must be suspended or terminated formally, in writing. But a conversation like the following may avert such an outcome:

SERVICE: Is this (name)?

CUSTOMER: Yes. It is.

SERVICE: (Name), this is (name) at (company). I'm calling about your account with us. It has gone 120 days past the invoice date for the (second, third, and so on) time this year. I have to tell you that I'm getting pressured by my credit people to put your credit on hold, and even turn the account over to a collection agency.

CUSTOMER: Oh, really.

SERVICE: Yes, (name). Now, I'd rather not do that. It is of much greater benefit to you and to me to work together to settle the account. Wouldn't you agree?

CUSTOMER: Yes, that's true. I'd like to.

Look at collections as a sales situation. You are selling your customer on the idea of paying you what he or she owes. As any good salesperson knows, effective sales pitches include questions that imply positive answers. If persuasion is the art of obtaining agreement, ask questions that are bound to create agreement.

SERVICE: Good. Now: Can you get me a check right away?

CUSTOMER: Well, uh. I've been meaning to call you guys. I've got some real cash-flow problems that I'm trying to get out from under. Can I call you, say, in a week or so to work this out? We've gone so far now, another week or so couldn't hurt.

SERVICE: The account is already more than 90 days beyond the net period, more than 120 days past the invoice date, (name). And, as I said, this isn't the first time this has happened. I know it's not going to help either one of us to press you for a snap answer now, but I can't afford to put off the discussion for a "week or so," either. What if I give you a day to review your situation and then call back on (day) at about this time? My concern is to get this account settled, to work *with* you in settling it, to *help* you settle it, and to keep doing business with you in the future. So, can I call you on (day)?

CUSTOMER: Yes.

SERVICE: Do you expect to have a definitive answer at that time?

CUSTOMER: Well, yes.

SERVICE: Because I just can't hold this account in good standing for many days longer.

COLLECTIONS: STOPPING SERVICE. THE CUSTOMER HAS NOT PAID FOR A COMMODITY PRODUCT, AND YOU WILL HAVE TO STOP DELIVERING IT

You can't keep supplying a customer who does not pay, but you can try to work with him or her to avert this serious blow to a business relationship.

Commodities, such as utilities, fuel, food ingredients, paper, raw materials, and so on, are generally sold to repeat customers, who are billed monthly for the amount of product they use. With today's advanced communications systems, many of these repeat transactions, including order entry, invoicing, and bill payment, are automatically handled by computers without human intervention. In many cases, contracts are reviewed at annual intervals only. When something goes wrong in the relationship, there are three goals:

1. Resolve the money issue.
2. Reestablish a positive relationship with the customer.
3. Prevent service/delivery interruption.

These goals are interrelated. The situation quickly gets critically uncomfortable and costs soar when delivery is discontinued.

SERVICE: (Name), I'm calling about the (commodity) bill. Our records indicate it still has not been paid. It is 60 days past due.

CUSTOMER: This makes no sense. I checked this on the first late notice. Our systems indicate this bill *has* been paid. There must be something wrong with your records.

Be prepared for this type of customer response. It is typical. The customer does not want the commodity to stop flowing. Don't get into name calling, and don't initiate an adversarial relationship. Instead, remain focused on the issue and its resolution. Build cooperation.

SERVICE: (Name), I am not saying you ignored your bill. We need, however, to resolve this situation. Our records show no payments for the past two months. Further, we have sent out a warning notice. The warning notice was sent by registered mail. (Name) signed the registered mail receipt. My point is we must get this issue resolved before your supply of (commodity) is stopped. Stopping the flow of (commodity) would be very costly for both of us.

CUSTOMER: Well, like I already said, we have paid the bill, and the problem is yours.

Go slowly with the discussion. Pace it. Be conversational, not threatening. Be a team member, not an autocrat. It *is* possible that the problem is yours. It is also possible the customer has embarrassing cash-flow problems. Stay focused on the goal, build an understanding of urgency without making any threats. Focus on your "limited authority." Find ways you can help.

SERVICE: (Name), I do have limited authority in this matter. We must protect all of our customers, and everyone must pay his or her share of the (commodity) cost. Let me point out what usually happens in these matters. We must have payment in our office, or proof of payment by (date). You may very well be right. Unfortunately, no system is perfect, and proof of payment by (date) is just as good as a cash payment. In these matters our procedures are pretty clear cut.

In most customer-service situations, it is usually not to your advantage to refer to policy or procedure. However, in this case, when trying to create a sense of urgency, it is useful to maintain some distance by focusing attention on the "procedure," over which you have only limited control. "It" is bigger than both of us.

SERVICE: Let me briefly discuss what will happen. On (date), assuming we still have no payment or proof of payment, an order to stop delivery of (commodity) will be sent to our delivery network. Delivery of (commodity) at your location will cease on (date).

(Name), this next point is very important: 98 percent of the time, our delivery team must go back and deliver (commodity) the very same day delivery is stopped, because customers who have lost service resolve these disputes immediately *after* service is stopped. This happens to us and people like you far too frequently. It is very costly and disruptive for both of us, and I'm trying desperately to keep it from happening to you. We provide excellent service, and virtually all of our customers come back to us. Even if you cannot make your regular payment for some temporary reason, there are several support systems we have available to help. They are (list). However, we cannot implement any of these systems unless we hear from you by (date).

Avoid making this a manifesto or tirade. Enumerate the preceding points in a clear but conversational style. Personalize the remarks with pronouns: *"I'm* trying desperately to keep it from happening to *you."* Allow plenty of time for the customer to speak. He or she may admit to a cash-flow problem. If the customer responds this way, implement whatever procedures are possible to help. He or she may also say, "I have proof of payment right here." In this case, apologize immediately, and ask for a copy.

If the customer offers only excuses, Customer Service has no choice but to enforce policy. Yet the representative should also stay between the customer and policy in an effort to persuade the customer of what is in his or her best interest.

CUSTOMER: Well, I insist it is not my problem. My bank makes the payments electronically. They must have misfiled the payment. I don't have a canceled check.

SERVICE: I need your help in getting the bank involved. You can get its attention; I cannot. What I am trying to suggest is that if the payment problem can be solved *after* the (commodity) delivery is cut off, it can also be solved *before* the (commodity) is cut off. Again, our records clearly show that, overwhelmingly, in similar cases the problem is solved the very same day (commodity) delivery is stopped. This is highly disruptive, a tremendous inconvenience to you, and greatly increases (commodity) service costs for everyone.

You should be totally clear and focused in these situations. Summarize key points and reconfirm the obvious conclusion.

SERVICE: Sir, we cannot call anymore, and we cannot send any more notices. All the dates are already in place. The matter must be cleared up by (date). If it is not, then the supply of (commodity) will automatically be discontinued, and I cannot stop the process. My only concern is that this is always disruptive, and I am certain the matter will be cleared up anyway. Can I ask you to please help us resolve this?

Even though this is a difficult situation, it can still be handled professionally. The general tone should be upbeat and focused on helpfulness. You do not want to stop delivery.

In private business situations, there are financing methods available to help a good customer get back on a positive footing, even though he or she may be having temporary cash-flow problems. These should be considered. In all cases dealing with commodities, be sure to review the total record with the customer. In most situations, there is more space for tolerance with those customers who have proven their loyalty over time.

Pitfall: State or other regulations usually prohibit cutting off "lifeline" utilities, especially to the disadvantaged. Usually, there are social agencies available to help those who can no longer help themselves. It is critical to avoid life-threatening mistakes.

COLLECTIONS: LEGAL ACTION

Nobody likes to get entangled in expensive, time-consuming litigation. And that goes for the plaintiff as well as the defendant. Customer service exists, in part, to avoid legal action. Yet the very fact that lawyers are held in dread by many makes the prospect of legal action a powerful motivator. Just be aware that warnings of legal action are double-edged. The courts may, in fact, be your only viable option for collecting on some accounts; however, the threat of legal action may either elicit payment or may cause your account to dig in his or her heels and force you to sue. Temper your threat by separating yourself from it. There is you, and then there is "company policy" or "our lawyers." Your communications should suggest to the delinquent customer that you, personally, are still on his or her side and would like to resolve the debt amicably and nonpunitively, but "company policy" and "our lawyers" will soon make this impossible. In other words, deal with me while there is still time.

Pitfall: Do not use a telephone conversation as a formal warning of legal action. This should be handled in a letter, preferably a letter from your legal counsel or legal department, written on their letterhead stationery.

SERVICE: This is (name) at (company). Am I speaking with (name)?

CUSTOMER: Yes.

SERVICE: Hello, (name). I'm calling at this time to save us both a lot of time and effort in the days and weeks to come. (Name), your account with us has been outstanding now for (days). We've tried repeatedly to contact you about this, but we've received no reply. (Name), I'd like to avoid turning this over to our legal counsel for collection. It seems to me, nobody wins once lawyers get involved. Wouldn't you agree?

CUSTOMER: I suppose so. Yes. I don't want any legal hassles right now.

SERVICE: Neither do I. We're in agreement on that. But I have only limited authority in this matter. And the only way I can keep from bringing in the lawyers is if we can, *now*, work out payment on this account. Here's what I need at minimum . . .

A variation on the informal warning:

SERVICE: . . . I'm calling about your account with us. It's way past due, more than 120 days since our invoice to you. I am getting tremendous pressure here to turn your account over to our lawyers. Now, (name), what I was hoping is that a simple phone call might make that drastic step unnecessary. The amount due is ($ amount). Can you get a check to us today?

CUSTOMER: Well, I guess you'll just have to sue me. Because I've been meaning to call you. We've had some problems here, and I'm afraid I've had to let some accounts go longer than they should. I just don't have the money to settle the account right now.

It is clear that the customer is fairly desperate. What do you offer to a desperate person? Help.

SERVICE: Maybe I can help. The total due, as I said, is ($ amount). What portion of this could you manage to pay right now? My concern is to hold off having to turn this over to lawyers, especially if you're in a crunch. Really, a legal headache is the last thing you need right now.

CUSTOMER: I need to speak to my accounting department.

SERVICE: Let's make a date for a follow-up call after you speak with your accounting department. If I call you tomorrow at this time, will you be prepared with an immediate-payment amount? . . .

Be persistent. Get a commitment now. Work out a payment plan. Keep the lawyers a looming presence, an entity neither you nor your customer wants to face.

Chapter
12

Training Customers

CONDUCTING TECHNICAL TRAINING

Any time Customer Service is guiding customers to some desirable conclusion, explaining or instructing customers in correct operations or use of a product or service, it is in a teaching role. When specific steps required to accomplish an objective are being explained, or when problems are being solved, or when questions about product performance, service requirements, and warranty are being addressed, Customer Service is involved with training. Modern market-driven economies are becoming ever more technically complex. Customer service responsibility for educating the public, already vast, will continue to grow. Importantly, customer-service representatives who explain company policies and procedures by discussing the rationale behind those policies and procedures, rather than just stating them, are teaching as well. This is one of the more critical, if widely ignored, teaching roles service personnel perform. Effective policy and procedure benefit the entire organization, including one of its most valuable members: the customer. Explaining the value of and persuading the customer of the benefits received from a particular policy or procedure leads to higher levels of customer satisfaction and future sales. Failure to explain policy invites disastrous customer reactions, leading to long-term customer dissatisfaction and negative word-of-mouth advertising.

This simple idea is frequently ignored, even at the highest levels of some major U.S. organizations. Consider this response I received to a complaint letter I sent: "I agree with you that the case is simple. The YMCA does not refund membership money and we go to great lengths to inform our members about this policy."

This classic line was placed on formal YMCA stationery by Mr. George H. Edmiston, president of the YMCA of Greater Cincinnati on May 4, 1990. He did not bother to discuss why I had requested a refund. It is certainly true my complaint as well as the amount of refund I requested are no longer important to the YMCA or to me; it is also true the organization no longer receives my support.

Growth in applied technical knowledge in the world economy is, like a hurricane in open seas, feeding on itself at an ever-accelerating rate. The teaching role for customer service is becoming more critical. The brightest customer-focused leaders are supporting, building, and cultivating training skills within their customer-service people.

Customer service applies teaching expertise any time it tries to get co-workers or customers to:

☎ Know something intellectually or conceptually they did not know before. Years of practical field observations have convinced me that the largest concentration of customer contact calls are not problems at all, but are simply requests for knowledge of some sort.

☎ Do something that couldn't be done before, such as operate a device, implement a procedure or install a system.

☎ Use a different combination of existing skills, knowledge, and concepts to form a more productive new behavior.

☎ Rearrange what they currently know about some thing or idea to develop a new understanding of that thing or idea. This is what any good salesperson or consultant does.

Training is a tough job because people are tough learners. Learning is hard for us because we bring strongly held convictions to our interactions with others. Aristotle, more than two millennia ago, observed: "We suppose ourselves to possess unqualified scientific knowledge of a thing . . . when we think that we know the cause."

Anyone who has ever talked to a customer knows that, many times, the customer thinks he or she knows the cause when, in fact, he or she does not. This human thing called perception makes the training job difficult, but not impossible. Organizations that do training well, that change customer perceptions effectively, will enjoy positive customer relationships, leading to future profits, while others will stumble and follow, if they survive at all.

THE KEY ISSUES

A few key issues always pop up in my workshops. Incorporate these major training ideas into your customer service strategy and leadership style.

☎ Just because a person knows all about a product, procedure, or system, he or she is not necessarily qualified to teach others. Training and technical skills are totally different. Too many in service management hire for technical competence and try to train for communication, presentation, and sensitivity skills, all vital for effective trainers. It is much easier to do the opposite: hire for communication skills, then provide the technical knowledge. Many service managers in high-technology industries tell me their best service technicians are those trained in psychology, not technology.

☎ Customer training is complete when the customer has understood the message, not when service has sent the message. Put another way: Just because you have something important to say does not mean others will listen. Your message must earn attention. Persuasion, or selling, is a big part of the job. Just saying something to the customer, even if it is the truth, is not good enough.

☎ Training means creating an observable and positive behavioral change. Care must be taken when undertaking this, because training, unfortunately, can also be negative. The wrong approach does create behavioral change (witness the change created by the YMCA president), but it is not the behavioral change you want.

☎ It's harder work than you might think. Most people just don't get it when first told. You probably know more than you think you do, and the issue is probably more complex than you think it is. Multiple deliveries using varying approaches, repetition, and reinforcement are all necessary for learning to occur.

Customer-service strategy cannot be organized around delivering messages efficiently; it must be organized around delivering messages effectively. Positive sales-building messages that are retained, assimilated, and passed along by word-of-mouth advertising are effective messages that build long-term marketing efficiency. The customer-service operation focused on short-term delivery efficiency rather than long-term sales effectiveness may very well be investing current cash to produce long-term negative advertising.

☎ Effective customer-service strategy allows for follow-up practice and reinforcement of training. Follow-up of phone training can be done with mailed reinforcement or additional phone contact several days after the initial training. Technicians training on site must allow practice time for customers. Each service contact will be longer and a more constructive investment in sales and advertising. If practice and reinforcement do not occur in some way, the training leading to future sales will be lost.

EFFECTIVE TRAINING *DO'S*:

☎ Be open and include your personality in the presentation. Your customers learn from you as a person; customers do not learn from a company institution or organization.

☎ Earn the customer's attention. Describe how the customer will specifically benefit. The customer is more likely to listen and absorb the training if he or she first understands the value you offer.

☎ Start out with an overview of the total training, then summarize specific steps or phases. Explain the general direction and overall goals before discussing specific details.

☎ Be interactive when discussing detail. Allow time for the customer to absorb the information, ask questions, practice the content, and provide feedback that proves he or she understands the message.

☎ Go slow, repeat often. The more unfamiliar the task, the more likely progress will be slow at the start. Basic concepts must be absorbed and a foundation built before more complex concepts can be understood.

☎ Test for retention and behavior change before moving to the next step.

☎ As you move through various phases and steps, take time to go back and review where you have been.

☎ Review and repeat the overall goals. Constantly remind the customer of the benefits and values he or she receives from your organization. Effective customer service is also effective selling.

☎ Be careful as you progress to more complexity. As the customer's learning capacity on a particular task or a given day is approached, progress slows down. If capacity is reached, it will take a great deal of effort to produce even a small amount of improvement. It is usually better to stop and try again another day.

EFFECTIVE TRAINING *DON'TS*:

☎ Don't ignore personalities. Your interaction with the customer is as important, and at times more important, than the subject material. Learning does require the customer to take a risk and be open about what he or she does not know. Take the time to build a relationship. Are you likable? If you are, the learning process will be smoother and the customer will be more willing to take risks with you.

☎ Don't underestimate the importance of leadership. Are you perceived as a knowledgeable leader? Even if the customer does not really like you, if you present yourself as a leader heading in a desirable direction, he or she can at least respect you and follow your message.

☎ Don't forget the total environment. Are you or your product a threat to this individual customer? Perhaps your new technology has cost this individual's best friend his job. The specific task or procedure you are trying to demonstrate is only one small part of the total environment.

☎ Don't assume your technical subject is the only agenda. Is the customer angry with you or your organization? If so, and you don't effectively deal with the situation, you could be set up to help the customer achieve some ulterior goal or objective.

☎ Don't ignore fear. This is especially true with technical training. You, your technology, your product, your knowledge all can be very intimidating to the customer.

☎ Don't speak in industry jargon or show off superior technical knowledge. This is always offensive. People who use jargon, lots of acronyms, or all the current industry buzzwords are only trying to impress others. Everyone sees through all the jargon. Professionals do not make simple things complex, they make complex things simple.

☎ Don't argue. Your ideas may be criticized. Listen, accept the criticism, but do not tell the customer he or she is wrong. Reposition your presentation, take another direction, be positive, explain why you are taking a certain position, and move on.

DEALING WITH CUSTOMERS WHO ARE FRIGHTENED OR LACK CONFIDENCE

Customers who fear the product or lack confidence in themselves demonstrate almost identical behavior. You can use similar strategies to deal with both behavior types. Fear and lack of confidence are serious customer-service concerns because both feelings inhibit the customer's ability to use and, importantly, receive maximum value from the product or service. If these feelings are not handled by effective service, the result is typically customer dissatisfaction and negative word-of-mouth advertising.

Customer service may have a frightened or insecure customer at any time with any type of sale, and business-specific scenarios should be sketched out and rehearsed: Panicked parents may not be able to understand label instructions on your product, which their baby just swallowed. What should your procedure be? Perhaps it is in your interest, for example, to always recommend the parents contact their doctor, even if your product has no known poisonous ingredients. An outline for such an important script should be developed in advance of the need.

WHY ARE CUSTOMERS FRIGHTENED?

Customers may feel anxiety about their learning ability. They may be afraid of causing damage to the new product. Your customer may have strongly recommended your product or service to his or her management team, and, after the product is installed, its performance may be less than expected. This condition creates very high anxiety. The customer may fear losing his or her job. I have seen managers who enjoy leading by humiliation and intimidation and get off on a real power high by demeaning their employees. If your customer has the bad luck to work for one of these egotists, he or she may very well feel insecure. These autocrats send a clear message: "Learn how to operate the system quickly or get off the ship." When your customer is in this position, your skills at being supportive and empathetic will be seriously tested.

Lack of confidence is a personal matter and customers can bring all sorts of personal baggage to the learning situation. Customer service is not expected to provide counseling; however, customer service cannot screen and preselect customers either. Customer insecurities are real, and these human feelings must be dealt with or you risk losing future sales opportunities.

Customers express fear by:

☎ Finding excuses for not participating or following your instructions.

☎ Simply stating: "I don't understand your instructions," and holding this position throughout the training.

☎ Breaking away from the demonstration or instructions by saying the equivalent of "Something important has come up and I must leave right now."

☎ Blaming the product: "I tried something similar to (procedure), and I don't want to try anything further; obviously, there is something wrong with the (product).

☎ Just stating their fear: "This new (product) scares me. I liked the old (product) better. I'm not at all comfortable getting involved with all of this." Or they may say something like: "I'm fearful of these new procedures. I just don't think this is going to work out."

When a customer expresses fear, address this insecurity. It is a good idea to put on your nurturing, "parental" hat quickly. Personalize the conversation and offer assurances using statements like:

☎ "James, this is a very simple operation, and I know you can do it."

☎ "Ms. Jones, I have confidence in you. This is easy; you can do it. I just know it."

☎ "Ruth, all of us have doubts at times. I still remember all the trouble I had when I first started with this system! But it's okay. If I can get it, I know you can. Let's go through it again from the beginning."

☎ "You're doing great with this. So far, you are catching on faster than many others. Let's review the (procedure) again."

In all cases, be sure to express confidence in yourself and exude charismatic leadership. Fearful and insecure people certainly will not follow wimpy leaders.

To avoid fear and help customers overcome feelings of insecurity, start with the conclusion or end result. The customer will get the immediate satisfaction of producing something. Further, by starting at the conclusion, the customer will know where all the steps eventually lead.

DEALING WITH THE CUSTOMER WHO HAS FEAR OR LACKS CONFIDENCE ONE-ON-ONE OR IN SMALL GROUPS

Assume you are training a customer in how to use a new (product) just purchased from your company.

SERVICE: We have invested a lot in making (product) very safe and easy to use. It is known as the best and most user-friendly (product) currently available. I have already set up the system for this demonstration. We can work through all the detailed setup steps later. For now, let's see what (product) will do. (Customer name), just press this button right here and watch it work.

Discussing a few advantages at the beginning sets the stage well and allows you to take advantage of a selling opportunity. Customers expect you to be proud of your products. Take advantage of all selling opportunities, but be subtle about it.

CUSTOMER: I would rather watch you do it.

Don't argue with the customer or challenge his or her feelings. Avoidance is a normal reaction to fear. Don't try to force the customer into the demonstration. You cannot make the customer's fear disappear. You, however, can create an environment that helps the customer overcome this fear.

SERVICE: Sure. Let me demonstrate for you. I'll just let the (product) run through its cycle. Let's watch together.

Build a relationship by maintaining a dialogue with the customer while the product cycles.

SERVICE: See what the (product) can do? Watch while it does (list). It was designed with simplicity in mind. Many fail-safe checks have been designed into the system. It has been designed to help you, me, or anyone avoid errors by checking itself if command errors are made.

Let me try to cycle the system again. Watch what happens when I deliberately give the (product) an incorrect command.

By proceeding with the incorrect procedure you are demonstrating the safety of your product, your own knowledge of the product, and simplicity of operation. This also demonstrates to the customer that error need not be feared.

SERVICE: Notice that the (product) refused the command and gave me an error message. It will continue to prompt me until I follow the correct sequence of steps. Watch. You see, we have implemented many steps to ensure safe, error-free operation. They are (list).

Okay. Watch while I clear the system and reset it. There. We're back where we started. Let me briefly review several fail-safe elements we have incorporated within the system. They are (list).

By reviewing several fail-safe elements, you help the customer overcome fear of the system. Be sure to allow the customer time to ask questions. Encourage a dialogue over these fail-safe customer benefits. It is important to go back to the beginning and push for involvement. The customer still is not participating in the demonstration.

SERVICE: Now, you try it. Hit cycle start.

Service must get the customer to participate and become actively involved in order to build confidence, involvement, and help him or her overcome the fear.

SERVICE: Come on, give it a try. You must do this, and I know you can operate this (product).

At this point, after you have demonstrated the system yourself and even discussed fail-safe items, push the customer until he or she is willing to get involved.

CUSTOMER: Okay, I'll try.

SERVICE: Super! See, the system is really simple. Go ahead and try it again.

Having the customer cycle the system more than once is a good idea. Confidence-building is a process, not a single event. Be sure to offer encouragement.

CUSTOMER: Okay, I think I got it now.

This is what you have been waiting for. Many times, it takes considerable effort to get the customer to overcome initial fear. But, remember, you must continue to build involvement throughout the demonstration.

SERVICE: Great! Let's move on with the demonstration. When we are finished in about (time period), I am totally confident that, in addition to operating the system, you will be able to perform a complete setup.

Service encourages the customer and estimates the learning time involved in understanding the total setup procedure. It is important to do both.

CUSTOMER: What's the first step? What should I do first?

SERVICE: Actually, there are (number) steps. What I would like to do is provide a brief overview of all (number) steps. After an overview, we can look at each step in detail.

This customer is now involved and expressing interest in the demonstration. Service deliberately ignores the customer's urge to dive into specific steps. This is fine. Service ignores the question and starts with an overview. This is a smart move. By providing an overview first, potential future frustration may be avoided.

SERVICE: The (number) steps are: (list).

If the customer expresses fear and lack of confidence at this point, don't continue. You will be just wasting your time. Go back and repeat the earlier script, pushing for involvement. Go through all steps and provide a brief overview of each. Describe why each step is important to the customer by explaining the value or benefit the customer receives from each step. Also, continue to build confidence in two ways: by reviewing all fail-safe systems, and by asking questions. This prompts the customer to participate fully in the discussion.

SERVICE: Let's now discuss the details of the various steps. Step one details are (list). What questions come to mind?

CUSTOMER: No questions, I think I got it.

SERVICE: Great. Let's move on. Step two details are (list). Let's review; what questions come to mind?

CUSTOMER: I got it.

SERVICE: Great. Let's check understanding further. In step two, I did (sequence). Feed back to me why we need to do this.

The "pop-quiz" idea is good when the customer is not asking questions. Use it frequently. You will need to adjust your approach depending on the complexity of your presentation. People can handle four or five steps before needing a significant practice and reinforcement period to make the training stick. If you have more than five major steps, break the demonstration into phases and then steps within the major phases, being sure to allow for much more practice time.

SERVICE: That, then, is a complete overview of the setup, and you are demonstrating a comprehensive understanding. Let's go back. You take the lead. Starting with step one, you go through the entire setup. Follow correct procedure and explain to me what you are doing each step of the way.

The only way you can confirm the quality of your demonstration is to test the customer and have him or her reproduce the entire setup. Observe and ask questions to confirm that the customer understands the logic of what he or she is doing.

DEALING WITH THE CUSTOMER ON THE TELEPHONE WHO HAS FEAR OR LACKS CONFIDENCE

The script and notes covering how to deal in person with those who have fear or lack confidence also apply to telephone service, with one exception: The telephone limits communication to one's ability to speak and hear. However, we know that most of what we learn and retain, perhaps more than 80 percent, comes through our sense of sight. Here are a few rules to help overcome the limitations of the telephone. When training on the phone:

☎ Use extra words to paint verbal portraits of what you are saying.

☎ Don't just do something, describe what you are doing.

☎ Avoid extended silence. Use this "white space" effectively by being descriptive or enhancing your relationship with the caller.

SERVICE: (Picking up phone call.) This is (name) at (company). How may I help you?

Establish a personal working relationship by using your name. The customer cannot see you and perceives the individual service representative as the entire company. While they know you are, in fact, not the entire organization, the perception persists. The customer expects you to make something happen.

CUSTOMER: I own the (product) and can't get it to work.

SERVICE: What is it currently doing?

CUSTOMER: Nothing.

SERVICE: I see. Have you had it up and running yet?

CUSTOMER: Well, no. I don't really know what to do.

Be inquiring. Do not criticize the customer or belittle his or her lack of confidence.

SERVICE: Well, I'm certain we can help. All versions of the (product) are very user-friendly. Let's get you going. Give me your serial number, so that I know which (product) version you own. Also, could I have your name, please?

Look for opportunities to express confidence in yourself, your product, and your customer. Get the customer's name as quickly as reasonably possible and use it often. Using names helps personalize the communication and helps the customer build confidence in his or her abilities.

CUSTOMER: The serial number is (number). My name is (name).

SERVICE: Great, (name). That is an excellent model and will give you years of very valuable service. The "on" switch is in the upper right-hand corner of the control panel. Turn the (product) on.

Take advantage of all selling opportunities with "years of valuable service" or a similar comment.

CUSTOMER: I don't want anything to break. I don't want to be responsible.

SERVICE: (Name), I have the (product) here in front of me. Just like you, I'm getting ready to start up. I will duplicate exactly every instruction I give you. Just follow my instructions and report what happens. That way, while we cannot see each other, I can still maintain good control over what is happening and help you learn how to operate this system. Further, by doing everything as you do it, I can be certain to include all necessary steps. Go ahead and hit the "on" switch and tell me what happens.

Use extra words, plenty of adjectives, to explain what you are doing, how your environment looks, and what kind of strategy for helping the customer you will employ. Remember, the customer cannot see you, and the communication is very limited. Be confident, yet professionally cautious. Avoid absolute comments such as "nothing will break," because comments of this type may be perceived as warranties.

CUSTOMER: The monitor is coming on. There are several codes on the screen. Is this okay?

SERVICE: Read what the codes are.

CUSTOMER: The codes are (list).

SERVICE: Everything is working correctly. Those codes should be on the screen at this point. (Name), let's stop for a moment. I'll hang on while you get your operator's manual and open it to page (number).

It's a good idea to offer coaching that fosters independence. You really do not need the manual, and by coaching the customer with the manual, the call will take more time. However, good customer service, and effective marketing, means taking the extra time now. This customer will likely call back. By encouraging the use of the manual on every call, you will eventually build the customer's confidence and some independence.

CUSTOMER: Why do I need the manual?

Expect this. Those who lack confidence may prefer dependence and resist those who push independence. You will need to sell your position.

SERVICE: I would like to review how and where some procedures are documented for you in the manual. It takes productive time for you to contact us with every minor operational problem. Also, at some future time, a broken phone line or other temporary problem may keep you from calling us in a time of real need. Under these circumstances, you may be able to solve a future minor problem without us and get greater use from the (product). That's why I wanted to discuss some of the manual contents with you.

CUSTOMER: Well, I really don't know where the manual is right now.

SERVICE: It really is important, and I do want you to get maximum value from use of your (product). The manual includes an excellent description of (specific values the customer receives). I can hold on for a few minutes while you hunt for it.

Focus on the advantages the customer receives by being independent. Do not focus on advantages, if any, your company might receive.

CUSTOMER: I've got the manual now, and it is open to page (number), as you asked. What do you want me to do?

SERVICE: On that page is the meaning of all the codes you see on your screen. Let's review the startup sequence together. The first code means (description). The second code means (description).

Position your comments to stress value the customer receives. Continue the dialogue as necessary until the customer's confidence builds and he or she is able to operate the system independently. It is important to take the time to foster independence by always referring the customer to the appropriate pages in the manual as the discussion continues. Customer satisfaction means getting this customer to get benefits from the (product), and this cannot be done very well if he or she is afraid to operate the product without help.

COACHING AN INEXPERIENCED CUSTOMER THROUGH A PROBLEM ON THE TELEPHONE

Coaching the inexperienced customer through a problem requires careful control. In addition to normal phone limitations, you also run the risk of making the problem worse. You cannot see when working with the phone, and, therefore, your experience, which would normally allow you to anticipate or sense the unexpected, will be of less use.

☎ Be comprehensive when asking questions, and be certain your perception of the problem is complete.

☎ The customer must be your eyes. Ask him or her to look around and search for the unexpected for you. Suggest what the customer should sense.

SERVICE: (Picking up phone call.) "This is (name) from (company). May I help you?"

CUSTOMER: I own the (product) and can't get it to work.

SERVICE: What is it currently doing?

CUSTOMER: Nothing.

SERVICE: Let's see if I can help. Could I have your name, please? Also, could you please give me the (product's) serial number? I will pull up history files and specifications on my computer. I will also be keeping notes on our conversation today.

Personalize customer contacts whenever possible. Don't just ask for information, explain why you need it.

CUSTOMER: My name is (name) and the serial number is (number).

SERVICE: Thanks, (name). Let me confirm: The serial number is (number)?

CUSTOMER: Yep.

SERVICE: Thanks, (name). Let me pull up some data on your product; this will take about a minute. How's the weather where you are?

The customer can't see you. Describe what you are doing with your system, including comments like: "This will take about a minute." Comments of this type help the customer generate a perspective of what you are doing and the total value you offer (generating databases and keeping files all costs money). The running dialogue also helps you build rapport. Be descriptive of your behavior. Use wait time to personalize the relationship. Some individuals can effectively use a bit of levity through the initial analysis. Levity is fine, if it fits your personality, the particular interaction, and the customer. However, be professional and do not belittle the customer or his or her problem. Avoid comments such as "you are the tenth call of this type I have received today" or "many of our customers are having difficulty with (product)." These comments are unprofessional and do nothing to enhance the relationship between you and the customer.

SERVICE: I'm now looking at (information about the product). Let's get into your specific situation. I don't want to be trivial. However, because we are on the phone, I need for you to help me get oriented to your situation. I must start at the very beginning. Have you confirmed that power is getting to the (product)?

You have no choice but to start at the beginning, wherever that happens to be in your situation. Further, you do not know anything about the customer's technical competence. It may be frustrating for the customer to go through these basic steps, especially if he or she has basic technical competence and has already been trying to solve the problem for a few hours. As the script suggests, offer reasons for your questions. Position your reasons so that the customer is helping you, not working against you.

CUSTOMER: Look, I'm no engineer. My job is to run this thing, and it just doesn't work.

SERVICE: Okay, please help me check a few basic things to narrow the problem, because I can't see anything. Look around at the back of the (product). Is it plugged into a standard wall outlet?

CUSTOMER: Yes.

SERVICE: Let's just make sure we have correct power into the (product). Perhaps we blew a circuit or something. This has happened before. Could you plug another appliance, a lamp, radio, clock or anything, into the same outlet and confirm that we are receiving power?

CUSTOMER: Okay.

CUSTOMER: (After checking.) No! Power is off at the outlet.

SERVICE: Well, that's important information. Do you detect any burning odors anywhere around the (product)?

Assuming the customer has not been factory-trained on maintenance of this product, if the customer detects burning, recommend the unit be unplugged and sent in for service to an authorized dealer or dispatch a service technician immediately.

CUSTOMER: No, nothing smells as if it has been burning.

SERVICE: Do you see any oils, fluids, or other signs of anything leaking anywhere on any control panels or around the floor? Perhaps something has gone wrong internally or, somehow, foreign fluids such as coffee, whatever, may have accidentally spilled onto or into the system controls. Look carefully, because we do not want things to get any worse.

Have the customer check specific things. Be detailed. A circuit breaker has blown, and you do not know why. Be careful with your words, and be sure not to accuse anyone of willful wrongdoing. Mistakes can happen. Someone willfully causing damage almost never happens.

CUSTOMER: No, there are no fluids or oils that are noticeable. I don't notice any spills, either.

SERVICE: Check closely again for strange smells, too. Feel around the panels and see if they are slightly hot. Be careful when approaching the panels in case they have somehow become hot. Even when the (product) is running at maximum load, they should be only slightly warm to the touch.

CUSTOMER: No, I have looked at everything carefully. Nothing seems unusual.

SERVICE: Our problem must be elsewhere, or perhaps we have no explanation for the tripped circuit breaker. Maybe it's just an electrical spike running through the line. While unlikely, it does happen. We need to determine if something else is wrong with the (product). Be certain the on/off switch is in the off position, and let's get the circuit breaker turned on again. I'll wait for you to flip the switch back on.

Service is explaining what it wants to do. By using "our" and "we," it is not blaming anything on any individual. This script may need adjustment for your specific application. If the customer does not know how to get the circuit breaker back on, or expresses fear about turning power on, you should recommend he or she get assistance from others and then call you back. If the customer must call back, he or she should be able to reach you personally. It is always better to have the person who started working on the problem finish the problem.

CUSTOMER: I've got the power back on.

SERVICE: Let's see if we can get (product) running again. We'll need to turn it on.

CUSTOMER: Will something go wrong? I don't want to start a fire or anything.

SERVICE: No. The worst that can happen is that the circuit breaker will blow out again immediately. If this happens, that unit must come in for repair. If the breaker does blow out immediately, you may hear a popping noise as it trips.

Customer is expressing some anxiety. Help the customer overcome anxiety with a nurturing voice tone. Be careful. If you detect too much anxiety, adjust the script. Suggest the customer get some help, or advise the customer to get the product in for service.

CUSTOMER: I've got the system on again, and it is coming up. Nothing seems unusual.

SERVICE: What does your screen show now?

CUSTOMER: Nothing unusual. It looks like it always does.

SERVICE: We need to run a few tests together.

CUSTOMER: I've never done that before.

SERVICE: It's okay. We're going to work on this together until we both get it. I'm going to give you some specific step-by-step instructions. I will be doing on my (product) exactly what I tell you to do on the phone. Using this procedure, I will be in control of what your system does. Working in this way, we should not cause any additional problems. Let's start with (test one). Punch in command (sequence) to start the test.

The pronoun "we" suggests how you and the customer are approaching a mutually beneficial goal.

CUSTOMER: I have punched in the (sequence). Now what?

SERVICE: Hit (key). Your screen should say "(test) running."

CUSTOMER: It does.

SERVICE: Good. My (product) here is running the same test. This test will allow us to check (list). We designed this test specifically for the (product) because of (specific value) it provides for you. After we confirm that (test) is not causing any difficulty, we will need to check (test two).

Be detailed and conversational through each phase of the diagnostic procedure. Avoid extended silence. Communicate, explain, and sell the value of your (product) and company as each test runs.

YOU ARE ON SITE TRAINING SEVERAL CUSTOMERS ON OPERATION OF THEIR NEW PRODUCT. TRAINEE DID NOT FOLLOW INSTRUCTIONS AND MADE AN ERROR WHICH SIGNIFICANTLY DAMAGED THE EQUIPMENT

People make mistakes while learning; but not all of these mistakes are a natural component of the learning process. A customer acting carelessly, for example, could cause considerable damage to equipment, and Customer Service may be helpless to stop the accident. Even though the damage was caused by a careless customer, service may find itself involved with resolution of the issue. The scenario that follows assumes considerable damage has been caused because of careless customer action. Training is under way, and the customer makes a serious error:

CUSTOMER: What's happening?

SERVICE: (Rushing to shut down the system.) Get away, get away!

CUSTOMER: Wow! What a crash!

SERVICE: Glad you're okay. I'm afraid the (product) is not, however.

CUSTOMER: How serious is this?

SERVICE: Very. Just a casual look suggests we've got damage to the (list of components), at minimum. I will have to check further; however, we will probably need to have parts shipped in. Further, we will need to disassemble the (main components) completely, check out all the detail parts, reassemble, and realign. I'm afraid this is serious and will take some time to get back on line. We will be down for awhile.

CUSTOMER: Man, what a mess. At least this is under warranty.

SERVICE: I'm sorry. This is not covered by warranty. We warrant the (product) against faulty workmanship. This was not caused by workmanship. This is an operational problem.

Try to avoid directly accusing the customer. Do not use words such as: "You really made a serious error." Language such as "this is an operational problem" allows the customer a bit more wiggle room. Avoid placing blame or criticizing as long as possible. Allow the customer as much room as can be found in an obviously uncomfortable situation. Don't take sides with the customer against your own organization by using terms such as: "Well, this is not covered, but I'll see what I can do." This type of language will make final resolution more difficult.

CUSTOMER: But I am in training, and you are right here. There was no intent on my part. I did not mean for this to happen. This is completely unfair! You folks have a responsibility to train us, and you are responsible for the equipment while we are learning correct operation. I'm calling my supervisor.

SERVICE: I sure am sorry this happened. It's probably a good idea for you to involve your management.

The empathy statement "I sure am sorry this happened" will do no harm and might do some good. There is no reason to create additional animosity between you and the technician who caused the accident. This issue will need management involvement, so let the technician call the boss. Let him or her take the lead in telling the story as well.

CUSTOMER: (To his supervisor.) ". . . So, anyway, the problem happened when I performed the (sequence). It was an accident, and they have the responsibility to train us.

SUPERVISOR: (To service.) Why did you let this accident happen? You are supposed to be training people in how to operate this equipment correctly, not in how to break it.

SERVICE: I'm sorry this happened. We do everything we can to help everyone avoid this sort of thing.

Empathize with the current circumstance without accepting responsibility.

SUPERVISOR: Well, you people will just have to repair all of this under warranty.

SERVICE: I will discuss all this with my supervision; however, warranty only covers improper workmanship in product manufacture. This is not a problem with equipment quality.

Keep the discussion narrow. Don't talk too much or offer too much explanation. Avoid placing blame and let the evidence and circumstance speak for itself.

SUPERVISOR: But you are here. You are responsible for the training of these people. You let them make the error that caused the damage.

If possible, agree with something.

SERVICE: That's true: We are here to conduct training. We never encourage risk taking and unnecessary chances with this high-powered and valuable equipment. In fact, our training reinforces the opposite by stressing caution and encouraging trainees to proceed with care.

Do not accuse.

SUPERVISOR: Are you suggesting our people are careless?

SERVICE: This type of accident can only occur because of operator error. Our design prohibits this, as protection is built in. The (product) would have stopped cycling and offered a fail-safe message to the operator before the accident. An operator would have had to perform (command sequence) in order to bypass the fail-safe message. That (sequence) would have caused the (product) to continue its cycle, thereby creating the accident.

Stick with the facts. Continue avoiding accusation.

SUPERVISOR: You are responsible for training them. If they did bypass something, it was because you did not correctly train them. I expect your company to repair this damage.

Avoid the argument. You do not need to directly address issues introduced by the customer.

SERVICE: Our training procedures are quite clear. Let me show you what we covered yesterday. Here in the training manual is the specific sequence I believe went wrong. The manual shows the correct procedure right here, and we practiced this procedure yesterday. Also, here in the manual is the exact fail-safe message, which would have been displayed. This specific message must have been bypassed. We discussed all of this yesterday with all of the trainees. As you can see, the message is quite clear.

SUPERVISOR: Well, perhaps something is wrong with the system and that message was never displayed.

SERVICE: That message is designed into the fail-safe system. If anything does go wrong with the safety system, the entire (product) shuts down. Restart is impossible until the fault is discovered and corrected.

SUPERVISOR: Where was (technician) when these issues were discussed yesterday?

SERVICE: I don't know.

SUPERVISOR: (To technician.) Did you hear all of these instructions yesterday?

CUSTOMER: No.

SUPERVISOR: (To technician.)   Did you need to leave the training yesterday?

CUSTOMER: Well, I had some important deadlines to meet on some other issues.

SERVICE: My notes indicate you were gone most of the afternoon when this material was covered.

SUPERVISOR: (To technician.) Where were you?

At this point, back out of the conversation, step away, and allow the supervisor to handle the employee. You have explained your position, and the supervisor should see why the accident occurred. What the supervisor does with the employee is a private matter between him or her and the subordinate. Respect the supervisor's need for privacy.

DISCUSSING SAFETY-RELATED ISSUES

Many times, service technicians must discuss safety-related issues with customers. These discussions can be difficult for customers and for customer satisfaction. Most of us want to do a good job, do not want to break things or risk harm to ourselves. When someone explains how something can go wrong, we find the discussions discomforting. Trepidation or outright fear is normal when we face something new, different, or unknown. Discussing safety-related matters is certainly critical, but the discussion must be handled with sensitivity. This scenario assumes training is well under way and the customer has already been operating your product effectively under your watchful eye. You must now review a number of important safety-related issues with the customer.

SERVICE: You're doing great with all of this technical instruction. You learn quickly.

CUSTOMER: Thanks.

SERVICE: The (product) has a number of fail-safe systems built in, all targeted toward eliminating the possibility of error. It checks your work to make sure you don't make any mistakes.

CUSTOMER: That sure is good to know. Does that mean all errors are intercepted automatically?

SERVICE: *All* is a pretty big word. If we eliminated all possible ways a mistake could be made, the (product) would not be very useful to you or anyone else. We have a number of safety systems that help, though. Let me demonstrate some things. Suppose I did something like this. (Performs sequence.) As we have already discussed, that command is well beyond the operating range of the (product). Watch what happens when I attempt to execute that sequence. See? I get the warning message, advising me that I am going beyond operating range.

CUSTOMER: Yes, I see that. I can see how that feature would be very helpful. Anyone could have punched in an incorrect number, setting up a major potential accident.

SERVICE: Correct. But watch this. I can set up this (sequence) like this. Now notice these numbers? I am well within operating range of the (product). But look over at the work zone. See that interference over there?

CUSTOMER: Yes.

SERVICE: The control has no mechanism to enable it to see that I have left that interference in the work zone. The control will allow me to execute this command sequence. As I am currently set up, if I pressed the button and cycled the (product), there would definitely be an accident, causing damage to the system. In the worst possible case, I could also hurt myself.

CUSTOMER: I don't like any of this. How can I be sure an accident of this type will absolutely never happen?

SERVICE: Nothing stops us from programming in an error like this. However, the good news is that most professionals never have a serious accident. That is because they know their own limits, understand the system's limitations, and have learned to check all of their procedures and setups carefully before actually starting to cycle the (product) in full production.

CUSTOMER: How can they do that?

SERVICE: Let me simulate a trial run. In this case, we obviously know I have made an error. But, for purpose of demonstration, let's suppose this is a real setup, I have just completed programming, and I am ready to launch full cycling.

CUSTOMER: But, we know this setup will not work.

SERVICE: Let's pretend we don't.

CUSTOMER: You're going to deliberately crash this system? That's crazy!

SERVICE: No. Watch. Professionals check everything to make sure serious errors don't occur. Anyway, assume I have completed my setup and am ready to go. However, because I have never tried this setup, I am first going to perform a dry run, which enables me to check my programming. That's what the professionals do. First, I will set the speed control as slow as it will possibly go, like this (set control).

CUSTOMER: Okay.

SERVICE: Now I will maintain my position right here, so that I can see all of the action. I will also place my hand right here on the cycle interrupt control. See, depending on what I observe, I can immediately shut down the system before the crash occurs. Watch as I start the cycle. Notice the upcoming accident can be clearly seen well in advance as long as I am operating at minimum speeds. I just press the cycle interrupt like this (interrupt cycle), and we are safe again.

CUSTOMER: It will always work this way?

SERVICE: Customers have operated these systems for many years, and the real pros never have accidents. However, those professionals are very careful, too. They always, without any exceptions, check every setup several times to make sure there are no programming errors. They check at very low speeds, just like we are doing now. It takes a bit more time in setup, but because accidents are avoided, it is well worth the extra time. This will be seen in the overall long-term savings. It just takes discipline to confirm every setup before running.

CUSTOMER: I believe these types of checks can be added to our standard procedures.

SERVICE: It will be well worth your effort. Let me suggest some other safety-related system checks. Let's look around back at the monitoring panel. Right now we are certain the (product) is operating correctly. See these twelve monitoring lights here? They all show green. These twelve lights monitor the (list of systems). The (product) will operate if these monitoring devices are disabled. Here let me show you. (Disables several checks.) Everything is still operating, yet notice the several monitoring lights checking systems I disabled have turned to red. The red lights indicate the (safety checks) are currently not operating. There are advantages and disadvantages to this design. The advantage is that the system will operate with these safety checks disabled, allowing you to (list). The disadvantage, however, is that you must check this panel frequently to confirm your operating status.

CUSTOMER: How often should I check the panel?

SERVICE: Considering past experience, we recommend the monitoring lights should be checked (number) of times per day to ensure safe operation.

CUSTOMER: So that's one more thing we need to add to our general operating procedures.

SERVICE: We have helped you with your general operating procedures. These prompt cards are reminders to you and others who will be operating the (product). We have defined all of the specific checks you and I are currently discussing. The cards are neatly designed and laminated. We recommend they be placed in strategic positions around the (product) after all other operators are properly trained and everyone else understands safe operation. We are not trying to scare anyone or restrict your productivity; its just a good idea to remind everyone that a few minutes invested in safety (number) times per day will produce good work habits and pay off in the long run with an accident-free work environment, something that benefits all of us.

DEALING WITH THE OVERCONFIDENT CUSTOMER IN PERSON

Overconfident customers cause many concerns. They can damage equipment or ignore important safety procedures; they can bypass important details, quality checks, or problem-prevention procedures; they can be error-prone. In dealing with the over-confident customer, service must be concerned about the equipment as well as customer safety. It is very important that the service representative be concerned about his or her own company as well, for when something goes wrong, the overconfident customer is notorious for finding excuses. Everyone, including you, your product, and your company will be identified as the cause of the problem rather than the customer him- or herself. Overconfident individuals are typically quite verbal, skilled with use of language, charismatic, and perfectly willing to express confidence in themselves, even if the confidence is unfounded. For this scenario, assume a demonstration of a new product is under way:

CUSTOMER: Show me how to get this up and running.

SERVICE: (Name), there are several important steps necessary for successful operations. Let's review all of them, what they do, and why they are important.

CUSTOMER: Look, I really don't need to know every engineering detail just to run this thing. Now let's get it cycling.

SERVICE: We can certainly do that, (name). Just press this button here and watch it cycle. However, there still are important operational procedures we must consider and discuss.

Service is demonstrating flexibility by bending with the customer. Trying to be cooperative with the customer is always a good idea. Ignore the brashness, and let him or her cycle the system. Try to get control later. Letting the customer cycle the system at least gets him or her involved.

CUSTOMER: This is simple. I've got the hang of this already.

SERVICE: That's true. You can cycle the system. However, running the system means setting it up and understanding all functions and alerts. The system, once set up, is very easy to operate. Virtually anyone can just cycle the (product).

By implying that "virtually anyone can cycle the system," service is taking a risk by mildly disciplining the customer. Directness with the overconfident individual is sometimes necessary to get the situation under control.

CUSTOMER: Well then, what do I need to know? I want to get production going on this thing.

SERVICE: There are (number) important phases in correct setup. Each phase has (number) of steps. While none of the steps is difficult, all are necessary for correct setup.

CUSTOMER: Those are all described in the manual, aren't they?

SERVICE: Yes.

CUSTOMER: Well, I can just look those things up when I need them, or I can just call you. Now, let's get production running through the (product). I pretty much understand what needs to be done.

SERVICE: We need to go through this demonstration, (name). Time is set aside for us to go through a complete training session while I am here on site. We need to focus on correct operations and make sure you can fully run the (product) when I am not around. Further, I am not always available for phone support. Your longer-term production losses could be serious if you are totally dependent upon telephone support. Many things can and should be handled without telephone support. That is what effective training is all about.

Customer service is holding to the plan, as it should. Further, the representative is using his or her personality, not "the boss" or other authority, to control the situation. He or she avoids such phrases as: "The boss said we must," "I'm not allowed," or, "We were told to." You must use your own personality to control the overconfident customer. Using some other authority will cause the overconfident customer to lose respect for you and your message. The overconfident person will only follow strong leadership.

CUSTOMER: Just what do I need to know?

SERVICE: Let's start with an overall view of all phases and major steps within each phase. (Provides a summary.)

CUSTOMER: That is not difficult. I pretty much expected all of those steps.

Just ignore the unprofessional comments, which you will likely hear from this type person. There are bigger issues.

SERVICE: Let's look at the details of phase one, step one. The details are (list).

CUSTOMER: Okay, I understand everything you said. What's the next step?

SERVICE: The next step is for you to explain and perform phase one, step one.

CUSTOMER: I said I understand it. Let's just move on.

SERVICE: I need to be certain I have not made any errors and that our communication is complete and comprehensive. Having you explain and actually perform the procedures as we go through this process is the only method available for me to check myself.

Don't argue with this person, and do not ask him or her to prove why he or she knows such-and-such. The customer can always say he or she understands everything and does not need to practice; however, it is far more difficult for the customer to argue with your desire to check your own work and your communications ability.

CUSTOMER: Well, this is simple. Here, I'll show you. (Customer makes an error.)

SERVICE: Great job. However, I see that a couple of points in the (procedure) require additional clarification. Let me review (procedure) again and try to clarify how it needs to be done.

Continue this approach through the training. When the customer makes an error, accept the responsibility yourself, review and correct, then move on. By accepting the responsibility for the error, you avoid a situation in which the over-confident person is constantly defending him- or herself. Further, you may avoid a lot of senseless argument and wasted time.

DEALING WITH THE OVERCONFIDENT CUSTOMER ON THE PHONE

Greater verbal description is required when using the telephone. With the over-confident customer, the inability to see can be used as an advantage to create better compliance.

SERVICE: This is (name) at (company). How may I help you?

CUSTOMER: I have the (product) and can't get it to run the (maintenance check procedure).

SERVICE: What is the (product) doing now?

CUSTOMER: I already started the (maintenance check procedure) and moved through step four. Then the (product) just hung up and stopped.

SERVICE: What procedure did you use getting to step four? What page are you on in the manual?

CUSTOMER: The procedure was pretty simple, really. I just figured it out on my own. I'm not using the manual.

It is a safe bet that the customer has more confidence than actual expertise. It is also reasonable to assume he or she has made errors in running and interpreting the maintenance procedure. However, as is always true when dealing with an overconfident customer, or any customer, being argumentative will accomplish little.

SERVICE: It is a good idea for us to restart the system and start over. That way we will be working together through all the steps, and I will be better able to help you interpret the signals we receive. Let's go through a shutdown and restart.

Try this optimistic approach. However, don't expect overconfident customers to comply. They are typically in a hurry.

CUSTOMER: That approach will take too much time. I am already at step four. Let's go from here. What should I do next?

Try optimism, but be prepared for this response.

SERVICE: It will take less time if we restart. There may be some problem with your (product). I cannot determine if something is wrong if we just continue from where we are. There are certain indicators and parameters we must review and interpret at each step of the (maintenance check procedure). Reviewing all the indicators at each step is the only way for us to determine if the (product) is working to all specifications. We must work together on this. Please hit shutdown and then restart. Could you also please get the maintenance manual?

By using "we" rather than "I," the representative avoids the possibility of developing an adversarial and argumentative communication. Further, there is no advantage in sharing with the overconfident customer that you suspect he or she might have made an error in following the procedures. Creating customer satisfaction is always easier when focusing on positive communications.

CUSTOMER: Okay, it is restarting. I don't need the maintenance manual if I have you.

Do not demand compliance. Sell the logic of your request.

SERVICE: We need to ensure you have the correct manual. Further, any special notes and parameters unique to your product would have been noted in your manual at the time of shipment. There may be a clue that gives us an idea of what has gone wrong. I can hold for a few minutes while you get the manual.

Sell the idea that both time and patience are necessary. The overconfident customer may lack both.

CUSTOMER: I have the manual now. The (product) has been cleared of the maintenance sequence and is running again.

SERVICE: Great. My (product) is also cleared, and we are ready to go. By working together, carefully reviewing each step, we both can keep up with what the (maintenance check procedure) tells us. Look at the product identification plate at (location). Confirm that the (product) version and release number is the same as noted in the manual on page (number). Please give me the version and release number, too.

CUSTOMER: The numbers are (numbers). The release and version numbers in the manual match the numbers on the (product).

SERVICE: Okay, I'm with you. Let's go. Restart the (maintenance check procedure). What is the screen showing now?

CUSTOMER: It is doing (description).

SERVICE: Look on page (number) of the manual. This page shows the display you should have on your screen, and my (product) now has that display. Does yours?

You are teaching the customer how to use the manual without making a big deal of the fact, which is a good strategy for this type of personality. They do not always make very good students.

CUSTOMER: It does. We really don't need to check all this out in the manual. I'll just tell you what I see on the screen, or you just tell me what might be missing.

SERVICE: That would work if we were together. Unfortunately, I cannot read your codes over the phone. There really is a lot of detail, and using the manual is the best way to ensure we are not missing details. Any missed step could indicate where our problem is. Let's continue to work this way, because looking at everything in detail is the only way we can be sure no detail is missed.

Continue in this vein. Don't make demands, sell what the customer should do. Do not focus on mistakes the overconfident customer might make or has made. He or she will likely get defensive and argumentative if you do.

DEALING WITH "SLOW" CUSTOMERS

Never ridicule the slow learner. Many of us struggle with alien ideas or procedures and could be considered slow learners in certain situations. The slow learner can get the job done, but may need extra time and energy. Typically, those who require extra learning time do not lack intelligence. They lack necessary prerequisite skills for the task at hand. Patience is the most important tool to use when training the slow learner. Intimidation or ridicule accomplish nothing. As soon as you detect the need for extra training time to help the slow learner, activate whatever contingency support plans are available to you. Get temporary relief from your immediate schedule, if at all possible, since this will reduce the immediate job pressure. Getting some relief also allows you the best opportunity for generating much-needed patience.

When training the slow learner, be very specific in describing what must be done. Also, take small steps, repeating and summarizing often. Allow for immediate practice while offering continuous reinforcement. Prompts in the form of note cards or other written references should be used liberally. Causing the slow learner to use the written references during the training session trains him or her to use them later when you are not immediately available.

SERVICE: (Name), there are four steps required to reset and activate the security alarm controlling the vault and monitoring system. To activate the system, they must be performed each day before the bank closes. Let me briefly summarize all four steps, what each does, and why each step must be performed in a particular sequence. (Lists and briefly summarizes all steps.)

Now I would like to go through some of the details in step one. But, before going into specific detail, do you have any questions about anything I have covered so far?

CUSTOMER: I missed some of that. Tell me again: how many steps are there?

This type of question suggests the customer is struggling. Don't criticize. Try another direction.

SERVICE: Let's review where we are. There are four main steps to setting up the system. As I discuss each main step, I will write down the correct code numbers on note cards. The indicator lights will be green when code numbers are entered correctly. We can discuss each step as I enter it, and then add any needed details to the notes. You can use these notes as reference tools. A summary of step one is (summarize).

Write the sequence on note cards, or review notes from previously developed note cards or from the manual. Take time. Don't just discuss the sequence. Be sure to review and read the note cards with the customer. Be careful not to use any language that might be construed as demeaning or belittling. Avoid terms such as, "I just covered that," or "let me repeat what I just said." Language such as this is unprofessional, may intimidate the customer, and will likely damage your relationship, making this training job even more difficult.

SERVICE: There are three more steps to cover. Before I continue, let's confirm that I have covered everything in step one completely. Explain to me how you would implement step one. Use the note cards, if you wish.

CUSTOMER: I'm not sure I understand all of this.

SERVICE: That's okay. That is why I am here. Start to repeat back what you think I said. It is all right to be unsure of some detail. We can discuss any points of confusion as we go.

The slow learner may lack confidence. Be nurturing or "parental" in your coaching and counseling. Build confidence in the customer.

CUSTOMER: Well, I think I should . . . (Customer explains step one and makes a mistake.)

SERVICE: Great. We have this step just about perfect. I need to clarify a few points. (Clarify and add notes.) Try explaining step one to me again.

CUSTOMER: Well, first we should . . . (Customer explains correctly.)

SERVICE: Let's confirm understanding. I want to make sure I have everything explained correctly. Why did you do (some portion of step one)? Feel free to use the notes.

CUSTOMER: (Answers correctly.)

This short quiz may seem like a lot of detail, but the slow learner requires a lot of repeating and review. Remember, when we have difficulty with something new, it typically is because we do not have the proper foundation for the activity at hand. The constant repeating and review compensates for the lack of foundation.

SERVICE: Great. Let's move on. The step two sequence is (describe). What is the purpose of (some portion of step two sequence)? Again, be sure to use the notes.

CUSTOMER: (Answers incorrectly.)

SERVICE: We need some more practice. Let me try this again. (Repeats step two sequence.)

If the customer cannot answer any part of the quiz, go back and review again. Use another approach or direction. Do not blame the customer. Use the "we" pronoun rather than "you."

SERVICE: Let's try again. What is the purpose of (step two)?

CUSTOMER: (Answers correctly.)

SERVICE: We have steps one and two down pretty well. Let's discuss step three. We will come back and revisit step one and two again later.

Continue this process throughout the exercise. After step three, revisit step one and step two with your in-process quizzes. After all steps are absorbed by the customer, go back and revisit all of them as a group. Some sort of follow-up is beneficial for all learning. Follow-up is especially important for the slow learner and would be most effective several days after the initial training.

DEALING WITH CUSTOMERS WHO DO NOT TALK ENOUGH

The nontalking customer is difficult to train because it is hard to determine if your message is being heard and absorbed. The nontalker answers yes or no to everything and typically avoids offering explanatory detail of his or her understanding. This person's general inability to offer input makes the training task difficult. This customer typically will neither ask questions nor state a lack of understanding. However, you must find a way to break through this shell of silence. If the customer truly does not understand, he or she will hold you responsible for poor training when something goes wrong later, and will be right to do so! The training job requires the service professional to work with many diverse personalities, including the nontalker.

The general strategy in training this customer is to create an environment that compels participation in the dialogue. Using open-ended questions is crucial for success. Open-ended questions cannot be answered with a simple yes or no. They create customer participation by causing the customer to describe sequences, events, feelings, or perceptions. Probing questions such as: "Why did you . . ." or "Explain what you mean by . . ." are also very useful in helping you to confirm that the message is getting through.

SERVICE: I would like to demonstrate the (maintenance procedure). Do you have any previous experience with maintenance procedures on this or similar systems?

CUSTOMER: No.

SERVICE: Do you have any related experience?

CUSTOMER: No.

Cryptic answers such as these are a strong clue that you are dealing with a nontalker and that a different approach is necessary.

SERVICE: Describe your previous experience with mechanical systems.

CUSTOMER: I have worked with (Systems A and B).

SERVICE: Yes, (System A) has some similarity to our (product). You said you worked with (System A). Explain what working with (System A) means.

CUSTOMER: I operated (System A).

SERVICE: I see. That helps. Did you do anything else with (System A)?

CUSTOMER: I had to go through setup procedures for (System A).

SERVICE: Could you describe what was required in the setup procedures.?

CUSTOMER: Setup required doing (list).

Even these answers are cryptic. However, continue to avoid the closed questions. At least you will get some needed details.

SERVICE: What about maintenance? Was any preventive maintenance required as a part of the general setup?

CUSTOMER: Yes.

Given the opportunity of another closed question, the nontalker will go back to the yes or no answer.

SERVICE: Could you describe the preventive maintenance procedure that was a part of the setup?

CUSTOMER: Preventive maintenance consisted of (list).

SERVICE: Thanks. That really helps a lot. I have a much better understanding of what you already know about mechanical maintenance procedures. With this information, I can save time for both of us and make things easier with a more targeted description of our (product's) maintenance procedures. I'll focus on procedures which are new to you.

Complimenting the customer rewards his or her participation in the discussion. However, the customer will continue as a nontalker when given the opportunity of a closed question.

SERVICE: Let's start with (description of procedure). Do you have any questions?

CUSTOMER: No.

It is a serious error to assume the nontalking customer who says he or she has no questions actually has no questions. The nontalker seldom has questions.

SERVICE: Perform the (procedure) for me so that I can check how well I explained the details.

To facilitate cooperation, use language that suggests you are testing your presentation, not the customer's learning. Further, asking the nontalking customer to perform something will produce better results than asking him or her to describe something.

CUSTOMER: (Demonstrates procedure silently.)

SERVICE: (While customer demonstrates specific things.) What did you accomplish by performing (step)?

While the customer actually performs the procedure, ask probing questions. Continue asking the customer open-ended questions throughout his or her demonstration to ensure the customer actually understands why the procedure must be performed a certain way. Repeat this script as necessary until the customer has mastered the procedure.

DEALING WITH CUSTOMERS WHO TALK TOO MUCH

The strategy for dealing with this customer is the reciprocal of that employed for dealing with nontalking customers. With the nontalking customer, one would use open-ended questions to encourage dialogue, whereas with the overly talkative customer, one would use closed-ended questions to discourage excessive communication. With the nontalking customer, one would use probes and positive reinforcement to encourage communication, whereas with the talkative customer one would use abruptness and discipline to discourage communication.

Sensitivity is the key, however. As with all customer situations, risk to future sales is everywhere. The talkative customer would certainly not hesitate to tell friends, prospects, or anyone who will listen about your bad service. Much worse, the overly talkative customer would not hesitate to embellish his description of just how bad your service is. Customer Service wants to control this customer without turning him or her off, and needs to be assertive without being confrontational, forceful without being overpowering, direct without being argumentative, and visionary in purpose without being condescending. When dealing with the overly talkative customer, service is on the edge. If you over-control, you'll create dissatisfaction. If you under-control, you'll listen to the customer all day without ever getting the training task completed.

SERVICE: (Name), thanks for calling, and I appreciate your order. I would like to take an extra moment to explain how you can now place your orders electronically, using our new electronic ordering system.

CUSTOMER: That is great, and I am anxious to learn all about this. I have been hoping for some time that all of our suppliers would incorporate such technology for us. You see, we have (number) of suppliers and dealing with all of them verbally and by mail is very time consuming. To date, we have (number) of our suppliers already working with us on electronic data exchange. Some systems are, of course, much better than others. For example, consider the system (Supplier XYZ) uses. It is really great because it allows us to . . .

This is a strong clue that you have a talker on your hands. You may need just to break in on this customer. Summarize a key point he or she has made and then move on. Get into your presentation and keep it moving.

SERVICE: That is interesting about (Supplier XYZ's) system. Our system is very similar. It operates with three specific steps. Let me explain all three. Step one does (description of system access). Step two does (description of order entry). Step three does (description of order checking and confirmation). Could you help me check my communications by describing the ordering steps back to me?

CUSTOMER: Sure, I can. Your system is similar to (Supplier XYZ's) system, and we have been using that system for (time period) now. I wonder if you could modify (steps) in your system so that it is closer to XYZ's?

Talkative customers can give you a lot of detail about competition, and you may wish to listen to all this and take competitive intelligence notes. However, it is also possible that you have no interest and must move on to other customers. Let's assume you want to move on.

SERVICE: That is an interesting thought, and I will make note of it for our MIS department, Now, however, for you to receive maximum benefits, our existing procedure must be used as designed. Let me make sure I have explained everything correctly. How you would implement step one, system access?

Be direct. Constantly bring the customer back to the task.

CUSTOMER: Step one says I must (description of system access). It's amazing what these new electronic systems can do. You know, at home I have this incredible sound system. Its digital capability enables me to enjoy superb sound quality anywhere in the house. I wonder where all this innovation will stop.

Keep your training specific and on task. Keep the communication tight. Closed questions, those which can be answered simply or with a yes or no, are best with this customer. Avoid open-ended questions. If you must ask for a description, be as specific and narrow as possible with your question.

SERVICE: I agree, electronic innovation will continue. That was great on step one. You can access our system. Help me check our communications on step two. What must you do to get the order entered?

Maintain the initiative. The talkative customer will drift about, taking the conversation in any number of directions. Maintain a powerful leadership position and do not be afraid to jump in to keep the dialogue focused. Focus on the customer's comments that support the task at hand. To discourage the customer's tendency to drift, avoid responding or dwelling on extraneous comments. Professionally overlook or place aside extraneous comments without being rude to the customer. Repeat this script format as you continue through the training. Success with this customer means maintaining a strong leadership position and keeping a focus on the task.

DEALING WITH THE DISRUPTIVE CUSTOMER

The disruptive customer is interested in revolution or chaos just for the heck of it. He or she is going to cause trouble because, erroneously, he or she perceives this is the way to get power and ability to influence others. This scenario assumes you are working in a training center, which has been set up for your customers. Several customers are in a class, and they are being trained on your product. One of the trainees is the disruptive customer.

SERVICE: . . . and that is why the procedure was designed in this way.

CUSTOMER: I have a question.

SERVICE: Yes?

CUSTOMER: Did your engineers consider an (alternative design)?

SERVICE: That idea and others were considered. The approach we chose was deemed to be the most effective for us and the (product). We believe this was the best method of those alternatives available at the time design concepts were frozen.

Tip: Always sell when possible.

CUSTOMER: Well, I think your engineers selected the incorrect design. They did not consider the (alternative design) correctly. If they would have performed a correct analysis, they would not have ended up with this inferior product.

Ignore and sail over the top of the slam. The class will follow you because, as head of the class, you are in the lead position.

SERVICE: Many designs were evaluated. We had to select only one design concept, and this is the concept we chose. Ultimately, the markets will decide the merits of the various design options out there, not we in this class. So far, our (product) has been well received by the markets, suggesting our design experts were correct. And now I would like to . . .

CUSTOMER: But wait. I'm just not sure I agree with your conclusion. Let me explain why your engineers are wrong. For example, notice . . .

You must take strong leadership action with the disruptive customer. You are not running a popularity contest; you are running a training program. You are not required to give the disruptive customer a forum, either. Cut him or her off as necessary and get back to the subject at hand.

SERVICE: I'm sorry. We must move on or we cannot get finished in time. Notice in your manual, on page . . .

CUSTOMER: (Product) design criteria is relevant to the training. For example, (item) would work much simpler if (alternative design) was selected.

Other customers will expect you to take firm action and keep in control. Everyone will know this individual is just trying to start a war for some reason; don't take the bait.

SERVICE: As I said, notice in your manual, on page . . .

CUSTOMER (as a general statement to the group): Well, these guys just can't admit they made an error. They know the (alternative design) offered on (competitive brand) is a better method.

SERVICE: Sir, we are all here to study how the (product) works. We are not here to evaluate competitive design strategies. Our respective companies have already evaluated the design strategies and made their decisions. Every company represented here, yours included, has purchased the product, and our organizations expect us to know operations at the conclusion of this training. I cannot accept any additional discussion about alternative design strategy, as all such discussion is irrelevant to the task at hand.

CUSTOMER: Not really, because . . .

Drop your voice volume slightly. Be very slow and deliberate with your words. Look right at the disruptive customer and fix eye contact. Use a monotone voice.

SERVICE: I will move on now. We have a goal to accomplish. You do not need to stay. (To the group): In your manual, please look on page (number). I want to review the (procedure) with you.

Taking this position should end the debate. If it does not, take even more drastic action.

CUSTOMER: You really can't cut me off. I have something to say about this product to this group.

SERVICE: Sorry, not in class. If you choose to stay, you must stay on task with the rest of us. Otherwise, you will just need to leave, because we must continue.

CUSTOMER: I just don't accept what you are saying. I have every right to be here and speak out.

SERVICE: Group, let's take a coffee break.

Your job is to defuse and regain control. This can best be done privately. The break enables you to convert what has been a public confrontation into a private confrontation. Allow everyone to go on break, which they will be happy to do at this point. Activate your security procedures and advise your supervision that you must expel this individual from the training. With security personnel as escort, approach the disruptive individual. Be brief and get it over with.

SERVICE: I do want to thank you for coming. Our security personnel will escort you to the door.

CUSTOMER: Wait. My boss said I had to come. I don't work for you.

SERVICE: We will notify your supervisors and advise them of what occurred. Thank you for coming.

Just walk away and go back to class.

SERVICE: (To the entire group, after it has reassembled.) I apologize for the customer, who obviously did not want to be here. Let's look in the manual on page (number). I would like to discuss . . .

The others in the class will respect your position and give you support.

HOW TO DEAL WITH THE CUSTOMER WHO HATES YOUR PRODUCT

Unlike the disruptive customer, this person, at least, has an identifiable reason for doing what he or she does. The customer erroneously believes that if your product did not exist, his or her friend would still have a job. You must deal with the situation. If you don't, it may develop into a problem for your product; a determined operator can find something wrong with most products, or make something wrong. Sometimes you can help this person develop a more positive attitude. Change always occurs and always will.

If possible, to get the best chance of winning this individual over, deal with him or her privately. The following scenario assumes that you noticed the customer sharing the negative attitude with others during training. During a break, you find a private moment and decide to take action:

SERVICE: Well, what do you think of the (product)?

CUSTOMER: It's okay I guess; I suppose it will work.

SERVICE: Sounds like you're not very optimistic about this new situation. These (products) are great. They really are quite productive and offer good potential for profit improvement.

Just dive in and get to the issue if you can.

CUSTOMER: Yeah, I've heard all about that. Everybody is talking about the increased productivity we're going to get. No one is talking about the people who don't have jobs any longer, though.

SERVICE: I know what you mean. Advancing technology always changes things. It causes displacement. It's tough to have to keep up with all the changing, to have to do all the learning. I guess we all need to keep learning forever.

CUSTOMER: People can't keep up if they don't have jobs. These advanced machines are putting thousands of people out of work.

SERVICE: They are also creating many new jobs, new, more advanced jobs. Did a friend of yours lose a job?

Try to move away from the philosophical discussion and get him or her to express the real problem.

CUSTOMER: Yep. They booted my friend right out of there and pulled this thing right in. It was just like my friend had no value at all to anyone, tossed right out on the street.

SERVICE: I'll bet that was painful to watch.

Express honest empathy. It is painful to watch the displacement advancing technology always creates.

CUSTOMER: It sure was. I saw a lot of good people get let go, all because of this (product). They had worked there many years. Now they have nowhere to go.

SERVICE: Sounds awful. But you have a job. You are part of the new team trying to make things go. The company will survive. It will be more competitive with the new technology.

CUSTOMER: I guess. But what about everyone else?

SERVICE: They will survive. We all do. Things can be tough, but most will adapt, accept new training, and get new jobs elsewhere. Some will even get more advanced jobs repairing, maintaining, and programming the new technology.

CUSTOMER: It was all fine before you people came in with your new-fangled (product).

SERVICE: Things were probably not as fine as they looked. If your company had not purchased the new technology, its competitors would have. They would have made competitive product at higher quality and at lower cost. Your company would have lost its customer base and would have been unable to pay salaries. *Everyone* in the organization would then be out of a job. There really is no choice but to change. It's not the product's fault. It's just what we all do, each of us finding some better way to do something. The best you and I can do is to keep on learning, keep on applying new ideas and new tools and contribute by improving the standard of living for all, even when it is uncomfortable to do so.

CUSTOMER: Sure seems there should be a better way.

SERVICE: There is. We're building it every day. Bit by bit, piece by piece. It just, per-haps, takes a lot longer than we think. Let's get to class and get the maximum out of the (product) for you and your company.

CUSTOMER: I guess that's all we can do.

SERVICE: Which is a lot.

DEALING WITH CUSTOMERS WHO CANNOT MEET CERTIFICATION REQUIREMENTS

There are many situations in which customer certification is required by you, the supplier. Customer service may be required to certify customers any time the company has liability exposure on its products. For example, training a customer to operate potentially dangerous manufacturing equipment would be a situation where certification might be necessary as well as wise. Instructing customers on correct operation of sensitive medical diagnostic equipment is another example. Further, service could be involved with customer certification in situations where mishandling equipment or procedures would have serious ramifications. For example, technicians have to deal with complex computerized checking systems covering interfaces between customer and supplier. Errors in operations can have serious business consequences.

Telling the customer he or she is not qualified to perform a task when training is complete is always sensitive. No one wants to tell another he or she has failed. But at times, there is no other option. When certification is required, the following suggestions will make this important customer-training responsibility easier.

1. The individual participating in the training should be told in advance of the training that performance will be evaluated and that he or she will be certified based upon performance. Do not assume the boss will advise the subordinate of the certification requirements and procedures. The individual participant should receive a personalized letter from customer service in advance of training. Get the participant's name from his or her boss.

2. Certification should be based upon specifically observable behavior the trainee will be required to demonstrate at the conclusion of the training. There should be no subjective criteria involved.

3. The certification requirements should be described in writing and provided to the trainee and management in advance of the training.

4. Any prerequisite skills necessary for successful completion of the training should be described in writing and provided to the trainee and his or her supervisor in advance of the training.

5. Be certain your boss is informed of the situation before you start discussions with the customer. You, as the trainer, should tackle the problem because you are closest to it. However, have your boss standing by to help, as he or she may be needed to support your efforts. This will be especially true if, as is likely, the customer expresses fear of losing the job.

Assume service has completed most of the training and is now in the final review and testing stages. The customer cannot demonstrate that he or she has mastered program objectives. This should be a private discussion with the customer:

SERVICE: (Name), sometimes this stuff is just plain tough. It looks like we're still having difficulty with the (specific procedure).

Move gently. The customer has been able to observe you and others. It is a virtual certainty the customer already knows he or she is failing. Further, it is likely the customer is embarrassed by being unable to grasp the necessary procedures.

CUSTOMER: I guess I need a bit more practice with all of this.

SERVICE: I understand your concern. This is a complex procedure, and this is an accelerated program. Many cannot grasp the necessary steps this quickly, no matter how hard they work, and you sure did put forth the effort. Further, much of what a particular person can accomplish within the constraints of this training is dependent upon the experiences they bring to the training program.

Service is attempting to set the stage and build the customer's ego.

SERVICE: I sure would hate for you to get back to your company and have difficulty getting this thing up and running, especially when they are expecting high production levels.

CUSTOMER: Well, I guess I'll just have to find time to practice.

By now you are aware that additional practice will not solve the problem.

SERVICE: (Name), in the longer term, that is probably true. With some additional help on prerequisite training, plus practice, you can probably master operations of the (product). However, I would hate for your boss to expect too much from you today. We did supply your supervisor with a listing of needed prerequisite skills. Did your supervisor discuss prerequisites with you?

Strategically, it is a good idea to find a way out for the customer, if a way out exists. If the customer came to the training without prerequisite skills, then, obviously, his or her inability to grasp the training should not be overly difficult for supervision to accept.

CUSTOMER: I really did not discuss much with the boss. However, my boss did tell me I would have to understand how to operate this (product). This will be my new job.

Be very careful not to take sides with the customer, his or her boss, or with your own company. Find middle ground, by staying with the facts and the problem.

SERVICE: It is not fair to you, your company, or my company for all of us to expect something that cannot be done now. Most importantly, when you get back on the job, I will not be around to help you anymore. I have a suggestion. Suppose I call your boss. I'll explain how hard you worked, mentioning we even worked overtime, and that you have started to understand the materials. I can tell him or her all of this and suggest you still need additional assistance, because you did not have all the needed prerequisites. I will explain to your boss that our class assumes participants come with certain prerequisite skills and has just been too brief for you. Without prerequisites, grasping all of this material in the brief time allowed is just about impossible for anyone.

Customer Service has created a reasonable explanation, allowed the customer to save face, and is asking the customer for permission to get involved with his or her supervisor. This is a better approach than simply refusing certification and leaving the customer to fend for him- or herself. If you just refuse certification without helping this person with supervision, he or she will likely claim your training effort was executed poorly.

CUSTOMER: Well, the boss did tell me before I left that I must learn these new job requirements. This is the only job they have for me to do, and if I can't do it, they may just let me go. I think I can get it with more practice.

It would not be unusual for the customer to express fear.

SERVICE: That's why we need to call and help your boss understand the total situation. For sure, I don't want you to lose your job. If you cannot perform, or if the equipment is damaged, or if someone is hurt, the entire situation will be much worse. If we don't talk to your boss, he or she will be expecting production just as soon as you return, and all of these other problems are far more likely to occur. Our training director, my immediate supervisor, has a lot of experience with these situations. We train (number) people at this center annually, and we frequently have difficulty with prerequisites. Let's get him or her involved with calling your boss. My supervisor can suggest additional training and, perhaps your supervisor can release additional funds to support further training. Let's go talk to the training manager now, and I will be sure to tell him or her how hard you have been working on all of this.

Having your supervisor talk to the customer's supervisor is usually a good idea. Corporate fiefdoms do exist. Supervision will be more detached from the actual classroom performance and can take a more businesslike approach in discussing related issues such as safety, production requirements. Further, it is the job of supervision to evaluate others. While you are trying to help the customer and create buy-in to your approach, you cannot allow the customer to actually make the decision. Avoid words that inflame or accuse; however, do not use words that imply the customer has a choice in this matter, either.

HOW TO TELL THE CUSTOMER'S BOSS THE TRAINEE IS NOT QUALIFIED TO OPERATE THE EQUIPMENT

Whether you are talking to the trainee's boss on the phone or in person, it is usually a good idea to have the trainee with you when you inform him or her of the trainee's limitations. No matter how good you are, this is always an uncomfortable discussion. If the trainee is not present to hear your actual words, it is very likely he or she will assume you are saying something awful. This scenario assumes you are talking to the trainee's supervisor on the phone.

SERVICE: Hello (supervisor's name). My name is John, and I want to discuss how the training has been going here.

CUSTOMER: Yes. Good to hear from you. I know we have Bill in your program. He was very excited and anxious to go down and see you guys. How's he doing?

SERVICE: I must say, Bill has been doing an outstanding job of staying with the program. He is sitting right here with me, and I have to give him a lot of credit. This is a tough program, and he worked harder than most to keep up the pace. Most come here with a much stronger foundation than Bill's and work a lot less.

Keep the discussion as positive as possible by finding positive things to say. Even when it is necessary to present bad news, present it constructively.

CUSTOMER: Well, that is good to hear. We have high expectations. Just as soon as Bill gets back, we need to get the (product) up into full production immediately. We already have a considerable demand loaded against it.

SERVICE: That's great. We want you to get maximum benefit from the (product). Bill and I have been speaking as this program has progressed. In fact, we even spent some extra hours in the evening, working to get him up the curve. Because Bill does not have some of the prerequisite skills he needs, some of the concepts are difficult for him to grasp. He is still going to need some additional support when he returns to work. Knowing your production demands, I wanted to be sure and discuss this with you in advance.

CUSTOMER: Are you saying he cannot do the job? We spent all that money sending him down there, and you did not train him?

SERVICE: Bill is doing a great job and is in a class with seven other trainees. We only have four days to get all important concepts covered and to allow everyone an opportunity to practice on the (product). Unfortunately, Bill is missing some of the prerequisite skills this type of training requires. This does not mean he didn't try, or that he can't learn. I just want to help you get maximum production as quickly as possible. Also, I don't want your expectations to be too high. Bill will likely be able to do a good job for you. He just needs more time.

CUSTOMER: What should I do?

SERVICE: Do you have others on staff who already know how to run this equipment?

CUSTOMER: No. Bill is our best guy.

SERVICE: Bill just is not ready to tackle this alone, and we are limited as to what we can cover in the class. I recommend that we schedule one of our best service people to visit your job site. I can explain this situation to our field service group. They can provide you with additional support during the initial setup. Further, they can provide additional training for Bill.

CUSTOMER: Is this part of our warranty, or part of our initial setup included in the purchase price?

SERVICE: No. The initial setup included in the purchase price assumes one of our people will be on site for one day. Based on my work with Bill, I would suggest you and he should plan for one of our people to be on site for about five days. That should be enough time to get you up and running and to get Bill up the learning curve.

CUSTOMER: At your prices, that is a lot of money.

SERVICE: Good training costs money. It also produces a high return. By having good setup and good system operators, you have a much better chance of achieving your production objectives with the (product). Further, skilled operators are far less likely to make mistakes that cause damage to the equipment. Viewed correctly, training is actually an investment in cost reduction.

CUSTOMER: Let's get our people scheduled in there and get this up and running.

SERVICE: Looking forward to a great program.

Chapter
13

On Site and Face to Face

When on site, up close and personal, the script starts to play out just as soon as you walk through the customer's door. Face-to-face communication is far more comprehensive than any other form of communication, because we all send and receive messages with all five of our senses. More importantly, we send the messages whether we intend to or not. Pay attention to the details; everything matters, there is no on/off switch, no neutral ground in communicating your overall customer-service attitude. When you are on site, a specific company image, either positive or negative, either planned or not, is always being conveyed to the customer.

All of us are turned off when we are around those who have "bad breath," those who don't seem to know who they are, understand how their looks impact relationships, or care about what they represent. Do not let the desired customer-focused image and message just evolve. Plan it. Develop training that defines the customer-focused image and message and their correct implementation. Teach employees how their behavior specifically complements and reinforces or detracts from what the organization represents.

LOOKING THE PART

Everyone agrees: the service representative must look professional when on site. However, "professionalism" is dictated by the specific customer-service situation at hand, and therein is the beginning of the endless "How-should-I-look-and-dress?" debate. A tuxedo may be necessary and appropriate while serving tables in a gourmet restaurant; however, it would certainly be out of place when performing preventive maintenance on oil-drilling equipment in the North Sea. Blue jeans and boots, while out of place when working on x-ray machinery at the hospital, or cash-handling machinery at the grocery store, or copy machines in the executive office suite, may be just perfect when rushing to bring the harvesting machine in the wheat field back on line before the fall rains begin. The surgeon's gown, appropriate and professional in the operating room, or when talking to an anxious family in the waiting room, is out of place while lecturing at the annual doctor's symposium. Appearance has always mattered to human beings and always will. Appearance must also fit the occasion and the work at hand. Do not just assume that the desired appearance will just somehow happen. Define and train for it.

No matter what the job, or how dirty the work, there is just no room for filthy or stained clothing in the contemporary world. When the nature of the job is such that extremely dirty conditions will be encountered, special clothing should be provided. Consider, as an example, insulation installers. They must frequently blow insulation into filthy attic spaces. However, these filthy attic spaces all too often are found sitting atop million-dollar renovated urban homes or offices appointed with distinctive and expensive furnishings. Full body suits should be provided for those working in such environments. The customer-service technician should arrive in a crisp, clean uniform and professionally discuss the scope and magnitude of the job with the customer. Assuming the access portal to the dirty area is from the clean area, the technician should prepare a work zone by protecting all clean areas near the access portal with plastic sheeting. Just before going into the dirty area, the technician should don a jumpsuit covering the total body as well as the feet, head, and neck. Reusable suits as well as low-cost disposable paper suits are readily available for this purpose. Masks and gloves are also readily available. When work is completed, the suit should be removed along with all the plastic coverings used to protect the area. After taking a wash break, and again in the clean uniform, the technician can approach the customer, summarize work accomplished, answer questions, fill out paper work, and discuss invoicing or any other related issues. This would be the minimum expected performance. After all, the customer is likely spending more than one hundred dollars per hour for this service.

Uniforms solve many problems for face-to-face service work and should be strongly considered for all businesses. Uniforms will enhance the image of any size technical staff, including staff for a very small business, such as the local grocery store, or the neighborhood fueling station. Some other advantages of uniforms are:

☎ The desired image for the organization can be planned in advance with public-relations experts.

☎ Consistency in appearance among all customer-service people is possible without stringent dress codes.

☎ Company logos can be easily displayed proudly and professionally along with a telling slogan.

☎ Badges allowing proper identification of technicians fit in nicely; shirts and jackets can be monogrammed easily.

☎ Gender differences can be minimized.

☎ A desired stature for technicians can be created. (The stature associated with the fire fighter, airline pilot, meter reader, judge, police officer, army captain, or teenage gang member is, in large part, created by the uniform.)

Do not assume everyone understands the importance of good grooming and cleanliness. Offer continuous instruction and reinforcement on how and why cleanliness, good grooming, and personal hygiene impacts the organization's service image. Remind everyone:

☎ that the customer is really the ultimate and only boss

☎ that there are alternative choices

☎ that consumers will make those choices

☎ that everyone can be fired by the customer

☎ that people are fired every day by customers

Generate codes covering appropriate use of jewelry and makeup. Develop codes covering acceptable hair styles, including facial hair. These codes need not be overly restrictive, such that they stifle individuality; however, they should tilt toward stressing a conservative appearance. As perceived by the customer, when the job is finished, the technician, his or her appearance, the work accomplished, and the organization itself should blend together as a positive unified whole.

Use the following as a general rule of thumb when developing codes covering appearance, styling, and general on-site behavior: A good presentation means that, at the conclusion of the service call, the customer will feel seven things about the service technician:

1. He or she felt comfortable with the service technician, trusted him or her, and would recommend the technician to others.

2. The technician was competent and demonstrated competence and leadership on the job.

3. The technician worked for a reputable company and expressed how important the customer is to that company.

4. The work was satisfactorily completed, and the technician kept the customer involved with effective status reports as the work progressed.

5. The technician offered helpful insights on how the customer could get better value from the product or service.

6. The customer's perception of the organization is enhanced because of how the technician performed while on site.

7. Overall, the technician was professional and appeared professional. However, the customer does not specifically remember anything in particular that the technician was wearing.

WHERE TO START, WHAT TO SAY

It's a good idea to start with the boss, manager, head of operations, or, as we like to say in sales and service, a "key-buying-influence" at the job site. A key buying influence is a person who significantly influences the buying decision and helps mold the overall perception a particular customer has of your organization.

Many service technicians hate hanging around bosses, management types, or other key buying influences. "It's too much like sales," they far too frequently report. Technical people prefer hanging around with their technical colleagues, out in the labs and shops and will often state: "That's where the customer really wants them to be, out doing the work." Besides, their instructors in college told them they need only focus on the technical job requirements and leave all that sales stuff to the other "sales types." Well, sorry folks, those college instructors were mistaken. Everybody is selling all the time. The only question is *what* is being sold, not *if* something is being sold. Effective service is effective sales, and, like it or not, buying influences make the decisions and write the checks. If bosses are required to write the checks, they have the right to be kept informed as to what is happening within their operations. Of course, the boss wants you out back fixing the darn thing. However, fixing the technical problem effectively and efficiently is just not enough to create customer satisfaction and long-term relationships. The boss also wants to be kept informed and wants to hear your money-saving ideas.

Stop by the office. Take the time to use a simple introductory script. Even if you can't see the boss personally, take a moment to leave a positive impression and a simple note. Even on repeat calls it is a good idea to drop by the main office to say a quick hello and offer an idea or two about how your product can be used more productively.

Try this as a rule of thumb: Good service technicians conduct themselves so that customers feel comfortable enough to invite them to use the "back door," or employee entrance, just like one of the family. However, good service technicians are always professional enough to continue using the front door.

ARRIVING ON SITE, RECEIVING AND HANDLING VALUABLE INFORMATION

This scenario assumes the technician arrives on site and approaches through the visitor entrance. Some contemporary operations have replaced the receptionist with a telephone and a set of written instructions. In these cases, just follow the instructions and contact the person asking for service. The following script assumes a human receptionist is on duty and offers valuable information. The service technician needs to deal with the information to ensure that no barriers to future communications are created.

SERVICE: Hello, I'm (name) with (company). Is (name) in today?

Service should ask for the person making the contact. If this is a routine scheduled call and no one specifically called for service, then ask for a key buying influence. Present your business card to the receptionist as part of the introduction.

RECEPTIONIST: She is in a meeting. Can someone else help you?

SERVICE: Yes. Is (name) in? I need to perform preventive maintenance on your (product) today. As part of your service contract with us, I want to ensure it offers maximum performance. I also want to check the systems and pressures as well as change fluids and check all alignments.

Service personalizes the conversation with the use of "I" and takes advantage of the selling opportunity by using words such as, "offers maximum performance."

RECEPTIONIST: Glad you are here. Some folks in the back have been complaining about the (product). They said it is really slow now.

Draw the customer out. This is valuable information, and service must talk to those who are complaining. Even if they are wrong about the product's performance, service still must deal with their concerns, since you cannot afford to have them offering negative comments about your product to each other.

SERVICE: Really? Thanks for telling me. I'm glad I came by today. Tell me, who commented about the (product's) performance? I want to be sure to talk to them. I need to understand what happened to be certain it is fixed.

Service exercises caution. The word "complaint" used by the receptionist is converted to "comment" by the service technician. Further, service does not just ask who commented, the representative explains why he or she wants to know. He or she is not indicting or putting people down for talking, but is problem solving and needs to make that clear.

RECEPTIONIST: I think Bill and Sue in accounting were complaining.

SERVICE: (Making notes.) Thanks. I'll be sure to talk to them before I get started. Could you call (customer's technician) for me? Let me just leave a brief note and my card for (manager or a key buying influence). I'll just say I am here in the lab working with (customer's technician) and that I will stop back later and give her a report of what gets accomplished before I leave. In the meantime, she will know where I am if she needs me.

Service would wait until the customer's technician arrives. This example scenario assumes the two technicians have worked together before and continues as the customer's technician enters the lobby.

SERVICE: Hi, (name). Good to see you again. It's time for quarterly routine maintenance on the (product). (Receptionist's name) advises that I should probably talk to Bill and Sue. They may have noticed the (product) acting up somehow. Is it okay to walk by accounting and get their view about what is going on before we go on out to the (product)? I want to make sure everything is okay here.

Service can and should be up-front with the information received and should speak, without being obvious, within hearing range of the receptionist. Service has the objective of positioning all comments positively and constructively. The receptionist and others should perceive that service is glad to receive any concerns about the product's performance.

CUSTOMER TECHNICIAN: That will be fine. Let's head on out there.

As the technicians walk to accounting, service should use the time in relationship-building. Service should assume there are no hidden agendas. With this assumption, Bill and Sue can be approached either simultaneously or individually, with essentially the same script. This example assumes Bill and Sue are approached simultaneously:

SERVICE: Hello. I'm (name) with (company). I'm here to do preventive maintenance on the (product). I understand you may have noticed it performing erratically or below expected standards. Could you help me? A few descriptive details on what it is doing may offer clues that could lead me to a potential problem.

Service draws the customers into the troubleshooting task without embarking on tangents such as "receptionist said that you said that. . ." Forget the "he-said, she-said" language. Service also focuses directly on the product and its performance, not the personalities of the customers.

CUSTOMER(s): It was doing several erratic things, such as (description).

Service has created a problem-solving discussion. Use open-ended questions; do not challenge input received; do not attack or discuss personalities; focus on the product's performance; clarify facts without challenging personalities; take notes.

SERVICE: This is great, and thanks to both of you. (Customer technician) and I are going over to dig into this situation right now, and your input will certainly make our job much easier. I really appreciate your help. Here are a few business cards. Your company has a service contract with us, and I am responsible for keeping that equipment running. If you ever feel it is not meeting your expectations, just give me a call. Usually I am traveling; however, you can reach me on voice mail twenty-four hours a day. Just leave a description of the problem on my recorder and be sure to leave a phone number so that I can follow up with you.

Bill and Sue are users and have already demonstrated their willingness to discuss the product's performance. It is always better to have the customer discussing the product's perceived poor performance with customer service rather than with colleagues at the job site. Service cannot guarantee it will call Bill or Sue directly. However, by leaving the business cards, the service representative improves the probability of being called. At this point, service should go to the equipment with the customer's technician, perform the planned preventive maintenance, and resolve issues discussed with Bill and Sue. The representative should discuss what he or she does, especially those adjustments directly related to issues addressed by Bill and Sue, with the customer's technician.

Customer satisfaction is enhanced when all communications started at the beginning of the call are closed at the end of the call. In this example, the service representative will report back to Bill, Sue, and the receptionist. Again, service can speak to Bill and Sue individually or together. The script would essentially be the same.

SERVICE: (To Bill and Sue.) Well, that is it. The (product) is running within specification now, and I wanted to just stop by to say thanks again for your comments. Based upon your observations, I checked the (subsystem) and found that a (problem description) had occurred. I did repair it and just wanted to say thanks again for your help. Please be sure to call me if you notice anything again.

Service should then close out the communication with the receptionist and again ask to speak with the manager in charge.

SERVICE: (To receptionist.) We're finished here. Thanks for your comments. I managed to speak with Bill and Sue, and based upon their input, I did locate a problem and resolved it. Thanks again for your help. Is (manager or other official) in?

RECEPTIONIST: Yes, she is. I gave her your note when she returned from the meeting and mentioned that you might stop by again. Just go on into her office.

SERVICE: (To manager. If the representative has not met the manager previously, then he or she should add an introduction to this script.) Hi, Ms. (name). I just wanted to drop by and give you a brief report on the (product). I performed a standard preventive maintenance procedure today. Further, based upon some helpful observations from Bill and Sue, I performed a troubleshooting sequence and found (brief problem description). I repaired the problem, checked out the system, and the (product) is performing well now. I also left my card with Bill and Sue so that they can contact me if they notice any other problems. Of course, (customer's technician name) has my number as well and can always reach me. Do you have any questions for me, or is there any other help I can offer?

If there are any other advantages for the customer such as product offerings, additional training, new services, recommendations on upgrades and so on, they should be offered at this time. If additional offerings are made, be sure to be very brief and do not use hard-sell persuasive tactics. These will likely turn the manager off. Consider the following:

SERVICE: (To manager.) Ms. (manager's name), let me leave this literature behind for your review. Your product is now two years old. We have developed an (upgrade) that offers additional advantages to users of (product). If added to your (product), this upgrade will enable you to reduce your operating costs by (dollars), because of (a simple reason). The upgrade's performance is defined in this handout, which you can review at your convenience. Thanks for allowing us to work with you, and I will see you again soon.

Service should also offer goodbye pleasantries to the receptionist before leaving as well. The sales presentation should be followed up as appropriate.

PUTTING TOGETHER AN INSTANT TEAM

On-site customer service technicians frequently need staff support help from the customer's technicians. Typically, the customer is required to prepare the site before service technicians arrive to install the equipment. In other situations, customers may be required to install the equipment before service arrives to check out, start up, and confirm operation. Further, service may be called on site to repair faulty equipment. However, when service arrives, the customer's production may interfere with the repair plan.

Any of these situations may require the service representative to ask for help, and asking for help on the job, which requires the customer to invest time, is always a delicate matter.

GETTING THE HELP YOU NEED WHEN ON-SITE

You have finished installation and have worked through your start-up procedures. The next step is to develop a support capability at the customer site. This sample scenario starts as you approach the subject of support with management:

SERVICE: Your new (product) is ready to go. Everything looks great and runs within specification.

CUSTOMER: Thanks for your help, and I'm sure the (product) will perform well for us. We have high expectations.

SERVICE: I want to do everything possible to ensure we meet our mutual objective of providing maximum (product) performance for you. To ensure that happens, I need to train four or five of your key people in correct operations and preventive maintenance procedures.

It is always a good idea to find and reinforce mutually beneficial objectives.

CUSTOMER: We are awfully busy right now, and I can't spare anyone. Just tell our technician, Betty, what she needs to know, and she will train the rest of us as time permits.

SERVICE: Training Betty would be a great start. She worked with me during the installation and has already learned quite a bit. I'm certain Betty will be an excellent lead technician for this system. However, this is the first time she has worked on this (product). It would be optimistic of us to assume she, or anyone else, can absorb all the necessary information so quickly. Our experience suggests training several of your people now significantly increases the likelihood of maximum productive output for you. Having several people trained gives you three specific advantages:

1. It increases the probability that backup is available if someone is off work or otherwise unavailable when a minor problem occurs. Saving one hour of downtime can result in significant dollar savings for you.

2. It allows for better assimilation of information. This is a new system, and everyone is learning for the first time. Each person will absorb something different from my presentation. The knowledge absorbed by a group will be greater than the knowledge absorbed by any individual. Having good technical skills on site means greater independence.

3. It increases the probability of greater up-time for you. There are always minor operational problems. Having several people trained means that more creative thought can be directed toward any unlikely significant problem that might occur.

The representative should attempt to sell his or her position by demonstrating clear dollar value the customer will achieve.

CUSTOMER: The (product) is under warranty. Betty, or someone else, can just call you if something happens.

SERVICE: And I, or one of my colleagues, certainly would respond. But, Mr. (name), our experience suggests that, far too frequently, one of my colleagues or myself shows up to fix something only to learn that a very small adjustment is needed. Unfortunately, our customer ends up with significant downtime and loss of use while waiting for us to arrive. On many occasions, when we have several trained people on site, we can use the phone, coach one or more technicians through the problem, and produce better uptime. Our studies on this subject have been conclusive and consistent for the past (number) years: Those customers who help us build and maintain an on-site team achieve, on average, (number) percent greater productivity from the (product). There really is a significant dollar return from training.

CUSTOMER: Well, we will just have to take the risk. I simply don't have the time right now.

SERVICE: I understand. Some risks we just have to take. Still, though, I hate to leave like this. Your production requirements are at risk. How about this idea? Normally, to get a good team in place, we need four people and four hours. Suppose we set aside three others to work with Betty, and I work with them for only two hours today. I expect to be back in the area around (time period). I can call Betty then, and depending on everyone's schedule, I might be able to do additional training when I return.

CUSTOMER: That seems like a reasonable compromise. Let's get Betty and the crew together, and I will explain our strategy.

Compromise is sometimes necessary. In the example, we did not compromise the ultimate objective, which is to get a trained team in place. We did compromise the amount of time it is going to take. If Customer Service elected the option of just training Betty today, the probability of getting back to the original objective later would be diminished.

WORKING WITH LAZY CUSTOMERS

The customer is paying your standard hourly rate for service support. As part of your long-term relationship with this account, and to hold down total service costs, on-site management has assigned technical-support personnel to assist you with troubleshooting and problem resolution. Over the past hour or so you have assessed the (product) and have determined the likely problem as well as a course of action for problem resolution. You have also had the opportunity to observe those assigned to work with you. It is apparent they have been avoiding any involvement, and you are now convinced they intend to do little or no work. Without their support, the job will take longer and cost your customer more than it should. The customer will likely hold you accountable for poor project management. After another extended absence, the two technicians wander back to the job site, again giving you an opportunity to solicit their help.

SERVICE: I've pretty much isolated the problem to the (component) area. It looks like we'll have to remove a good bit of shrouding and shielding to expose and replace the bearings. Here, you guys start here. Remove (description of what to do), and I will start around back.

Throughout this script, assume either of the customer's technicians responds.

CUSTOMER TECHNICIAN: Sounds okay. We'll get right to it. We do, however, have other areas to check on and maintain at the same time we work on this job.

Many who accomplish little or nothing are always willing to share how busy they are. If you observe them acting as duffers, they are likely duffers. Don't be a pushover.

SERVICE: Sure, I understand that. However, we do need to get into this project and get it up and running. (Manager's name) made it clear this morning that production is urgently needed. Further, I have the overall responsibility to hold down total cost. I have already invested more than an hour in diagnosis. My tests indicate a likely source of the problem. I know what must be done, and I do need your help to get everything done in a timely manner. Without support, this job could take all day.

Service assumes leadership and clarifies the joint responsibility to hold down total cost.

CUSTOMER TECHNICIAN: Well, like I said, we'll help out as best we can. Management around here is so screwed up, they never get the schedule right. They always do this to us. We just have too many things assigned, and everything must be completed at the same time.

Do not give these guys wiggle room. This is not enough of a commitment.

SERVICE: I really can't comment on your total work schedule. But I do have a specific responsibility, and I need help here and now. I do need specific things done. I expect the three of us will be working on this problem, and this problem alone, for the next several hours, perhaps even through the lunch break.

Get this problem resolved before it grows further. Without threatening the technicians, clarify the tasks and estimate the time required to complete them. Call for a firm commitment. Those more interested in getting out of work tend to avoid being pinned down.

CUSTOMER TECHNICIAN: We are trying, but we also have other responsibilities. We will do the best we can to help you. But like we said, these other problem areas just come up, and we have to deal with them.

SERVICE: We had better get things clarified; this could cost your company a great deal of money. We must commit to the general plan I suggested in order to bring this system back on line in a timely manner. Further, to keep the overall project under control, I need to work with the same support team until this total repair is completed. We will experience even more problems and delays if the three of us start work and then I need to get others to help me finish. I understand your situation, however. If you have too many other responsibilities then, obviously, you cannot commit to this problem. Let's get your management to clarify priorities.

Define the range of your authority. You have a responsibility to the customer's total organization, not just individuals within the organization.

The customer expects you to manage the project as well as perform technical work. Seeking clarification based upon limited authority is at times necessary. If the project takes longer than expected, the customer will ultimately blame you. The veiled threat suggesting that higher levels of management are needed to clarify priorities should be enough to keep the duffers in line.

CUSTOMER: Let's get at it. There is no need to call in our management, since they don't know what's going on. If they did, we wouldn't be in this fix anyway. What do you want us to do? We will hang in here, and other problems will just have to get worse.

SERVICE: We agree. This is the main priority, and we will all work together on only this project until the problem is resolved. You start with the (description).

These types won't jump on board with enthusiasm, and you will likely have to keep pushing them throughout the assignment. You can, however, get them to perform at some level. Supervise them closely. Keep a tight rein on them, as they will likely try to wiggle out of work again.

CALLING THE CAVALRY:
WHAT TO DO IN RARE BUT DIFFICULT SITUATIONS

Despite our best efforts, situations can get out of control. Service must be sensitive to the total environment and know when to call in the cavalry for additional help. Many in service erroneously think that calling for help is an admission of personal incompetence or failure. It is not. Indeed, it suggests the opposite: a high level of professionalism. No one can be expected to know everything there is to know or to think of every possible problem or cause. Professionals are always ready to discuss their limitations with colleagues and to call for additional expertise and support. For example, assume a service technician is on site to repair a radiation therapy machine used by the hospital to treat cancer patients. If the machine is down and unavailable, then patients will need to wait for their prescribed treatment. Under these circumstances, how long should the service technician work alone on the technical problem before calling for help? Obviously, the doctor wants prescriptions administered expeditiously. One would think the patient does as well.

How long should a customer lose real production dollars while a service technician fights a technical problem alone? Again, Customer Service must be aware of the complete environment and evaluate total losses to the customer in order to gauge correctly when to call for reinforcements.

The technician has several perceptual problems that must be overcome. First is the tendency to become overly involved in the particulars of the technical problem, or said another way, making the problem a personal contest. Technical problems can be a challenge, almost fun, like a jigsaw puzzle. The thinking goes something like this: "This problem is not bigger than I. I'm determined to beat this thing. I know I can find a solution."

Second, there can be a real fear of significant embarrassment. The thinking is something like this: "I've worked on this for eight hours with no luck. Suppose I call in for help. A colleague just listens to my description and sees an obvious problem instantly. Or even worse, sees an obvious problem that has been staring at me all along."

Some companies have macho service cultures that make these personal perceptual issues even more difficult to resolve. Service representatives can be found at chest-thumping sessions around coffee machines, chortling on fuel such as: "Bill worked on that XYZ problem for eight hours. Yeah, they had to send me out there. I loved it. I just looked at the readout and told Bill to (description) and that just fixed it. It was great! He just stood there, stammering like a dummy, as the customer watched. I just let him drift."

Institutionalizing the customer-focused perspective, many companies have ironclad procedural rules, "automatic escalators" for how to call in the cavalry. For example, many of our clients use an automatic escalator worded something like this: "If the service technician has not correctly isolated the cause of the problem after a two-hour diagnosis, he or she must contact and alert local supervision of the situation. Local supervision will then provide back-up support in locating the cause. If the technician working with local management cannot determine the cause of the problem within the first four hours, then divisional management must be notified. If divisional technical support, working with local technical support, cannot determine the cause of the problem within eight hours, then . . ."

Escalators are usually linked to locating the cause of a problem, not to implementing the solution. This makes perfect sense, since it is always more difficult to estimate the time involved with finding something unknown. However, once a cause for a technical failure is identified, then typically, a technical solution is known and executed easily.

Short of automatic escalators, there is no magic that ensures service will always know exactly when to call for reinforcements. The best practice would be to communicate your plan of action with the customer and ask questions to understand his or her unique situation. Some sample scripts follow.

CUSTOMER DESPERATE: WILLING TO COOPERATE

Immediately upon entering the job site, you are met at the door by three or more managers. You get hit with questions before you can get to see the product. You have no time to check anything.

CUSTOMER: We have a failure, and the screen indicates a code (number). How serious is the failure? How long will it take you to get us up back up and running? We have hundreds of people standing by waiting for production right now.

Being met like this at the door is a clear sign that the customer is desperate. Saying: "I don't know yet" or "let me get to the (product) first" will only increase anxiety. The customer wants action and professionalism; he or she wants you to take control, so take *immediate* control.

SERVICE: There are several reasons for that particular code. I will need about thirty minutes to look at a few things over at the (product's) control. There are ways you can help while I check the control outputs.

Someone can alert people waiting for production that, at absolute minimum, we will be down for another thirty minutes. They have to survive without us at least that long, maybe longer. We will give them another status report in a half hour. But we don't know what we are up against yet. To be prepared, they should start immediate planning for a delay that runs for several hours. If we get back on line quickly, then nothing will be lost. If we discover we need more than thirty minutes, then at least they will have preparations under way.

Can someone locate the available spare parts kit for the (product)? I don't know what I need yet, but let's identify all the parts we have on hand. It could save us time later after a diagnosis. Someone can also check which airline flights between (the parts depot and the customer's location) are still running today. Again, we don't yet know if we need to fly parts here, but if we must, at least we will have the information available. This will save us time, too.

I will head to the (product) and start my diagnostic tests. Is a telephone extension located near the (product)? Perhaps a couple of technicians could be assigned to me to assist with disassembly and assembly.

The most urgent two answers we need right now are: What parts are on hand? What is the airline flight schedule? Just as soon as we determine the problem, answers to these questions will control our estimates of how long it takes for us to get back on line.

Don't be glib; be serious. Take immediate control by giving specific assignments others can do. You must approximate some sort of time schedule, as noted to run your tests. Don't just think about the technical problem with your product. Think about all the details that must be addressed in order to resolve the total crisis. The technical problem is only one small part of the total cost pressure the customer feels at this moment. Break the crisis into small pieces of work and involve others by delegating the work. Getting people involved in resolving the problem will tend to build a problem-solving team and help defuse tension and anxiety. In an emergency like this, management people will hang around. Don't try to make them go away; they won't. Giving the observers tasks will decrease the pressure as well as the total time required to get the product up and running again.

SERVICE: (Thirty minutes later, speaking to the observers.) We have progress. I am virtually certain we have a (description of the problem). However, there are no replacement (parts) on site. Can someone notify those downstream depending on us that there will be an additional delay? We can estimate a time for them. Who checked the flight schedules?

CUSTOMER: The next flight is leaving your (part depot location) in one hour.

SERVICE: (Calling the depot.) First things first. Let me get two sets of (parts) on that plane.

The customer will likely want to keep a spare set on site after all this. Also, something could still go wrong with the new parts being shipped. At this juncture, you may or may not know why the old part failed. Extra shipping costs are small when compared to all other costs caused by the emergency.

SERVICE: (After calling in the parts order.) Our people at the depot are fully informed and working on this. They will meet that plane, and our needed parts will be enroute within the hour. Could someone meet the plane for me? I could go; however, I would like to use the time to check out the system. I am trying to determine why the failure occurred in the first place.

CUSTOMER: We will have someone meet the plane. They should be back here one hour after the plane lands.

SERVICE: That sets our plan, and we should inform others waiting downstream for production. I will use the next two hours while the parts are enroute to check everything possible. Once the courier returns with the parts, it will take us another hour to get the parts installed, bring the (product) back on line, and perform a system check. Those waiting for production can expect to see us back on line, optimistically, in three hours, around four hours at the outside. Hopefully, that should do it. If another major problem is going to occur when the new parts are installed, we will know in about three hours and can advise everyone at that time. If they do not hear from us again in three hours, everything is going according to plan, and we are coming back on line.

Continue keeping the customer informed of the approximate time schedule as the problem is resolved. Always advise the customer of the risks in your estimates. Many in service avoid estimating time intervals because of the risk involved. However, the customer must worry about more than the immediate technical problem. By providing time estimates, you are helping the customer control the total operation, which is what he or she wants you to do. Customer Service is much more than solving technical problems.

CUSTOMER DESPERATE: UNWILLING TO COOPERATE

Assume you are bombarded with "When-is-it-going-to-be-ready?"-type questions just as soon as you enter the door. Further assume the uncooperative customer, insecure and frightened, is more interested in placing blame on you and your company than in resolving the problem.

CUSTOMER: We have a code problem (number). What caused it? How long will it take you to fix it? When will we be back on line? People are waiting for production. You know the (product) is still under warranty. This should never have happened. We were operating exactly the way we were trained by you people.

SERVICE: I'm sorry this has happened. There are several problems that could have created that alert code. I will need about thirty minutes to run diagnostics and investigate. You could help by alerting those waiting for production that there will be a thirty-minute delay, minimum. They should start making preparations for an even longer delay, though. Depending on what I discover, the delay might even be longer than that.

CUSTOMER: Hey, I'm not getting involved in your problem. This thing is under warranty and should be running perfectly. I'm not running around here passing out bad news.

SERVICE: Other people must continue without us for a minimum of thirty minutes, perhaps longer. I cannot eliminate that initial time requirement. Those dependent upon us should be kept informed of our status and progress. They won't like the delay, but at least, they will be informed. Interruptions to production are always stressful. They get worse when others are not given information. I will be glad to give status reports. However, I should really get to the product as soon as possible. Let's keep talking while we go there.

Our status is this: It will take me at least thirty minutes to run the diagnostic tests. Hopefully, but I cannot guarantee it, I will determine the problem in that time frame. Once I determine the problem, I will then need to confirm the needed parts are on site in the spare-parts kit. If they are not here, I will need to ship them in from our depot. Those waiting for production should be kept informed of our progress. Assistance with some of the details will help me speed up the problem-solving process.

CUSTOMER: Look, I don't want to take responsibility for your problem. I didn't really do anything.

To make progress, you do not necessarily need to address what the customer is saying specifically. Try to look over the nonessential issues, and dodge the issue of responsibility for now.

SERVICE: I know the system is under warranty, and we will fulfill our responsibilities. However, your people are waiting for production, and you did ask how long it would take to get the system up and running again. I can give status reports to those waiting for production myself. However, they would likely be concerned, because I would be talking to them and not working on the technical problem.

Other support could be needed later after the problem is determined. Perhaps there is someone else who could assist me.

CUSTOMER: This is under warranty and your responsibility.

SERVICE: I agree that the (product) is under warranty. How do you suggest I keep others informed of our progress? We really don't know how long it will take to resolve this problem.

CUSTOMER: I will advise them of our status.

Asking a question draws the customer into the situation and the potential solution, making it more difficult for him or her to continue the uncooperative behavior. At this early stage, do not accept that this is a warranty problem, as you really don't know the problem or its cause yet. Acknowledging that the product is under warranty, as suggested above, is not necessarily accepting that this particular problem is covered under warranty. Use the: "How do you want me to handle this?" idea every time the customer becomes uncooperative.

CUSTOMER DESPERATE: GETTING HELP FROM OTHER CUSTOMERS

Service has recently arrived on the scene. The failure occurred approximately twenty-four hours ago. This scenario starts with Service in a troubleshooting discussion with the customer. The customer has defined what the (product) did just before the failure occurred:

SERVICE: What you have described thus far does not give me a very clear indication of where the problem is. It looks like we are going to have to get into some diagnostic testing.

CUSTOMER: Let's get going. We need this up and running right now. We have already missed a complete day of production, and work is piling up.

SERVICE: Help me understand how serious the production situation is. Diagnostic work can take some time. I will need to run various tests and don't know which one will produce results for us.

Service is attempting to understand the customer's business problem, not just the technical equipment problem. This strategy will help service get to the real issue, which is always creating customer satisfaction. Satisfaction does not necessarily occur just because service fixed the technical problem.

Pitfall: Service should not use phrases such as "production losses"; such language suggests culpability.

CUSTOMER: That sure doesn't sound very promising! See that sign? We promise our customers their film will be developed in one hour. We, obviously, try to get them to shop our store while they wait for photo processing. We were down all day yesterday. Look at all those rolls of film waiting for that development machine! Look at the business I'm losing! Those customers dropped off their film and left as soon as we told them the machine was down. This is causing lost sales. This (product) is under warranty, and we expect better service than this. How long will these tests take?

SERVICE: There are several tests. The first test I'm planning to run will take about two hours. It is the most comprehensive test and most likely will produce results. I can estimate the time required to repair any problem uncovered by the first test at the end of the run time. However, I cannot guarantee success. If luck is running against us, and the first test is negative, I will need to use a second test, which will consume another hour of testing time. Again, I will need to assess our position at that time.

Even though there is no easy way out of this situation, it is best practice to involve the customer in your thinking. Service is arranging the scope and limits of a contract with the customer. The customer may not like to hear bad news, but it is better to lay out the truth with a constructive direction than to allow false expectations to build. Bad news, unlike fine wine, does not get better over time.

CUSTOMER: I just can't live with that prognosis. The way you're talking, this thing may be down for another full day. We're losing a fortune!

SERVICE: Maybe we can do something else. I have another (product) installed several miles from here. What I can do, assuming my other customer does not object, is to take all of your film over to his machine and buy some time from him. That does not solve our technical problem here, but it does get some of the pressure off you. At least the film will be developed when your customers return. Resolution of this particular technical problem will likely take somewhat longer, though.

CUSTOMER: I understand. But, you can't fix the machine here and run production elsewhere for me at the same time.

SERVICE: That is true.

CUSTOMER: I have a better idea. Why don't you work on your system here, and I will send one of my technicians over to your other customer?

SERVICE: That would save some time. However, I had better call and pave the way. I can't guarantee my customer will work with us. But I think I have a better chance of getting cooperation from him if I call. He may perceive you as just a competitor.

This strategy assumes Customer Service has an excellent relationship with customer number two. However, this strategy can backfire, and service should keep expectations with customer one low.

SERVICE: (On phone with customer two.) (Customer two), I'm in a bind, and I need help. I have another (product), identical to yours, installed across town. Unfortunately, I have an unknown problem and must run some time-consuming tests. I have production seriously backed up. Assuming you have time available on your (product), I would like to rent (hours) from you.

CUSTOMER TWO: Are you asking me to help a competitor?

SERVICE: (Customer 1) is not really your competitor. His product mix and target market here are different from yours. The two of you only compete on film developing, and you are across town from each other. Your respective customers are likely deciding where to develop film based on location more than anything else. Besides, I'm asking you to help *me*. I've got a problem with the (product) that I can't yet define. Hopefully, the situation will never be reversed. However, if it ever were reversed, and I had a similar situation with your (product), be assured that I would do everything possible to help you as well.

CUSTOMER TWO: I see your point. Bring the production over and run it off.

SERVICE: Thanks.

SERVICE: (To customer 1.) The good news is that I have rented production space for you. The bad news is that I have to run the production personally. I will start test one before I leave. Your technician can watch the test cycle for me. I'll call (technician name) in about two hours and we can discuss the next best step.

The technician used his or her personal integrity to rent time on the (product) from customer two. Under the described conditions, it is wise for the technician to run the production personally. You had the option of suggesting to customer two that customer one's technician would be coming to run the production. As this scenario unfolded, customer two expressed reservations. Given these reservations, it is wise not to push the issue. If customer two had expressed no reservations at all, then pushing a bit further would probably have been okay.

There will be expenses for the rented time. Who should pay? Service or customer one, the owner of the machine? Here are several things to consider. Is the machine under warranty or service contract? If so, what rules exist? Even if the machine is under warranty, it is unlikely the warranty guarantees production flow-through. However, if it is under warranty, it would be a good gesture for service to pick up the rental tab.

What is your advertised service response? Are you within limits? If so, then asking the customer to pick up the rental cost would not be unreasonable. It is the customer who will get the profit from the production. However, if you missed your service response, then a gesture may be helpful.

How angry is the customer? Is there a list of other unresolved problems with the equipment? Again, if there is, a positive gesture may be appropriate.

There is no hard-and-fast rule on who should pay for the rented production time. In general, customer one should pay as he or she would have had to pay for production on his or her own equipment if it were running, and stands to receive all the profits from the developed film. Further, your company sold customer one a product and promised to keep the product running; it is unlikely that your company promised any customer a specific level of business from any products sold.

CUSTOMER DESPERATE: TAKING RISKS WITH EQUIPMENT

The first part of this scenario might unfold similarly to the preceding scenario. This scenario assumes the customer is already expressing serious concerns about lost production:

CUSTOMER: I need a stronger commitment from you. You need two hours to test this system. And then, your diagnosis will depend upon the test results. Even after two hours of testing, you still may not know what is wrong with this (product). We have serious production requirements, and I absolutely must get up and going. I just can't live with these losses today.

SERVICE: I understand the need for production, and I sure am sorry this is happening. But there is little I can do to decrease the test time needed. I could ignore proven procedure, try to guess what is wrong, dive in, and start exchanging new components for old. That would represent a risky and potentially high-cost approach. I might be lucky, guess correctly, and have the (product) up and running in fifteen minutes. That would be great. Conversely, I could also spend the next two hours exchanging parts, run up a large parts bill for your company, and be totally wrong with all of my guesses. The (product) could still be down two hours from now.

Easy roads seldom exist. Expressing empathy without assuming culpability with statements like "I'm sorry this is happening," keeping the customer factually informed, and involving him or her in the risk assessment is the high road and the best road to travel. While this road does not guarantee customer satisfaction, it does produce the best possibility of getting there. No road can guarantee satisfaction.

CUSTOMER: This is just awful, and I can't accept all these risks. I don't have the budget to authorize randomly replacing any and all parts. There must be more you people can do. You should not need all of that test time.

SERVICE: (Name), this is a highly complex state-of-the-art (product). When it is running, it produces tremendous productivity for you. It is the complex control system, which enables the productivity. But that control has a lot of built-in intelligence. The diagnostic tests were the best technology available when the system was designed.

Do you have a nearby colleague who can help us? Perhaps we could borrow or rent some production time from him or her. Or perhaps you could borrow competitive product and replace it later with some of your own production. I will be glad to help you make either of these situations work.

CUSTOMER: No, neither of those ideas will work. There is no friendly competitor close by with excess capacity, and no one will be willing to loan me product. The entire industry is sold out right now and has been for about the past year. There is not a shred of excess capacity anywhere. Everyone is desperate for production increases. They're all late on delivery, too. I can work around some lateness for the next few days. This one job, though, I urgently need run time right now.

SERVICE: There is one more thing I can do. I don't like what I am going to propose. It is risky to your (product), and I do need your approval and support. This job currently running is the most urgent and must be done now?

CUSTOMER: Yes.

SERVICE: What is the run time to finish this job?

CUSTOMER: We need another two hours to finish.

SERVICE: I can disconnect the (description), which disables the (protection circuits) for the (product). Disabling the circuits will enable me to operate the system manually. We will need luck to keep going for two hours. The (protection circuits) kicked in because something is seriously wrong. If I run manually without the (protection circuits), we will certainly produce even more damage to the (product), creating greater repair costs for you. This is not a great idea, as even more time will be required to do all the additional repair; but, if at this moment production output is more important than the system itself, then bypassing the (protection circuit) may be worth it. I should also mention that this is an option only because there is no increased chance of physical harm to ourselves as operators.

CUSTOMER: How much additional damage might occur?

SERVICE: I will be right here and do an emergency shutdown if necessary. However, I'm sorry, there is just no way I can predict what the (product) will do to itself once I override programmed protection systems. Additional damage could be extensive or slight. With monitoring systems disabled, there is no way to know. Further, I cannot even guarantee we can limp along for another two hours. We can just try to relieve the pressure for you.

CUSTOMER: Let me contact my management and discuss all this with them before we let you go ahead.

When the customer decides to involve others, he or she is probably aware of the seriousness of what you are proposing. Neither Service nor anyone else can legitimately offer to put human safety at risk. However, putting equipment at risk to accomplish an important objective may, at times, be necessary. When this action is contemplated, Service must be careful in choosing words that explain the situation as well as the risks to the customer. This is important: Service wants to partner with the customer in solving the production problem without accepting responsibility for any additional equipment damage that might occur. Service has the responsibility to keep the equipment running, not maintain the production schedule. Service does not want the responsibility for the customer's production output unless an existing contract requires Service to accept this responsibility. For this scenario to be effective, the customer must understand that he or she will be expected to incur the additional repair costs.

WHAT TO DO WHEN NOTHING CAN BE DONE

Sometimes it just is not going to work, there is nothing more Customer Service can do, and the customer is going to experience losses. In these unfortunate situations, even if Customer Service cannot solve the problem or temporarily relieve the pressure for urgently needed production, it still can be empathetic and offer longer-term solutions, which might prevent the problem in the future. This scenario assumes a technical-service representative is on site, the problem has been diagnosed, and all methods for achieving a temporary solution have been exhausted and have failed.

SERVICE: (After analysis of problem is complete.) That is it! I have nowhere else to go. I tried to activate the (last special procedure) and still could not get us up and running. There is nothing more I can do that is a quick fix. As we discussed, parts will be arriving by special air carrier later this afternoon. The best I can do right now is to get the (main component) disassembled and have it ready when parts arrive. We're looking at two days of work to get you back on line. I know you don't want to hear all this, and I sure am sorry this happened; but this is the reality we have to live with.

CUSTOMER: This may be the reality, but it is also a disaster. This is going to cost us a fortune. Even worse, our relationship with our largest and oldest account is going to be hurt. They were depending on us, we promised we could perform, and now we're going to let them down badly. This is about as awful as it can be.

SERVICE: I really am sorry. Is there any way one of your competitors can help? Perhaps you can purchase some production? Even a small amount might, at least, relieve some of the pressure.

CUSTOMER: There is no chance for any help from competitors. The industry is flat sold out now. Everyone is under pressure just filling requirements for their own customers, and they sure are not going to help us with ours.

SERVICE: Then we just have to sweat it out. You can tell your customer that the problem is diagnosed and repair is under way. Assuming nothing else creates difficulty during reassembly, we should be running full production again in about forty-eight hours. If it's any help, tell them we are on overtime to get you back on line as soon as possible. We can give you periodic status reports as the reassembly work progresses as well.

CUSTOMER: I appreciate all that, but it is not going to help. They are still going to be livid. They are under severe strain themselves right now.

SERVICE: There is one more thing we could offer, although it will not help the short-term problem. We could work with you to put together a plan to minimize this type of situation in the future.

CUSTOMER: How is that going to help my customer?

SERVICE: It does nothing to help your customer right now. However, it may help you maintain his or her future confidence.

CUSTOMER: How so?

SERVICE: Right now, we are in a negative position. We must tell your customer that he or she is going to be hurt and that we can't do anything to keep this from happening. This is a tough position to be in, and, at the moment, the conversation stops right there. However, if we develop a plan to minimize this in the future, then at least we have something to talk about that's positive. We would in essence be saying something like: "This did happen now, and there is nothing we can do about it right now. However, there is plenty we can do to make sure this does not happen in the future." And then we could explain the plan. As I said, it does nothing for your customer today, but it is at least something positive, which may help your future relationship with him or her.

Tip: Using the "we" pronoun suggests a partnership. It tends to forge a bond.

CUSTOMER: What kind of plan do you have to keep this from happening in the future?

SERVICE: There are two possibilities: the purchase of redundant equipment, and our Smart User Group. Many customers purchase either new or rebuilt redundant equipment for critical operations such as this. Redundancy gives you added value of greater assurance for your customers. With redundancy, you cannot be unresponsive to your customers unless catastrophic failures occur with both pieces of equipment at the same time. That is an unlikely occurrence. However, the main roadblock to duplicate equipment is the capital cost involved for initial purchase and the continuing maintenance upkeep. We designed our Smart User Group to offer critical support for customers who are too small to justify the purchase of new or rebuilt redundant equipment.

CUSTOMER: How does the Smart User Group work?

SERVICE: Smart User customers are organized into a network that owns a small piece of redundant equipment. This situation, for example, would be one of those conditions where it would be an advantage for you to own a portion of some additional productive equipment. Now, for example, you could call on that productive capacity to support this urgent shipment.

CUSTOMER: Who maintains this productive capacity?

SERVICE: We do. All customers in the network pay for a portion of the machinery. We try always to keep some salable production running on the (product) in order to minimize the program's operating costs. However, the (product) is mainly available as emergency backup to all of the customers in the network.

CUSTOMER: How do I know productive capacity will be available for me when I need it?

SERVICE: Nothing is totally perfect, including the network. But it is better than nothing for those customers who cannot afford redundant systems. All customers in the network are on maintenance contract. Further, we constantly track who is using the backup and how it is being used. As the network grows, we add productive capacity. All load against the network is tracked, and trend lines are constantly plotted. Again, nothing is perfect. But offering some assurance to your customers is better than offering none at all.

CUSTOMER: I want to know more about how this works.

SERVICE: I'll call our sales representative and ask him to get in here first thing tomorrow morning. That way you will have all the information you need when you call on your customer.

FINDING AND QUALIFYING A WARM LEAD

This scenario assumes the service representative is giving the customer a follow-up report at the conclusion of preventive maintenance. The service representative decides to take advantage of the opportunity to determine if the customer is considering additional purchases.

SERVICE: I wanted to stop by and give you a brief update before I left. The (product) is in good shape; it's obvious your people care for it well. Today I performed standard preventive maintenance procedures. Further, I took the opportunity to do some additional training for your new operator, Jackson. Your people have done an excellent job; he is already well trained. I just filled in a few small gaps and answered a few remaining questions he had.

CUSTOMER: Great. I'm glad we're doing something right. Thanks for stopping by.

SERVICE: Glad to help, and thank you for the confidence in us. I couldn't help but notice all the work piling up over in department 27. It looks like your business is booming.

CUSTOMER: It sure is. This is turning into a banner year for us.

Words like these suggest the customer has a potential buying attitude.

SERVICE: The (product) is running at capacity and has provided (number) years of service. You already have received an excellent payback on your initial investment. However, maintenance requirements will be increasing in the near-term future. This booming business cycle may offer an excellent opportunity for you to consider investing in additional capacity.

CUSTOMER: We have been discussing capacity constraints around here. A breakdown leading to significant downtime would cause us serious problems.

SERVICE: I agree. It would. I'll discuss all this with Judy. She will be up here next week, and I'll ask her to make a call on you to further discuss some additional benefits we are now building into new versions of the (product).

CUSTOMER: That might be worthwhile. Thanks.

Don't just tell Judy about the lead. Share specific details. Share how you positioned the lead. Discuss with Judy how you brought up the subject of return on investment and so forth. As Judy assumes responsibility for the sales call, the customer should see a seamless transition between you and her.

HANDLING THE UNEXPECTED SUPER-HOT LEAD

The service representative is completing a maintenance procedure on site. The customer comes over to talk and, unexpectedly, drops a super-hot lead on the service technician.

CUSTOMER: (Approaching the work site.) How is everything going over here?

SERVICE: Good. I resolved the problem; it was in the (component). I'm just cycling, testing, and fine-tuning things. You are up and running, and I should be out of here in thirty minutes or less.

CUSTOMER: Great. Glad everything is okay. But, look, there is something I need from you. I know our salesman, Bill, is on vacation. However, I need some sales help now. I'm finishing negotiations on a major new contract and need to expand my production capacity quickly. This deal I'm working on just came up, and it's hot. It will go, and I'm committing myself to a very aggressive delivery schedule. Currently, I do not have enough capacity, even working three shifts. What are you currently quoting for delivery on (product)? What options do you recommend for me? Before you answer, assume I am going to be performing (list of operations). What is your current pricing? What is your current leasing program?

Do not say you don't have the answers. This customer wants to buy now, and it is important to maintain control. It is always to your advantage to focus on the positive side, discussing what you know. Discussing your limitations and tilting toward them can damage the confidence the customer has in you and your company.

SERVICE: Congratulations on the new contract! I'm certain we can help you with the expansion. Let me finish this test and turn this (product) back over to production. Then I will get on the phone and get some details resolved immediately for you.

CUSTOMER: I need answers now.

SERVICE: And I intend to get them for you. I'm scheduled to be elsewhere. However, the schedule was created before this came up. As I said, I intend to get the answers you need right now. I am finishing up here and will call in immediately. Which phone should I use? Let me talk to my office people for about half an hour and get some current details. I will come to your office at (specific time) and let you know what I have learned, especially on current deliveries, since that number changes continuously.

CUSTOMER: Okay. But, I need answers now, not when Bill returns.

SERVICE: Let me get on the phone.

If possible, find a quiet space to talk on the phone. You will need to convey a strong sense of urgency, and you don't want your customer overhearing you *persuading* your people to move quickly.

SERVICE: (Talking to boss.) I am at (customer's name). Management just came over to me and told me they need to buy from us right now. They just nailed a giant deal and desperately need additional productive capacity. They need specific and immediate answers on pricing, delivery, option content we recommend, and so forth. I don't know all the answers. Bill is their sales rep, but he is on vacation.

SERVICE MANAGER: That sounds like a sales responsibility. You have got to get to the next service call. (Customer 2) is down right now and needs your help. Tell them thanks for the interest and that Bill will get back in touch with them.

Just because the boss speaks, that does not make his or her position correct. That does not mean he or she automatically understands, either. It is not unusual for all of us, including the boss, to be "internally focused." Your boss is focused on the service problems, not the sales problem you found. Maybe he or she shouldn't be so narrowly focused, but no one said the boss was perfect. You must change the boss's focus by selling him or her on the urgency of your situation and the ramifications for the company. You must paint a verbal picture of your position.

SERVICE: I know I am needed at (customer 2). However, I am needed here, too. We have a big order at stake, and our service reputation is on the line. I can see it clearly: this guy is desperate. He knows Bill is on vacation. However, he landed this deal now, which forces his need for an immediate purchase. He needs information and needs it now. If I walk out, he will certainly go ballistic, and I sure couldn't blame him. I'm certain he will complain to the higher ups. Count on it: our top-floor management is going to hear about this one, one way or another. If we do this right, we in service get positive strokes for moving the dinosaur and making something happen. If I walk out of here and blow this off now, our top-floor guys and the entire sales force are going to be trashing us in service big time, and we would deserve it. They will all know it was me and you that missed this ball. I've got to do something for this guy. I'll bet that if we don't act right now, this guy calls the president before the day is out. He is going to tell the president we in service are turning down sales.

Customer service must challenge the boss to think and understand the urgency involved, and this can be done without being insubordinate. It is the service representative on site who feels the urgency, not the supervisor. The service representative must convey that sense of urgency and red-flag the boss to take action. To get attention, embellish your position as necessary, but not so much that you lose credibility. Carefully send a message that your boss will be embarrassed along with the total service organization.

SERVICE MANAGER: I am not really up the curve on all that new product pricing information and other stuff. We don't have current delivery information in the office, either.

SERVICE: Try getting the regional sales manager on the phone with us. I have got to stay on the line. Just as soon as I get off, I've got to give this guy a report with hard answers.

SERVICE MANAGER: Okay, hold the line.

There is now a three-way call. The field service representative takes the lead, since he or she is the one on site with all the urgency. Service should repeat and describe the on-site situation for the sales manager.

SERVICE: . . . So, we have got to do something quickly. This guy needs answers today.

SALES MANAGER: Great job on getting our attention. I think you're right. We have to give this thing a priority. Let me check our status and fax our current delivery situation. I'll also fax you some sales information and include some options we usually recommend for his situation. Tell him we are tentatively holding a slot in the delivery schedule for him; I will circle his slot on the schedule I fax to you. This general strategy should cool things down a bit and buy us a few days. Avoid getting into a price debate with him. I want to be in that discussion. I can't be there tomorrow, but tell him I will be there day after tomorrow, and we can discuss final pricing and leasing packages at that time. To gain a few days, keep reinforcing the fact that we are holding a delivery for him. What's your fax number? Or give me his on-line address, and we will e-mail the information you need directly to his computer.

The service representative should get the fax number or e-mail box number from the customer's receptionist and get the literature in hand. Then service should report back to the customer.

SERVICE: (To customer.) I've got great news. We have a delivery slot available. See this schedule? Your (product) is now scheduled for delivery on this date. I talked to the sales manager and service manager, and they fixed that date in place. Further, I had the office fax literature, which includes option configuration. This list includes the options we currently recommend for your type of application.

CUSTOMER: Can I lease from you? For me cash is short. What is your current pricing and what about financing programs?

Tip: Focus on what you can answer. Avoid what you cannot answer, but do not proclaim ignorance.

SERVICE: Our sales manager, Judy, wants to get involved to make sure our recommendations on options are okay before she calculates the final price for you. She wants to use her experience to confirm the actual configuration you need. She understands how urgent this is and has rearranged her schedule to be here day after tomorrow, in the afternoon. At that time, she can confirm the option content and pricing. She will also bring all the details on our leasing and financing programs. More importantly, however, none of this impacts your production requirements, as we are holding a delivery position for you now. All you need do is resolve the final details with Judy.

CUSTOMER: Thanks for all the help.

SELLING A SERVICE CONTRACT

The service representative is working overtime to repair a residential furnace. The failure was complete, leaving the customer without heat. Plunging outside temperatures forced the customer to ask for and pay premium overtime rates, the only way the customer could ensure a service call before nightfall. The service representative arrived one hour ago and has diagnosed the problem. The concerned customer is, understandably, shadowing the service representative.

SERVICE: I believe we have this pinned down to a broken white lead from the thermostat. Red and white shows an open circuit. However, connecting blue and red shows solid continuity. We will run blue-red to the furnace, and that should resolve this problem. You should have heat again in about thirty minutes.

CUSTOMER: Sounds good to me. I'm just glad we have the unused blue lead running back to the thermostat. I would hate to see you running new leads at this late hour.

SERVICE: Sorry I couldn't get here earlier. It's the beginning of the heating season, and we are flooded with calls. Our contract customers get priority. Do you have a contract with us?

It is always a good idea to seize any opportunity to probe for a sale. The customer is shadowing the service representative, and the discussion can proceed while the service technician completes work on the heating unit.

CUSTOMER: No.

SERVICE: You should consider one. There are several advantages.

CUSTOMER: Like what?

SERVICE: As I mentioned, all people on service contract get priority service. Their problems move to the top of the list. Further, there are no overtime charges. If we must work overtime, it is all at straight-time rates.

CUSTOMER: That might be worth something. What are the rates?

SERVICE: I have all the paper work in my car. I'll get it as soon as I finish here. In addition to no overtime charges, contract customers have a guaranteed same-day response. Further, we come out and clean your heating units annually and get them ready for the heating season. We look things over and try to anticipate problems before they occur. We don't want situations such as this to happen.

CUSTOMER: Could you have anticipated and prevented this?

SERVICE: Frankly, probably not. A broken wire is tough to predict. However, we might have been able to shorten the diagnosis time.

CUSTOMER: How so?

SERVICE: This is the first time I have seen this installation. I had to check and confirm operation of valves, relays, and transformers. If we had a maintenance contract on this installation, I would have been here earlier to do a preseason system check. If all of those important components checked out okay a few weeks ago, then I probably would have invested far less time checking them out today.

CUSTOMER: That sounds reasonable.

SERVICE: The contract does pay off for you. That is especially true when you consider the flue and boiler cleaning, which we do at the beginning of each season. Most people only call for service when something goes wrong. The flue can clog, allowing carbon monoxide gas to escape into the house. The potential for a serious accident is there.

CUSTOMER: You make a good case. Let's review the contract and pricing.

SERVICE: Thanks for your interest. You won't be disappointed.

SALESPERSON OVERPROMISED

You have installed a system that enables the customer to transfer orders direct to your central computer. While training the customer in correct operations, he or she tells you the salesperson has promised more than the system will apparently deliver. Your role is to defuse the situation and build customer satisfaction without attacking the salesperson.

CUSTOMER: But I thought the (product) allowed me to produce inventory control reports in any format I choose.

SERVICE: There is considerable built-in flexibility. The (product) allows you to choose from seven general report formats. Additionally, each format can be further modified to fit your specific requirements.

Accentuate the positive and try to avoid a confrontation, if possible.

CUSTOMER: Your salesperson told me I could develop any report format I wanted.

You do not need to accept the comment as stated, nor do you need to address the exact issue introduced by the customer. Do not take sides with either the customer or the salesperson. Getting into a discussion of: "he said/she said" is always unproductive. Work around the direct attack on the salesperson by focusing on the here and now. Stay on the positive side, discussing what you can accomplish for the customer.

SERVICE: We certainly do have a lot of flexibility. Do you have some sample report formats here that you would like the (product) to produce? I'm sure I can duplicate them for you.

CUSTOMER: Even if you can, suppose I want to do something completely different in the future? The salesperson said I could do anything I wanted to do.

The customer may try to draw you into a debate. Focus on the work at hand. Be nurturing.

SERVICE: All systems have some limitations. Right now we need to get the (product) to produce the reports you need as quickly as possible. At our other installations, customers have found more than enough flexibility in the structure of report formats. Let me show you how easily this works. Where can I get some sample reports the (product) will have to produce for you?

CUSTOMER: But your salesperson said I had infinite flexibility with formats.

SERVICE: "Infinite flexibility" seems a bit strong. Let's try to set up one of your more complex existing formats.

You must get to work on setting up the reports. If the customer continues to focus on the flexibility issue, you will need to acknowledge something. Acknowledging his or her position as noted above is probably safe. You are not agreeing or disagreeing with the customer about what the salesperson did or did not say. Keep pushing the idea of getting the system working now.

CUSTOMER: But I still feel cheated. I was promised infinite flexibility.

Be nurturing to build confidence.

SERVICE: We will stand behind the product, and I am confident of our ability to produce the reports you need. The best way to demonstrate the (product's) flexibility, is for me to produce a report for you. We can discuss any additional needed flexibility after we first determine the current system's limitations, if any. We need to move on and get the (product) working for you. Who should I contact to get some sample report formats, so that we can move forward?

The service technician sent a signal suggesting he or she may need to go elsewhere to get the information needed. Sending a signal that you intend to get the sample reports elsewhere should be enough to get this customer moving toward completion of the task at hand.

CUSTOMER: I don't think we can move forward until we get the issue of infinite flexibility resolved. I need assurances that the base software will be modified so that I have the promised flexibility to produce any report I want.

If the customer becomes a bottleneck, find a way around the issue for now. You must move ahead.

SERVICE: I am attempting to demonstrate the flexibility you need. I can't comment on software limitations unless I locate them. Our respective companies need this (product) up and running as quickly as possible to reduce costs for both of our organizations. For now, let's set the issue of report formats aside. We need to get some orders placed with the new system now. That will start producing immediate savings for both companies and ensure the system works smoothly. More importantly, it will further ensure your raw materials orders will be in place. I'm sure you agree our respective managers, at minimum, expect us to get the orders placed. I will then produce some sample inventory reports and modify them as needed. If there are problems with the report layouts, it will then be apparent, and I will be able to address those problems. I'll get over to the order-entry department and get things rolling.

CUSTOMER: Okay. But I will still insist on infinite flexibility in report formatting.

SERVICE: Great. Let's go to the purchasing desk and make something happen.

About all you can hope for is to get around the obvious bottleneck and start working with your product and produce results. Many of these bottlenecks disappear as your product flexibility and usefulness is demonstrated.

SALESPERSON DOES NOT SHOW FOR SCHEDULED DEMONSTRATION

CUSTOMER: Where is John? He told me he would be here during this presentation.

SERVICE: I don't know. John was scheduled to be here, and I did not receive any messages suggesting otherwise. Where is the nearest phone? I can check my messages again.

Be up front, honest but objective. Lying to cover John's absence will probably not be effective. Throwing bricks at John would not be helpful, either.

SERVICE: (After checking messages.) Still, there are no messages from John. This is strange. I really don't know what happened. Suppose we just forge ahead and start going over the system? Hopefully, he is just temporarily delayed and will arrive as we get started.

CUSTOMER: No, I would rather wait. I had several things to discuss with John before we start. You know, you just can't trust those salespeople to keep promises.

It is best not to participate in the jabbing. Putting John down also puts you and your company down.

SERVICE: Perhaps I can handle those outstanding issues.

CUSTOMER: No, my concerns deal with promises made between me and John. I would rather wait for him to arrive.

SERVICE: Sure. Let me quickly check the sales office to see if they have any messages from him.

CUSTOMER: Okay.

SERVICE: (After contacting the office.) This makes no sense at all. John has not called into the office with any problems, either. I did leave a message and explained we are waiting. I left this phone number for him.

While there is no reason to lie and cover for John, there is no reason to persecute him either. Stick with the facts and state them simply. Degrading John in the customer's eyes will do nothing to create satisfaction or enhance your image. However, an empathy statement is appropriate.

SERVICE: I really am sorry this has happened, and it is unusual. This is not representative of our company's commitment to the customer. Unfortunately, things do not always work as planned, and I do hope everything is okay with John.

Let's proceed and hope for the best. What did John promise? I can either resolve your concerns or get them resolved through the office or through John later on. Again, I am sorry this has happened.

Keep it positive and upbeat. Keep things focused on the product and the task at hand, not on John's behavior.

CUSTOMER: John promised (list of items A through F).

SERVICE: I can confirm that (A, B, C) will occur. Let me make some notes on (D, E, F). I want to make sure I get your understanding correct. I will need to check these out. While I can't guarantee a total resolution within two days, either John or I will get back to you on these matters with a status report.

Be careful with your choice of words. There is a difference between evaluating information correctly and agreeing with the customer that "John promised" something. When clarifying the perceived promise made, be certain to focus on information-gathering with your questions. Get information, but avoid agreeing with the customer. Also it is critical that you get back to the customer within two days as promised, with or without the final solution.

CUSTOMER WANTS TO BUY, YOU'RE NOT QUALIFIED TO SELL

You have completed maintenance or repair on your (product) and are giving a final report to the manager before leaving the site for your next call:

CUSTOMER: Thanks. I really appreciate your support on that (product). Our sales have been growing consistently, and we are experiencing bottlenecks in our production operations. Recently we have been discussing the purchase of another new (product) manufactured by you folks. Tell me, does it have the capacity to do (list)?

SERVICE: It is designed for your purpose, and I believe it is a fit. However, because I do not sell the (product) daily, I am not qualified to discuss its complete applicability. Let me gather some information on what you are trying to do. I can get additional support on this.

It is never a good idea to stretch your knowledge of applications, since there are always problems when products are misapplied. Dissatisfied customers are the typical end result. You can, however, still move this sale closer to a successful conclusion. Be sure to take notes!

SERVICE: (After questioning and note-taking on the specific application at hand.) This helps. I have a pretty good understanding of what you are trying to accomplish. Now I need to do some homework. I'll send you literature on this (product). I will also share my notes with your salesperson, Susan Jones. Either Susan or I will be back in touch with you by (date). Even if we do not have a complete answer and recommendation, we will give you a progress report. Is this an acceptable plan?

CUSTOMER: That sounds great.

Be sure to follow up with your salesperson, and be very specific about the agreements you have made, especially the promise for the follow-up call. You made the commitment, which was the right thing to do, and you must make certain the follow-up occurs as planned, even if the final recommendations are not completed by the promised date. It would be best for the salesperson to make that follow-up call. It remains your responsibility, however, to sell the salesperson on the importance of keeping the commitment.

SERVICE: (To Judy Jones.) I wanted to let you know about what happened at (customer name). I was there working on (product), and (customer name) asked me about our (new product).

JUDY: Sounds great to me. Do you think they are seriously interested?

SERVICE: Yeah, it's real. They are experiencing good growth and running into capacity constraints. Judy, they asked me several questions, which I could not answer. Specifically, they needed to know how the (new product) would handle (list of issues).

JUDY: That list is not so bad. We can address all of that.

SERVICE: That's what I told them. Here's where I left things: I told the customer I could not address all of the issues, but that I would find the answers. The customer was obviously interested in action, so I mentioned either you or I would get back to him or her by (date), even if we had not resolved all of the questions. Are you going to be able to grab the ball and run with this?

JUDY: My calendar is okay on the date you promised. No problem.

SERVICE: Super. About the customer's questions, give me some background on what the answers might be. Some feedback on your overall strategy would help, too. I usually go in there once per week or so, and I want to be prepared to support you if I get hit with more questions.

JUDY: Good thinking. I'm going to say . . .

Tip: Make periodic contacts with your salesperson about this sale and keep informed of the progress. Effective servicing is effective marketing.

SURVEYING AND ASSESSING: YOU SUSPECT YOU ARE BEING CHEATED

You service equipment such as copy machinery, x-ray machinery, part-making machinery, and so on. Your service contract is based on usage, and your prices increase as the equipment usage increases. The equipment has an automatic cycle counter. While doing preventive maintenance, you notice the counter has been rolled back. Someone on site is cheating, but you can't prove it. What should you do? Let's assume you are just closing out the call with the manager:

SERVICE: I have completed the preventive maintenance, and everything looks good.

CUSTOMER: Great; thanks for stopping by.

SERVICE: I want to make you aware of one irregularity I discovered.

Be careful with your position and the words you use. Do not accuse the customer of violating the service contract, if nothing can be proven. Further, the individual you are talking with may be involved in the scam. You do, however, want to signal the customer that you are aware the scam is under way. "I want to make you aware" is a good neutral phrase. Your purpose is to leverage the minimum knowledge you have into maximum power.

CUSTOMER: What's that?

SERVICE: From experience, I can judge approximately how many copies have been created with the (product). Under normal running conditions, each individual cycle produces extra powder, which builds up in the fusion system. Keeping the fusion system clean is a major portion of our service agreement. On this call, the fusion system was very dirty, indicating a heavy usage rate, say in the tens of thousands of copies. A notation on my service report of the current cycle count is required for every maintenance call. When I compared the current count to the count taken last quarter, it indicated only several thousand copies have been run through the system. It really didn't make any sense. I even went back and checked the past several reports, and for some reason, this quarter count was extremely low. Yet the condition of the machine clearly indicated the count should have been higher.

State your observation without accusing.

CUSTOMER: What are you suggesting?

SERVICE: The condition of the machine suggests many cycles have been completed, yet the cycle counter indicates only a few cycles have been.

CUSTOMER: Well, maybe the counter is faulty, or maybe the machine just dumped extra powder.

SERVICE: This maintenance call has been quite routine. Everything is functioning properly. Only cleaning was needed, because of the heavy usage.

CUSTOMER: Are you implying someone has tampered with the counter?

SERVICE: I don't know why or how this occurred. I am making you aware of it, because, as manager, you should have knowledge of what I observed.

CUSTOMER: Well, let me assure you, there is no possibility anyone has tampered with the counter. We have no cheaters around here.

SERVICE: I would hope not. I just wanted to make you aware of my observation. I will note the irregularity and our discussion on my service report.

CUSTOMER: What does that mean?

SERVICE: We keep comprehensive histories of our manufactured equipment, its usage, and all important observations. We also note all irregularities or other unusual events on our reports. The database enables us to track trends and find ways to improve our business and our customer service.

CUSTOMER: You can note anything you want. However, be sure to note that no one tampered with that counter.

SERVICE: As I mentioned earlier, I will note that you and I discussed my observations. Thanks again. Be sure to call if any questions or problems arise. Otherwise, see you next quarter.

This is about all you can do. But you have accomplished a lot. You did not accuse the customer of any wrongdoing. You did, however, inform the customer of your observations, and he or she is now aware the scam is noticeable by you and others on your team. You also advised the customer your observations will be recorded for future reference. If the customer continues to tamper with the equipment, it is probably wise to end the relationship. Just allow the service contract to expire and do not renew. It is never a good idea to escalate the confrontation with accusations, even if they can be proved.

The Customer Is a Thief

The customer claims the item was purchased last week by others and the sales receipt was accidentally thrown out. You, however, know the product has been stolen, because it is a store exclusive item, new to your department, having just been placed on display this morning.

CUSTOMER: I would like to return this, please. My wife bought it, and it does not fit.

SERVICE: All right. When was it purchased?

CUSTOMER: Last week.

SERVICE: Do you have your sales receipt?

CUSTOMER: No, I'm sorry. It was accidentally thrown out.

SERVICE: I'm sorry. May I have your credit card, please? I will credit your store account the full retail price.

This works to your advantage. If the person wanted the product, he and the product would already be gone. He actually wants the cash, and is trying to return the product for cash. This works to your advantage another way as well: The thief probably does not have an open account with your store.

CUSTOMER: My wife paid cash for this (product), and I would like a cash refund.

SERVICE: I'm terribly sorry, but I can only refund cash when I have a sales receipt. When the sales receipt is lost, I can only credit your store account.

CUSTOMER: *What?* That is the most screwed-up rule I ever heard! The law says I can have my money back, and I demand cash immediately: Right now!

Continue to express limited authority, always focusing on what you can do.

SERVICE: Sir, I can only refund cash if you have a cash receipt. But I can fully credit your store account.

CUSTOMER: Outrageous! Just outrageous! I have never heard of anything so absurd in my life. I insist on a cash refund immediately. My wife purchased with cash, and I want cash now!

SERVICE: I'm sure she did, sir. I am sorry, but I can only refund cash with a sales receipt that shows a cash purchase. Perhaps your wife can help you find the receipt.

CUSTOMER (as he stomps away with the product): I have never been so humiliated in my life. Never have I been treated with such poor service! I will never shop in this store again, and I intend to tell my friends to stay away as well. I intend to make a full report to the Better Business Bureau.

Your behavior will not make the customer happy. However, you are not in business to satisfy thieves. Hiding behind a policy or procedure is obviously good practice in a case such as this, when you are attempting to thwart the thief's efforts. It is unlikely the thief will go to your store manager. If he does, be certain your manager is aware the product has been stolen. In this situation, by only crediting store accounts, you at least ensure your out-of-pocket losses are, at maximum, the cost of the merchandise, not the full retail sales price, including taxes. Confronting the thief directly and taking legal action is a security matter and should not be done without support from store security personnel.

SAFETY FEATURE DEACTIVATED: CUSTOMER COOPERATIVE

SERVICE: (Speaking to a supervisor at the customer site.) I noticed as we walked by (product B) that the safety interlock on (feature) was disconnected. I would like to reconnect it for you.

A personal approach will be more effective. "I would like to reconnect it for you" will sell better than, "I must reconnect it" or "Our policy says I must reconnect it."

CUSTOMER: Yeah. The operators got tired of having to push both buttons for every cycle. The interlock made things run too slowly, and they asked our maintenance staff to disconnect it.

SERVICE: Having to push both buttons may slow production; however, it certainly is a lot safer. The (safety feature) forces the operator to keep both hands away from the cutting zone and eliminates the chance for human error. I really would like to reconnect it for you.

CUSTOMER: If you do, they'll just disconnect it again.

SERVICE: This is better for all of us. Thanks, I will reconnect the (feature).

Service should go back to the supervisor after the device is reconnected.

SERVICE: Sir, we recommend management prohibit operators from disconnecting the (feature), even if they complain about the inconvenience. If someone were hurt, your company might be held liable for negligence. Perhaps individual supervisors could be held liable as well. Someone could argue that management allowed, and even encouraged, operators to work in a dangerous environment. If management is aware the (feature) has been disconnected, and it has not done anything about it, then it could be argued that management is participating in and supporting dangerous working conditions.

CUSTOMER: You have a point, I guess. Thanks.

SAFETY FEATURE DEACTIVATED: CUSTOMER UNCOOPERATIVE

SERVICE: (Speaking to the customer's management.) I noticed as we walked by the (product B?) that the (safety device) was disconnected. I would like to reactivate it for you before I leave.

Just stick with the observable facts. It is obvious that management knows the safety device is not operating, so it is probably best to avoid a discussion of how the device came to be disconnected.

CUSTOMER: Oh, that's okay. The staff is careful with that machine. They are quite experienced and don't need all that stuff. Leave it running as is.

SERVICE: We, like you, are very concerned about operator safety, and we really can't leave that interlock disconnected.

Using "we" in this context builds your authority level. "We" suggests the issue is larger than you or this particular individual at the customer's site, which is exactly the message you want to send.

CUSTOMER: Everything is okay. Just leave it as it is. They will just disconnect it again anyway. Besides, you did not come here to work on that (product).

SERVICE: It's true that I did not come here to work on that (product). However, it does carry our brand name, and I did notice the safety device disconnected. I do need to reconnect the interlock.

CUSTOMER: It's our system and our responsibility. Leave it as it is.

SERVICE: I understand, and I agree that this is your (product). But I must protect myself and my company from unnecessary liability exposure, and you should know what we must do to protect our own interests. I must note in my service report that the (safety device) on the (product) is disconnected and that you and I discussed the issue. I must explain that I offered to reconnect the device and that my offer was refused. Our service manager and safety director will send you a letter explaining the significant hazards and risks for your operators being caused by this unsafe equipment. They will further recommend you reconsider your position. My management usually waits a couple of weeks for you to contact them. If they do not hear from you, they will send a similar letter to your company owners explaining our recommendations. We keep the letters in our files and send copies to our attorneys. If in the future, and we certainly hope this never occurs, someone is involved in an accident and our company is named as a party in a negligence case, we will use the letters to demonstrate that we were operating in good faith and made you aware of the risks you were incurring.

CUSTOMER: That sounds pretty pompous. This is our (product) and our work site. You do not have the right to threaten me with your lawyers.

SERVICE: I have no means or power to issue threats, and I'm not trying to threaten you or anyone. I can't in any way issue threats, because you are totally correct: this is your (product) and your work site. I am, however, trying to give you information and am only trying to keep you informed. Because we are design experts on this system, we have certain responsibilities. Those safety interlocks are required by our safety engineers, and they are clearly not working right now. We would be negligent and naive if we did not protect ourselves against unnecessary liability exposure. You are our customer, and you have a right to know what we must do.

At this point, the customer would most likely allow you to reconnect the safety devices. If the customer continues to refuse, implement your plan. No sane person risks liability exposure in this litigious age. Safety and negligence are serious matters in all developed markets. It is probable this person will be reprimanded or dismissed when the company owners receive your letters.

INSTALLATION ISSUES

Confirming Preinstallation Before Dispatching Service

This scenario assumes you are responsible for the actual installation. However, the customer is required to have everything ready for the installation. Specifically, the customer is to have water, air, and power available to the equipment for your hook-up before calling you. The scenario assumes the equipment has been shipped. As prearranged with the customer, the equipment is to be unpacked and all utilities should be in place before calling for final installation procedures.

CUSTOMER: (Calling on the phone.) I wanted to make contact and schedule your people in for the installation.

SERVICE: Sounds great. Let's look at the schedule board. We can get someone there on (date). How does that sound?

CUSTOMER: It sounds good to me.

Tip: Make the commitment and give the customer a date before going through your check procedure.

SERVICE: While I have you on the phone, can I have a few minutes to go through our preinstallation procedures?

CUSTOMER: What's a preinstallation procedure?

SERVICE: I just want to check a few details to be certain that everything is okay before our technician arrives. I need to check and see if we need to bring anything and confirm that we will be able to complete the entire installation.

CUSTOMER: I said we are ready.

SERVICE: Yes, and we have you on the schedule. Can you confirm that (volts) of electrical power is available on a dedicated line?

CUSTOMER: Yes.

SERVICE: Is the circuit breaker box within fifteen feet?

CUSTOMER: Yes. What difference does it make?

SERVICE: We need to be certain the power . . .

Continue the checklist. Have your specific questions written out in advance. Be brief, and make notes. Offer explanations only when the customer asks specific questions.

SERVICE: That is the entire list. Sounds like you have everything ready for us. Let's confirm our notes. To summarize, then, everything is okay, and all that remains for you to run is the air supply. Bring a 3/4-inch hard line, and secure it to within three feet of the pneumatic manifold block located at the (product's) rear. Run a 5/8-inch flex line to the manifold itself. Be sure we have 30 psi at the manifold block.

CUSTOMER: That's what we discussed, and I'll get it done.

SERVICE: We will need that supply available on (date) when we arrive to install. Can you get it in by then?

CUSTOMER: Sure can.

SERVICE: Thanks.

Assuming you have not worked with the customer frequently, you may wish to make one more call to confirm the utility has been run before you are scheduled to depart for the installation. If your history with this customer is a good one, the additional call can probably be skipped.

Confirming Full Installation Before Dispatching Service

You have shipped the product to the customer's site, and the customer is responsible for constructing the foundation as well as hooking up utility requirements, such as electrical power, air, and/or water. Standard procedure is that the customer calls, asking for service to dispatch a technician to supervise the product startup and conduct operator training when installation is complete. Service must confirm the installation has been performed correctly.

CUSTOMER ONE: (On phone.) We need a service representative to assist us in the startup of the (product).

SERVICE: Great. I'm glad to get you on the schedule. We're anxious to start producing results for you.

Sell value enthusiastically every chance you get. There is always a payoff.

CUSTOMER ONE: We're anxious, too.

SERVICE: I currently have you scheduled for (date). I would also like to review a checklist of some preinstallation procedures. Can we do that now? Can you confirm that certain specific tasks have been accomplished for me?

CUSTOMER ONE: I'm in purchasing and am involved with vendor scheduling. Our technical people have confirmed to me that everything has been completed as required. All your instructions have been followed.

SERVICE: Could I have the name and number of the lead technician handling the project? I would like to call him or her, do a phone review, and discuss how the installation went.

It is unlikely that purchasing or other administrative types will be able to help you with the technical specifics.

CUSTOMER ONE: As I said, our technical people have confirmed that everything is completed and ready for you. They asked me to schedule your technician in for startup.

Defensiveness is not uncommon: fiefdoms still do exist among us humans. You will need to get around this individual without discounting him or her.

SERVICE: Great. We have someone scheduled for you. As I mentioned, our people will be there on (date). I would still like to talk to the technicians who actually completed the work. We always seek perfection, yet things still go wrong no matter how effectively everything is confirmed before the (product) is shipped. Also, some minor thing may have gone wrong during installation. Perhaps something was overlooked; perhaps even a small part is damaged or missing. Your technicians might be assuming our people, when they arrive on site, will always be prepared to correct these small eventualities. They would be correct; our technical people can fix any number of small things most of the time. However, there is that rare occasion when things go wrong, and they do not have what they need. In those instances, technicians call us from your location, everyone must scramble, emergency shipments must take place, and we all live with confusion and delay as costs soar. Both of us must explain poor efficiency and poor planning to our respective management teams. A minor error, which can easily be corrected now over the phone, may require us to repeat the entire trip. It just makes good sense to confirm as much detail as possible with a phone review before our technical support people actually arrive.

CUSTOMER ONE: I see your point. (Customer two) is the lead technician on this project and is responsible for all installation procedures. His phone number is (number).

SERVICE: Let me repeat that. The spelling of his name is (spelling), and his phone number is (number).

CUSTOMER ONE: Correct.

SERVICE: Let me call him and perform a technical review. I will get back to you with a status report after our discussion. For now, let's assume our scheduled date for on-site startup is firm. I will let you know if there are any necessary changes in the schedule. Thanks for calling, and I will be back to you in a few days.

Suggesting the follow-up call helps this individual save face and that is a good enough reason to make the call. There is no value in putting this administrative person down by freezing him out of the communications loop. He may not be able to help you technically. However, he did initiate the contact, and he will be able to help you in some future capacity. This scenario continues with service contacting customer two.

SERVICE: (Customer two), we have been scheduled to come in for startup. Purchasing advises installation is complete.

CUSTOMER TWO: Yes. That's what we told them to say.

SERVICE: We have scheduled technical support into your location on (date), and we're looking forward to working with you. To make sure startup works as planned, I would like to review the installation with you.

CUSTOMER TWO: We're all ready for you. Everything went fine.

SERVICE: Thanks. I would like to have a telephone review to confirm some specifics. It will take about thirty minutes or so. I just want to make sure everything went according to plan.

Ask for permission to conduct the review. Don't just launch into the discussion, assuming the customer will give you thirty minutes.

CUSTOMER TWO: I don't really have thirty minutes. We followed all the instructions you provided and performed all preliminary checks. Everything is ready to go for you.

SERVICE: I realize looking over details will take time. I am relying on past experience. We install about one (product) per week. Far too often a very small thing has been overlooked, and the entire startup trip needs to be scrubbed and rescheduled. The (product) will produce a lot of value for you. It is also complex. Perhaps something was overlooked in our final checkout procedures. Perhaps one of your people missed a technical detail. Maybe an important specification or instruction was lost in shipping, and your personnel do not even know they were supposed to do something. My experience teaches me that a telephone review can help us find small, unforeseen but, at times, important problems. If we can uncover them now, our technician will arrive on site ready to resolve them immediately, saving valuable time for both of us. Is there a better time in the next few days for me to get back to you?

CUSTOMER TWO: There is no good time. Let's go ahead now. Fire away with your questions.

SERVICE: I have (number) questions to review. Did you do (specific installation procedure A), and did the system do (output)?

CUSTOMER TWO: Yes, we did that, and the system performed correctly, producing (output). Why did you ask?

SERVICE: Because if the (product) does (output B), it might be indicating a possible problem with (installation procedure A).

Be very specific, short, quick, and businesslike with your questions. Do not waste time. Only offer explanations for the various questions when the customer asks for it. Be descriptive when necessary. Note difficulties, but do not suggest that the customer made errors; avoid phrases such as, "You should not have done . . ."

SERVICE: Thanks. I really appreciate your making time for this review. Let me recap: we reviewed two faulty outputs, apparently produced during installation steps (number and number). These are minor. I will advise our technician, and we will simulate the faults in the lab, plan whatever fixes are needed, and be prepared when we arrive. There is no reason to change our current arrival schedule, and I will reconfirm with purchasing that we are on schedule as planned. If we run into difficulty with the lab simulation and need additional data, I will get back to you. If you do not hear from me, we will arrive as scheduled.

CUSTOMER TWO: Sounds great. We'll plan accordingly.

SERVICE: (On phone with customer one.) I just wanted to get back to you with the follow-up report I promised. The technical review has been completed, and we are still on the schedule you and I developed. We did identify two minor problems, but I am fairly certain we can get those resolved and still maintain our existing schedule. I have advised (customer 2) that if he or she does not hear from me, we will be arriving as currently scheduled. We will keep you informed of our progress as well.

CUSTOMER ONE: Thanks for the follow-up.

A brief letter confirming your plan would also be helpful. Address it to customer one with a copy sent to customer two. See my *The Complete Customer Service Model Letter and Memo Book* for some ready-to-use examples.

CUSTOMER HAS NOT INSTALLED PRODUCT CORRECTLY

This scenario started earlier when service first arrived on site. We assume that service has already talked with management and is now at the new installation site with an on-site technical manager. Service has inspected the installation and has observed several significant problem areas. There is no possible way service can perform initial check-out and start-up procedures. Service must discuss and resolve the problems with on-site technical management.

SERVICE: I've looked over the overall installation of the (product), and, generally speaking, things look pretty good.

CUSTOMER: Thanks. Our installation team really worked hard on that job.

SERVICE: And the effort clearly shows. This is a complex system. For a first effort, your team has done a great job.

The representative is proceeding cautiously, as he or she should. It is always a good practice to start with the positive side.

SERVICE: There are, however, a few adjustments needed. Are the installation drawings close by?

CUSTOMER: Adjustments? What's wrong? Our team went crazy trying to get everything right.

SERVICE: And they have done a great job. But this (product) is complex, and they have never installed it before. For a first effort, they have done a super job. Perhaps we could meet with the installation team. Using the installation diagrams, I can explain a few things that need correction.

CUSTOMER: Well, if there are only minor adjustments to make, why don't you just make them so we can get this going?

SERVICE: A few adjustments need be made. They are not necessarily complex, but they will consume a good amount of time. The time involved would exceed the current planned startup schedule and budget. On your project, installation was not part of the initial sale. Usually, users who choose to install the (product) without our support do so to develop in-house technical skills while holding down initial costs. However, I am sure we can change the initial agreement. If it is better to change the agreement and have us take over, I would recommend the following steps: First, I would call the office and discuss the requested change with my supervision. Second, I would create time estimates and budget to cover the necessary work. Third, after discussing the estimated budget with my supervision, and with your approval of the estimated budget, we would reschedule the installation and startup. Depending on current conditions in the field, we may be able to schedule additional time today. However, I cannot promise time today without first checking with the office.

Service must not imply the customer messed up the installation. However, middle ground must be found; for there is no reason for service to perform the additional work involved without compensation. Service needs to remind the customer of limits in the initial agreement as well as define and offer a solution to the new problem, all without creating an adversarial relationship with the customer. As suggested above, an effective method is to remind the customer why his or her management may have opted to perform the installation without your assistance in the first place.

CUSTOMER: I don't want to get into all of that. For now, let's stay with the initial plan that everyone agreed to. I'll call the installation team together for a meeting. You explain what must be done. We will correct the installation and then reschedule your startup.

With the installation team, just as noted in the above example, focus on the positive side of what was done well. Define specific things they must redo. Be certain to use the supplied documentation to demonstrate correct installation procedures.

UNCOOPERATIVE CUSTOMER TEAM STALLS INSTALLATION

You've got a serious problem with an installation that must be resolved with the cooperation of customer engineers on site. Unfortunately, Jim and Sue, two of six technicians involved in the project, neither work well together, nor even seem to like each other. Of course, neither Jim nor Sue works for you. They work for the customer. But they're still very much your problem, because you are responsible for this installation. Normally, you'd begin to resolve the technical difficulties at hand by calling a meeting involving yourself and the six technicians. In this scenario, however, do not begin by calling the meeting. It is almost certainly doomed to fail. Jim, Sue or, more likely, both will ensure the failure. For you and your company, failure would translate into inability to resolve technical problems; damage to your reputation or credibility; and on-site a product that may never perform well, since most high-technology equipment needs a "friend" on site who wants it to work effectively. Potential friends will want to stay away from both Jim and Sue. Instead of calling a meeting, visit with Jim and Sue individually.

SERVICE: Jim, we've got a problem with the installation I need to discuss with you. The problem is (description). How do you think we can handle this?

JIM: Well, I think we should do (Jim's idea). That does require Sue's cooperation and a resource commitment from her, however. I don't think she will support this idea, as she is already heavily committed to other goals.

SERVICE: That sounds like a reasonable approach. I'll discuss this approach with Sue. Thanks for your suggestions.

Service would then go to Sue with the same approach.

SERVICE: Sue, I would like to discuss a problem we have with the installation. The problem is (description). Jim suggested we might try (Jim's idea). How do you think we should handle this?

SUE: Jim's idea sounds reasonable. Unfortunately, the resources he is recommending we commit to a solution are all committed elsewhere. Another idea we could try is (Sue's idea). You may want to discuss this with Jim, since he would need to commit some of his resources. He may likely tell you that those resources are already committed, however. But I think it is worth a try.

Service should then go back to Jim and share Sue's idea. It is highly unlikely that running back and forth will resolve the technical problem, because you need all six engineers together. But take the step anyway. Without it, the general meeting will probably fail because Jim and Sue might start a useless argument. Running back and forth between Jim and Sue may require several discussions, which will consume time. You will be frustrated at times; but, then, whoever said customer service or resolving issues was easy? It is important to remember that your time and effort are being invested to ensure an effective meeting and a good solution. Sue may tell you how bad Jim is and vice versa. Listen, but don't agree, disagree, or in any way reinforce negative comments that one might make about the other. Instead, use neutral responses like "I see" or "uh huh." Then, as you go back and forth, continue to bear down on the technical problem, using such phrases as: "Jim, can you suggest how I might resolve . . .?" or, "Sue, do you feel we could get support if we . . .?" or, "Jim, do you have any ideas on how we could get through this problem more quickly?"

Your objective is to get one or, better, both of them to suggest that you call a meeting including all concerned parties. By getting one or both of them to initiate the meeting idea, you will reduce the name-calling that will likely occur later. After all, the meeting was their idea, not yours.

Planning the Meeting

You must have an agenda, which includes what you already know about the specific problem and whatever reasonable suggestions, if any, have been offered. The agenda should be in writing, using a bullet-list format. You might even consider defining specific time allotments for each topic. This meeting must be tightly controlled, because there are explosive personalities invited. However, the control comes not from you as a director, but from you as a facilitator, who focuses discussion on the issues at hand rather than the personalities involved. An effective agenda might include such written phrases as:

☎ The problem as it exists is having the negative effect of (description) on our ability to (description).

☎ Projections indicate we will not meet our assigned objective if we do not change direction.

☎ Several possible solutions have been suggested, and they are (list). All possible solutions impact all of us, and our purpose today is to discuss the pros and cons of each in order to reach consensus on which option is most acceptable to all departments and still enable us to meet our assigned goal of (description).

It is important that the assigned goal be specifically defined; keeping everyone focused on the goal will help you control the aggressive personalities in attendance.

Conducting the Meeting

Jim and Sue should not be permitted to sit directly across from each other, since this will only reinforce their adversarial relationship. Service must arrive at the meeting site first. If possible, secure a round table for the meeting. As people enter the room, Service controls the seating arrangements. The best situation would be for either Bill or Sue to sit to the immediate left of Service, while the other sits to the immediate right.

SERVICE: Cheryl, why don't you sit here? And we can put Bill in this seat. You and Bill will likely have some side comments to share with each other about the (description). Charles, sit on the other side of Cheryl, since you and she share similar concerns about the (description). Perhaps you can share notes. Sue, how about sitting here? Jack has notes on the (description), which will be of interest to you.

Service must be positioned in front with the chalkboard or flipchart, the most powerful position in the room. After everyone sits down, remain standing to start the meeting. This establishes you as the leader of this session. The weakest positions in the room are to your immediate left and immediate right, and, hopefully, Jim and Sue occupy these seats. The spots directly across from you are the second most powerful positions; avoid seating Jim and Sue in these places.

SERVICE: We are having difficulty with the installation because of (description). Continuing our current course will cause us to miss our goals and incur cost overruns because of (description). Obviously, this likely outcome is unacceptable to everyone. Working with each of you individually, I have generated a list of possible alternatives. They are summarized in the agenda. All alternatives have limitations as well as positive elements. All available alternatives will require us to compromise our individual requirements in order to achieve a greater goal. You all have recommended this meeting so that we can share concerns as a group. By the end of today, we should agree on one of the options or on some modification of one or all options. Please note your agenda. Let's start our discussion with a review of (first option).

Be goal-directed at the beginning and establish the meeting as a positive discussion focused on a specific task. Make clear that the meeting is not a forum for general discussion of personalities or anything other than the task. Define success for the group by specifically defining the work that must be concluded during the meeting. It is a good idea to raise the issue of financial impact. Finances always help keep business meetings focused on the agenda.

JIM: I agree we have a problem here. Some time ago I proposed a solution, which would have solved this problem and reduced our installation costs. Unfortunately, we could not get the needed support from Sue's operation.

The first jab could come from Jim or Sue. No matter who attacks and no matter how subtle the attack, don't let the other respond. Jump into the discussion and take control.

SERVICE: Jim, I'm not sure I understood. Could you explain the potential cost savings?

Employ this tactic every time Jim or Sue attacks the other. The stratagem forces the attacker to move away from the personality of the intended victim and back to the problem at hand. Also, by jumping in before the attacked person responds, you absorb the blast and prevent the intended target from retaliating. The tactic forces the attacker either to call off the assault or to attack you instead. The latter is less likely to occur because, you are, in effect, a guest; you don't have a "history" with the attacker and you are also the leader, occupying the most powerful position in the room.

JIM: (To service.) Wait, this is important. You are our guest here and don't understand how frequently this occurs in (Sue's department). Yours is just one problem. We must put up with this all the time. Poor performance in (Sue's department) is something the organization must resolve. It's costing us too much money.

Should Jim or Sue start to attack you, avoid a direct response. Instead, stand up and start writing a brief summary of the attack on the flipchart or chalkboard. In doing this, modify the attack into a relevant concept for the whole group.

SERVICE: Let's summarize where we are. We need to resolve (description). Let me make a note or two to help us focus. Cheryl, any ideas on where we go from here?

Calling on another person in the room and asking an important question tends to redirect the discussion back to the problem at hand. If possible, ask a question that is dollar-related. Remember, just by standing, you automatically assume more power, and the written notes on the board are a very powerful tool, focusing attention on the topic. After your summary defuses the attack, sit down again and ask another question related to the topic. Do not direct your question to Jim or Sue.

YOU ARE ISOLATED: DEFECTIVE PARTS SHIPPED—TWICE!

You are in a very bad position. The system has been totally down for two days: blown power supply and motherboard. New parts were shipped to the customer yesterday in advance of your service trip. You arrived as scheduled to replace them, made the installation, and discovered that the new parts shipped were themselves bad. You rush-order more parts, and your factory support team flies them out. Even using "counter-to-counter" shipping, the parts do not reach you until the next day. The customer has now lost three days of production. You start the day at the airport, waiting for the parts. They arrive, and without unpacking them, you rush to the customer's site. Desperate to be up and running, the customer is right at your elbow just as soon as you get in the door. He watches as you pull the new advanced electronics out of the special shipping carton. There is a note taped to the board. It reads: BAD BOARD! DO NOT USE!

Yet again, you have been shipped a bad part, this time with a note proclaiming it defective! And your customer has watched it all happen. Based on your experience from yesterday, it is a certainty that your customer is going to lose another day of production, making a total of four days lost.

Your tactic? Cool, be very cool. There is no question that your company is wrong, and there is no question that the customer is going to stomp on you. You don't deserve it, but your company does. Today you are the whipping post. Brace for it.

CUSTOMER: What kind of a !@#$% jerk outfit do you work for, anyway? They sent a bad part special counter-to-counter handling, and they knew it was bad! There's a !@#$% note on the stupid thing saying it is bad! I want this stinking (product) out of here right now, and I want to be paid for all my lost production. I'm calling my lawyer!

If there is ever a time for great empathetic skills it is now. As bad as things are, and they are bad, you can express concern and be comforting without placing blame. You should be upset. Use voice modulation, express emotion, but do not toss disparaging remarks at your own company.

SERVICE: It is unbelievable that this has happened to us, and it happened twice! I just can't believe it!

Using the "us" allows you to put yourself, your company, and the customer on the same side. "It is unbelievable that this has happened" does not necessarily blame your company or any one person, but it does acknowledge a horrible state of affairs. It is very important not to start blaming departments or "others." You may feel like saying, "I can't believe those idiots at the factory . . .," but if you express personal frustration in this manner, this out-of-control situation will only get worse. Hurling invectives at your own company or staff will not help. Accept your fate, and deal with the issue. As far as the customer is concerned, at this moment, *you* are the company. Period. Let the customer vent while you continue to express empathy.

CUSTOMER: !@#$% . . .

SERVICE: This is really a terrible circumstance.

CUSTOMER: !@#$% . . . This should never have happened.

SERVICE: I agree. I just cannot believe how everything is going wrong. This is really embarrassing; certainly, no one could have ever wanted this to happen.

Such phrases allow the customer to vent, and they acknowledge the error that has occurred. These phrases can be used without throwing bricks at your company. Neither agree nor disagree with the customer about who is at fault, since fault finding is not solution finding. Fault finding will only create additional problems.

Pitfall: Do not agree that you owe the customer money for lost production. While you and your company may choose to offer some compensatory gesture, and especially during a disaster such as this, doing so is a good investment, it is unlikely that your company will want to be in the business of guaranteeing production output to its customers. As quickly as possible, move beyond frustration to action.

SERVICE: I must get to a phone immediately. We have many quality-control steps to prevent just this sort of mess from occurring, and all of them failed miserably. I must get to my supervisor immediately.

With voice modulation and gestures, express urgency, but not panic. Acknowledge that the situation is serious, but that you are still in control and capable of taking positive action. Get your management involved quickly. This is a classic case where you must get management involved. Even if you are certain you can create a solution alone, it will help calm the customer if he or she perceives that you are cracking the whip back home. It would be best if you could speak to your boss privately. However, it is unlikely the customer will be calm enough to leave you alone. Chances are the customer may want to pound on your boss as well. Who could blame him or her? If the customer is going to listen to every word you say, it is important to tip off the boss immediately that this is the case.

SERVICE: (On phone to boss.) (Boss's name), we have a major disaster here at (location). (Customer) is right here with me.

It is a safe group of words, yet quickly alerts the boss that the language you are using to describe the problem will be more or less censored. Nevertheless, use enough emotion to tell the boss that you are in a real mess.

SERVICE: This is a total disaster, and I wanted you to know about it immediately. Can you believe this mess? (Explain what happened and express urgency.) There was even a note attached to the thing saying it was bad. Can you believe this is happening to us?

Take action now. But just where to go from here is a tough question. New parts cannot be delivered tonight, and the customer is way behind on production. Is there related equipment in the general area that you can lease? Can you subcontract the customer's production requirements somewhere? Perhaps another customer is nearby, and you may be able to borrow some slack time on his or her equipment. Can you make the system limp along in some fashion to do at least some work? Even at the risk of additional damage to the system, getting some of the production pressure off may be worthwhile. In the real world, these solutions are practical and effective. Whatever options are available, it is important for the customer to see that you are doing everything possible to offer a solution. You have two bad boards in your possession. How good are you? Can you salvage parts from both of them and make one partially good one? The point is this: Stopping the customer's production hemorrhage is now more important than fixing the equipment. And even if there is no way to stop the hemorrhage, still put forth a gallant effort. It is critical for the customer to perceive that you are trying to do something, anything, to relieve the production bottleneck. Putting forth effort to relieve production pressure is the best option for defusing this very legitimately angry customer.

Let's review up to this point:

1. Express empathy with the customer's position. In this case, the company is clearly in the wrong. Do not, however, toss invectives at your own company. This does nothing to resolve the issue, and it destroys your integrity.

2. After the customer has had time to vent, take constructive action. Act to resolve the customer's problem of lost production, and act to get your boss involved and alerted to the bad quality control in the spare-parts group.

3. How can you deal with the customer who insists that he or she must be compensated for lost production? Try to dodge the bullet. Be like the politician who answers the question he or she wants to answer, not necessarily the question actually asked. If you focus on the steps just discussed, in most cases, the question of compensation will simply go away.

You should consider doing what most companies do in a case this bad, however. Give away the value of the service call and all expenses. Some companies, but not as many, would also give away the parts or, at least, discount them. Many who sell supplies for their own equipment might give away some supplies as a positive gesture of apology. I know of no company, however, that will make cash payments based upon perceived production losses unless a contract specifically defined such a penalty in advance of the occurrence.

In a crisis, when the customer is panicked and angry, it is all too easy to lose your perspective on the real world. When your company sold the system, it did not promise the customer any particular level of production. You warranted the system to run, not necessarily to produce anything. Furthermore, even if the customer chooses to make a legal claim against your company for lost production, he or she would have to prove that the business losses were actually incurred and that they were directly related to your problems with the machine. This is always a tough thing to do. But do not get into a discussion of the legal ramifications with the customer. Our purpose in Customer Service is to retain this customer and, ultimately, to create satisfaction. It is not to make more money for the legal profession. Discussing legal issues is inflammatory. If the customer keeps bringing up compensation for production losses, focus on what you can do.

CUSTOMER: Fine, you are getting parts here tomorrow. However, I am losing money today, and I expect your company to pay me for my losses. I have lost four days' worth of production.

SERVICE: I understand your concern. I have discussed the issue with (boss). Parts will be on the first commercial flight tomorrow. I have received assurances that my supervisor is personally rechecking the parts. We do not know where quality assurance broke down at the plant. However, we can be certain your particular parts will be functional when they leave the plant. First thing tomorrow, I am going to meet the plane. I will be here about (time) o'clock. After getting this up and running again, I will spend (hours, days) helping you catch up on production.

Service is focusing on what can be done, which is a lot, even if not exactly everything the customer wants. Also, Service is answering the issues it can answer, not necessarily all the issues. If the customer insists, then Service should fall back on the idea of limited authority.

CUSTOMER: No, that just is not good enough. I must insist on a cash payment for the lost production.

SERVICE: This is all very embarrassing for us, and I am going to waive all travel and service-call expenses. Your only expense will be for the first set of parts ordered. This represents (dollars) in savings to you. Further, I intend to stay over and help you catch up on production. Additionally, I will also leave behind some (standard supplies) at no charge. I have no authority to offer cash.

Leaving consumable supplies plus helping the customer with production should be enough. Keep the customer focused on the idea that everything possible is being done. If the customer repeats the demand for cash, just continue to repeat what you can do, always defining in detail your efforts and the cash value they represent. Continue repeating that you have no authority to offer cash. Do not recommend that the customer call to discuss the issue further with your boss or his or her lawyer. If the customer really wants a court fight, let him or her make that decision independently and without your recommendation.

F Part
our

Within Your
Business:
Satisfying the
Internal
Customer

Chapter
14

Customer-Oriented Leadership

GETTING ATTENTION FROM OTHER DEPARTMENTS

Some, maybe too many, believe that customer-oriented change can be driven from the topdown only. The thinking goes something like this: If the boss doesn't believe it, sell it, and drive it, then the troops below will never fall into line. This is obviously one approach and, in fact, probably the best and even the most effective approach, but the boss is not always supportive of needed customer-focused change.

As I travel about, I am always amazed at the number of people I meet who feel that, because the boss is the boss, he or she is somehow blessed with competence and intuitively cares about the business and its customers. Many express considerable frustration and surprise when their personal observations prove their assumptions to be incorrect, even though history records numerous leaders, in business, society, or government, who cared little or nothing about those they led. In my own consulting experience, I have met many customer-focused people who must work with completely incompetent bosses, bosses who care nothing about the customer, or even the business. Like most, I have worked for a few incompetent bosses myself during my corporate tenure.

This may all be true, yet you still have to manage the customer focus because you, correctly, assume the business is greater and more important than the existing boss's whims. I have several client companies in which operational vice presidents, directors, and managers successfully set up strategies that enable them to manage the business around the incompetent CEO. The reality of our world is that anyone can cause a revolution if he or she can create a following. The reality is that you may need to get customer-focused attention from other departments on your own, without support from the top. The reality also is that both front liners and managers have the power to cause customer-focused cultural change if they want to. And as with everything else in life, the reality is that modest risk-taking is involved.

Two key points to remember about customer-focused change are:

1. Change is continuous because humans have never been satisfied with the status quo. Most individuals within an organization are trying to improve that organization in some way. Everyone in the organization says he or she is working for the customer's best interest. The endless debate among us is over which specific idea will create which specific improvement, how do we know this improvement will occur, and when the improvement will happen.

2. All change under way in the organization is being sold or pushed by someone who believes the change is necessary for the organization's long-term benefit or his or her own long-term benefit, and that someone has mustered a constituency. The pushers are creating incentives and reasons for the constituency to grow and follow them. Those who follow the change agents are being rewarded in some way.

Everyone says they are customer focused, but careful observation suggests something quite different. Groups are interested in pursuing what they are rewarded to pursue. Production is interested in shipping product, preferably shipping the same product forever; for its rewards are based upon meeting the shipment schedule at the lowest cost. Predictability is the best way to achieve lowest production costs. Sales are measured on new orders produced, so the Sales Department chases new orders, not necessarily the best customers. Engineering is measured on new drawings produced, the mail room is measured on pounds (or tons) of mail moved, and so it goes.

The organization as an entity obviously has an interest in the customer, as everyone will agree the customer feeds the organization. Individuals, or individual departments within the organization, however, have personalized goals and objectives.

So, like it or not, the customer-focused manager, running around saying this or that should be done because the customer needs this or that done may not make many things happen. Customer-focused managers who accomplish goals must tilt their messages to suit the various communities of interest within the organization. Those who choose to drive the customer-service message must create a following, like everyone else. People follow what they perceive is in their best interest. Therefore, the customer-focused message must be tilted to the listener's best interest, not the customer's best interest. If you want to be heard, position your message so that the listener's personal objectives are supported.

DEALING WITH PRODUCTION: CONTINUING LATENESS

Production operations are notorious for always "making-up" the lateness accumulating on the project. Here's the way it works: some problem has occurred, usually in final testing; production "just knows" the solution is near at hand, and they are always "certain" to pick up the lateness with a bit more overtime. Unfortunately, this same statement was made last week, last month, last year, or on the last project. This scenario assumes customer service wants to change this endlessly repeating cycle. Service is in a discussion with production control management.

SERVICE: I wanted to provide some follow-up on my discussions with (customer's name). We had a wrap-up review meeting on the project last week.

PRODUCTION: Great. I sure am glad we finally got that job shipped. We had several problems with it, but everything worked out. I'll bet they're happy we finally got everything resolved. I know they'll be happy with the performance.

SERVICE: They were definitely happy we finally shipped and that all the problems were resolved, but they are not very happy with our performance. They don't feel we handled the job particularly well.

PRODUCTION: Well, why not? We were a bit late, yes. But that thing is running beautifully now. They are going to get a lot of value from it. I'm sorry about the problems, but we couldn't very well ship with the problems still occurring now could we?

SERVICE: No. Obviously, shipping with problems would have been much worse. They just did not like how we managed their expectations throughout the project.

Go slowly with the discussion. Let concentration on the subject build. Don't just attack the production operation. Remember, production people normally do not deal with customer-focused nuance; they concentrate on technical and measurable daily problems. No one was intentionally lying.

PRODUCTION: Well, I guess you people in Sales and Service need to improve in that area. It is your job to manage the customer.

Expect this kind of comment. Not everyone perceives how his or her individual performance links to the total team performance.

SERVICE: I agree. It's our job, all right. But, we do need your help.

PRODUCTION: Sure, we're glad to help. What can we do, though? We never talk to the customer.

SERVICE: That's true. We're the folks in constant contact with the customer. The problem we have is in developing and controlling the customer's expectation. We can only build a company response based upon input from yourself and others throughout the company. In our review meeting, most of the customer's concerns were with the ship dates promised and then missed. We had to reschedule our ship date three times.

Don't say the "dates production missed" or something similar; this would be adversarial.

PRODUCTION: There's nothing we can do about that. We never lied to you or anyone else. Every date we promised was exactly the date we were trying to meet at that time. It's just that when problems arose, they had to be dealt with. Before we can evaluate problems and solutions, the problems must first exist. That's a fact of life and has always been true. We'll never be able to tell you about stuff that doesn't exist.

SERVICE: I understand, and I agree. However, our customers still need to plan, and they are planning using the shipment dates we promise. When we miss the promised dates, we mess up promises they have made to others, their customers. Sometimes customers believe we are scheduling phony ship dates just to keep them from complaining. They feel trapped. They can't throw us out. It's too late to get another supplier once the project has started.

PRODUCTION: Look, that's all baloney. We're not giving out any phony dates. I have my hands full trying to get the technical problems resolved. The customer is constantly asking us to make promises, and we only have partial data. We're giving the best estimates possible when we give them. Your problem is putting up with all this from the customer.

Stress cooperation and the need for help. Don't fight him or her.

SERVICE: But we need your help. How about an adjustment in the way we work together? We can avoid this problem in the future by increasing communications with the customer. Customers will always be demanding scheduled ship dates to plan their own operations. How about if we offer them more than a specific date? We could offer a promised ship date as well as a list of assumptions we use to produce the estimated ship date. With this kind of estimate, the customer can factor a degree of uncertainty into his or her own plans.

PRODUCTION: Look, I don't want the customer down here underfoot every week reconfirming the ship date. It is your job to handle the customer side of this thing.

SERVICE: I agree. You should not be giving the customer reports continuously. It's our job to manage the customer. I'm talking about how you and I can work together more effectively. Each week at our production control meeting, you and I can discuss the planned ship dates for the various projects. If your people could also supply me with a list of assumptions they are making to project the ship dates, I can then develop a more complete presentation for the customer. Essentially, nothing is changed, and everyone is doing the same things. We're just communicating with each other, and with our customers more. By projecting assumptions as well as ship dates, our customers will have a better overall view of the project, including risks. They will have greater confidence in us.

PRODUCTION: But most of the time we can correct for problems when they occur.

SERVICE: And we can share that with the customer as well. I am only lobbying for more communication. By keeping the customer more involved, I believe we can increase his or her confidence in us. He or she will be better able to understand why ship dates may possibly be missed.

Keep selling this concept to production. Use different approaches as necessary to make your point; not everyone supports the idea of open communications. Increasing communications, explaining projections, assumptions, and risks is the best way to increase the customer's confidence in you.

DEALING WITH REPAIR: THEY WON'T GIVE ESTIMATES

How can you cause the repair department to be more customer focused? It is difficult to estimate how long any repair will take, especially when the problem has not yet been fully diagnosed. Many in technical repair services, having been burned in the past making estimates they could not keep, refuse to make any estimates at all. They simply maintain the position that "It will be ready just as soon as I can get to it." In this scenario, customer service wants more cooperation and greater communication from technical support.

SERVICE: Our customers are complaining. They need better estimates on how long they will be without their (product) when it is left in the shop for repair.

TECH: They always ask for estimates. But we cannot make estimates on how long things take to repair until we first figure out what is wrong. I have been burned before by giving estimates I could not meet. Just tell them it will be ready when we are finished. They have to accept the fact that we cannot predict the unknown.

SERVICE: I agree that we cannot give estimates on how long it will take to fix something until we know what it is we are trying to fix. But we can involve customers in the process of diagnosis and analysis. We can explain how we are going to go about getting the product checked out, and we should be able to share benchmark checks and status reports with them.

TECH: But that does not tell the customer when it will be ready, which is what he or she really wants to know. We have tried involving the customer in the past. We have given estimates and placed contingency assumptions around those estimates. They don't want to accept the idea of contingencies. So, they ignore the contingencies and assume the estimates are etched in granite. Look, I have been burned on all this before.

SERVICE: I agree. Ultimately, the customer wants the product back and wants to know when it will be coming back. I also agree we can't commit to that. But at least his or her being involved in the process is better than having no information at all. It is up to us to create understanding about the contingencies we must face and how those contingencies impact our estimates.

TECH: So now I need to train all our customers in technical repair technique? Look, we have traveled this road before. No matter what I say, the customers will ignore the contingencies and remember the estimate as a promise.

SERVICE: Well, we still need a strategy. Let's involve him or her in the process, not the conclusion. Let's talk about the steps we are going to pursue and provide status reports.

TECH: The customer will be here *every day*.

SERVICE: Not if we tell him or her about benchmarks. Look, the customer will say "When will it be ready?" We respond with: "Can't say yet. Based upon what you describe, A, or B, or C could be wrong. I will need to check to be sure. I am going to run some tests, which will take about four hours. I can contact you with a report on what I found. When we have a review, I can then give you another status report.

TECH: That is not telling the customer what he or she wants to know.

SERVICE: True. We can't tell the customer what he or she wants to know. But we can try to stop some of the "unknown" the customer feels, which leads to complaints. I am not suggesting a perfect solution; perfection would mean the product did not break at all. This solution, however, does keep the customer involved in our processes. While involvement will not stop every complaint, it will stop some of them, and that is an advantage.

Continue pushing this general idea. It will work for your more rational customers. A few customers will not accept this strategy, but do not le t a minority of your customers control your perceptions. Design a strategy that works for most.

DEALING WITH MARKETING: DEMAND EXCEEDS SUPPLY

The company just launched a new product. Demand was wildly underforecast, and customers are screaming for product that simply does not exist. Customer service is being overwhelmed with complaints, and production is swamped. Marketing wants customer service to "come up with excuses, "yet protect the wonderful sales figures. How should customer service handle this?

At first glance, this looks like a sales bonanza with nary a hint of a customer-service problem. Sales exceeding projections can be hypnotic: "Just tell them to drop off the orders, and we will ship when we get around to it" is the thinking that takes over. But the apparent bonanza is deceptive. Beneath the rising sales numbers, customer frustration could be building and might explode with volcanic ferocity.

The inspiration for the script that follows comes from a pharmaceutical company service manager attending my service leadership seminar. The company had developed a new drug to help in treatment of a particularly insidious and common chronic disease. The drug, while not a cure, was positioned as offering significant benefits to sufferers. Marketing wildly underestimated demand, and sales poured in right after launch, completely outstripping supply in just a few days. Product availability evaporated, and customer service was besieged with complaints.

Overwhelmed by customer complaints, Service went to marketing for guidance, which ultimately proved to be a strategic error. Marketing, drunk with the nectar of sales success, was blind. It recommended that customer service "create an excuse" and shift the blame for the product-supply problems to the raw material suppliers. When angry customers insisted that names of the raw-material suppliers be released, customer service, again under misguided instructions from the marketers, informed them the raw-material suppliers were all off-shore and that the needed materials were held up in U.S. customs.

The "house-of-lies" strategy collapsed when the company's president received a call from a U.S. Senator. The Senator wanted to know exactly where evil government bureaucrats were stopping such valuable raw material from entering the country. He insisted on getting this information immediately, as his constituents, judiciously using the press, had alerted him to the problem. He had every intention, with story-hungry reporters looking on, of using the full legislative powers of the Senate to break through the red tape immediately. What was initially a strategic and tragic marketing error became, within thirty days or so, a full-blown public-relations disaster. Marketing was wrong, and so was Service.

SERVICE: (To Marketing.) We have a strategic problem. The introduction of the new widget last month is greatly exceeding our wildest dreams. We must do something. Incoming order entry lines are jammed, production is losing ground even on overtime, lateness is accumulating, and distributors are running out of product.

MARKETING: Yeah, its grand, just grand. We've hit a home run.

SERVICE: We may have hit a home run, or we may have bitten into an elephant. Distributors are starting to scream because their customers are starting to scream. We've got do do something.

MARKETING: Like what?

SERVICE: First, let's stop throwing gasoline on the fire. The campaign is a national one heading east to west. We've got to stop the marketing campaign now.

MARKETING: What! And lose all momentum? That's crazy. No way. It would cost millions in lost new business. All the marketing dollars are committed. We would lose millions in cancellation fees. Distributors are expecting the campaign, too.

The obvious tendency here would be to grab the nearest brick and knock this person off his or her cloud. However, resist using muscle and try persuasion first.

SERVICE: We certainly don't want to lose momentum, but we must slow demand as the risks to our reputation are much too high. Distributors want the campaign, but they're assuming we can deliver product. They will quickly start complaining when their shelves are empty, and they face the angry crowd. Those frustrated customers will not create sales numbers, they will create negative public relations. The distributors won't support us, they will side with the customers and blame us for the whole marketing mess. We've got to take the heat off and slow this thing down before we do any serious damage. As I said, distributors are already hearing customer complaints.

MARKETING: We just can't stop the campaign. Promotions, Advertising, everything is committed. It's your job to handle the service side of this thing.

SERVICE: Can we bring in alternative raw material supply for production? Even supply from a competitive source would be better than nothing.

MARKETING: Forget it. That's what makes this whole thing a home run. There is no competitive supply.

SERVICE: But there must be consideration for customer satisfaction here. The new business numbers you see are an illusion. We don't have new business, because we have no product to ship. All those new-business numbers will go up in smoke next month when angry distributors send us cancellations. We're just shaking the cage, creating false expectations, and disrupting our customer base. Right now we are training customers to contact distributors about wonderful new product that does not exist. Those false expectations are going to damage our long-term reputation for no reason. Competition is going to pick up on this and use it against us; they would be fools not to.

MARKETING: Well, as I said, it's up to your people to handle the service side of this thing. We've just got to take advantage of this selling opportunity. Can't you take the heat? Buy a little time. Just tell the distributors our truckers messed up on deliveries temporarily. The production guys will catch up. They always do. Their lateness problems are not that serious. You're too much of a pessimist. Production always cries wolf about everything and then just solves it.

Ignore the slam and maintain a customer-accountability focus. The put-down may be childish, but even the best of us lose focus from time to time. Besides, you have more important things to worry about. You need to position the idea that customer accountability is as important as sales. You will also need to decide just how much risk you must take. How many allies do you have? How good is your past record? How good of a relationship do you have with Mr. or Ms. Big? A good relationship with the big boss as well as a good track record will give you confidence as you handle this important scenario. Try to be casual, but firm. Do not attack him or her personally.

SERVICE: It's just not there, (name). Production is not crying wolf this time. I'm charged to make sure we maintain customer accountability, and accountability is what we're discussing. All programs, including marketing, sales, service, and otherwise, must ultimately yield to the test of customer accountability. I can take risks like everyone else. However, this is more than a business risk. We are making promises with the marketing campaign that we absolutely can't keep, and we know that we can't keep them. Strategically, shifting the responsibility for our failure to the truckers will not work. The truckers will fight back, and they will, successfully, rally the distributors for support. Besides, and most importantly, we don't need to take these risks. The strategy I have proposed is very positive. Just stop the unfolding campaign. We can justify that. We can make the following points to customers from states we cannot support:

☎ the market loves the product, and interest is very strong

☎ because demand is outstripping supply, we are temporarily not accepting any new customers from west of wherever we decide to cut off distribution

☎ our production operations are running flat out, and we are searching for alternative manufacturing sites to expand our capacity

It really is the best way to protect our fundamental customer accountability, and it won't cost us anything in sales. The sales will come just as soon as we can get production ramped up.

MARKETING: Look, it's just too big. I can't shut this whole thing down, there are too many people involved. The approval and support must come from the top. You will just have to handle it.

SERVICE: This is positive, not negative. Let's go to the top together and tell the boss what we must do. We can explain that we are in agreement on strategy. We can position the whole thing so that he or she understands how positive customer accountability really is and why we have stopped the campaign. The small costs incurred to stop the campaign will be much less than the costs to our reputation. We can explain how successful the campaign is, how we will handle the customers in states where product will not be available, and how we are trying to boost production. Let's go to production together and be sure it is on board with the strategy as well. Production will certainly join us in the meeting.

MARKETING: Let's try it your way.

This strategy will work. Unfortunately, it is possible that you have an irrational leader who does not appreciate the importance of customer accountability. My experience suggests there are a few out there. If this describes your personal situation, then you have a personal decision to make. Perhaps your environment is unhealthy for your career aspirations and you should find another. The ultimate beauty of our market-driven society is its self-cleansing capacity. The leader who cares little about customer-accountability will be pushed aside eventually; they always are.

DEALING WITH MARKETING: ERRATIC PROMOTION STRATEGY

Often, in my consulting experience, I have seen customer-focused leaders face this scenario. It can happen in any industry, especially where product differentiation is difficult. As an example, the following scenario might happen in the airline industry: airline X decides to boost sales volume by discounting the fare between city A and city B. It could have decided to improve value for the customer, but it chooses the easy "price-discount" road instead. The promotion runs for a few days, and the order-entry department enjoys logging a slew of new business. Airline Y must respond with a better promotion (which is why customer-focused strategists hate discount-based promotions). Airline X must respond to the retaliation from airline Y and comes along with an even better "new and improved" price reduction. And the price war is on.

But unfortunately, all wars produce casualties. The customers who went for airline X's initial promotion are now irate. They proceed to increase the work load in airline X's complaint department dramatically. They call in with all sorts of angry comments, scream that airline X has no integrity, and claim it is a cheat and a liar. They demand the "new and improved" price reduction for themselves. Customer service, trying to gain back lost integrity, dives into appeasement mode and rolls back the previously discounted price to the "new and improved" discounted price for the irate customers. Customer service, of course, must do all this while it is trying to take orders from new customers seeking the "new and improved" program. Phone lines cannot support the increasing influx of calls, creating even more irate customers.

And so it goes, until the competitors have run out of energy and margins. The dollar losses are staggering. This cycle is endlessly repeated, and it is up to customer-focused leaders everywhere to defeat it.

SERVICE: (To marketing.) The new promotion strategy is causing us great pain in Service. Our systems are bogging down. Phone lines are jamming, and we're getting a lot of complaints.

MARKETING: Look, what do you want me to do? I've got my own problems here. We're under pressure to fill seats, and the discount strategy is the best way for us to fill them quickly.

SERVICE: It's also the best way to ruin our reputation in the marketplace.

MARKETING: Our customers don't care about our integrity or our reputation. They only follow low prices.

SERVICE: They follow low prices because we and the competition tell them to follow low price. Even if they don't care about our integrity, we don't need to make it worse.

MARKETING: We're not making it worse. We're just trying to be competitive on price.

This dialogue may seem confrontational. You do not intend it to be. You do, however, need to be direct, get attention for an important idea, and establish a peer-to-peer relationship.

SERVICE: We are making it worse. The message we hear from customers over the phone lines makes it clear we're making things worse. Customers believe we are lying to them and making suckers of them. We offer a special discount, and they respond. Then a few days later, we offer an even deeper discount on the exact same route for those who have not responded. Everyone who trusted us and accepted the first discount feels cheated.

MARKETING: Look, that's just a fact of life. Business is business, and that's just the way things work.

SERVICE: That's just the way things worked yesterday. Maybe we can make things work differently for tomorrow.

MARKETING: I'm listening.

SERVICE: Let's change promotion strategy. Let's tie it into something other than a low fare between cities A and B. We could probably produce the same increase in demand with some other linkage.

MARKETING: What linkage do you have in mind? You'll have to be more specific than this.

SERVICE: If we have no choice but to discount prices, we could offer discount coupons for use on a future flight to those customers who have been most loyal in the past, for example.

MARKETING: How does that strategy help us compete on a particular route?

SERVICE: It doesn't. Competing on route A or B does not build the airline. Loyal customers supporting us over the long haul build the airline.

MARKETING: How does that idea help us get new customers when we need them quickly?

SERVICE: Nothing helps us get new customers quickly, including what we are doing now. Today, we discount to buy a new bunch of customers in support of a particular route. That only disrupts the existing and loyal customer base. The negative phone calls we're receiving make that clear. Don't worry. Our existing customers will help us get new customers through word-of-mouth advertising if we stop hassling them.

MARKETING: Maybe we can try this.

SERVICE: This is one idea, not necessarily the best or only idea. Maybe there are even better ideas that do not involve discounting at all. We would all like that. What I am really suggesting is that we work with your group, brainstorm, and consider accountability to our existing customers as part of our ongoing marketing strategy. We can create lists of marketing ideas that will help us build the business without running the risk of creating dissatisfaction with existing customers. We may even be able to use these strategies now before the pressure for discounting builds. Our competitors will likely be grateful, too. They probably hate the price wars as much as we do.

MARKETING: I guess it's at least worth a day of planning and thinking. Perhaps you're right about that, with your input, we can do a better job of keeping customer accountability in perspective.

This positive debate should produce constructive results for you. Try this strategy, even if you believe your company, or your marketing director, is not receptive to the service contribution. If your company is not interested in your input, it is better for you to know now rather than later.

SPEAKING THE LANGUAGE OF BUSINESS: COMMUNICATING WHAT CUSTOMER SERVICE DOES IN DOLLARS

Too often in my travels, I find that customer-support operations are positioned as a "necessary evil," something, like taxes, which must be endured in order to do what we really want to do, which is sell products and rake in the profits. Too often we conceptualize about how the customer leads to profits, while we position customer-support operations as costs that could (and should) be eliminated if we could only build the perfect mousetrap, or find perfect customers who would understand the mousetrap's natural limitations, stop complaining about them, and buy new mousetraps when we tell them to.

I recall a service manager who told me his boss, the company owner, wanted him to keep pay for service-support technicians below market averages so that they would leave the company within two years. This "visionary" company owner believed service could contribute nothing to the organization, and the support technicians would "burn-out" in a year or so. The owner felt support operations should be positioned so that technicians would leave right after burn-out. Considering his attitude, the owner was probably right: technicians would burn-out in a year or two. This individual, we can only hope, is the exception.

Positioning customer service as a cost and nothing but a cost is hardly exceptional. Customer-focused managers must shoulder some of the responsibility for this corporate attitude. Far too often, I hear customer-focused managers who preach with eloquence about what the organization should or should not do for its customers. They ramble on about the good, bad, and the ugly, somehow concluding that a god from on high will bring their "shoulds" and "oughts" into reality. And they must think this can all happen without finances, since their presentations are typically devoid of financial analysis. If customer service is ever to be perceived as the strategic business function it is, it will be because rational customer-focused managers learn to demonstrate the contribution Service makes to the bottom line.

If you want to have second-floor executive credibility, communicate what you do in terms of its contribution to cash flow. Business is not an altruistic entity, it is a profit-maximizing entity, and it listens best to those people who express their demonstrable and positive impact on cash flow and, ultimately, profits.

When service creates satisfaction, which causes customers to buy again or recommend the organization to others, then service has created positive goodwill, which should be documented and claimed. If service eliminates a recurring quality problem, and all the customer contacts the problem has produced, then it has eliminated a negative cost or a drain on cash flow. This is also a positive event, and credit for the contribution should be claimed.

COMMUNICATING THE CUSTOMER SERVICE CONTRIBUTION TO MARKETING

Develop a budget for service and determine a cost-per-customer service hour. This cost is much more than just payroll cost for the service technician. It includes the total cost to support every hour a technician is available for talking to any customers. Total costs include payroll, benefits, administrative, overhead, computers, telephone, and everything else required for support. Sick time, vacation, study time, research time, training, inefficiencies, and other responsibilities must be deducted from total hours available for servicing customers. Using this cost-per-service hour gives you credibility as you discuss the contribution service makes to the organization.

Approach marketing with financial analysis in hand. This should and must be an upbeat, nonadversarial discussion.

SERVICE: I wanted to share with you our contribution to the widget marketing initiative. I've performed a resource allocation for us to look out.

MARKETING: Let's see what you got.

Use your charts as visual aids.

SERVICE: Here's the launch of the marketing campaign. You created a lot of interest. Note the spike in the number of hours directed to inquiries. On average, we invest 100 hours per month directed to customer inquiry or requests for more information. Here, one week after launch of the national advertising campaign, that number doubled to 200 hours per month. Therefore, at an average cost of $100 per service hour, our service contribution to the widget marketing campaign is running at $10,000 per month. The campaign looks like a winner. As you see on the chart, the spike in our inquiry load is being sustained at the 200-hour-per-month level. The numbers have been fairly consistent for the past eight weeks or so.

MARKETING: This is great, good feedback. I agree, this suggests the campaign is working well.

SERVICE: We're glad to contribute, and it's good the campaign looks like a success. $10,000 per month in resource allocation, though, is a pretty hefty number. I thought it might help our overall marketing strategy if we did a bit more service analysis, so I had our people take a closer look at the characteristics of the spike. Fifty percent of the inquiries are exactly what we want. After answering the prospect's questions, we convert these callers to orders.

MARKETING: That sounds good.

SERVICE: Yes, however, the other 50 percent of contacts are false hits. After answering their questions, the callers decide the widget is not for them. $5,000 every month in false hits is a fair amount of cost, so I asked our people to do some research to determine what attracted the prospect's attention and why we ultimately ended up losing them.

MARKETING: Great! What did you learn?

SERVICE: Look at this breakdown of why they called, what they expected, and why they ultimately said no: (Review lists and charts).

I realize the campaign is already under way. Yet if we can incorporate a few modifications in the advertising effort, we could perhaps eliminate some of these calls.

MARKETING: It will cost some bucks to modify that campaign now that it is launched.

SERVICE: Sure, and maybe it's not worth changing. I'm just suggesting it might be worth a look. My costs will continue as long as the campaign continues. Perhaps that is the lesser of the two costs. I really don't know. I'm just suggesting it's worth looking at so that we can compare the costs associated with changing the campaign to the costs I am going to incur continuously.

MARKETING: Let's get Bill from advertising and look at this.

SERVICE: Okay. While we wait for Bill, let me bring up one more thing. The service contribution to our bottom line does not always get noticed around here. The whole world, though, is focused on the marketing effort. It makes sense: you bring in the new dollars.

How about if I add a Service segment to your monthly report? A page or two of words with a few charts describing how we contribute to overall marketing would help educate the masses to what we do. If it's okay with you, I would be glad to discuss the Service contribution to marketing every month.

MARKETING: Do you think we really need that? I'm not sure we need to broadcast problems to the whole company.

SERVICE: I'm not talking about discussing problems. I'm talking about discussing a positive contribution we are making to marketing. The organization is full of problems. I need to broadcast what we in Service are doing to help with continuous improvement. We could easily publish our own report focused strictly on the service contribution. However, it may just look like we're working alone. Adding a complementary segment to the marketing report shows how we are constructively supporting the sales plan.

Continue this line of dialogue. It is unlikely that Marketing will reject your positive overture. If it does, publish your own report. Be careful not to toss bricks around the company. Keep your report focused on positive service contributions. That is, do not just discuss the cost of problems, discuss the problem and the action you are taking to correct it.

USING DOLLARS TO COMMUNICATE PROBLEM SEVERITY

There are many scenarios wherein Service can create cost studies and ally with other departments to help focus scarce resources, or new resources, toward a much-needed solution. This script assumes a product such as a copier, engine, x-ray machine, toaster, automobile, or any other device needs a component failure fixed. Service is addressing the issue with Engineering:

SERVICE: The hydraulic problem we have discussed is continuing. Technical-support costs are now averaging $5,000 per month. What's most alarming, though, is the rate of increase. The number of failures we're getting is growing at a rate of 3 percent per month and the trend has been consistent for the past three months. At that growth rate, we cannot sustain our service support. We just don't have enough resources, and we do not have authorization to grow the service force at that speed.

ENGINEERING: You're going to have to take the heat and support the effort for awhile. We're cranking on this as hard as we can. We are in the lab testing several new cylinders right now to find a solution.

SERVICE: Within a few months, our costs will be over $7,000 per month. We just don't have the needed resources. What are the lab tests currently showing?

ENGINEERING: Still inconclusive. We need at least two months for more testing.

SERVICE: What do we know after the tests are concluded?

ENGINEERING: We will know the course of action. With a solution in hand, we will then need to change the widget design to incorporate the fix, get production going, and get new parts to your people in the field. You're probably looking at six months.

SERVICE: We won't make it. We just can't support the load that long, and it's growing. Can the plan be expedited with more resources?

ENGINEERING: We don't have more hours to throw at the problem, either. We're flat out, too.

SERVICE: Let's get an analysis together, go to management, and get additional resources dedicated to this problem. Maybe we can get some temporary help in here. Production and sales will support us, too. They know this problem is growing.

ENGINEERING: New people aren't the solution. We will need to do training and everything. More help may even slow us down. By the time we bring new people up the curve, we might as well do everything ourselves.

Defensiveness is a common reaction. Expect it. There are several interacting reasons which create defensiveness. First: pride of ownership. Engineering does not want others messing with their designs. Second: engineering does not want to give the problem any more attention than it is already getting. After all, it designed the bad component into the widget in the first place, and that, obviously, was a bad decision. Third: by agreeing to support a crash program to get the widget fixed, Engineering is admitting it cannot handle this new situation and things are getting out of control. Ignore the defensiveness, instead focus on, and create understanding for, the larger business issue.

SERVICE: We need to do that analysis now and get our recommendations together for an executive review. This is a business issue, not an engineering or technical review. Service will be out of control within four to six weeks. Our response time will be intolerable. Customers will start complaining to executive management as well as the board of directors. More importantly, they will also bad-mouth us to anyone else who will listen, including the trade press. Executive managers will then be coming to us for recommendations, and they will want to know why they were not informed in advance.

ENGINEERING: You're painting a worst-case scenario. Those lab tests could be producing positive results as we speak.

SERVICE: And that possibility, too, needs to be part of our overall analysis and recommendations. I have no choice but to alert management to our vulnerable position. Trends strongly suggest a near-term failure. I need your support to produce a comprehensive analysis. By going to management together we reduce the possibility of an invective-filled major argument around here. We need to lay out a time line, evaluate the cost of support, and recommend a course of action, including bringing in temporary help as necessary. It may be uncomfortable; however, it is better for us to do it now rather than wait for management to demand it. We both lose if management asks us why they were not informed earlier.

Continue this line of discussion, making clear your resolve to go alone if you cannot get support. Engineering will likely realize that working with you is better than working against you. Be sure to bring on Sales as allies, too.

The same script could be used if a process needed to be fixed. For example, instead of a component failure, we could have been discussing a process failure, such as problems caused by mis-picks in a warehouse, problems caused by poor response from production, problems caused by exaggerated sales or advertising claims, problems caused by poor availability of spare parts, and so on.

MOTIVATING THE STAFF WITH CUSTOMER-ORIENTED MEETINGS

Many meetings are a waste of time and money, since they address such things as announcements, key current events, review of policies, procedures and regulations, and/or other informational issues. All of this communication is much more efficiently and effectively handled with written or electronic words. Avoid calling these meetings. Meetings are costly forms of communication and should not be wasted. If invited to such meetings, politely find reasons why you cannot attend.

Most of the hustle within the customer-service workday is spent on issue resolution. This or that crisis occurred and needed attention. Yesterday's problems were resolved, only to be replaced by today's new package of problems and so on. The customer-oriented meeting is an opportunity for everyone to stand above the fray, meet as a team, and redouble effort on the ultimate objective, which is creating high levels of customer satisfaction. The meeting is an opportunity to discuss strategy, to relate satisfaction-oriented tactics to specific scenarios, and to inspire the troops. Use customer-oriented meetings only for these high-value purposes. Use them as discussion forums focused on redirecting energy and vision. Meetings are the most effective form of group communications; they are also the most expensive.

Just how is customer satisfaction created? If you do not deliver product quality, or keep your service promise, you will certainly create customer dissatisfaction. And, as we already know, much customer-service effort is focused on eliminating problems that cause customer satisfaction. However, creating customer satisfaction requires something in addition to eliminating the problem. While customer service is eliminating the product or service problem, it must also cause any one or all of the following to occur:

1. The customer must perceive that he or she is receiving an individualized response to an inquiry, as opposed to a "by-the-book" response.

2. Service must recognize the unique challenge the customer is enduring at the moment of contact and do something to help him or her resolve that challenge, even if the problem that caused the challenge cannot be totally eliminated at that moment.

3. Service must acknowledge some objective the customer is trying to achieve and cause the customer to accomplish that desired objective, or some portion of that desired objective, even if it has nothing to do with the product, service, or problem.

Contacts between Service and the customer are not contacts between organizations. They are contacts between human beings, who may or may not represent organizations. Creating a satisfied customer means creating satisfied human beings, no matter why the contact was originally made.

No matter what the context of any particular meeting, ultimately the customer-focused meeting should be used to coach people and reinforce them in the continuing challenge of creating and maintaining high levels of customer satisfaction.

MEETINGS: REINFORCING POSITIVE CUSTOMER SERVICE

Satisfied, positively enthusiastic customers can only be created by enthusiastic customer-service representatives who communicate positively with those customers. In addition to solving problems, the service representative must convey that he or she is glad the customer called, and that he or she appreciates the opportunity to serve the customer's interest. The customer-service representative must convey this positive message enthusiastically many times per day. It's a tough job.

Enthusiasm is delicate and fragile. It is easily stifled by insensitive supervision or unappreciative business cultures. It can easily be dissipated in the sometimes frustrating sea of corporate cynicism. Ultimately, enthusiasm comes from within the individual customer-service representative, but it must be endlessly reinforced by the culture and customer-focused leadership within the culture. The inspired customer-focused leader is always circulating among the team. He or she is upbeat, talking with team members, working with the group, suggesting novel approaches, expressing empathy, continuously consulting, coaching, and counseling the team. He or she recognizes that enthusiasm does not just happen, it is created, and built over time upon an open, trusting foundation. He or she gathers notes continuously on these observations and uses meetings to review notes, reinforce positive attitudes, and refocus the team's attention.

As I travel about, I hear many people arguing that positive public recognition and reinforcement is not really necessary in the workplace. Too many argue that adult workers should not be singled out and rewarded just for demonstrating what is commonly called "expected customer-focused behavior."

Those who argue these positions are just plain wrong. Does anyone argue that the Academy Awards, the Malcolm Baldridge competition, the Nobel Prize, and dozens of other recognitions have no value? We have known about the importance of positive reinforcement for ages.

Reinforcement meetings must always be positive, upbeat, refreshing. As part of open communications, allow people to bring up concerns that should be addressed in other discussions; however, do not allow this important session to deteriorate into name-calling, complaining, or general grumbling about work conditions. Many of my clients leading better customer-service teams find time to hold these meetings weekly. Whenever possible, introduce a new twist, a small surprise, or something special in the meeting. One client brings doughnuts purchased with her own money. Above all else, believe in what you say. There is nothing that destroys enthusiasm faster than phoniness. Be certain you are sincere and authentic in your approach to positive recognition before calling this meeting. It can backfire on you, if your team detects insincerity.

MANAGER: (Starting a regular Monday morning customer service review session.) Welcome back, everyone. I hope your weekend was as great as mine. You guys, as usual, look great, and I'm looking forward to another super week. Good things are happening for us.

Be light, warm, friendly, and upbeat, no matter what your opening words. Find positive words to use that fit your own personality. Most importantly, be sincere.

MANAGER: I've got a bunch of notes, and I wanted to review some super stuff I watched you folks working on last week. It's obvious to me that we are all learning from each other. Take the situation Bill was involved in as one example. Let me give you some background to set the stage: (describes situation).

Do not just lecture; talk with your team as you describe the situation. Be interactive, using interjections that create excitement as you describe the events. Be specific, using some graphic detail that will bring the situation to life. The more specific the detail, the more learning you will achieve.

MANAGER: So, as we can clearly see, this was a tough one. Bill really did do an excellent job handling this, though, and, Bill, I just wanted to say thanks for a great job. Let me review several things he did that we can, and should, all emulate. (List and discuss each item with the team).

Thanking Bill personally is a nice touch. Again, you cannot fake authenticity. If you don't truly believe the words you use, neither will anyone else. Be detailed with the review, focusing on Bill's specific behavior. Do not just say he did a good job. Describe why what he did made his performance a good one.

MANAGER: For example, in response to the inquiry, Bill specifically used these words with the customer. They were great and I wrote them down for you. Bill commented: "I understand the question, and I have written some good notes on this situation. However, I can't comply with your request right now, because I must first check on (issue). What I can do is check on this, clarify what I can get done, and call you back within two hours. I can't guarantee what the resolution will be; however, I can guarantee that I will get back to you again with clarification." This is doing a great job, because Bill explains why he cannot comply while also accepting personal responsibility for taking some constructive action. He does not use words like: "I'm not allowed" or "you will have to talk to others." He uses the pronoun "I" throughout the discussion and specifically accepts responsibility for managing his piece of the business. He states what he personally will do and makes a commitment to get something done without making false promises to the customer. Great, Bill. That's what excellent performance is for all of us.

Keep your reinforcement meeting focused on learning and building enthusiasm. To build enthusiasm, discuss specific behavior, which others can emulate. Here is an example of how a specific event should be handled:

MANAGER: Judy handled the National Investments account in a super way as well this past week. They called in a panic, unable to bypass the software roadblock. Somehow, they had improperly set the password coding. They were in a panic because they couldn't execute any transactions for their customers.

Judy stayed with this tough one, and I wanted to draw your attention to some of the things she did and hard decisions she had to make.

First, and most important of all, she needed to protect National's security as well as our own. As you all know, we cannot easily solve these problems on the phone because of a possible security breach. What is really superior about Judy's performance is that before resolving the problem, she successfully took the time needed to maintain security protocol, and this is important, without irritating the heck out of National.

Judy had to follow all the rules and get all necessary confirmations from National to ensure she was speaking only to authorized people at the company before helping them get through the roadblock. In stressful situations like this, when time is critical and the customer needs immediate action, it takes thought to focus on the right direction. Often in these situations, the customer puts us under pressure to by-pass the safety rules. Judy, however, did a super job. The president of National called, and, Judy, she said your performance was exemplary. Congratulations on a job well done. You get an (award) for this one, your fifth this year.

We can learn a lot here. I've got some notes on some of the great things I heard Judy doing. But I would rather she tell you herself. Judy, tell us. How did you keep your focus? What specifically did you say to National?

JUDY: I'm really not sure why it worked. At first they seemed defensive and just wanted to get into the problem, as they needed an immediate solution. I remained calm and explained why it was in their interest for me to follow security protocol.

MANAGER: How did you get them to accept your need to follow protocol?

JUDY: First, I apologized for needing to check for a security breach. I then explained why I needed to check and discussed the value to National. I also reassured them I did not believe they were hackers, and I commented on the fact that their internal security, combined with our systems, formed a tough shield for their customers and gave them a selling advantage.

Judy will probably tell you what she did in an abbreviated manner. Listen for the critical points and draw the strategic lesson for the group.

MANAGER: This is great. Judy's approach worked because she did not just follow security protocol; she strategically positioned the value of security protocol. There is a big difference between following protocol and, when necessary, selling the reason for security protocol. She does four strategic things very well.

First: Recognizing she is working with a frustrated person, she first expresses empathy and apologizes for the current circumstance. Anyone can say "I'm sorry this has happened." This does not make her responsible for what happened.

Second: She did not then say: "I am following procedure" or "I'm just doing what I am told to do." Instead, she explained what value she was offering. She explained what kind of disaster could occur if, per chance, National's computers had been somehow breached and we were accidentally duped into helping the hackers.

Third: She reassured the customer, explaining that in no way was she accusing the person on the phone of wrongdoing.

Fourth: She then explained how the customer could use the value Judy offered to better position his or her business with his or her own customers.

Judy, you can't get much better than this great job. We can all learn from her, since this is exactly what kind of value we offer in our company and exactly how to demonstrate that value to our customers. We won't all be this good all of the time. But we all can be this good some of the time.

Continue the meeting in this vein, always focusing on a specific incident and why the specific incident was good. My experience suggests that most people will positively respond to this approach. Generally, this meeting should go on for about one hour or so, giving enough time to review several excellent examples in depth. Allow ample time for questions, discussion, and clarification. This meeting works best when it is interactive. Have these meetings once a month or so.

PROBLEM WON'T BE FIXED: KEEPING THE STAFF ON TRACK

This is a difficult meeting to handle. There are many reasons why the company may not fix a problem with a product or resolve a particular customer-service issue. Some typical examples: perhaps the "mis-pick" problem in the warehouse may be too costly to fix. Maybe the needed new warehouse computer cannot be justified. Perhaps the lowest-cost thing to do may be just to live with a modest customer-service problem forever rather than redo the entire product offering. Or, in one of the most difficult situations, perhaps you personally have not yet discovered a way to get corporate attention directed to a pressing problem.

These are but a few of the many reasons why you may be asking the service-support team to endure continuing customer complaints. This meeting is still very difficult to handle, though, because no matter how valid the many possible reasons for continuing problems, it is the technical customer-support teams that have to endure the constant hassle from the customers, and they know their fate.

Candor is the most important way to make these meetings successful. More communication and involvement is required, not avoidance of the situation.

Do not try to hide the decision, make excuses for the situation, or paint rosy word pictures. Do not defend the decision or put it down; stay with, and communicate the facts. Explain what is happening, either good or bad, behind the scenes. The organization does not always do what is good for customer service; the organization does what it perceives is good for itself. Explain the business rationale and express empathy for the situation. Then state how everyone must move forward and climb over the situation.

Above all else, do not treat the team as a bunch of children. Treat them as contributing adults, capable of understanding, and accepting, that this is an imperfect world. Even in an imperfect world, you can still maintain a following and drive the customer focus. Be certain to define and explain the positive role you intend to play in the continuing search for a solution in undesirable circumstances, people will still follow if they perceive you are still moving, or attempting to move, in some positive direction.

MANAGER: I called everyone together to discuss the current situation with mis-picks in the warehouse and the customer complaints the problem is causing.

REP: Man, I sure hope something is done quickly. The mis-pick problem has been driving us nuts forever. We're choking, and the screaming customers are consuming all our time.

If you are managing a healthy and open environment, and you should be, virtually anyone on the team might blurt out a comment. A comment of this type should not be considered negative. It is merely an expression of frustration. It is better for frustration to be expressed among team members rather than with the customers.

MANAGER: No doubt about the stress this is putting on us. I hear from all of you continually and read your reports. The problem has been around for more than a year, and it is consuming about 20 percent of our total service capacity. It is costing us a lot. This thing has had my top priority, and I have been chasing possible solutions all over the company. But I do not have good news to report. A fix for the warehouse problem just is not in sight at this time. We're going to have to absorb the complaints.

REP: That makes no sense. Customers are constantly complaining, repeat customers especially, as they have to put up with this every month. They just don't know why we can't get this resolved.

MANAGER: The simple reason is cost.

REP: What about the cost in customer relations?

MANAGER: Right. No doubt about it. I know it is costing us in goodwill and in customer satisfaction. Sometimes this job is just plain tough. I'm hoping all of us as a team can minimize the damage this problem is causing, even while we know there is no solution.

REP: That's crazy, just crazy. This thing is causing damage. We know it, and we won't fix it? Brilliant!

ANOTHER REP: Why is there no solution?

ANOTHER: What is the cost problem, anyway? What is more costly than customer satisfaction?

Do not be threatened by this kind of tough talk from the team. In a controlled and constructive, discussion-focused meeting, this type of communication does not suggest insubordination. This is the way we all talk and act when frustrated. The team has the right to be frustrated; after all, it has been taking the heat for more than a year. The team is venting. Under positive circumstances, frustrated employees should have the right to comment upon and feel comfortable criticizing the imperfections in their own company. Considerable creative improvement stems from constructive criticism; so does coping power, something you need right now.

MANAGER: Hold off. I know you're all upset. I am, too. Any thinking person would be. Just like you, I wish everything were perfect. But I can't address all your questions at once. Let me start with the cost issue. This is no small problem. I have been working closely with Craig in the warehouse on this one for months. He, like us, is well aware of the problem and the solution. Unfortunately, a solution requires an investment of about one million dollars. That's the boxcar estimate for a new computer system. Craig just does not have the budget approval power.

REP: Someone does.

MANAGER: Of course, the president does. Let me finish. Craig and I have made a number of calculations. We have talked to several computer vendors, and we have analyzed the current cost situation based upon input from your weekly service reports. We also created savings estimates from streamlined warehouse operations, obtained support from finance, and took our analysis to the president. All of us have looked at this problem. Here is the deal and the bottom line: our current business levels and margins just do not give us enough cash flow to support the capital expense needed to get the new computer purchased and installed. The project dollars just aren't there until we somehow change business conditions.

REP: Right. We don't have and can't get the money to solve the problem. But we will continue wasting dollars harassing customers.

MANAGER: It may sound that way. But the world is a practical place. The facts are simple. We cannot spend money we do not have. If we borrow the money, it must be paid back with interest. That means we need to increase cash flow and get our margins up. Perhaps in a year or two, we can look again at the new computer.

REP: What are we supposed to do in the meantime?

MANAGER: We're supposed to keep doing our jobs as constructively as possible. We're supposed to continue building the business, and that is exactly what we are going to do.

REP: What in the world are we supposed to tell customers? Are we supposed to say: "Yeah. We know we are making a mess. You'll just have to live with it, because we don't intend to fix it."

MANAGER: Certainly we are mature enough to speak more constructively than that. Our customers are likely more tolerant than that, too.

When customers call with mis-pick problems, we should do what we have been doing. We should express empathy, apologize for the problem, and resolve it as quickly as possible. Repeat customers will be a bit more difficult. They will want to know when the problem is going to go away.

REP: Should we lie to them?

MANAGER: That's never a good idea. We should tell them we are working toward a solution. Be up front, but you do not need to discuss every internal problem detail. Also, positioning the message is important. You can say that the problem is occurring because of an overloaded information-processing system. Business conditions over the past years have changed, and we need to change with them. We are planning an upgrade just as soon as the capital budgets will support the new computer and software we need. All statements similar to these would be appropriate.

REP: Some of our largest customers will push. They are already sick of this constant hassle. They will want to know when the new system is budgeted to be on line.

MANAGER: Tell them it is not currently scheduled because of budget constraints. We are striving to get a new system in the long-term plan.

REP: That sounds pretty weak.

MANAGER: Positioning is everything. You have a responsibility to demonstrate our total responsiveness to the customer. We all do. It may be a weak answer; however, it would be much weaker for us as a corporation to recklessly blow the capital budget and jeopardize our financial health. If we bankrupt the company, then we can serve no customers.

REP: I guess that's a good point, too.

MANAGER: And depending on how the conversation was going, I would make the same points to the customer.

REP: This strategy will hold us for a while. But our largest customers will not accept this forever.

MANAGER: I think you are right. I'm working with Craig to set up a temporary fix. I'll be asking some of you for help in implementing this idea. What we are planning to do, if possible, is to identify those select largest users, isolate their shipments, and then add extra checking procedures to their orders only. If this works, we will be able to reduce the mis-pick problem on an exception basis. But, you can't share this idea with the customers yet for two reasons. First, we don't know if we can set up a system that can isolate selected repeat customers. Further, assuming we can isolate their orders, we don't know if we can find the extra resources needed to do the extra checking required.

REP: That will be an expensive idea to put in place.

MANAGER: It will add cost, yes. But, as you have correctly noted, we are already paying a price in bad customer service. We may need to add part-timers or temporary workers. We will also need to add more work load to supervision in the warehouse because of the additional diligence that will be required. The extra costs will be added to the operating budget, which is a bit easier to justify on a short-term basis. However, all of these costs combined will be far less than the million dollars of capital needed for the new warehouse computer system.

One more point. We're not giving up on the new system. We will reevaluate the project in another year or so and see what can be done at that time. All of these extra costs we incur to support our best customers will become part of the total justification for the future new system. We will be able to reduce these special checking costs once the new system comes on line. So, in a very real way, these temporary measures will be supporting our longer-term objectives.

So, I can't offer a perfect solution, but I can offer ideas, general direction, and continued pursuit of a plan. I still need your best efforts on the firing line, as the road ahead will be tough. It's up to you to help us keep this thing afloat as we continue striving for longer-term, more comprehensive solutions. I will contact some of you individually to help me determine how we can isolate our best customers on a temporary basis. Thanks for the support.

It is a good idea to end on a positive note with a personal plea for support. The team is going to take some heat, and it knows it. There is no need to ask for its agreement with words similar to, "How do you all feel about this?" This would be foolish. A soldier may accept that part of the job means he might die for his country, but it would be stupid to ask him to like that part of the job description. We already know the team does not feel good about the situation. The members will, however, accept it. Be certain to keep them informed as the plan emerges. Keeping them informed will help them endure the additional stress.

KEEPING THE STAFF FOCUSED LONG-TERM WHILE LIVING WITH SHORT-TERM PROBLEMS

This situation is easier to handle than the previous one, because there is at least some solution in sight. There are many problems that simply do not have a *short-term* solution. For example, fixing a faulty baggage-handling system may require a very long time. Perhaps the entire mechanical system may need to be rebuilt. Still, though, the customer-service team will have to take the heat. In the short term, they will be the individuals putting up with the customer who is constantly suffering from and grumbling about the problem. The simple fact that the team is being hassled must be understood and recognized by management.

It is not good enough to send the message: "Well, that's just a characteristic of the job" or "You must take the good with the bad." Simplistic messages like these must be avoided, since they will serve to increase anxiety among team members. Show real concern, and don't try to fake authenticity. Stay involved with the team. People do not do better coping with adversity when they are kept ignorant. The opposite is true. Keep your people informed, while emphasizing the need for team members to support each other.

MANAGER: I wanted to give you an update on the baggage handling problem you have endured for so long. First, a sincere thank you to all of you who have been putting up with this problem for so long. Candidly, our performance on this one has been significantly less than it should have been. Even worse, we are hurting some of our best customers; tragically, those who travel with us weekly are being hassled the most. There's no doubt about it. All of your personal efforts at controlling the damage is keeping the defection of our best customers to a minimum. Thanks again.

This personalized message will carry more weight than saying: "The company thanks you," or "on behalf of the company, I would like to thank you," or similar comments.

MANAGER: We have been working with the vendor who built the system. Its service technicians have been here for months, trying to get this problem resolved, and it just looks like there is no simple fix possible. Frankly, they are failing. The large lower belt feeding the upper six smaller belts needs to be eliminated. The general plan is to feed all six belts independently.

General design plans are being worked up now, and they will be reviewed by the CEO next week. However, whatever the final decision and no matter when it is made, we are talking a major error. It just does not look very good at all. It will take millions of dollars to rework the system, and it looks like a solution is more than a year away.

There's no reason to sugarcoat anything. For us, it means finding a lot of lost luggage and working with disenchanted customers for some time to come.

We are going to get more help during this difficult period. We will have more customer-service people up on the floor working with the customers. Baggage readers are misreading the tags, and baggage can come up on the wrong carousel. We can have extra people to help customers who are waiting too long for the baggage. The extra people can check other carousels. We are also going to have extra people below checking on the automatic system. It seems that, at times, the bags just disappear on the lower belts and never come up. Extra hands can look for these situations and remove bags manually. This is not a perfect fix; however, extra help will alleviate some of the pressure over the next year.

REP: Why did it take so long to get action?

MANAGER: I'm not going to make any excuses. There just is no easy way to say it. We blew it. We, I, my boss, executive management, whomever; we just couldn't, or didn't, get management attention focused on this thing soon enough.

By way of explanation, I guess we thought the vendor was going to get the thing working, and we lost focus. We still should have added extra people.

REP: Where are we going to get the extra help?

MANAGER: Overtime has been authorized and will be immediately implemented, effective tomorrow. We are also talking to several temporary-help agencies. Our people will be given overtime priority, but a year is a long time, and I am certain some temporary people will be needed.

REP: What about the customers? Helping them find the lost luggage quicker will not keep them from being aggravated. Can public-relations people help?

MANAGER: Any ideas?

REP: Can't we build some models or put up some signs or something?

MANAGER: Not a bad idea. I'll work on that. Sketches, signs, and so forth will help. Again, thanks for your efforts, and I'll let you all know what the advertising and public-relations people suggest. I'll insist we must do something to help communicate the message.

GETTING THE TEAM INVOLVED IN SOLUTION-FINDING

MANAGER: I wanted to give you a status report on the difficulty we are having with the invoicing software. The problem blossomed when we merged the Jacoby and Smithton accounting systems last month. Some of our charge-account customers are getting faulty invoices when they use their charge cards. The computer can randomly duplicate an actual purchase. It only seems to happen on much older accounts, those open longer than ten years.

The good news is that we pretty much have the problem identified. The bad news is that getting the software fixed will be a major hurdle. I wanted to discuss our current strategy with you and invite any suggestions you might have.

Don't just announce the decision with words like: "We have made the decision not to fix the problem." Take the time to build understanding for the decision. Also, the team may have something to contribute to the decision.

MANAGER: The new invoicing system is quickly coming on line. The software is about ready for testing and should be completely debugged in about one year. Our software designers assure us this invoicing problem has already been checked out and will not be in the new system. But not everything is perfect. Here is the bad news: The problem with the existing software has been located. Our designers have studied it, and there just is no simple way to fix it. Unfortunately, significant code rewriting will be necessary.

Here is what would happen: Diverting resources to fixing the existing problem will cause a three-month delay in installation of the new software and, of course, a three-month delay in the features we so desperately need and want. I'm sure you will all agree that we just cannot accept a delay. It would waste entirely too much valuable resource for a very short-term gain. We would then trash the old software anyway in about a year. So, in lieu of fixing the old software, we've decided to maintain our focus and bring the new software on line as soon as possible. We need your support, no doubt about it. The glitch will continue for about a year, and we are all on the firing line.

REP: What are we supposed to tell the customers?

MANAGER: Tell them the truth. I don't think they want to hear endless detail on our internal-systems problems. But giving them a summary would be appropriate. Simply tell them the problem occurred when we merged the two divisions. As part of the merger, we were able to avoid a general price increase by combined invoicing systems, which reduced administrative costs. That's when the software problem appeared. The problem is known, and a solution is under development. I think if we position the message correctly, we can ask our customers to be patient with us and tell them a solution will be coming in about one year.

REP: That strategy should work most of the time when the customer first encounters the problem. However, this glitch is hitting our best and most loyal customers, those with old charge card numbers. That solution won't work very well as they get hit the second and third time with the same problem. They're going to scream.

MANAGER: I think you're right. When this type of service call comes in let's agree to take extra time with the customer. Discuss the situation and be sure the customer understands we must still live with the problem for a while. Find out how often they use the card. Maybe the easiest thing to do is, with their permission, kill off their existing account and give those frequent users new accounts. That will cost us a few dollars, but it is better than hassling the customer with this recurring problem.

REP: What about those customers who just pay their bill without checking for accuracy? Some of them might be overpaying, and neither we nor they will know it.

MANAGER: That's interesting. I don't like that thought at all. I guess we hadn't considered that possibility. You guys talk to customers every day. How often does that occur?

REP: Probably more often than we think. A number of customers blindly assume the computer is correct. They glance at the invoice, it looks generally good, so they just trust us and pay it.

Assume the group agrees.

MANAGER: That's not good news. Are you sure? Think carefully, because this changes our thinking considerably. In fact, what you describe could have already happened.

REP: I've talked to many of our customers. I'm certain it's true. I just know they trust us implicitly. Many never give the invoice more than a simple glance. In fact, our best customers may check on us least of all, as their experience suggests our invoices are always correct.

MANAGER: Maybe we will be forced into spending money on repairing the glitch after all. We can't run the risk of cheating our best customers and potentially creating all sorts of negative publicity. This definitely changes things. More importantly, we now need an immediate fix. We have to alert our customers to the potential for error. Unfortunately, if we send out some alert message, that's really going to expose us to a flood of incoming calls. Customers are going to demand we go back months to confirm they have not been overcharged.

REP: Let's not wait for them to see the problem. Why don't we just open new account numbers for all older customers, say those who have been with us eight years or more. If we are certain it only occurs with old account numbers, let's just kill all the old ones and replace them.

MANAGER: That would be costly, but it may be less costly than fixing the software glitch. Maybe that is our best choice. I'll take this to the marketing and software people, and we will do a cost analysis. For now, any customer with an older account who calls with this problem should be switched to a new account number. We will go back and rethink this idea as to what is lower cost: fixing the glitch or just replacing the account numbers. Thanks for all your input.

GETTING TEAM MEMBERS TO POSITIVELY REINFORCE EACH OTHER

Everyone knows the most powerful form of reinforcement is peer reinforcement, either positive or negative. Your continuing leadership challenge is getting individuals on the team to continually reinforce each other positively. This is a difficult objective. If you play favorites, focusing, for example, on personality rather than performance, then cynicism, negative reinforcement, and poor morale among the unfavored team members will be the outcome. In such an environment, this sensitive meeting will do more harm than good.

This meeting works well when controlled positive competition is encouraged within the work group. Everyone enjoys a well-designed contest, and positive competition helps achieve desired results, just watch how the players treat each other on any good team playing your favorite athletic game. Goals that focus the service representative's attention on achieving posted and measurable performance standards serve to enhance team formation and cohesion. Healthy competition means that all service representatives feel they at least have a reasonable opportunity of winning a particular competition. Individuals working in these healthy environments are always willing to reinforce each other. However, unbridled competition can allow individual members of the work team to run amok. It can be highly destructive to group cohesion and morale. I have observed many situations in which customer-service representatives, and everyone else, for that matter, are allowed to enhance their personal standing by ripping apart their colleagues. This type "survival-of-the-fittest" negative competition builds alienation and destroys team cohesion. In such an environment, calling a meeting that encourages customer-service representatives to positively reinforce each other will likely produce the opposite effect, breeding even more cynicism.

Skills are important, too. Team members who do not have the needed job skills can't compete. They will not be accepted as viable team members, and this type meeting will do more harm than good. It would be better to focus your attention on training or realignment of job responsibilities.

You will have the most success getting customer-service representatives to reinforce each other constructively when:

☎ group members respect themselves, their colleagues and you

☎ you create fresh air and brightness in the team, and service representatives genuinely receive at least some satisfaction from working with each other

☎ a sense of camaraderie and cohesiveness exists

☎ individuals perceive they are making a positive contribution to customer-focused goals and objectives

This meeting would not normally be a stand-alone event. Make it a subset, or the last few minutes, of another meeting. An element of surprise works well, too. Do not tell anyone in advance what specific incidents you are going to describe. Describe the specific behavior you observed and want to reinforce without a lot of fanfare. The incidents you select to relate to the team should be specific enough and obvious enough to stand alone.

MANAGER: Before we close, Beverly, Jerry, and Andrew, I want to extend personal thanks on behalf of the entire group for your positive efforts.

Folks, let me be specific about what these three did. All of us know this job can be really tough at times. I was walking by just as Bill must have been finishing a very tough call with a customer last week. His expression spoke volumes. Beverly, with prompting from no one, had apparently heard portions of the call. She walked over to Bill's station, pulled him off line, and offered to buy him a coffee. She just took a moment to help a colleague in a tight spot. It's not a big deal, but it helps keep us all on track. Thanks, Beverly. That's the way we should all do it.

Jerry, your initiative with Sharon in production control paid off, too. Her boss told me all about it.

Folks, apparently Jerry had a rapid response situation last week. He absolutely had to get chemicals shipped in a hurry, and he went to Sharon for help. She managed to move the production control dinosaur, find the needed product, and get the shipment out. But she had to really climb over several mountains to do it. That is, of course, the performance we all expect from our friends in production.

In this case, our customer, Alford Chemical, told Jerry that getting the emergency shipment to them enabled them to keep three of their large hospital accounts supplied in a timely manner. Alford Chemical had made an error in calculating inventory on hand and fell a little short. Jerry and Sharon helped them around the error and, because of their efforts, three of Alford's hospital customers never noticed the chemical shortages.

What Jerry did that I think was exceptionally helpful was to follow up with Sharon after the emergency ended. He took a few minutes to jot a simple memo, explaining to Sharon how her efforts eliminated a problem and improved our relationship with Alford Chemical. He also sent a copy of the memo to her boss.

All of us can follow his lead. Production is a long way from Customer Service. Often the folks in Production comply with our requests and do what's right for the customer. The whole company is better off when, like Jerry, we take a few extra minutes to convey to them and others exactly how their help resolved a particularly difficult customer problem. Gestures such as Jerry's memo build cooperation, flexibility, and team cohesiveness. Thanks again, Jerry.

Andrew's performance deserves a thank you, too. Andrew and I were visiting his account, Jacon's Chemicals, several weeks ago. We were doing a simple audit over there, talking to both Jane, our contact at Jacon, and Jacon's manager, Charles. This one is a little embarrassing for me personally. But no one, me included, is perfect, and we all must learn from our mistakes, no matter how painful. No one can learn from mistakes, though, unless someone helps you learn, and for that I've got Andrew to thank.

During our discussions over at Jacon's, I said something that was particularly offensive to Charles. I don't really know exactly what I said; however, it bugged Charles enough so that he felt compelled to say something to Jane about it. Fortunately for us, Jane's relationship with Andrew is good, and she shared the entire matter with him.

For the past week or so Andrew has been doing exactly what we would expect him to do. He has been going about patching up my mistake, whatever it was. This particular thank you is not for doing what's expected. It's for telling me about my mistake. Andrew, thanks for having the courage to come to me and share my mistake and its results with me.

Andrew could have just patched things up with the client without saying anything to me. Right? But then I wouldn't have learned anything. I appreciate the fact that he felt good enough about our relationship to share a sensitive situation with me. Many of us do not feel that good commenting on errors our bosses make. I guess many of our bosses don't want to hear about their mistakes, either. Andrew, you helped build our team, and I appreciate it.

To pull this off effectively, you'd better be a person of high integrity, and your people must be aware of your integrity.

BUILDING AND REINFORCING CUSTOMER-ORIENTED BEHAVIOR

Customer-oriented behavior is not innate. Most of us, though, learn to be customer-focused to some degree, since survival in virtually any job requires some of these skills. Some of us, though, are better than others at customer-service work. Start by hiring the right people. Those hired to do customer-service jobs must be capable of learning, developing new skills, understanding information, creating ideas, and explaining things. They must be socially adept. That is, they must have a fundamental interest in others and the circumstances surrounding others. They must be willing to work with and help people resolve problems.

Customer-oriented skills, the communication skills needed to deliver empathetic messages, solve problems, create compromises, and defuse situations, can be learned by most who have the right aptitude and good speaking skills. Learning, though, occurs over time, so the needed skills must be built over time through constant coaching. Learning must also be reinforced; it's a constant process, not an event. Positive reinforcement is best done by managers on the job. Give considerable attention to this important management function. Customer-service people protect your next sale and your future business. Years of travel and thousands of conversations with service representatives and managers in all sorts of places have convinced me that much more energy could be and should be invested in this important job function.

You cannot reinforce customer-oriented behavior from your office, just by looking at performance statistics, no more than the manager of a baseball team can manage the game from the locker room by watching the scoreboard on closed-circuit television. The baseball-team manager builds and reinforces his or her player's skills on the practice field and during the game. Good customer-service managers do the same thing.

Objective measurement of customer-focused performance is important, and more measurement should be done. Coaching in real time builds the behavior that is worth measuring.

COACHING THE SERVICE REPRESENTATIVE POSITIVELY

Center the dialogue around positive events and position areas to improve within a positive framework.

MANAGER: Pamela, I liked what I saw in that demonstration. You really do have good language and coaching skills. You made nice use of questioning techniques, too. I'm glad you're in this department and this organization. The company and its customers are better off with you being here. Nice job.

Tip: Focus on specifics for greater impact.

MANAGER: Many customers are intimidated when they first see our control. I really can't blame them. There are a lot of buttons, and this is a large and expensive scanner. The strategies you developed to get your message across, all those ideas that made everything seem simple, caused that customer to feel comfortable with the control and with you. I could see it in his face. He really did like you and your style. How did *you* feel about the demonstration?

REP: I felt good about it. He seemed to respond well. There were a couple of areas where I had trouble explaining myself and I was struggling to get my point across.

MANAGER: Everyone can improve. I thought your performance was good. The customer-feedback evaluation is good, also. Keep it up. Where do you think you were struggling?

It's a good idea to get people to describe their own limitations when possible. Keep this script tilted toward positive reinforcement, though. Otherwise, the representative will miss the positive intent and only see this scenario as a critique session.

REP: I was struggling to explain why it was necessary to run the redundant scan check every time before cycling. He asked me several questions about the logic of that sequence, and I'm not sure I addressed his concerns effectively.

MANAGER: I remember that sequence. I think you did fine with it, and it seemed to me he understood. As you explain abstract things such as the redundant scan check, consider drawing some block diagram sketches. When I'm explaining, I always sketch a lot. My experience suggests the sketches enhance understanding. Go review our sample scripts covering presentations again. I'm sure they will give you some good ideas on how to present that type of data. After you review those sample scripts, let's sit down and have another discussion. I'll help you develop your notes.

For maximum effect from both scenarios, separate the coaching discussion from the positive-reinforcement discussion.

MANAGER: But, for now, I just wanted to say I think your overall performance was super, and I appreciate your efforts. Thanks, and I intend to share some of the good things I saw here with others on the staff.

COACHING: SERVICE REPRESENTATIVE NEEDS TO IMPROVE TECHNICAL SKILLS

MANAGER: Steve, it's good to be out on the road looking at the real world and making calls with you. I don't get out as much as I should. How to you feel about that call at Alcon? What's going on there? Jones did not appear particularly pleased with us.

Get to the point; state your opinion. Don't wait for the service representative to express the view that everything was great, only to hear you disagree with him or her in the next sentence. Using phrases like "pleased with us" is a better entry into the subject than words like "pleased with you." Words like "us" make it clear you are going to be supportive of Steve's efforts. Get the service representative involved in critiquing his or her own performance as soon as possible.

REP: Last week I was there and took several hours to troubleshoot a problem. Sometimes you just need a little time getting to the cause.

MANAGER: Describe what happened.

REP: I just needed time. Sometimes things just aren't obvious. I guess Jones thought I should have been able to get him back on line faster.

Take your time and draw the representative into the discussion. Pride and ego are at stake here as well as technical problem-solving skills. Creating buy-in from Steve for his own self-improvement is important, since you cannot monitor him, or any other representative, continuously. Each service representative must judge, police, and seek to improve his or her own skills and performance.

MANAGER: There's always a trigger, though. Give me more detail on how this particular call worked out. Maybe I can offer some suggestions on process.

REP: I first checked and cleaned the mixing valves, and that took a while. The problem actually turned out to be with chemistry formulation. It took me some time to get to formulations, though. I don't know, maybe Jones thought I should have found the chemistry problem sooner.

MANAGER: What do you think? Was he right?

Keep the representative involved in analyzing his or her own behavior.

REP: Maybe yes, maybe no.

MANAGER: Explain that. What does that mean?

Keep probing. The representative's perceptions are more important than yours.

REP: Well, I really don't know. I just went in and tackled the job to the best of my ability. Perhaps if I would have started with chemistry, I would have noticed the formulation error more quickly. However, dirty or clogged valving does produce the same type of inaccurate readings. So like I said, I really don't know. Maybe even if I had started with chemistry, I might still have gone back to clean the valving. It's hard to say. It's really a judgment call.

MANAGER: It's always a judgment call, that's true. We still have to maintain customer confidence, though, and we still need to get the systems up and running in a timely manner. The systems are complex, and customers are demanding.

Steve, maybe there is some help available. Troubleshooting complex systems effectively and quickly is always a problem. As you know, effectiveness and speed are not the same thing. For the past several months, Engineering and Research have been reviewing service reports, brainstorming, and evaluating different ways we sort through potential system problems. Perhaps they have created some ideas that might help us.

It is probably not a good idea to suggest that others can "teach" Steve his job. Steve is an experienced person, and such comments might seem belittling. Anyone, though, can accept new ideas and knowledge. Using terms such as "might help us" is good. This language makes clear that you are helping, not indicting the person.

REP: I have ten years of experience; I already know how to troubleshoot the system.

MANAGER: Of course you do. There's no question about your technical skills. You're good. I know that, and so does everyone else. Continuous learning today is a reality, though. The knowledge base constantly changes. Let's get a trip to the office on your schedule. You can review what strategies these folks have developed. Perhaps they have something helpful, which you can bring back to all of us.

Don't discuss the decision endlessly. Once the decision is made, get things done.

COACHING: SERVICE REPRESENTATIVE LACKS CONFIDENCE

Behavior such as longer customer contacts, an increase in performance-related complaints from customers, repeat calls from a customer involving the same service representative on the same recurring problem, a service representative continually seeking help from his or her colleagues, or a service representative always asking you for guidance might, be indicative of poor decision making or lack of confidence in decision making. Don't wait to "see if things improve." Take action when these or similar performance changes are observable. If you don't, the situation will likely get worse. The individual who cannot make decisions needs a lot of coaching and counseling.

REP: (To manager.) This is Susan out at the Lonken site. I need some help on how to handle this glitch I've found with the company's software.

MANAGER: What's the issue?

REP: I think the problem is with how they are building the files for their database. Our diagnostic checks all show that everything is okay. However, they are still crashing the system.

It would be easy to tell Susan how to go about confirming her deduction. But if you take this easy road, you will not be helping her with decision making. More importantly, if you just tell her what to do, she will continue relying on you for support. To help her develop skills, you must work with her through a logical thinking process.

MANAGER: What do you think you should do?

REP: I really don't know. That's why I called you for some suggestions. I already watched one of their people building a file, and he seemed to be doing everything by the book.

MANAGER: We've had similar discussions in the past. Think of what we've discussed on previous occasions.

REP: But this is different. I really haven't been out on this type of problem before. As I said, I watched one person build a file, and he seemed to do everything right.

MANAGER: Many problems are unique, and to solve them requires a totally new and creative approach. Many others, though, have similar characteristics and can be resolved using experiences learned previously in other situations. What other options do you have? You watched one person build a file correctly. But you still feel the problem is with the way Lonken is building files. What should you do next to prove if your theory is right or wrong?

REP: I'm not sure.

MANAGER: Just think about it. Come up with something.

Let silence fill the space for a period of time, if necessary. You must send a message that you are not going to make this decision.

MANAGER: There must be something that comes to mind.

REP: I suppose I could go and discuss my theory with the boss. Maybe he or she could give me some insight.

Do not just stop here. Take the rep through a process of decision making, which includes establishing several potential courses of action.

MANAGER: That sounds like a reasonable next step. What might be another next step, if the boss is not able or available to help?

REP: I suppose I could watch others load files into the database. Watching others may provide me with clues also.

MANAGER: Susan, that sounds good, too. What you're saying is exactly what you should be doing. Suppose those you watch do everything correctly. What else could you do?

REP: I guess I could discuss my theory with some of these people. Perhaps they, too, may be able to provide clues.

Take the advantage and drive to some conclusion. Explain how taking initiative is part of the job.

MANAGER: This is exactly what you should be doing. Susan, you do not need me to approve these decisions. The folks at Lonken know something is wrong, and they expect you to be making these decisions. They want you to take the lead, talk to them about your views, tell them what to do, and explain why they should do what you say. In short, they want you to take control, be decisive, and lead. They will do what you say.

REP: I suppose.

MANAGER: There is no "supposing" about it. If I did not have confidence in your decision-making ability, you would not be there. I want you to take action and so does Lonken or any other customer. The customer has confidence in you because we have confidence in you. He or she assumes you are competent because we sent you there. The customer will not let you fail, unless you cause them to lose confidence in you. Go after it, tell them what to do. The steps you described are all reasonable and logical. Follow them, and they will ultimately lead to a conclusion.

REP: Okay.

MANAGER: Try everything we discussed. If these steps still do not lead to a solution, develop similar steps with the customer. Try similar steps without calling in for approval. I'll trust your judgment. Fair enough?

Self-confidence builds slowly. Don't get frustrated. You will need to repeat this script many times with this individual. Each time you go through this script, focus more strongly on the fact that logical problem solving and decision making are part of the job. Continue to insist that the representative think problems through and make appropriate decisions. Eventually, though, if he or she simply does not respond, you may need to take other actions and find something else for him or her to do. If you do not take action, your customers will force it with their complaints.

COACHING: SERVICE REPRESENTATIVE WON'T DO RESEARCH

Seeking knowledge and experience requires logical thinking skills. It also requires individuals to take the initiative for learning. Some do not know how to gather information and experience. Compounding the issue, not everyone knows how to, or wants to, take the initiative. But the modern world requires customer-service people to operate in ever-expanding influence spheres. There is a volumetric explosion in the amount of information available to individuals within the organization.

Continuous learning is part of every job description, and you must build in all team members the skills required to do effective research.

REP: (To manager.) I need some help. I really don't understand our procedures on order tracking (or any other sequence or procedure). Several customers have asked me about this, and, candidly, I don't really think I answered their questions very well.

MANAGER: What don't you understand?

REP: I don't understand what happens to the order after we load it into the system, or how we track its movement through our operations.

You could just explain your business processes and how you track order movement through them all. However, your goal is to reinforce the idea that each of us is responsible for self-development. The service representative is responsible for educating him- or herself.

MANAGER: We reviewed order-tracking procedures and business processes as part of your initial basic training. That information is in your operating manuals. You can use your manuals for reference at any time.

REP: Yeah, I know. That is the stuff I explain to our customers. But they seem to want more information than I am able to give. It seems they don't trust my answers or something.

MANAGER: Maybe they don't have confidence in your answers or, perhaps, your overall presentation. It's one thing to have the technical knowledge you need. It's another thing to use that knowledge for effective communications with customers, and to cause that customer to have confidence in you and your presentation.

REP: I'm not sure I understand the distinction.

MANAGER: You have basic knowledge, or academic knowledge, but not experiential knowledge. We gave you basic knowledge through formal training. You have got to go and get experiential knowledge on your own.

REP: Where?

MANAGER: Out in the "real world." For our work, the real world is in the manufacturing plant, or the warehouse. It's over in inventory control and the production control offices. It's in receiving, shipping, accounting, and so forth. You need to get out and see what happens to the order. You've got to follow it, feel it, and see it. Our customer-service product is service. You've got to live with the order so that you can understand just what service to the customer actually means through all of the company's processes. By living with what we do, you learn to do a better job of explaining what we do.

REP: Your method takes an awful lot of time. You can just tell me what happens out there.

MANAGER: Creating experience does take time, and time is money. It takes effort, too. Unfortunately, we can't give you experiences. We can't make company processes part of your basic personality. Yes, I can tell you what happens. We have already done that. We can also create opportunities for you to go out and create experiences. But only you can go out and actually have experiences. Experiences are things you must do for yourself.

REP: Where do I find the time to do all of this?

MANAGER: Like all of us, you make time. Bit by bit, piece by piece. We find a few slack moments here and there in the schedule, we cover your responsibilities, and you take off and do your research. You get yourself educated, build your confidence, and bring something back. On some other day, you cover responsibilities for someone else, and they go out to explore our processes. Then we all share notes with each other. We build our skills and confidence based upon our combined departmental experiences. Learning, and creating new knowledge is everyone's responsibility.

COACHING: HOW TO INVESTIGATE PROBLEMS

REP: (To manager.) Man, we must have received a zillion calls on order confirmations today.

MANAGER: A "zillion" sounds like a lot of calls.

REP: Well, maybe not that many. But it seems we are getting too many order-confirmation inquiries from customers. They are calling to confirm an order has been received and to get a promised ship date.

The general formulation of this script may start in any number of ways. The strategy for handling the issue is essentially the same.

MANAGER: Answering customer inquiries is part of the job.

REP: Sure. But it seems there should be a better way.

MANAGER: There might be.

REP: What is it?

MANAGER: I really don't know. There may be many better ways, or maybe the current method is the best method. We don't know what other options are available, so we really can't evaluate what, if anything, is better. That's where you should start. Research the potential options available.

REP: How do I do that?

MANAGER: Invest some time and thought. Create a list of possible ways to solve the problem differently. For example, one solution would be automatically to send every customer a confirmation letter, fax, or e-mail after every order. This may or may not be a helpful low-cost solution. There may be other, better ideas. Talk to your colleagues here in Customer Service and get their input. Go to Accounting, Shipping, and Sales. People working in those departments talk to customers, too, and may have other options for your list. As you talk to people about potential options, some you interview will suggest others you should see. Visit with these other folks, too. Keep interviewing until you have created a comprehensive list of options.

REP: Is that all we need to make the decision? A list? Do we then just pick the right solution?

MANAGER: It's never that easy. We will need to do more research than that.

REP: Why is this my job?

MANAGER: Because you uncovered the potential problem, which is good. I'm glad you noticed the problem. It shows you are paying attention and taking initiatives. Customer Service is a job for those willing to think. When you uncover a problem, you have the responsibility to do the research and develop potential solutions. Gathering information, creating knowledge, and developing improvements is part of everybody's job.

You will have higher morale when you involve your customer-service representatives in continuous improvement projects such as this.

REP: What other research is necessary?

MANAGER: It depends on what you learn. Look over your list. Most of the potential ideas will probably be no good. They will either be too costly or just unworkable. Review your thinking process with me and some others in the department, and narrow the list to include only the best ideas. Then go back again to the interested parties, such as Accounting and Shipping. Discuss the best options with these folks and refine what should be done. Get their suggestions on implementation strategies. List the potential costs. Build some estimates of these implementation costs. Maybe an excellent solution will jump right off your list itself, and all we need to do is just implement it. That would be great.

REP: And this project will be finished?

MANAGER: Yeah, if we come up with an obvious solution. But obvious solutions are not found that often.

REP: Why not?

MANAGER: We aren't the first people in these jobs. These processes have already been well-defined by our predecessors. We get lots of orders and have many computerized tracking systems. Current systems and processes are quite sophisticated and have incorporated many incremental improvements over the years. That makes the research job more involved, but not necessarily harder. The best ideas remaining on your list will most likely be additional incremental improvements. That's not bad. It just means additional study will be necessary. We really won't know until further along in your analysis, until you have a list of possible solutions. We will have reviews periodically as your research continues, and I will be able to help guide you with some of this.

REP: What other type of study might be necessary?

MANAGER: If a solution is not obvious from your list, comparison cost studies may be required. They usually are. You will likely need to compare the cost of continuing business as usual using current methods versus the cost of implementing the new methods you and others develop.

REP: How do I do all that?

MANAGER: You should already have some idea of implementation costs for a potential solution to the problem. This information would be developed and charted as part of your initial research into the problem. You should also have calculated some estimated savings implementing these new methods would produce. I will help you lay out your information. The costs associated with this proposed change must then be compared to our existing business methods.

To calculate the cost of our current methods, look back at historical time sheets. See how many total hours are dedicated to this unique problem. Look back over the past six months or more to create a trend. Then we can compare the cost of implementing your new solutions against the cost of continuing business as usual, using the current methods. That's the way we fix things around here.

REP: Where do I get the time to do all of this?

MANAGER: We take the time. We create a few hours to start an analysis. We constantly analyze the individual steps you are taking to be reasonably sure they are leading us to reasonable solutions. As long as the general direction looks positive, we keep moving.

REP: That will take forever.

MANAGER: Not forever. But, it will take some time. We must continue to manage the business, to keep the business going while we investigate different ways to improve the business. The business must continue to support us, its customers, and stockholders while we change it. To change faster increases risk. As you continue your analysis, we can change faster if the evidence suggests we should. We will just have to see how things progress.

REP: Who does my job while I do all of this study?

MANAGER: You do. You, all the rest of us, we're all always accountable for our key routine responsibilities. Yet solving problems is also part of all jobs. In all jobs there are busy times and slack times. There are times when short-term responsibilities consume all the time available, as well as other times, when special project work consumes all available time. We must all learn to do several things at once. You must complete short-term responsibilities, do problem research, and problem resolution as well as special project work. That's the way it is.

REP: But what about the individual who does not always want to justify changing things? What about leaving things as they are?

MANAGER: I don't know about those folks. People have never found things okay as they are.

COACHING: SERVICE REPRESENTATIVE WON'T LEAD CUSTOMER

If you want to guarantee having infuriated customers, just keep them out of the problem-solving loop. There is no real experience that suggests people want to be kept ignorant of problems which can impact their well-being. Yet, everywhere I travel, customer service representatives, and unfortunately, too many of their managers, come up with lots of reasons why they should not keep customers informed during the problem-solving process. It's silly for so many to do this. As customers, we may wish for perfect products, yet as customers we are human, too. No rational person expects perfection, and, long ago, we all learned to handle the imperfections in our world.

Unfortunately for our sound-bite-oriented society, many problems cannot be solved instantly by using one's memory or by simply reciting information found in a manual or electronic database. Research may be required to find a lost order, payment, insurance policy, or some particular specification. Diagnostic tests to determine what went wrong surely must be conducted before the widget can be made right and put back to work. Customers, while they may not like it, can live with some of this. They have to. But to maintain at least some predictability and control over their personal circumstances, customers must be part of the problem-solving process. From the customer's perspective, the broken widget, lost shipment, or lost specification is part of some process, and the current problem is interrupting that process. For example, the customer is using your equipment to manufacture his or her products. These shipments, the results of the customer's total process, are more important than your equipment. Or, as another example, the customer urgently needs your shipment of tomatoes because he or she featured them in a big promotion, which starts this weekend. The late shipment of tomatoes, from the grocer's perspective, has an impact on the warehouse workers as well as the stocking clerks, all being paid overtime while waiting for the shipment. If the tomatoes are not received quickly, the problem is going to have an impact on the grocer's customer, his or her standing in the community, and so on.

Informed with timely progress reports, the customer can better gauge the problem's potential impact on his or her total business process. If the customer knows the solution is off in the future, he or she at least knows to find some way around the problem to keep the overall process moving. Informed customers may not be thrilled with you; after all, no one wants the problem in the first place. However, they are less likely to get irate; at least they have information about what is going on. They can create alternatives as needed.

So why do so many in customer service choose not to involve the customer with timely progress reports? The chief reason reported to me over the years is that, far too often, customers misinterpret progress reports. A progress report becomes translated into a prediction of success. A positive progress report such as "I'll give you a status report in one hour and tell you what I have learned" is too often interpreted to mean: "I'll have a solution for you in one hour." This, however, is a communications problem, which must be overcome if your ultimate goal is creating satisfaction. Coach your people in how to overcome this important communications problem. Using a limitation in our ability to communicate as an excuse to avoid communications with customers can only lead to irate customers.

MANAGER: (To service representative in coaching session.) Eric, I received a call from the production manager at Beta Company yesterday. Let's sit down and discuss it.

REP: I'll bet she's getting upset with us because of that system problem we've got over there. You know all about it from the updates I've been giving you. We're still trying to duplicate the problem in the lab. I just checked again a few hours ago, and we're still having no success. As you know, we got the problem early yesterday and have been in the lab with it ever since. Several people are working on it, and this is our second day chasing this thing.

MANAGER: I'm familiar with the problem. Marilyn, Beta's production manager, called me for a status report. She wanted to know how we were coming with a possible solution.

REP: I don't have anything you can tell her yet, as we still don't have a solution. Heck, we haven't even been able to duplicate the problem yet. We're still ignorant.

MANAGER: I know where you are in researching a solution. You've kept me informed. But, Eric, you have got to keep Beta Company informed as well. Marilyn should not have had to call me.

REP: I didn't tell her to call you. I talked to her early yesterday morning, just a few minutes after we learned about this hangup in her system. I told her I would get back with her just as soon as I possibly could, and I will, too. I'll call her just as soon as we duplicate the problem in the lab and determine the cause. Then, at least, I will have a chance to predict when a solution will be possible.

MANAGER: She can't live with that for an answer. She feels left out. That's why she called me.

REP: That's not leaving her left out. That's the only answer I have. I still don't know what's wrong. What can I tell her?

MANAGER: She needs progress reports. She needs to plan her production requirements based upon how bad this is. She needs someone to communicate with her, to keep her informed. Input from you is needed so that she can create a reasonable plan.

REP: But I don't know anything. How can I have any worthwhile input for her?

MANAGER: You know a lot. Several tests have already been run. The results of those tests have eliminated the potential range of possible problems. The search is narrowing. You also know the additional tests you are planning and how long these additional tests will run. Further, you also know what problems these particular tests will eliminate. Even if you randomly are trying to duplicate Beta's problem, and have no idea how long it will take to accidentally duplicate the problem, you still have valuable information. You can still call her with an appropriate review every several hours or so. You can make an agreement with her on how often you should make contact. The important point is that once we take ownership of the problem, neither Marilyn nor anyone else at Beta Company should have to call us again. We should be calling them with progress reports. That's what being proactive in Customer Service means.

REP: But I know what happens. Just as soon as I call her and say we are running this or that test, and it will take so long for the test run, she will tell all her people at Beta that the solution is almost at hand. I know she will. It's happened to me before. It happens all the time. Everyone assumes I am giving them a promise.

MANAGER: Understood. And you must live with that. It's a fact of life. People hear selectively all the time. But ignoring the human limitation does not make it go away. Dealing with human limitations, though, is a job requirement. If you feel misunderstanding is possible, then you must fight to be understood. That requires more communication with the customer, not less. That's the job.

REP: You're saying I am responsible for what she thinks?

MANAGER: Of course not. You are responsible for what you think, and for conveying what you think. You are responsible for a complete communication with the customer. Help her to understand. Ask questions that clarify her concerns. Explain what you are going to do. Use enough words to clarify the limitations of your promise. Estimate how long the various tests will take, and explain the likely outcomes these tests will produce. Communicate your problem-solving plan and advise the customer of the plan's limitations. Explain what you do and do not know. You are responsible for keeping the customer involved with the total process and for helping her evaluate her options during problem solving. You have to do more than just give her results when they are ultimately available.

REP: But she really only wants results.

MANAGER: Sure. And if you could just give her results, you would; if you could make the problem go away, you would. You can't, though. So the next best thing is to keep her involved with the process.

REP: She won't like not getting a commitment from me.

MANAGER: True. She will dislike being kept in the dark a lot more, and she won't accept it. She will continue calling me, I will have to contact you constantly, and she will get more and more irate. True, she does not like the idea that problem resolution is illusive, but at least being kept aware of progress is better than nothing. She can at least plan around the issue, if she must.

Next time, try it this way: Discuss the results you get with me, and I'll give you the best support I can give.

COACHING: POOR PERFORMANCE MUST RESULT IN TERMINATION

There are two types of poor performers: the service representative who does not care about the job, and the service representative who cares, is trying, but simply cannot do the job. The interview strategy for handling either personality is quite similar, and usually quite uncomfortable. When coaching these individuals, stick to discussing job requirements and performance. Avoid discussions of personality. Stay tightly focused on the measurable performance shortcomings and explain that the unsatisfactory performance has been discussed before. Be specific about the time and place of these previous discussions. There is no reason to be apologetic, as long as you stick to measurable performance. State clearly that this is the last review session and explain that your intention is to release this person from the payroll unless a dramatic change in behavior occurs quickly. Write a summary of this discussion, and tell the service representative you are keeping the written summary on file.

If your company's systems require it, discuss this individual with your personnel manager before conducting the counseling session and follow any special rules your company may have established for these situations. Do not ask the personnel manager for his or her permission to dismiss this person, but make it clear that dismissal is your intention, if the behavior does not dramatically change.

Plan your comments. Write an outline of key ideas to cover. Keep the outline on your desk for reference during the discussion. Plan to focus on measurable performance standards required of everyone on the team, and describe how this service representative falls short of the particular standards. Keep the discussion tightly focused. State specifically what measurable things must occur, how this individual must make these particular things happen, and when the improved standards must be met. Make certain your boss is informed.

MANAGER: Daniel, I want to discuss your performance again. As you know, we have been averaging two conversations per week for the last three months. All that counseling was to help you improve performance, yet you still score below our minimal standards.

REP: I have been working very hard trying to meet our planned objectives. I think I'm going to get my performance scores up.

Do not challenge the representative's perceptions. Ignore perceptions and judgments, as you have already had many discussions focused on the representative's view of events. Stay focused on the job-related issues for this final session.

MANAGER: This job has measurable standards, and I must be concerned with the total team and the objectives assigned to our team. As you and I have discussed before, each team member must make a positive contribution or our overall customer-satisfaction statistics will sink. We all need each other.

Daniel, look at these performance charts. The number of problems you resolve is about half the team's average. The amount of time you require to resolve a problem is about twice the group average. Also, you call for backup help far more often than others on the team and have an above-average number of customer complaints. You are not performing at an acceptable performance level, and I cannot keep you as a staff member. I must have an immediate improvement.

REP: But I'm trying. I've been working very hard lately, studying our systems. I just need more training time; I need a little more help.

You should have given all the extra time and counseling you can afford before this session. There is no reason to rehash everything you have done again. A sparse summary might be appropriate.

MANAGER: Daniel, this job is not for everyone, and you should consider finding a more suitable job. All of us have different skills. Look around for job opportunities elsewhere. We have been discussing your performance for three months. That's a long time, and I don't think things will work out for you here. You have participated in all available training and have repeated several training sessions. Further, I have provided extra coaching for you. Nothing is working.

REP: I need one more chance.

Take responsibility for the decision you are making.

MANAGER: That's all I can afford. I must be fair to the company, your colleagues, to you, and most importantly, our customers. I can only give you another thirty days. The turnaround in your performance must be complete. Let me be specific. I will be looking for the following things:

1. The number of problems you resolve must be at or above the departmental average.

2. The time required to resolve a problem must be at or better than the departmental average.

3. The amount of backup assistance you require must be at the departmental average.

4. The number of customer complaints you receive must also be at the departmental average or below.

Daniel, I think if you could meet these standards, you would already have done so. I still think your best option is to seek employment elsewhere. If you want to stay here, I need an immediate turnaround. You must implement all you have been trained to do. Your performance must improve to an average level and remain there over time.

REP: That's being unfair. I need a little more time. I need this job.

You will be better off with a direct approach. This is usually uncomfortable for both parties, but dragging this discussion on forever just makes everything worse.

MANAGER: Let's set a date now to review your performance numbers. See me on (set date a month or so away). You and I will both know if your performance is improving up to departmental averages. The statistical summaries are always posted. I'm still recommending you do the best you can here, and use the next month to find another job. If, however, you feel you can apply what you have learned, you can have the next thirty days to do it. Otherwise, I will remove you from the payroll in our next meeting.

Keep the communication specific, focused on performance, and very tight. Make sure that you specifically state that he will be removed from the team.

GETTING THE POOR PERFORMER OFF THE TEAM

This should be a short scenario, perhaps fifteen minutes or less. The decision to remove this person from the payroll has already been made. Counseling and extra training should have been going on for months. Some time ago, the employee should have been told that he or she was going to be removed from the payroll if specific improvements did not occur within a specific time frame (see preceding script). This script is the final departure discussion. It should be specific, state that the decision has been made, and then be ended. Do not apologize, say how you wish things were different, or state regrets. None of these words will help. It is over, and this script is only a statement of that fact. Do not talk around the subject. Get immediately to the subject at hand and stick to it. Dragging out this discussion can only increase the potential for additional problems. Besides, once the decision has been made to sever the relationship, there can be nothing gained from making this script into a full-fledged dialogue. Keep it essentially a proclamation. Take responsibility for the decision and end the relationship as graciously as possible. Above all else, avoid placing blame, and don't tell the service representative what he or she should have done to create a different outcome.

Follow all company rules. Advise your personnel manager, if applicable in your situation, and be sure to write all required notes and fill out necessary documents. Past performance failures should already have been documented. Your supervisor, attorneys, or others as applicable should have been involved with all the previous steps you have taken.

MANAGER: Daniel, your performance has not improved over the past month, and I've decided to end our working relationship.
REP: But I have been trying.

Do not get into an argument. Further, there is no need for a reminder that some time ago you suggested the representative pursue employment elsewhere. If that message was understood when given, you would not be in this situation now. Ignore the argument and proceed with the topic at hand.

MANAGER: A change is necessary. We will provide (state, do not discuss, whatever severance arrangements your company has available. Two weeks pay is customary if he has been on the payroll longer than a new-employee probation period).

REP: But what am I going to do? Where am I going to go to get a job? I must work.

Avoid comments such as: "I'm sorry" or "I know how you feel" and so forth. You are not losing your job; the employee is. Comments such as this will be insincere and invite retaliation. The representative will say: "If you are so sorry, why are you doing this?" Do offer whatever tangible help is available.

MANAGER: To help with your job search, personnel has provided this list of placement agencies. There are a number of jobs open in our area, and some of these agencies might be able to help you get placed. You should also get out and meet people in the business community and let them know you need work.

REP: How do I know where to go to find these business groups?

MANAGER: The chamber of commerce or library will have indexes that show all the business clubs and organizations in our area. Also contact everyone you know personally. Build a network of people who are willing to help you find work.

REP: But what about my family? What about medical insurance?

Avoid paternalistic comments such as: "You should have a savings account" or other similar words. These kinds of comments are antagonistic and add tension to an already difficult script.

MANAGER: Contact the healthcare provider directly and ask them to maintain your policy. You can pay them directly to keep your medical coverage until you get another position. Daniel, here is your severance check, and I do wish you the best of good luck.

COPING WITH STRESS IN THE CUSTOMER-SERVICE FUNCTION

Stress, a part of everyone's life, is more prevalent in some jobs than in others. Customer service can be a high-stress environment because no one doing this work can completely predict daily events, and unpredictability produces stress. This is a job for those with inner strength, discipline, and a positive, creative outlook on life. There are always unique customer situations bubbling to the surface as well as angry or distraught customers. And it's not just customers. It's also impossible to plan for all the problems that occur inside your own company; many of these internal problems exacerbate problems already existing with customers, thereby adding even more stress.

Pay attention to your body, and encourage those around you to do the same. Customer service is a job for thinking persons, and your brain certainly won't function very well without a healthy body to support it. Exercise burns off excess tension produced by stress. Get lots of it. A life-style including consistent rest, sound diet, and long intervals of rigorous aerobic and weight-training exercise will help reduce stress and increase success in customer service.

The more successful service operations I have seen are led by managers who pride themselves on being active team builders. They take time with the team, are great team players, good cheerleaders, and are always involved with their staff. These leaders create harmonious teams of representatives working in relatively stress-free environments. Their service representatives are not isolated or buried in problems, but see direction and purpose and are integrated within the total organization. Be one of these leaders.

Mornings can be a highly productive time, when people are at their freshest. So, manage by example. Get there early, but don't always dive straight into your own work. Start your day away from your desk. Get on the floor with your people. Walk around, see what's going on, meet and greet, and stay in touch. Let everyone know you're human. Don't just talk shop; ask about families, how the kids are doing, and so on. Keep the early-morning conversations light, including talk about the rumor mill and its recent proclamations. Use this time to feel what's happening. Just walking around and demonstrating your availability to your team helps reduce the pressure.

Stay in touch throughout the day. Remember, stress starts with the little stuff. Observe the pace and tempo. Be around to laugh at the silly things that always happen, or to express empathy when someone has to handle a particularly disagreeable customer, or, even worse, a disagreeable individual in another department. Don't assume people will just come to you when they are starting to feel stress. Create involvement, get close, and be friendly. Facilitate communications using lots of informal scripts. Say things like the following:

☎ "How's your husband (wife, girlfriend, boyfriend, and so on)?"

☎ "How's everything going?"

☎ "What's happening?"

☎ "You look great."

☎ "Can I help in some way?"

☎ "You look troubled. Is there a problem?"

☎ "What's new?"

☎ "How's the day going?"

☎ "How are you doing with (issue)?"

☎ "Where's the bottleneck?"

☎ "Who's supporting us?"

☎ "Who's helping?"

☎ "Are you struggling?"

Most of your time, perhaps 60 percent or more, should be spent with the customer-service representatives or technicians, helping them with problems they encounter while doing their jobs. The best way to reduce the stress inherent in customer service is to build a trusted team empowered to take constructive action and capable of reinforcing itself.

If you have a field-service operation and your service technicians are scattered in remote locations, your job will be more difficult, but not impossible. Talk to your people several times a day on the phone. Spend time traveling with your technicians. You will need to be well organized in order to make this special effort to be with your people. If you can't find the time to be available to your representatives, to build a team, examine your job responsibilities. Is your time being consumed by too many administrative reports and such? Are there too many meetings of questionable value? If the answer to these questions is yes, then work to get control of your job. Delegate some administrative details. Ignore other details. Don't wait for your boss to join you in risk taking. Do something creative. What have you got to lose? You must make time, invest it in your team, and create strategies that get the job and related stress under control.

Consider this scenario: A service manager inherited a stressed-out demoralized customer service department. Within a few weeks she learned the operation mostly produced burnout and chaos rather than customer service. Turnover was 100 percent per year, overwhelming training needs for the endless flood of new employees were impossible to meet, and customer complaints of poor performance were rife throughout the day.

Immediately classified as "just another boss," she commanded no respect from her team. Neither did any other manager. No one felt any sense of accomplishment or pride in the organization. The customer-service team believed it was nothing but chum fed to hapless customers foolish enough to swim near the worthless products produced. The manager's people and her operation were out of control.

She developed a simple creative-recovery situation. Each service representative would have fifteen minutes of her time each week. They *owned* this piece of her time and were allowed to discuss any topic, business or personal, they wished to discuss. A schedule was arranged. If individuals had something to discuss at their scheduled time, great. If they offered no agenda, their fifteen minutes were forfeited; she did not take over the time to discuss issues she deemed important.

She had about forty people, so something like ten hours per week were invested in these private meetings. Trust builds slowly, and the initial response from her team was cynicism. However, after a period of persistence and continuity, some service representatives started bringing up real issues. They watched. She took notes and acted. Some things she resolved quickly. Others became longer-term projects. Still others were beyond her control. When she could not act, she explained why.

Relationships started to build, cynicism declined. She was patient. She let her integrity with the team grow over time. Six months or so were required for results to show. Team building started, while stress and turnover declined.

When I first met this manager, she had been leading her team for several years. I vividly recall her sharing this story with a group of customer-service managers in my seminar. Enlightening was the fact that others in the group, perhaps too many, could not understand where she found the time to do all she had done. They could not understand how she could still "get her job done" if she was spending ten hours per week talking to her staff!

But there must always be time for constructive team building, for allowing the staff to vent, for creating new ideas and better ways to do the job. Such activity is vital for a healthy stress-free work environment.

To get another department under control, another manager took this simple approach. He said:

> Look, we are overloaded. There is no time for us to share ideas or come up with creative solutions to our problems. The workload continues unabated. This Thursday I will be here at 7:30 A.M. I will talk about things with whomever is here. No one is required to attend. I can't offer overtime pay or anything. But at that hour, at least the phones won't be driving us nuts. I will bring in the doughnuts, and I intend to continue this practice indefinitely.

A few of this manager's customer-service representatives joined him during the first meeting. In time, the entire staff started to attend. Within a year or so, word of his weekly problem-solving meetings had spread. The company president became a regular attendee and contributor to this meeting, which had now evolved into one of the most important practices in the company. The president also took over responsibility for supplying the doughnuts.

Coach service representatives continuously in ways to be more effective. Listen to what they tell you and to what they are saying to customers. However, secretly monitoring telephone performance increases stress. Service representatives feel that secret monitoring means you do not trust them. However, publicly listening in on conversations they have with customers and offering helpful suggestions has the opposite effect. Good coaches assume their service-support teams are always trying their best. They monitor performance through public observation and constantly offer helpful suggestions. They trust the service representatives and act accordingly.

Here are methods and activities many managers use to reduce stress:

- ☎ *Company picnic.* This is the most common, and the best ones seem to be when the bosses cook all the food for the first-level customer-support teams.

- ☎ *Gags and jokes.* These are great stress relievers. I have clients who perform a practical joke on birthdays. Jokes can take many forms: messing up your office, wearing funny hats, having dancing bears, gags involving your family, and so on.

☎ *Trading places*. Managers hold a first-level position a minimum of one day per year. Service representatives have a field day dreaming up practical jokes for them to endure.

☎ *Prizes for heroes*. There are tons of these programs. Virtually any form of prize or recognition for excellence works. One word of caution: These programs are disasters when they lack authenticity and sincerity.

Chapter

15

A Rock, a Hard Place, and You: Scenarios for the New Office Politics

DEALING WITH A POLITICAL TRAP

Politicking, like so much else in life, can be either positive or negative. We all spend a good bit of time selling. Conversely, and perhaps too often, too many of us try to advance the ideas we hold by trashing ideas held by others. Bigger organizations mean more people and more political debates.

The best way to avoid becoming the target of some aggressive politician looking to enhance his or her position by destroying yours is to ensure that you have a good support structure in place. Who are the people held in high esteem in your organization? Surround yourself with these folks. Sell them on the importance of following your ideas. Be a champion for their ideas. Get the right job, one which produces high value for the organization. Do it well. Make sure you work for a good leader who can muster resources and powerful political support if a tiresome turf battle breaks out. Find the corporate sharks. Make them your friends. Manage relationships with sharks carefully. Watch them carefully. Follow their lead, be on their teams, but don't use sharks as mentors or confidants.

Circumstances do not always fit some ideal model. You are most likely to become shark bait if either you or your boss is holding a high position, either of you is incompetent, or your overall business unit is in trouble. To some standing in line for promotion, derailing you may be nothing personal, just a necessary step toward advancement. Your career may be merely food for some shark's next career move.

Here's a classic setup. The person who selects you as a target will approach with some serious problem he or she has uncovered. Being the very judicious employee that he or she is, concerned only about the welfare of the organization, of course, this fine person has already taken the liberty of widely reviewing this

339

important problem with several higher levels of management. Naturally, this skunk he or she uncovered lives within your area of responsibility. Yet this very judicious person never once discussed this important problem with you. He or she simply carried the skunk to the lofty heights of the organization and let it spray.

There may be subtle variations, twists, and turns to the classic setup, but you get the general idea. The scenario will unfold something like this:

The attacker will just drop in on you unannounced. He or she does not want you to have time to develop a strategy.

SHARK: Over in Research, we have been doing some analysis of that new-customer support option you people introduced last year as an add-on to the widget product line. Development costs were well over $300,000, so we have put it under a rigorous analysis.

MANAGER: It's doing quite well in the marketplace, being well received. We're excited, it looks good, and fills out the product line nicely.

SHARK: Our analysis indicates that the new program cannot do what it was designed to do. In fact, our calculations indicate customers would be better off not purchasing it.

MANAGER: So far it has been well received by the marketplace. Users are excited about the program.

SHARK: That's what concerns us in Research. We already went and reviewed our findings with Frank (the super-big executive). We're concerned that the company image will be hurt as soon as the marketplace learns our customer-support operation is less than it should be and, worse, that we're not capable of doing what we promised with the program.

This is a pretty big clue. Like it or not, you're in a political fight. There are several concerns. This person is trashing you and your operations at the highest levels of the organization. When someone takes a potential problem with your operations to anyone other than you, that someone is not concerned about you or your views. He or she is far more concerned about him- or herself and whatever advantages sought. Or he or she may feel you are just incompetent and is trying to get you out of the job. Either way, it does not look good for you right now. This shark has you in a tight spot.

Be careful how you respond. It is not wise to take this person on head-on, or to discount him or her. First, he or she has the jump on you, and obviously has been working on whatever analysis for some time. You have just heard about this thing, and you do not know what his or her people have put in writing. Second, whatever the skunk found was smelly. The analysis has enough merit to hurt, at least to some degree. It must have. He or she put something in writing, and grabbed the skunk, and carried it to the lofty heights without mentioning anything to you. Only a fool would do that without checking. Homework has been done; he or she has proven something. No matter how weak the argument developed, it is best to assume this person's analysis makes some sense. Third, big and public political fights hurt your career, the company, and everyone around. People are political animals, yet we don't much like politics. Nasty political debates have a slimey underbelly; the worst case is called war. So, what to do?

Stall. Take time to think. Use silence. Do nothing. Stare into his or her eyes, or look off into the distance. You may want to rock back slightly in your chair, but don't look down or do anything that might suggest weakness. The employee is very aware that he or she has just sprung the trap.

Don't ask what you should do or anything like that. He or she will tell you soon enough, and is already taking the lead position. Don't help him or her gain more influence; make your adversary talk next and take the time to think.

MANAGER: Mmm. Interesting observations.

SHARK: Frank wants a report. He wants you to develop a report that describes our marketing strategy. He wants to know how our sales people are supposed to sell this program when it does not work.

Expect something like this. The skunk will tell you he or she is innocent and only the messenger for Mr. or Ms. Big. Simply doing a good job. Of course, that's why he or she went to Mr. or Ms. Big with these concerns rather than to you in the first place.

Your market strategy has long since been developed, and salespeople are already selling your new program. There is no need for this time waster. Even if you do write this report, it will not be well received. He or she will poke holes all through it, converting it into more fuel for his or her ultimate objective, whatever it may be. You could ask to review the findings in this report. He or she might comply. But this action tends to give your adversary's position more weight also. He or she can give you the analysis and tell the world of this important discovery, and can then announce that you are "reviewing" the very important discovery for the purpose of correcting your errors and developing a new strategy. You won't look very good. Telling him or her to get lost or inviting your boss into the debate are not great options either. If you tell this person to get lost, he or she will run straight to Mr. or Ms. Big and whine. This won't help.

Think things through before confiding in your boss. He or she is weakened for some reason or other and won't be helpful. The attacker is making a move because there is vulnerability in your plan. The report your adversary developed says something, even if it is something small. If your boss were on top of things, he or she would have helped you correct this long ago. If your boss were on top of things, this discussion would not be occurring.

The best option is to stall, allow your market strategy to unfold, and let observable success kill off this attack. However, don't give the shark the opportunity to develop countermoves by sharing the outline of your plan. You must contain him or her for a while.

MANAGER: If Frank needs a report, he will get one. Unfortunately, I'm jammed because the new program is so well received. Developing a marketing plan takes more time than I have right now. I just can't get to it.

SHARK: When will it be ready?

The shark won't let you off the hook easily. Ask for the maximum amount of time. Don't ask for too much, however. Asking for too much time will send him or her running to Mr. or Ms. Big howling about your stalling tactics. The exact amount of time you can get depends upon your specific circumstances.

MANAGER: We're awfully busy. It will be several months before I can address this topic.

SHARK: That's a lot of time.

MANAGER: It's the best I can do right now. The urgency must be on supporting the customers who are purchasing the new program.

Position yourself correctly, and you can stop the shark for now. If luck runs your way, a well-executed stalling tactic, combined with market acceptance of your new program, will resolve the issue and stop him or her forever. The need for the report will die a natural death, and your attacker will search elsewhere for fodder.

If you are unlucky, the markets will slip a bit or remain flat, people will be looking for scapegoats, and the attacker will return in three months. Next time, be ready. Get tough; plan for his or her return. Get your homework done. Develop graphs and charts. Show how much you are doing. Document how successful the program is.

SHARK: (Three months later.) Frank still needs that report on marketing strategy. How are you doing with its development?

MANAGER: Have we been busy! The new program is so well received that I just haven't had time to focus on anything other than new customers. We've been too busy working with customers and making deals.

SHARK: Frank is still waiting for the report.

MANAGER: I'm not sure we need it. Look at this chart showing the current workload. This new business is all created from the new service option we introduced. We're just shoveling in new work. Obviously, the sales force knows how good the new program is. I'm not sure we can write any plan that improves upon anything they are already achieving.

I've put together a rough plan, and it will take us approximately 300 hours to develop a complete set of marketing instructions for the sales force. I just don't have surplus hours available. I can only take hours away from all of these new customers we're pulling in. Maybe you can help. Look at these charts. They show how well our new service program is being received by the market. Here are some additional charts, which show our performance costs and the levels of customer satisfaction we're achieving. As you see, our margins are good, and customer satisfaction is high. We're moving. Perhaps you can revise your initial report to include these charts.

Language of this type may get rid of this person, and the political problem. Use words that send the message that you can and will fight back, if necessary. Be sure your homework is well done. Make sure your charts explain your success in clear terms.

SHARK: The analysis in our study is still valid. We anticipated initial sales would be good because of an unsophisticated market. The problems are going to come later. The sales force is bringing in the easy business now. Shortly, they will be bringing in more advanced customers, and those people will put pressure on our support capability. That's why we will still need a new marketing strategy. Without one, we won't be able to maintain our margins with our more sophisticated and demanding customers.

If he or she presses the debate, you will have to fight back.

MANAGER: This presents us with a serious dilemma. I just don't have the resources to accomplish what you want. They are all dedicated to paying customers we're bringing in with this new service option. These charts show that. To do what you are asking, we must turn away paying jobs. I don't have the authority to turn customers away.

SHARK: Frank just told me to get you working on this needed new strategy. You'll have to discuss your resource constraints with him.

Just because the shark says something, you do not have to respond. Pick your words carefully. Do not threaten him or her, but do not let him or her take the lead position, either. Use words that make it clear you are holding the shark, not Mr. or Ms. Big, responsible for this discussion.

MANAGER: Go ahead and discuss the constraints with Frank. You're anticipating a future marketing problem, which is not predictable from our current activity. However, you could be correct. Tell Frank our current status and have him send us a memo stressing the need to develop this new strategy you feel is necessary.

When I receive the memo from Frank, I'll tell him how many customers we will lose when I divert resources to the project you think should be done. I'll also show him these charts reflecting the effectiveness of our current strategy and explain that you and I have already reviewed these facts.

Continue working this strategy. If you have done your homework well, he or she will back off. The shark does not want just any political fight; he or she wants a political fight that can be won. As the scenario unfolds, as suggested above, your attacker will realize the battle has been lost, and will retreat. Mr. or Ms. Big will support the existing marketing strategy and the customers you are bringing in. Your attacker will see the outcome and back off. The shark will say he or she is going to discuss everything with Mr. or Ms. Big, but won't. You will never hear anything about this issue again.

THE PROJECT IS A DUD: HOW TO AVOID BEING THE "FALL GUY"

Major projects tend to develop constituencies, even when they evolve into disasters destined to be sink holes for large sums of money. People are assigned to the project. Full of promise, they start to execute the plan. The project starts to grow and swallow money. Those working on the project become dependent upon it and develop pride in it and allegiance to it. A constituency builds and assimilates power as more and more money is pumped into the project. The constituency defends the project and fights for more resources, even as evidence mounts to suggest the project should be scuttled.

Individual team members may also fear their jobs will be lost if the project is stopped. In many organizations, these fears can be well supported with the historical facts. Market-driven economies are self-cleansing, however, and the sink hole's appetite must eventually be curbed. If the project can't produce an ROI (return on investment), or other suitable objectives cannot be developed, the project must be killed. The larger the pile of bucks in the sink hole, the more critical the organization's need to throw a few bodies in as sacrificial scapegoats. Finger-pointing will start.

You are the most likely sacrificial lamb when the project grew within or near your area of responsibility. The worst scenario is when the project is in your area of responsibility, you know the project is a dud, it's gobbling up big bucks, and your boss is its biggest fan. We'll explore this twist.

The earlier you become convinced the project is a dud, the greater the probability you can avoid being a scapegoat and wiggle out of the mess. But don't expect an easy time working things out. So, how should you proceed?

It would not be prudent to go directly to your boss and challenge his or her support for the project. If he or she is the project's biggest fan, the boss will only reject your arguments anyway. If you protest too loudly, he or she may cut off other escape routes you may be able to cultivate. Take subtle action. Raise doubts about the project. Gather statistical evidence to form a factual base. Express your doubts in casual public debate around the coffee machine, and find some way to put your doubts in writing. Develop some sort of progress report, which may be part of a larger departmental report or a new report discussing the project only. Sample reports can be found in my book, *The Complete Customer Service Letter Model and Memo Book.*

The distribution list should include some group called the Project Team. Build this project team by listing names of individuals working on the project under the title "Project Team Members." Be sure your boss is a team member and that you are not. Diminish your authority and role. Be the recording secretary, not a team member. In these reports, you need to distance yourself from the project and the decision-making process. You need to make clear the project is a sink hole without starting a war that could jeopardize your career. You want to kill the project, not lose your job. Use language such as: "Review the figures attached. They suggest there may be errors with some assumptions originally developed for the project." Or: "Please review the following market statistics. They suggest the vision and initial goals for the project should be reevaluated. Perhaps the statistics suggest a market shift since this project was launched."

Do not use your name or become someone who attacks the project. Continue referring to analysis that should be done, but be nondescript about who should do the analysis. Reflect on new information or new circumstances. Show the team the way out. Identify circumstances that have changed since the project was launched, and make it easy for the team to pick up these clues and get out of the project before someone starts looking for sacrificial lambs. Do not mention individuals by name. Consider this language:

1. The following competitive facts have recently been discovered. See the attached chart. They suggest reevaluation of the project's goals may be necessary. If the competitive intelligence is correct, the project's objectives may be optimistic.

2. There seems to be a shift in objectives. Current trends would suggest the project should be reviewed. Three months into the mission, the foundation upon which the project's launch was based may have shifted.

3. The project will still require a significant commitment of resources for completion. $100,000 has already been invested in the project, and current projections suggest $150,000 more will be needed for completion. This is a good opportunity for a project review, considering all the changes observed in the markets recently. There have been significant market shifts reported. Perhaps the project cannot fulfill its initial potential.

4. There has been a shift in our business objectives. The project may no longer be able to deliver on its promise. A review of goals and objectives may be appropriate.

Avoid pronouns "we" or "I." Speak in the impersonal abstract, but make clear there should be reason for doubt. Make suggestions, not demands. Use statistics, and base your opinions on these statistics. Raise questions, and avoid opinions that cannot be supported with statistics: "Our customers are always shifting. Review the attached chart, which suggests our markets may have shifted away from the goals initially established for the project. The project still requires significant investments before completion. Perhaps funding should be redirected."

Send copies of your reports to other parties outside your immediate influence sphere. Don't ask permission. Just add these people to your distribution list. Take a modest risk and send copies of your reports to your boss's boss and other important people on the same level with your boss. Grow your distribution list slowly. It really doesn't matter if everyone reads these reports or not. What does matter is that they are on the distribution list, are part of the project, identified with the project and are perceived as part of the decision making system. You cannot stop the project singlehandedly; but you can reduce your role. Distance yourself slowly.

While you are developing this contrary point of view, others will likely be defending the project. Do not attack these project champions directly or specifically refute the positive things they are saying. War is not the objective. Ignore their reports and build your reports using totally different logic with customer-based statistics. If war is to be the outcome of this debate, let that decision come from others.

Be certain to keep a project book. It's also important to keep copies of all the reports. Date all reports, document all statistical evidence, and include reference notes. Change your behavior. Miss project meetings. Have other important things to do or important places to go. Whenever possible, try to get your boss to cover meetings for you. Remember, he or she is a project champion; you are not. Miss as many meetings as possible while maintaining the power to develop reports that continue to express doubts about the project. Become a follower in project-review sessions. Express doubts in the meetings, being careful not to antagonize. Use phrases such as:

- ☎ maybe this won't work
- ☎ I'm not sure
- ☎ the rationale may have changed
- ☎ goals may need review
- ☎ the markets look different
- ☎ there seems to have been a shift
- ☎ customers are moving away from this perspective
- ☎ this project may not produce the planned value

Continue this general behavior. Ultimately, the project will fail, as you predicted, and finger-pointing will start. Lie low, say nothing, and wait. If you are to be the designated fall guy, you will get signals. They will likely come from a political opponent several levels above you. Some important person, perhaps your boss's boss, will approach you and start a conversation:

MR./MS. BIG: Bill, I'm concerned about that new project we just launched. It's been out there for several months, and the results are very disappointing. The markets are not responding well at all. What's wrong? I expected much better results, and we have historically achieved better results.

BILL: I think there was a shift in the market. For the past year, my reports have been calling for a review. But the review never happened. I think the shift I was discussing all along in my reports has in fact occurred.

MR./MS. BIG: No, I want more than that. I want to know what went wrong. How was the marketing mistake made? We always do better than this.

You have been sending Mr./Ms. Big reports for a year. Suddenly he or she knows nothing. None of the questions you raised over the past months exist. Everything is new, a complete surprise. Even worse, he or she is asking you personally for a written report, even though you have been distancing yourself from the project for months.

Congratulations! You have been chosen to take the fall. When you develop your report, everyone will say: "If only we had this information earlier, we could have made better decisions." And, of course, you are the one who did not provide the needed information in a timely manner.

As bad as things may seem, you are actually lucky. You have just been given some time to maneuver. You have been protecting yourself all along, and now is the time to use whatever muscle you have developed. You'll need to muster all your strength. Those around you are playing hardball.

You could just ignore this request for the report, but that would be dangerous and might hasten your demise. He or she would use your behavior as additional fuel to prove your incompetence. You have been targeted to take the fall, and ignoring the request for analysis will only serve to prove that this disastrous project is all your fault. So develop the report.

Take your time. Spend some money. This has been a major project, and a fortune has been lost. The report must be formal, neat, well done, and well argued. It should be comprehensive, at least fifty pages, and must include charts, graphs, and other statistical detail to prove your logical decision. Pitch the report, and give it a positive spin. Do not be defensive. Develop it as a learning tool for the organization, a tool to help the organization grow and avoid a similar error in the future.

Present your evidence, including all the past doubts you have raised about the project. Use lots of footnotes, refer to specific dates, previous reports, and so on. This is most important: be sure to note the number of times you have called for a project review. Also identify how much money would have been saved if the review had actually occurred as you suggested. Explain how decision making should be improved. Don't take all the credit for good and blame everyone else for the bad. Yet make clear that the decision to proceed was not your decision, but an organizational executive decision. Use all the muscle you have, as there is nothing left to lose. Someone has already decided you are going down. You are just trying to slow the process and explain how messy your assassination is going to be for them.

List names, if you can. Describe who should have done what. If you don't have the courage to move this far, then list job titles and departments. Design the report so that your antagonist and your boss are revealed as more involved with the project and its decision-making structure than you were. Use language such as:

> In September, it was clear from the marketing analysis that an executive review of the project should have occurred. The marketing data was distributed to everyone on the project team, and the recommendation for a project review was made. However, the current decision-making process did not allow the analysis to go forward.

Or perhaps this:

> By October, three different studies suggested the initial goals for the project had shifted. All three studies were made available to the project team. However, the goals were never reviewed. The project's inherent momentum continued to move it forward.

Be even stronger with your statements, if you can:

> In June, we recommended that project funding should be reevaluated, as evidence clearly demonstrated its foundation was being challenged by changing market conditions. Published reports at the time recommended Mr./Ms. Big order a project review. The review was not ordered.

Prepare a wide distribution list, which includes all the high officials in your organization. Be certain the distribution includes your boss, your boss's boss, your antagonist, his or her boss, and so on. But under no circumstances should you send the report to the distribution.

Instead, take two copies of this document to your boss. Explain that Mr./Ms. Big suggested you develop the report so the organization can learn from its mistake. In a nonthreatening manner, let him or her know that copies are ready to be mailed. Ask your boss to give the document a final review before it is distributed to all concerned management in the organization. Explain further that you want the organization to receive maximum benefit from the review. So suggest he or she also ask your antagonist, Mr./Ms. Big, to review the report, add additional educational comments as necessary, and sign off on it before you mail copies to the distribution. Be certain the extensive distribution list is attached to the copies you give your boss.

This should be the last time you hear anything about this report. Don't say anything more about it.

This is the best you can do for now. Someone wants you to take a fall, but they don't want a big mess. They just want you out. Your antagonist will probably back off. But he or she will be back at some point. Your problems are not over.

If you start a shooting war, you will lose. There is too much muscle above you, and someone with clout has already targeted you. If he or she doesn't get you today, there's always tomorrow. But he or she knows you can fight back, and also knows that you're wise to being targeted.

It's easier to save yourself if you feel secure about your future. These situations are always quite difficult, and you should be prepared to walk away from this job at any time. In these situations, being right matters less than having enough muscle to deflect the attack. Having power, arising from goodwill built upon your previous reputation and performance, and using that power effectively does matter.

Using this method should get you time to get control of your own career. You have won the battle, but not the war. Use your time wisely. Get away from Mr. or Ms. Big within your existing organization, get a sponser bigger than Mr. or Ms. Big, or take control of your future, go another direction, and get another career start with some other organization.

WHAT TO DO WHEN YOUR BEST MENTOR BETRAYS YOU

We all need to trust others, and it is extremely painful when someone we trust betrays us. Unfortunately, betrayal is part of the human condition.

Here's an unfortunate scenario: For some reason, you are feeling insecure in your position and need a mentor or confidant. Perhaps you made a significant error, or a political opponent has just won a major battle, or you received a poor performance review from some important person. Whatever the problem, it bothers you a lot. Someone in power is after you; perhaps it's your boss's boss.

This scenario assumes you cannot confide in your boss for whatever reason. Either he or she is insensitive, incompetent, unconcerned, or maybe you just don't trust him or her. But the stress is running high, and you must talk to someone. So you go to another mentor, one you have trusted for years. Maybe this other mentor has even helped you get a promotion or two. You approach this other mentor, ask for his or her confidence, and you receive it. After all, this is your mentor. Then you open up, spill your guts, and discuss all career concerns and doubts openly. The mentor does his or her job; you are consoled. The conversation yields some comfort, and your thoughts are clear. Back on track, you return to your office. Then the worst possible thing happens.

Your boss is waiting at your door as you return. He's all over you with words like: "Why didn't you share your concerns with me?" "Why did you go to another?" "Your relationship with me should be a private matter." "You should have come to me with your doubts." "In the future, you must share with me first."

Your great mentor, the one you were just talking with five minutes ago, contacted your boss just as soon as you had left. This individual, who so many times before was your trusted mentor, disclosed every detail of the personal and private conversation you had with him or her.

Why would your mentor and friend do this to you? Has he or she been evil all along? Was your relationship always corrupt?

Maybe not. Organizational relationships are complex. This person is your mentor, and the relationship you had with him or her was probably honest and worthy of your trust. The key to the betrayal resides in his or her relationship with your boss. This mentor is probably older than you and likely at a higher level in the organization. Perhaps he or she is on a peer level with your boss, and therein is the key. If this mentor knows your boss well and trusts him or her, he or she may think a favor was done by breaking the confidence. Your boss is now informed of deep concerns you have. In the eyes of your mentor, your boss can better help you with counseling, coaching, and so on if he or she is aware of your concerns.

This sounds sort of crazy, but the reality is that you are the winner in this mess. You feel awful about the betrayal, but you are ahead. Swallow the pain and take some time to think.

Consider that your mentor plays a double role. He or she is your mentor, but is also your boss's confidant, or would never have betrayed your confidence in the first place. Your mentor certainly asked your boss, *his or her* confidant, to maintain a confidence, just as you asked the mentor to maintain a confidence with you. Your boss blew it by telling you everything, and you now are the winner.

When I share this scenario in my customer-service leadership seminars and ask the class what they would do if they were the manager betrayed, they usually want to bash the mentor for betraying the confidence in the first place. But you win more by staying quiet. Why? Because you have gained knowledge, and knowledge is power. Only *you* know that *both* people violated confidences. One betrayed you, and one betrayed the other. This is critical information, and you can use it forever. You can act as if these people are still your mentors. You can still grow and learn from them. But because you know they cannot keep confidences, you should never share intimate information with either of them again.

Tip: In the future, be more careful about selecting mentors. Most people have mentors and confidants in the workplace. It is better for you to generate some of these intimate relationships outside the workplace as well.

ORGANIZATION IS TOP HEAVY: HOW TO SAVE YOUR JOB

Management is always fighting a battle against management levels. This particular managerial morass usually evolves something like this: Organizations grow, adding many new and inexperienced workers. There is insufficient time for training.

Personnel problems emerge, mistakes happen, and layers of supervision are added to supervise the legions of new workers. The workforce is new, and many supervisors are added to provide tight control.

Then, because of shifting markets or changing competitive positions, cutbacks in the workforce are required. Supervisors and managers eliminate those below before eliminating themselves. After a major reshuffling, too many managers are suddenly managing too few workers. Presto! Another top-heavy organization is born. Communication slows, stagnation builds.

This brings us to an important organizational rule: To avoid this morass, avoid management levels. If you are pushed by those above you to add levels, resist the pressure, even to the point of becoming a bottleneck for your organization. If you are the top dog in the organization, it is still a good idea to avoid levels if at all possible. The top person is not invincible and can be pushed aside by lower levels.

Does your organization have a problem? To get an idea, look around and estimate the average supervisor/subordinate ratio. There is no perfect number, as the ideal ratio is dependent upon the job, the objectives, employee skills, risks, and so on. But you should be able to approximate something reasonable. Most jobs are not that complex, and one supervisor should be able to manage about twenty subordinates. Automatic information processing and a well-educated workforce tend to push the ratio higher every day. If you are in an organization where the ratio is something like one supervisor for every five subordinates or so, then it may have a problem. Flat or squeezed profits would certainly exacerbate the situation.

Assuming you are in a top-heavy organization, the best way to protect yourself is to be certain your own organization is as flat as possible. Be sure you are managing ten or more people. If you have three or four supervisors under you, and each of them has two or three subordinates, move your supervisors. Get them transfers or promotions and don't refill the positions. Expand the responsibilities of your first-line workers. Use self-directed project workteams to get things done. The best way to protect yourself is to clean up your own organization before someone else does it for you.

HOW TO AVOID ADDING SUPERVISORS

This is the reciprocal problem of scenario number 4. Say, for instance, you take over customer service when it only consists of two or three people. Then, because of a big corporate push to get better focus on the customer, you are asked to grow the department to thirty people or so. Human-relations problems emerge, as they always do. You, however, are caught up in resolving individual customer's issues. To gain more planning time, your boss suggests supervisors are needed to help you manage the expanded operation.

The organizational error starts to occur after you add this layer of supervision. Organizing into five teams and adding five supervisors answering directly to you gives you the best-looking organizational symmetry and much greater supervisory control. However, if the organization is not planning to triple the first-line staff, say up to 100 first-level people or more, so that each of your new supervisors will be managing twenty or so people, you have just built a very top-heavy organization. A moment ago, the manager-to-employee ratio in your organization was 30:1. Now it is 5:1. A moment ago, communications from you to the first line were clean and direct. Now they will be much slower. Communications will travel from you to your supervisors, who will discuss things among themselves before sending the message on. Filtered messages will travel to the front line. The same will be true in reverse. Communications coming to you will slow, even if you have an open-door policy and encourage first-level people to go around their supervisors and come directly to you. My own consulting and training experience suggests that organizations with the most difficulty are those with the tallest, most narrow hierarchies. Another important political consideration is the number of people who answer to your boss directly.

Suppose your boss has five people answering to him or her. Assuming this to be the case, your position is considerably weakened if you create the new organizational structure. Just think of this: If your position were eliminated, then your five supervisors would report directly to your boss. He or she would have a very manageable nine people who report directly and would receive corporate kudos for flattening the organization and eliminating bloat. Great for the boss. But what about your job?

Customer-focused managers with confidence in their leadership and management skills can easily avoid building these top-heavy organizations.

How do you stay away from these political problems? Don't create them in the first place. Stay focused on the correct things, which are leadership issues, not operational issues. As leader, your job is coaching and leading. Your job is helping the team find direction and teaching team members skills needed for working well with each other. Your job is not to resolve this or that technical problem; it is helping others develop the skills to resolve this or that technical problem.

You are most tempted to add supervisory levels during times of rapid growth. The workload is high, customers are demanding, hiring is in fast forward, many inexperienced people are running around asking lots of detailed questions, and the demand for training is high, as errors proliferate. Yet this is when the best leaders excel.

Whenever a group of people work together, informal leaders evolve. You can borrow from the informal structure without making it a formal leadership hierarchy.

Rely on your most experienced people to resolve the technical problems. Others will come to them with detailed questions, and they will evolve as informal group leaders. Give these experienced people special projects. Let them perform the research, talk to other managers, and develop recommendations for resolution of the technical problems, which will constantly crop up. Lead them, don't tell them what to do. Let them develop training sessions, manuals, and written instructions for the newer people. Don't reward with promotions that bloat the organization. Reward with job diversity, special projects, and dollars. Experienced people will take longer in resolving issues, and they will need coaching from you. But by breaking down the larger technical problems into manageable projects, you are expanding the job, developing their skills and freeing up time for yourself.

Assign two or three people to a group project as well. Don't assign the group leader. You focus the team's attention on the goals and objectives. Let them, as a team, handle process and team-leadership issues.

And what of the boss who insists you promote supervisors and create more levels? Buy time. It will happen something like this:

BOSS: Jim, that little group of yours has grown quite a bit over the past year.

MANAGER: We're at thirty people right now.

BOSS: You need to consider another level of supervision between yourself and the others. You can't handle thirty people alone.

MANAGER: Sometimes I'm stretched, but we do pretty well. I have a lot of teams set up. The teams manage themselves quite well.

BOSS: But when you're out, I really don't know who to call with questions.

MANAGER: Call any of the senior people, and they can get you the information you want. Our information is public to everyone, and we all know what others are doing. Any senior person can either get you an answer you need or get you in touch with whomever has the right answer.

BOSS: Well, all that is good for now. But if you get sick or something, the organization would be better off if another layer of supervision was in place to help manage that operation.

Words like these are a clue. The boss is concerned about the organization. He or she is also concerned about him- or herself, and is worried that perhaps you may depart the organization, leaving a leadership vacuum. Be careful with the words you use. Your tendency may be to proclaim proudly that any of your experienced people could replace you. Don't say this, as he or she will likely tell you to make these folks supervisors. Buy time on this issue.

MANAGER: You have a point. I'll make a note of it and start thinking about the subject. I don't really have anyone ready for supervisory positions right now, but I will give your suggestion some thought.

BOSS: We should have some additional supervisors in place in three months or so.

Let the conversation die off, and don't bring the issue up again. But prepare for the fact that your boss will bring it up again later. Keep building your team-management skills, and keep building the skills of your people.

BOSS: (Five months later.) Have you decided on a new organizational structure?

MANAGER: No. Everyone is working so well together, I hate to break it up. They really like the teams we have in place. It's a lower-cost organization, and communication is smoother and easier.

BOSS: Those supervisory levels are important, though. We have been working toward establishing those supervisory positions for some time now. We need to get moving.

MANAGER: We will need to keep developing our people toward that objective. Some have the potential to grow into a leadership position. However, no one is ready yet.

BOSS: Come up with a developmental plan, which should produce the supervisors we need in the next three months.

Continue buying time and begging off this situation. It would be difficult for your boss to overrule you if you maintain the position that no one is ready yet. Also consider finding a better position for your best person in another department.

GETTING RID OF WORK

Most operations attract some trash work. Customer-service departments, eyes and ears for the customers, seem to be especially vulnerable. Everyone with a question or political agenda will ask Customer Service to help conduct a study and learn more about what the customer wants, or prove what the customer wants. People need reports covering what the customer thinks of products as well as effectiveness of promotional campaigns. Others need to know about error rates, faulty engineering, production problems, difficulties with the published schedule, changes in complaint levels, failures, and so on.

Don't fight against all the absurdity you see. The simplest way to get rid of work that should not be done is simply to ignore it. If the request comes through the mail in memo form, set it aside and let it age for a period of time. Many things can be allowed to die a natural death. If no one asks about it, forget the memo altogether, and throw it out in a few months. If someone comes along and asks for it, you can always say you have been very busy, apologize for your negligence, do the task (if necessary), or move the task to another holding pen and hope it dies next time.

What if the boss asked for the work, but the task still is not worth the effort? In my consulting work and seminars, I hear a lot about the paper-shuffling boss, the one who is always sending around one or two more forms for people to fill out, all of which are utterly unnecessary. I worked for one once. There is also the boss who needs just one more analysis before the decision is made. Follow the same suggestion: Ignore it.

Yes, at times, even the boss can be ignored. This is especially true with the paper shufflers as they forget about all the paper they are shuffling. As with everything in business, there is risk. Before you ignore a request for something, make sure you know the importance of that thing to the person who is doing the asking. The task may seem trivial to you. You may even think it is something you should not be asked to do. Yet, the task may be a critical link in some larger goal or objective that impacts the company and your operation. Ignoring an important task of this type will quickly get you a reputation for being uncooperative and a poor team player.

Sometimes you can't ignore the task; the requester follows up. If this happens, try tossing the work back to the requester. Suggest that the requirements aren't clear and ask for clarification, preferably in writing. Ask for more than one clarification, too. You can usually plead ignorance for a fairly long time. Say resources are not available to get the special project done. Ask the requester to get you the people you need. Even your boss can be held accountable for the tasks he or she creates. If the boss asks for something silly, ask what should be ignored in order to do this new silly thing. Suggest some things that could be ignored, so that you have the resources to do the silly thing he or she wants done. Make sure the things you offer to ignore are manifestly critical to the business.

Another alternative is to "sell" the routine task to someone else or to another department. The manager of this other department may actually like doing it. For example, suppose you are head of customer training and are required to handle travel logistics as well as training content for all your customers. Obviously, your real concern is for the training quality, not the travel logistics. Invite your transportation department or travel agency into the problem. Your job is training. They handle logistics as an end product; you handle it as a means to an end. They may be glad to help out. You get rid of work you should not do; they are able to justify their existence and make a greater contribution with their end product.

Don't think of just special projects, either. A routine task can be reassigned to another department, too. To avoid infighting, always approach these political situations on a cost basis. Study the task, and determine costs for performing the task, using current methods in your operation. Approach the sister department and calculate the costs, assuming the sister department performed the task. Recruit the sister department as an ally and present the savings to management. As long as you and the sister department agree on the transfer of responsibility, these situations are almost always approved.

Be prepared to transfer the people doing these jobs. This would normally be expected and is a sure way to get the sister department to join you as an ally. At times you have an exceptionally good person doing a job. You want this person to stay in your operation, but not the work he or she is doing. Be sure to transfer him or her off this task well before, perhaps three months or more, any analysis that might lead to a transfer gets under way.

Some routine tasks can be allowed to die a natural death just by following the rules mentioned above for projects. Stop doing the task and see what happens. Many tasks and routine responsibilities are started in organizations, develop a following, and simply continue for no apparent reason other than to support the constituency that does the task. Be suspicious of any task that costs money but does not support the customer. Question written policy, too. At one of my client's operations, service technicians are assigned company vans. Before being dispatched to the field for use, brand-new vans were routinely repainted to ensure they were the correct company color. Five hundred dollars per van was routinely spent on every new van. We had to come from the outside to question this wasted cost.

At Cincinnati Milacron, the billion-dollar machinery company where I worked from 1967 to 1985, the white side-wall tire option was never purchased for new company cars. It was too costly. Replacement tires were all the lower-cost black side-walls as well. However, during the seventies and eighties, many new cars shipped with white side-wall tires as part of the standard equipment package. Some bureaucrat in finance at corporate headquarters issued a policy: Immediately after cars were delivered, sales and service technicians had to take their new cars to their local gas station and have all the tires removed from the rims. The tires were to be reversed on the rims so that, when mounted on the car, the white-walls faced into the wheel well. Hundreds of employees blindly wasted tens of thousands of dollars in time and service station fees performing this absurd task. The policy stayed in effect for years and years.

Enhance your own career. Keep control of any tasks that add value for the customer. Add any new task to your operation that adds value for the customer at no new or additional cost. Find budget money to develop new tasks that add value for the customer.

Any tasks that do not directly add value to the customer should be ignored. If you can't kill the skunk outright, let it die a slow death. If it won't die a slow death, get it out of your operations. Delegate it somewhere. Otherwise, sooner or later, it will become an anchor on your career.

If you can't get the skunk out of your operation, do the task very poorly. Every time you do the task, gnaw on it. Be sure to point out what important things for the customer are not being done because you have to focus on the skunk.

WHEN TO IGNORE COMPANY LOYALTY

People agonize over loyalty. I do not advocate being disloyal to your organization or to your superiors. Yet, consider: Engineers who understood the cold-temperature risk tried to stop the tragic *Challenger* launch. They were overruled by their superiors at both the principal shuttle contractor and NASA. I'm sure we all agree the world would be a better place if those same engineers had tossed loyalty to the wind and gone screaming to the news media. Certainly, the victims' family members must feel this way.

There is no easy answer to where loyalty stops and the greater good begins. You must let your conscience guide you.

If you do decide to go public, there is no risk-free way to do it. Here are a few guidelines to help with your thinking process:

☎ Select a well-known reporter, someone who has a stake in the community and the issue you need to leak. Be certain he or she has a vested interest in the community. Such a person will be more trustworthy about maintaining the confidence if things get hot later.

☎ Call him or her anonymously and outline the issue. Be sure to *avoid* the critical details needed to create a story. Tell the reporter that you want guarantees of anonymity before you meet and to give out the critical information.

☎ Make the reporter guarantee anonymity. Depending on the issue at stake, you might choose to involve the reporter's boss and have him or her support the pledge. You may even ask for a written guarantee of anonymity.

☎ Tell your story. Be certain to have your résumé ready and start looking for another job. You don't want to stay here any longer than absolutely necessary.

STOPPING THE PUBLIC REPRIMAND POSITIVELY

These scenarios are always embarrassing, because they have a public tilt. They unfold something like this: A particularly insensitive detractor will write one or more memos complaining about something your department is doing. Or he or she may write about some service your department should offer in the future. While your detractor may have good suggestions for improvement, the memos are direct or abrupt in tone. You may like this person, and he or she may be quite competent. The problem is with tone; he or she uses tough, perhaps even condescending, language in these memos. He or she seems to be disciplining you in writing. While not pleasant, this is all acceptable. Many in business play hardball.

But true insensitivity comes into play, and heat is really cranked up in this scenario, because of the distribution list. The detractor sends copies of the memo to your boss, his or her boss, and everyone else within mailing range. The message in the memo is not so horrible, and even the tone would not be so offensive if it were sent only to you. However, the distribution list makes it appear as if you and the detractor are in some sort of dispute, that you are wrong, and that he or she is reprimanding you for the mistake you have made.

Your initial reaction may be to jump on this person. Well, don't. It's better to do nothing for awhile. Keep the memo, because you may need it later, but exercise some patience. Buy a little time. Don't respond in any way; don't send the memo back with margin notes or anything else that might encourage him or her. Just sit still. Usually, your detractor will simply go away. Memos are difficult to write, and he or she will probably just tire and find something better with which to occupy him- or herself.

However, the memos may keep coming, and, if they do, additional action is required. If you do nothing, these continuing public criticisms will damage your career.

Arrange a few impromptu coffee-machine meetings with this person. Be friendly, courteous, and upbeat. Don't bring up the memos. If he or she brings them up, just acknowledge you have them and that you appreciate the positive suggestions. Don't thank him or her for the input or provide any other form of encouragement. Try to slide into the conversation a word or two about the tone used. Try something like:

> Right. I like the suggestions you make. We're already implementing ideas similar to yours. Thanks for the support. I'm always looking for ways to do things better. Style of presentation is another issue. We have a lot of work to do, and, certainly, our whole department has a long way to go. If you have any other suggestions, just pick up the phone and give me a call. We can have lunch or something and discuss your suggestions in more depth.

Be subtle. You don't want to make a big deal out of this. Drop only one or two modest hints about presentation style. There is another reason for caution. The detractor, either on his or her own or with coconspirators, maybe even with the boss, may have a master plan. This whole memo campaign may be a plot designed to make you the fall guy for some project failure. At this stage, you simply don't know, so it is best to be cool and lie low for a while. A few coffee-machine meetings are fine for now. Follow this trail as long as you can, though with each memo it will get tougher to stay quiet. Collect the memos, continue to drop hints about the style, and be friendly.

Above all else, make this detractor fall in love with you. You have everything to gain and nothing to lose. At best, this individual is insensitive and makes inappropriate statements. You do not want him or her making inappropriate statements at the wrong times about you.

At worst, he or she is part of a conspiracy that will impact you later. In any case, the closer this person is to you, the better for you. The closer he or she is to you, the easier for you to observe his or her motivations, movements, and associations. Also, if the person is close to you and sees your competence, he or she may cease the memo barrage without further action. However, if the public reprimands continue, this trail will become unbearable. It's time for a different tactic. A bold but controlled confrontation will be necessary. You will have your best chance at success if, through past encounters, you have caused this protagonist to respect you and your performance.

Gather your energy and all the memos you have received. Walk over to his or her office unannounced. Be sure he or she is alone. Just walk in, drop the memos on one corner of the desk. Remain standing, use your bold and authoritative voice, look your detractor straight in the eye:

(Name), could you please stop reprimanding me through the mail?

Pause, maintain silent eye contact for a long moment, and then sit down. Immediately take the initiative in the discussion and be totally positive. You are trying to change behavior, not start a war. Tell this person how much you appreciate the positive suggestions. Comment on how helpful the ideas are to your goals and objectives. Talk about the positive contribution made to your operations. If possible, express where you agree with the criticisms and outline remedial steps you are taking to improve your operations. Mention that the constructive contribution, while helpful, is undermined because of the continuous pubic criticism and recrimination. Focus on the importance of your cooperative relationship with him or her. Explain that your only concern is the method of presentation, not the content, which is helpful:

Please don't stop the constructive input. It's needed. It's just the public reprimands I'm concerned about.

Your ideas are always needed. But the way they are presented in the memos makes it difficult for us to focus on the constructive content.

Experience like yours is always needed and very positive. It can help me build a new department.

(Name), everyone on my staff thinks people from your department are very helpful. I'm trying to build on that and need your help to accomplish the important cooperative objective.

It's not your ideas, or even the public nature of your memos. It's the tone of the language used. We already know we're not doing a good job. We're trying to turn things around. We need help not criticism.

(Name), we know our performance is less than exemplary. Our department has been underfunded and ignored for years. Now, with the new organization, we have to build an infrastructure. It should have been done long ago, I agree. But, we're doing it now and it will take time. We need constructive support, not continuous criticism.

That operation has been ignored forever. I'm newly assigned and trying to build morale. The team is currently weak and it will take time for me to rebuild. I need for my people to hear encouragement about what they do well from other managers, not continuous criticism about yesterday's problems.

(Name), you know I'm new to the service function. We're working overtime to turn that department around over there. I need your expertise and support. I want to work with you. But I really don't need a public debate. Can't we work together more closely?

Your detractor will be set back with this pointed discussion. If the whole thing was an honest mistake, and he or she simply has a poor writing style, the memos will stop immediately. Expect him or her to make amends somehow, perhaps even saying a few positive words to your boss, apologizing, and stating that he or she was only trying to be helpful. (The colleague in my corporate life who was the inspiration for this scenario did exactly that.) Spend a good bit of time building a relationship with this individual. He or she will be helpful to you in the future.

The memos will stop, even if the antagonist was plotting a conspiracy of some sort. He or she may want you out of your job, but does not want a bloody public war. Your direct approach indicates you are prepared to fight back. This he or she cannot handle.

If you suspect a conspiracy, as the ensuing weeks pass, start taking cautionary defensive moves as quickly as possible. Build a containment strategy; for your adversary will return again. Next time, the tools will be more subtle, and perhaps more effective.

SUBORDINATE DOES NOT LIKE YOU

Corporate secrets are difficult to maintain, because informal corporate communication channels are always well lubricated and running in high gear. The protagonist ridiculing your startup mistakes thinks he or she is communicating only with selected friends. Not so. You probably discovered this emerging problem through the grapevine. Supportive mentors or confidants have picked up gossip he or she is spreading and have tipped you off about the emerging problem.

The initial reaction most think of is a confrontation before things get worse. One may be inclined to go to the protagonist directly, tell him or her what you know, and get the grievance out in the open. This strategy is usually a mistake. Obviously, this person has not developed respect for you. Why else would he or she be talking to others about you? If he or she is not sharing feelings with you now, it is unlikely that he or she will respond to a direct approach. Use it, and you will likely succeed in driving the emerging problem underground. You are then destined to await its appearance elsewhere, at some other time and place.

, But there is a plus: You now have discovered a valuable source of feedback. Don't lose it. A much better strategy is for you to cultivate this important feedback channel. As a new leader, you do not have the benefit of the department's history. You have not yet learned about all of your people, their perceptions, their abilities, their attitudes and their relationships with each other. You do not yet know what everyone thinks of you. This new communication channel can give you information in all of these areas and more. Learn from it. Use information gleaned to refocus your presentation to the staff, to evaluate how your message is being heard, and to help you restate and clarify goals. This communication channel can help you learn what is perceived behind the scenes.

The first step is to be certain your mentors and confidants are working overtime for you. Thank them for their support. Ask them for additional efforts. Tell them you need their help, and be certain they do everything possible to listen and gather data. But be sure they take no actions that might cut off the communication channel. Talk to these confidants frequently. Cultivate long-term relationships with them. You need information and time to study that information. You may want these confidants to help you cultivate this communication channel for a period of time, perhaps a year or more. Remember, this antagonist is doing a good job for you. If you can save him or her for your operations, you should.

Watch what you say and do around this antagonist and his or her associates in the department. Maintain a positive attitude, being sure to give no indication that you have another communication channel providing you with feedback on his or her views. Give this person assignments as usual. Be available. Open impromptu communications with him or her by frequently asking about family, hobbies, and so on. Offer suggestions. Be a good coach and counselor. Get as close as possible. Offer him or her a maximum opportunity to open up to you and seek your guidance. Offer him or her every opportunity to criticize you, your goals, objectives, style, or everything else that may be liked or disliked.

This, then, should be your posture. Follow these two paths simultaneously:

1. Do everything possible to build a relationship.
2. Evaluate the progress you make with your informal communication channel.

You can maintain this position for a very long time and do quite nicely. Remember, his or her job performance is satisfactory. It's just that this person cannot be trusted as your ambassador. It's not the best of circumstances, but it's not that terrible, either.

It usually boils down to a tolerance contest. The best outcome is that your relationship with this antagonist improves. If this hopeful and desired outcome occurs, it will be easily confirmed by the informal communication channel. Mentors and confidants watching your backside will report that the stream of criticism has gone dry. In the best case, they will even report hearing positive comments about you.

Far too often, though, the back-stabbing comments continue, and your tolerance level will be exceeded, even though you're putting forth your best effort to turn things around. Something must be done, as you cannot run your operation effectively knowing that a team member is always there standing off-stage, just waiting to sabotage your every effort. Living with the status quo indefinitely will ultimately cause you to reduce your risk-taking. You will start watching your back and operate too conservatively. Unresolved, this situation will ultimately have a negative impact on your own performance. Try arranging a transfer for this individual. Find a colleague who has a new employee requisition and try to sell your protagonist to this other manager. Be sure to pick the correct job and the correct manager, as you do not want simply to pass your antagonist on to another department in the company, where he or she will cause difficulties for another. Too often, we find that people unsuited for any job in the organization are passed from department to department because no manager wants to make the difficult decision and go through the necessary process of releasing this individual from the payroll. Yet off-loading the skunk onto an unsuspecting colleague ultimately causes the entire organization to suffer. Be open with the other manager:

> Don is doing okay with the technical job requirements. It's our personal relationship that is not developing.

> Larry, don't make your decision by talking to me alone. Talk to Don first. See if the potential for working together is there before accepting him. He had a strong relationship with my predecessor, who was moved aside. Perhaps he somehow blames me for the management change. Maybe that's why he can't or won't respond to my style.

> I'm new to the department and making a lot of changes. The changes may be too tough for him. A new position might be just what is needed to get him turned on again.

But what if there are no other job openings? I still recommend you transfer this individual. You must be able to trust the people working in your department. Look around the organization. There is always someone who needs help but has not been able to get approval to hire new employees. Approach this manager. Describe your situation and offer him or her the antagonist and the associated payroll through the existing budget period. You can lobby for a replacement requisition during the next budget cycle. Moving this person would be better than having someone in your department who continually tries to sabotage your effort.

After you have lined up an interview, you will need to introduce this job change to your protagonist. Make sure to use positive language, since the objective is to create a painless change, not a war. The object is to resolve a personality conflict, and there is no reason to create harsh feelings that will impact the organization far into the future. Your words need to create a delicate balance. The antagonist has no choice in this matter, yet you should not send the message that he or she is being pushed out of the organization:

> Don, Larry over in sales has an immediate need for experienced help. I suggested you for this position, and he's very interested in talking to you. Our workload is in

a lull over here, which will continue for a while. Call Larry. He's anxious to see you. It will be a new experience for you and, overall, we can create some efficiency in the company, because our workload is declining.

Don, I've got some great news for you. Judy over in accounting has an urgent need for some assistance. Your background is perfect for what she needs to get done. Go talk to her; I think you are going to really like what she has for you.

Don, as everyone knows, our workload has been declining for some time. I've really been worried about keeping all of us busy. Larry over in sales has an urgent need for help, and your skills fit his requirements exactly. It's a new adventure for you and a great way to help the entire division. He is overloaded and we don't have enough work. Go over and listen to what he has to say. I'm sure you will like what you hear.

I need your help with an out-of-balance situation between us and Judy's operation. We're two separate departments, but we're in the same division. We're busy, but she's swamped. I told her we could find some hours to help her out. Your experience fits her need exactly. Go talk to her and listen to what she has to say. Don, it's a new experience for you and a great way to help out the entire division.

YOU MESSED UP AND HURT SOMEONE: REBUILDING YOUR INTEGRITY

No one is perfect, and all good people go out of their way to avoid hurting anyone. However, our human condition seems to dictate that at least some judgment errors are inevitable. You would be brilliant indeed, in addition to being awfully lucky, to conclude a successful career without making any serious mistakes. Unfortunately, an error in judgment can hurt other good people. The worst of all possible scenarios is when your error hurts one of your best customer-service representatives, one who truly admires and supports your style, one who makes a major contribution to your goals and objectives. Making this situation even more difficult is that your error may be very painful for this good person. To save face, he or she may be forced to leave your organization and seek employment elsewhere. The best people usually have other employment choices available.

Even if you do make a gut-wrenching error, you still are the leader of the customer-support team. Others depend on you. You must do more than just live through the situation. You must rise above it. You know it's your mistake, but somehow, you must swim through the emotional muck and climb out of the abyss. While doing this, you must also convince others on your staff that you still are a person of integrity and that you and your vision are still worth following. Just how can you accomplish this?

First, start with the good person you hurt. Do everything in your power to save him or her for the organization. This may take several conversations and a good bit of time.

Be open with your boss and solicit his or her support, too. Receive counsel from your mentors as well. All these folks will be able to offer experience and advice. Even if you can't save the injured person for your department or the company, others on the team will need to know later that you did everything possible to try.

MANAGER: Jim, I'm sorry about (summary of the incident). It was an error in judgment on my part. I know I hurt you, but I hope you can look beyond it and forgive me. I really do want to work something out with you. I've talked to my boss, and he or she, too, is offering all the support he or she can. You're a good person, and we both want you to stay.

Use this type of language during several meetings. Keep the dialogue personal, but do not dwell on the specifics of the mistake. You did it, you have accepted responsibility, you have apologized, and it's over now. There are bigger issues at stake, and your focus should be on getting Jim to focus on these larger issues.

REP: I want you to fix the error.

Expect comments of this type. He or she thinks there is something you can, or should fix. Things would not be so far out of control if he or she felt otherwise. Use a lot of empathy. But remember, you have no integrity with this person right now.

MANAGER: I can't undo what has been done. Please understand that if, in my judgment, I could find a way to make things different and rectify this situation, I would. But you have made your position clear. I know you believe there is something I can and should do. On that point, we must continue to disagree. I can't do what you ask. I know what I did was painful for you, but I cannot rectify it in the way you feel I should.

Jim, you are an excellent performer, and we all need you on this team. However, I also understand that you may not respect me enough to stay with us in customer service. I also believe strongly that you have a future with this company. I am only one employee, and there is no reason for you to leave. There is plenty of space for you in this organization.

Tip: Be humble.

MANAGER: I have contacted two other managers and have explained to them that you are one of the best people in this department. Further, I have briefly outlined my error to them and have asked them to talk to you. You have my highest recommendation, and both of them are eager to offer you a position.

REP: No, I don't really want to stay.

MANAGER: You have been with the company for five years and have created an excellent track record. This organization rewards tenure highly, especially for high performers, and you are one. There is no reason for you to throw away five years of seniority and start over elsewhere.

REP: We have had several conversations. It's true that initially I was hurt and angry with you. That anger did cause me to look elsewhere. But I'm over the anger now. I don't want to interview for those other positions. I have another job offer, and I think it's an opportunity I can't afford to pass up.

MANAGER: I don't want you to leave the company because of me or any other single person.

REP: Originally, it *was* you, but it's not you anymore. Now I just want to try this new opportunity. This new job is here and available now, and I don't want to turn it down and regret it later.

Continue this dialogue long enough to convince yourself you have done everything possible. This may take several conversations.

MANAGER: Jim, I'm sorry you have to leave, but I do understand and wish you the best of luck.

A few things are likely true:

1. Jim is carrying a major load for your department; good people are always carrying major workloads.

2. Everyone in the department, and in neighboring departments, knows everything that has happened. You have said nothing to your subordinates, but Jim has told all.

3. Your integrity is not worth much right now. Jim has told this story from his perspective, not yours. He has been undermining your integrity. It is your error, and you won't fix it the way he thinks it should be fixed.

4. Jim is angry with you and trying to do as much damage as possible. You hurt him. He will pick the worst possible time to quit. The day he quits, he will be committed at a maximum customer load, and you will have very minimal flexibility to cover the labor shortage.

What should you do when he hands you his resignation letter? Do not make an immediate announcement. Jim is not the only good person you have in your department. First, gather three or four other trusted colleagues and have a closed-door meeting somewhere. This meeting will be a little rough on you, but worth it.

MANAGER: Jim just turned in his resignation. He is leaving in two weeks.

CONFIDANT: What the hell did you do to him, anyway?

Expect a reprimand of some sort. This scenario has been brewing for some time, a good guy has been injured, and everyone knows all about it. The rumor mill has been working overtime; Jim has made sure to keep it well fueled. Importantly, these other confidants have only heard Jim's point of view, but they still want to follow your vision.

They are very frustrated good guys. Since this mess started, they have been unable to discuss any details with you. At the same time, they have watched Jim use the rumor mill to undermine the entire department. Your integrity with this team is shaken, but not broken. This is the first opportunity for open communication. Be open and honest with these people. You need them.

MANAGER: Look, I screwed up. (Give a brief description of the mistake you made.)

CONFIDANT: Okay, you screwed up. Why does Jim have to pay the price?

Stay with this topic as long as necessary. You are rebuilding your integrity.

MANAGER: He doesn't have to pay. I've had several conversations with him. I apologized to him for the mistake and did everything possible to keep him with us. Further, I told him I would understand if he could no longer work with me or this department. I even got him several job offers from other managers. He has talked to my boss, too. He won't accept anything we offer. He has locked in on the idea of leaving us, and that is exactly what he has done.

They will ask you questions until they are certain you did everything possible to save him. Don't rush things, and be open with your comments. This discussion may go on for some time, as you are rebuilding your integrity with them. Eventually, the conversation will run its course.

CONFIDANT: What do you want from us?

MANAGER: Jim was loaded to the hilt, and he picked the worst time of all to leave. The team is going to have to bust butt to handle his load as well as their own until I can find some additional help for us.

Right now, I have no integrity with anyone, and I need your help rebuilding. I'll gather everyone together, announce Jim's resignation, and wish him the best of luck. Then I will head into my office.

I need for you guys to handle the rumor mill for me. Handle questions people may have. Use your judgment, strike a balance, and resolve their concerns about my integrity. I also want you guys to lead the effort needed to fix the schedule. Take over after I make the announcement, reshuffle things, and make sure the workload is covered. You will need to book people very heavily to accomplish this. Can I depend upon you for help?

If you have been open and honest enough, you can pull this off. As long as you did everything possible to save the injured party, you can get over the top of this. Your team will not let you down. They will say yes. You are allowed to make mistakes, even those that hurt others, as long as you do everything possible to undo and compensate for the error.

HOW TO SAVE THE OTHER WHEN YOU CAN ONLY PROMOTE ONE

Only one person can be promoted to the leadership position at a time. Making the decision is always difficult. Once made, though, it must be implemented positively. The entire team must accept the decision and the new relationships it brings, even though team members were not a part of the decision-making process. Some who were not in contention for the promotion will accept the promotion of their colleague from within rather easily. They knew they were not contenders. Those who were in contention will have a more difficult time.

Managing the transition is a very important process. Too often, promotions are handled poorly. They are simply announced, and the close contenders who were considered but not selected are forced to reconcile their personal feelings alone. Often, pride forces the key runner up to quit the organization, creating huge costs for all. The good person who quits must search for a new career elsewhere and loses all the valuable seniority and goodwill she has created with your organization. Additionally, your organization loses a highly skilled and valuable employee. This need not happen. The outcome can be significantly influenced. With careful planning and thought, you have an excellent chance of keeping the runner-up on the payroll as a motivated and productive employee, both interested in and competing for future promotional opportunities as they arise. To make this happen will require some careful private coaching, with all the team members involved. Start first with the lucky winner. His or her behavior during the transition will be critical.

MANAGER: Beverly, I've been given an advancement, and you have been selected as my replacement.

BEVERLY: Thanks for the vote of confidence. I appreciate the opportunity and certainly hope to measure up to your expectations.

MANAGER: And I know you will. For now, I want to discuss the transition period, which must be made seamless. You need the entire team. I want everyone to work with you just as hard and effectively as they have worked with me over the years. You will have to earn their support, and I am going to help you get in the correct position.

BEVERLY: What role do I play?

MANAGER: Right now, do nothing. Trust me, and let me handle things. Here's the way we're going to do this. First, I'm going to talk to all the supervisors privately. I'm going to explain my decision to them and take full responsibility for it. I want to leave your future relationship with them as clean as I possibly can. You should do nothing for a period of time, say a few weeks or so. Take no initiatives. Call no meetings to discuss strategy or handle issues. Let business go on as usual. Let people come right around you and directly to me if they so choose. Don't worry about it. You and I will have plenty of private time to discuss things, and I will keep you fully informed about what everyone is saying.

BEVERLY: What if they come to me with questions and concerns?

MANAGER: That would be perfect. Answer the questions, coach your team members, build relationships with them. Be the leader I know you are. It would be great if they do come to you. That's what we want. But I want you to do nothing if they don't. Give them time to adjust to the new situation, and trust me to give you the information you need and help you build your relationship with them. You know I will do this for you. I promoted you. Obviously, I am going to do everything possible to make this work for you. If it does not work for you, it won't work for me, either.

BEVERLY: That all sounds fine with me.

MANAGER: Good. Now I want to talk a little about Pat. She, too, was lobbying hard for this promotion, and she came in a close second in the decision-making process. I want her to accept the decision, be happy here, and continue to work here. I want her to continue making the excellent contribution she has always made. I expect you to help me to make sure all this occurs. She's an excellent person. This company needs her, and you do also.

BEVERLY: I will do what I can.

MANAGER: Let's discuss a strategy. I'm going to have a conversation with her. I'm going to acknowledge that I know she wanted this job. I'll talk to her about how tough the decision was, then I'm going to make clear that in no way should she consider that this decision in any way suggests her performance is anything less than exemplary. I don't want her personal pride to take over. We don't want her to feel forced to leave. We want her to know she is still on the fast track. I'm going to do everything possible to make her stay here in the company. I'm even going to encourage her to go around you and directly to me if she feels the need. I'll let her know I'm going to work as hard as possible to get her another promotion in the company.

BEVERLY: How can I help?

MANAGER: You should do pretty much the same thing. I will talk to Pat before the announcement. After the announcement, make it a priority to get to her as quickly as possible, perhaps in a day. Take her to lunch or something; start a private conversation. Essentially outline for her that, while you are happy to have been selected, you had nothing to do with this decision. Be humble, very humble. Tell her you need her and want her to stay. Don't say "the company needs you." Make it a personal plea for help. Say: "I" need you. Ask for her support, and tell her you intend to lobby hard for her if she wants a promotion outside the department.

Explain, though, that it will take some time and that you need her patience as well as support.

Follow this type of script until you are both comfortable. Then you will need to have meetings with Pat and the others. Let's discuss what might happen with Pat, which will be the most difficult meeting:

MANAGER: Pat, I've got some news for you. I've been promoted to the director's position, and Beverly has been selected to replace me. I know you have been striving for a promotion, and you were clearly in the running for the job. The decision was difficult, very difficult. In no way does this mean that your performance is anything less than excellent.

PAT: If I have an excellent performance record, why wasn't I selected?

MANAGER: There is never just one answer to such a complex question. What is more important is that there can be only one promotion to a particular job at one point in time, even when there is more than one good person available to get that promotion. The good news, though, is that there are many more promotions in the future. You are excellent and have a long career ahead of you. You are still in line for advancement. I know you want to advance, and I am going to do everything possible to make sure that happens. I want you to stay, and I am asking you to give Beverly the same support and loyalty you have shown to me over the years. Help her become successful in her new leadership position.

I'll still be watching, and I promise to be looking all over the company to find a suitable promotion for you. I don't want you to lose confidence in me or the organization. You are an excellent employee, and there are many other opportunities in your future.

PAT: When might another opportunity come along?

MANAGER: That, of course, is the big unknown. I can't predict the future. I can influence it, though. What I intend to do is make your performance known to everyone I know and respect. I'm going to sell you around the organization. You can help. You can demonstrate your salability by continuing with your excellent performance and by helping Beverly produce results right here. Make Beverly want to promote you as well. Right now, I am your advocate. I believe you are ready for advancement, and I am committed to make that happen. You can support the entire effort by making Beverly do the same thing for you.

PAT: Thanks for talking to me. I'll try.

MANAGER: I'm sure you will. After the announcement, you will be working for Beverly. But, and don't forget this, my office door is still open. Come and see me directly any time you want to talk. Beverly will not complain. She's a good person and will understand. Give her your loyalty and support and make me proud to be your advocate within the company. We'll get you that promotion you need and deserve.

WHAT TO DO WHEN CALAMITY STRIKES

In this situation, we're not discussing the relatively minor things that plague us, such as fender-bender car accidents or the occasional broken toe. We're talking about disasters: an employee who gets involved in a permanently disabling accident, or an employee who is diagnosed with a fatal illness. There are also the calamities that can hit the employee's family, such as the loss of a child, which can have significant impact upon the team's stability. Major disasters hit hard and remind all of our common vulnerability.

Too often, when disaster strikes, management employs no strategy. Everyone looks the other way, and the issue is only discussed in whispers around the coffee machine. This should not be allowed to occur. People do not separate their work lives from their personal lives. If they are not handled constructively, personal disasters impact morale negatively. The team is left with the impression that company management is cold, aloof, and insensitive. Disasters are always awful. But handled correctly, they can serve to help bond the team together. Inspired leaders recognize the total team suffers when calamity strikes any one member. They accept the new reality, react quickly, and focus their energies on team bonding and building.

As soon as practical after you become aware that the disaster has occurred, tell some of your closest confidants within the department to spread the information throughout the department as positively as possible. The information will spread anyway. Take control of the rumor mill and start sending constructive comments:

> Talk to your colleagues. Bill was in a horrible accident and lost his arm. He will be okay, though. We're all grateful he's going to make it. I'm going over to the hospital to see how he is doing.

> The Russells lost their home to fire last night. They lost everything. But, thank God, no one was hurt. Right now, they are with neighbors. I'm going over for a quick visit to see if there is anything we can do.

> Judy's baby was born with Down's Syndrome. He is otherwise healthy. With early intervention and special training, they are doing a lot for these kids nowadays. They start pushing them early, so that they keep near their peer group. I'm going to make a quick trip to the hospital to see Judy and her new baby.

Advise your best employees to start looking at the upcoming work schedule, too. A person who must deal with a serious disaster will miss about one week of work. If the disaster occurs late in the week, he or she will likely miss the remainder of the present week as well as all of the following week. Obviously, if the team member has been personally injured in some debilitating accident, you may be without his or her service much longer than a week. If practical, go in person to visit the employee who is facing this new circumstance. Go to his or her home, to the hospital, and so on; be open, available, and constructive. Express empathy to your employee and his or her family members. Spend some time visiting, perhaps a few hours or more. Listen and invite your employee to talk. Create communication, don't just wait for him or her to volunteer communication. Be sure to tell the employee that work responsibilities will be covered by others and that his or her first responsibility is to be supportive of his or her immediate family. Then get back to your team.

By now, all of them will know what has happened. Call a meeting. In a perfect world, it will be early in the day. The early meeting is better for you, as you can be available throughout the day. Cancel meetings that will take you away from your office. Employees may want to talk privately with you during the day. In this meeting, share a few personal thoughts about your visit with their colleague. Make this meeting an informal close-knit discussion, if possible. Covering the issues that follow will be most helpful to your employees.

Give a prognosis for the calamity. No matter how serious the disaster, life goes on. People will adapt. Focus on whatever positive thing you can find.

> As you know, Bill lost his arm in an automobile accident last night. I just got back from the hospital. He is doing quite well. His spirits are up, and he is optimistic.

Some will feel uncomfortable. They will want to know what to say when their colleague returns to work. Advise them that neither the employee nor the circumstance should be ignored. Team members should be encouraged to approach their colleague to express empathy and other positive sentiments as appropriate.

> Bill is not afraid to talk about the accident. When he returns, just focus on his positive recovery. He may even want to talk about his loss, and I suppose that's okay. He's working with professional counselors now. Like all of us, he spends a considerable amount of time at work. We're all close to him. By being good listeners, we can facilitate the healing process.

> Bill is going to be away from work for a while. Be sure to stop by the hospital and visit him. Seeing all of you guys will lift his spirits and help his recovery.

Mention a word or two about the work schedule, being sure to advise everyone that, with others, you are already studying revisions and adjustments. Tell them you will appreciate their extra effort, which you know they will put forth.

> Judy, Ken, and Joe have been reviewing the work schedule. I asked them to assume Bill will be away for a while. I also told them to assume that all of us would be willing to put forth the extra effort necessary to keep the operation under control. I know I can count on everyone for the extra effort, which will be needed.

Most progressive companies now have relationships with professional counselors. Your personnel office will have the needed information. Professional support is also generally available to the public through social-service agencies in the community. Before implementing a strategy for the absolutely disastrous calamity, such as someone being murdered, bring in whatever professional support is available and follow their advice for building a suitable team recovery strategy. Traumatic stress can be serious, and the professional counselors will help the team control what can be debilitating stress.

WHAT TO DO WITH THE PRIMA DONNA

Hiring the super-person always causes general excitement. You have been looking everywhere for him or her, and success has finally been achieved. The super-person is the one everyone dreams about working with, and the team is excited about this new asset. He or she is perfect in every way. Excellent vocabulary, good looks, impeccably dressed, perfect personality, wonderful job-related skills, excellent experience, and so on. He or she is a natural fit for your job opening and can perform in a superb manner. Life is good, the future is bright.

Unfortunately, far too often, the super-person, always aware of his or her unique blessings, becomes cocky, and quickly learns of these superior attributes. He or she feels superior to others and may start to act the part. This person can become isolated, condescending, and seek extra favors, or special dispensation. Unfortunately, all jobs have certain routine, but undesirable, tasks that everyone hates. These undesirable responsibilities must be completed, though, and in most organizations, they are simply shared equally by all. Super-person may decide that such sharing is beneath him or her and should be done by others. He or she may refuse to carry a full load. Suddenly, there are extra meetings to attend when the dirty work must be done. Often, the super-person needs to leave the office early, has other things to do, or doesn't feel well, and is always asking for help with the dirty stuff.

In summary, super-person is less than super, and fails to mature as a bona-fide team player. Usually, if the problem with super-person is going to arise, it will start to arise quickly, within three months or so from the date of initial employment. Be alert with all new employees. Spend extra time in the department. Monitor performance continuously. Listen carefully for signals. You will pick up comments from your staff. They will probably *want* you to overhear their comments:

Bill doesn't like to get his hands dirty.

Judy, give me a hand. Bill is too busy; he's always too busy for the dirty work.

Did you see that over at the copy machine? Alan was struggling with a mess of toner, and Bill didn't even lend a hand. He just turned and walked away.

As soon as you start to hear this stuff, take action. Don't wait for things to get better without intervention. They probably won't. Coach and counsel the prima donna. Be tough, and take him or her down a few pegs. Don't be intimidated by this one. Get the following concepts across:

Bill, there are a certain number of dirty and nasty jobs in this operation. None of us likes these tasks, so we all equally share the responsibility for getting them done. I expect you to do your fair share.

You're good, and we have high hopes for you. But we all start at the bottom around here. You will certainly be promoted, but you have got to go through the steps first. Going through the steps includes doing your fair share of the dirty work around here.

Bill, I'm hearing words I don't like. Rumors are floating about you. I'm not going to tell you the source, but some of the others around here are getting the message that the dirty work is beneath you. They're talking about you, and I don't like it. They are saying you aren't a team player. They're saying you aren't pulling your fair share of the load. The gist of the message is that when dirty work needs to be done, you go elsewhere. Let me make things simple: I want the messages to change. I want to start hearing others say more positive stuff about your performance, your attitude, your willingness to dive in and help out. I want to start hearing more positive words now, immediately.

Stay firm, and observe things closely. If you are going to save this person for the team, the most direct approach is probably the best approach, so go after it. If this direct approach won't work, then it's time to move on and encourage the prima donna to seek employment elsewhere. Do not wait too long to make your decision. If the behavior does not change immediately, within days, then it probably won't change at all. He or she is a die-hard prima donna, and you will have to move him or her off the team.

The strategy to employ is straightforward. Watch him or her closely and look for the appropriate opportunity. Some completely awful task will come along, and he or she won't want to do it. Get ready; he or she will come to you with some statement like:

The wonder widget is an awful mess. I need to get it cleaned up before I demonstrate it to my customers. They are arriving tomorrow morning. How do we get that sort of work done around here anyway?

This is your golden opportunity. Get your lab coat and simply say something like:

Here, Bill. Let me show you how we get these wonder widgets cleaned up around here.

Then go out to the wonder widget and dive into the filth. Get your hands dirty, do the task yourself, and don't let the prima donna help. Keep him or her next to you, though, and go through every step, solo. Describe what you are doing in detail. When you are finished, drag him or her into the locker room with you and watch you clean up. Look the prima donna in the eye, and end the whole scenario with a simple comment:

There now. That's how we get those jobs done around here.

Then simply walk away. If the prima donna did not get your message before with counseling, he or she will get it now. If the behavior was going to change, it would likely have changed when you were doing all the counseling. With this last demonstration, you are sending a completely different message. You are suggesting he or she leave, and my guess is that you will have his or her resignation within a few weeks. Accept it when it comes.

SUPERVISORS ARE SLOWING DOWN: "SPARKING" THEM BACK TO LIFE

Several service supervisors answering to you are losing their dedication and commitment to the customer. You would like to send a strong message to them and perhaps a number of their subordinates. Coaching and counseling these folks should be enough. They are your chosen leaders. Do not have any group-counseling sessions, though, speak to them only one-on-one. Go after them individually and be specific with your complaint. You have a right to demand a high degree of excellence from them. Speaking to them individually, try the following:

The staff looks to you and me for guidance. They follow your example and mine. They follow what we do, not what we say. I expect you to be out front and visible when problems arise. I want people to see you and me putting out extra sweat for the customer. Yesterday, during that crisis, you were not around. I didn't like that. If you have an important meeting or something, at minimum, everyone should have known about it. I should have been told, too, so that I can cover for you.

Lead by example. I want you to be the first one here in the morning and the last one to leave, especially during busy times. When there is a crisis, be out in front. Be seen in the fray. I want you to be informed and involved in the action.

The staff learns more by observing than it does by listening. They're always watching, and, like the rest of us, they keep score. Everyone has to take off once in a while. If you are going to miss some work, make sure you have ten days of extra work in the bank for every one day that you must miss. Make sure everyone knows you are working harder than everyone else, too. That's the way it is. Nobody said it was fair, but that's the price of leadership. We lead and mold our subordinate's behavior by example, and we have to set that example. If you don't want to pay the price of leadership, then we need to put you in a nonleadership position.

Well, to be honest with you, the answer is yes. Our customers at times do come before our family responsibilities. I don't like it, and neither does anyone else, but the customers don't ask my opinion. They don't ask yours, either. That's the price we pay for our leadership positions. You might say we leaders have extended families. We have our personal family, but our customers and subordinates also consider us family. All look to us for guidance and support.

Taking advantage of situations where you can positively share words similar to these with your supervisors should be enough. But there are cases where words are not enough. A demonstration is necessary. You may be forced to drive the message even harder in order to get cultural change. If, after repeated coaching and counseling, the sense of urgency still fails to develop, it's time to rework your strategy. Continue the very directed coaching and counseling, but start searching for the right dramatic incident.

Say some disaster occurs. A big one. You didn't plan it, but it did occur. Yesterday, you shipped some very important thing to a customer. Unfortunately, what you shipped was faulty. It did not meet the customer's required specifications and cannot be repaired. This morning, the customer, panicking, called, and would speak only with you. Understanding the ultra-serious situation he or she is in, you give the customer your personal assurance that the issue will be resolved before the day ends and that his or her operations will not be interrupted.

Immediately, you gather your three lieutenants, the same three you have been coaching and counseling, for a strategy session. Everyone agrees on what must be done to ensure the desperate customer gets the shipment before the day ends. The meeting adjourns. The team is focused. The only thing left to do is implement.

The day goes by. It is late afternoon, near quitting time. You stroll around the office and into the shop area to check on things. You notice the customer's needed product still has not shipped. Also your three lieutenants are nowhere to be found. With a few discreet inquiries, you quickly learn they are probably gone for the day.

This is your dramatic incident. This would be the perfect situation for creating significant cultural change. It is a great time for a demonstration. Turn this into the moment you have been waiting for.

Don't start ranting and raving about your hapless key lieutenants. Say nothing about them. Better to be calm and collected. Act as if your lieutenants don't exist at all. Gather together the remaining first-level people you need to get the shipment out. Say something like:

MANAGER: Look, this is very serious. (Customer) is absolutely desperate to get a duplicate of this (product) today. They have to have it. There are no possible exceptions. I spoke with them this morning. If we don't ship tonight, their operations will be stopped before morning. They will suffer major losses, and it will all be our fault. It's a disaster. (Customer) is one of our best customers. We simply must ship this tonight. In fact, I thought the (product) had already shipped.

I don't know what happened, but I need your help now. I personally cannot perform all the operations necessary to redo the (product). You can. I just don't have the skills, all of you do. Right now I work for you. Just tell me what to do, and I'll do it. But we have no choice. We must ship tonight.

Now be their slave. Ditch the formal suit and tie. Get dirty, work like a dog, harder than anyone else. Do all the worst jobs. Be subservient to your team. Do anything for them and be everywhere at once. Let everyone know you will do anything to help them get their jobs done. When the job is finished, take everyone out for pizza and beer. In whatever appropriate way, savor the moment and celebrate this accomplishment for your customer.

And now comes the next day. With it comes your opportunity to deal with your dense supervisors, those fine folks who just can't seem to get the message about customer-focused flexibility. What should you do?

Your initial reaction might be to call them in for additional counseling. But you have greater impact by ignoring them. Be abrupt with them, cold. Say little or nothing to them. Talk only business. Above all else, say nothing about what happened the night before. They already know all about what happened. In fact, they probably knew all about what happened long before the night was over. Their buddies called them last night; count on it. They were totally briefed on the entire incident. In fact, every person in your operation knows about everything that happened last night. This is fine. Let the rumor mill carry the customer-first message for a while. You have tried on numerous occasions to get through to these three. Now let others carry the message.

Your supervisors may come to you. They may want to offer an apology, or explain where they were the night before. They may even make more than one attempt to speak with you in the upcoming days. Just tell them you have nothing to discuss. Every time any of them brings up the subject of their absence, ignore him and say you don't want to discuss it. You have tried the easy road. Now they owe you.

There is no need to discuss this issue with anyone on the team. The story will be told and retold. Let folklore build in the department. Everything that needed to be said was said by your behavior and the impromptu team you put together to solve the problem. Do no more coaching and counseling on customer-service philosophy with your supervisors. Do, however, continue to issue instructions. Be a distant leader for a while. With your demonstration for the customer, you have drawn a line in the sand. Keep it there and clearly marked. You have delivered a strong message on what customer service means. Now everyone understands. It is time for your supervisors to make their move. Watch them and let them know you are watching. There is no more room for words. Everyone on the staff now knows what a customer-first operation means to you.

Your message has been made perfectly clear. Look for and expect positive customer-focused change. If your supervisors are the right people capable of change, your message has been heard, and you will get the change you need. You will be able to see it. They will be out front on critical issues. They will start to lead. When they do, you can start to loosen up again.

And what should you do if you don't see the change you need? Don't bother with coaching and counseling anymore. If they did not hear the message delivered so strongly with your demonstration, they cannot hear any coaching and counseling, either. Start looking around and plan three leadership changes.

YOUR PREDECESSOR WAS DEMOTED: BUILDING RAPPORT WITH YOUR TEAM

You are being brought in to replace the existing manager. The person you are replacing is being demoted because of poor performance. However, the team likes him or her. When the announcement is first made, expect some poor morale. The team does not know you. No matter how poor your predecessor, he or she was at least a known entity, and had some sort of relationship with everyone on the team. Further, you have been brought in from outside the team. Perhaps some existing team members, who now find themselves working for you, felt they should have been promoted to the manager's slot. Competent individuals within the department were probably passed over because of poor overall departmental performance. Their individual competence was overshadowed by the incompetence of their leader. When evaluating the leadership change, your management probably did not even consider promoting anyone from within. Management wanted a clean new beginning, or you would not be in this job. You cannot discuss any of this with your subordinates. Your incompetent predecessor created this shadow, but you will have to live with it. You will have to take small rebuilding steps.

Start by sending a brief but humble message at the time of your promotion. Tilt toward the team and away from your boss, who made the final decision to remove your predecessor:

MANAGER: I really appreciate this new assignment and the opportunity to work with all of you. I'm looking forward to our future together and toward making a positive contribution. I want to help you fulfill your individual objectives while we work together to fulfill the departmental objectives. We must work together to perform at high standards, help management understand our contribution, and lobby for needed resources.

Be a fast learner and continuously available to your new team. Find out what is going on as quickly as possible. Be the first one there every morning and the last one to leave every evening. Work on weekends.

Stay with the staff during these first few weeks on the job and learn the details. Watch them do their jobs. Find out what they do, how the operation currently runs, and where they feel the problems are. Let them coach you on specific issues. Have lunch with them and listen a lot, but don't make a lot of "hip-shooting" decisions. Chances are excellent that a few good performers exist and that some others are duffers. Also chances are that the good people are overworked and underpaid. Get quickly involved in administration. If they are underpaid, fix that immediately. Money will keep the overworked folks moving for a while longer.

Then focus on the overworked few. Learn the nature of their programs, be visible with these people, and get them some immediate relief. Everyone, even the duffers, knows the overworked few have been carrying the workload. We all like to see leaders support someone on our level. Getting some relief for the downtrodden few will be the quickest way for you to build your image and reputation with your team. It is the quickest way to demonstrate that you can take action and make things better.

Take very targeted action and get the good performers some help, even if you have to temporarily beg, borrow, or steal the help from other departments. To accomplish this, you must sell your organization on the idea that your problems are greater than those existing in other departments. Get your boss to support this concept. They removed your predecessor for good cause; you will likely get their ear. Even bringing in temporary help will tell the entire team how capable you are. Getting immediate relief for some also tells everyone the company cares about what your department is trying to accomplish.

Getting immediate, if temporary relief is your highest priority. While doing this, make your second priority finding out why your predecessor was demoted. Don't discuss this issue with your new department. Build a relationship with your boss and find out from him or her. Find out what the key issues were and what your predecessor did not do. Get an understanding of what executive management expects from your new department. Develop overall goals and objectives.

As a second priority, get these goals defined into projects and routine tasks as quickly as possible. Assign the tasks to your best individuals. Keep a list of projects to be done. Post it publicly on some "to do" planning board. This will help you establish the future direction. By this time, you should already have built a lot of support within your new work group.

GETTING RID OF THE "PROTECTED" IMCOMPETENT

None of us is permitted to discriminate against another because of ethnic origin, age, religious belief, physical disability, or gender. This is as it should be. However, none of this has anything to do with a person's ability to get the job done. What people *are* is different from what people *do*. Dealing with an incompetent subordinate who may also be in a protected group can be a very tough job. Making matters worse, the person may know how to use the system well. The incompetent person in a protected group seems to know his or her rights and your responsibilities better than any well-paid lawyer. These kinds of scenarios are constant topics of discussion in my leadership training programs. Such situations create high stress, as you will likely find yourself standing alone on your principles. If you are, unfortunately, in this situation, the road ahead will be hard, and everyone around you knows it. If you choose to fight this battle, don't assume you will get a lot of support from Human Resources or from your immediate manager. While no one will state it overtly, your work culture may subject you to subtle pressure. If you embark on this mission, you may very quickly get a message similar to this: "leave well enough alone, and just live with the limitations of organizational life; no one will ever complain."

This person is essentially your problem, and count on it, all the decisions will be yours. My own experience is that you will get little or no support as you work through this situation. Before deciding to travel this road, make sure you are right in your conclusions. Rethink everything long and hard:

☎ Make sure you have done everything possible to get this individual to perform. Have you been perfectly fair?

☎ Check and recheck your perceptions and the past assignments given to this person. Did he or she have the ability and opportunity to perform?

☎ What about his or her working relationships with others in the department? Has anyone done any harm? Has anyone discriminated against him or her?

☎ What about counseling? Have you been a good coach? Have you effectively described what must be done?

Think carefully, make notes, and set them aside. Then go back a week or so later and review them. Make certain you have been more than fair. This is going to be a long, tough fight. Be certain fighting is your only remaining recourse. Check his or her work history and add this past to your evaluation. The worst possible case is when the person has been with the organization for years and years. Usually, a quick look through the incompetent's personnel history shows the awful truth. Far too often, the incompetent who has been with the organization for many years has been incompetent forever. In these worst-of-all situations, many managers before you have merely been playing "pass-the-skunk." No one before you would tackle the issue. Your predecessors all knew about the incompetence, but instead of solving the problem by getting rid of the skunk, they simply looked the other way, gave adequate reviews, and moved him or her to another department and unsuspecting manager who, in turn, did the same to someone else.

With the long-tenured incompetent, there is usually no doubt that many managers before you have been derelict in their duties. If you have this worst possible situation, your company is clearly in the wrong. Moving this person or changing his or her behavior is going to be significantly harder. After all, if he or she never had to do any work for anyone else, why should he or she have to do any work for you?

In our discussion here, we will assume you are dealing with the worst possible case. You have inherited a department and an incompetent who has been passed around the company forever. Where should you go for your first move? Before talking to the employee, go to your boss. Find out what he or she knows.

Your boss probably knows all about this. You will likely hear the "good-ol'-boy" story. He'll rock back in his chair, roll his eyes, and say those wonderful words you jsut love to hear: *"Everybody knows old Gordy . . . that's just the way he is . . . he's always been that way . . . you'll just have to accept him . . . that's the way things are . . . everybody has tried to get something out of good old Gordy."*

So, push on the boss a bit and find the bottom line: "Look, if you climb the mountain with old Gordy, you will certainly climb back down alone. He just is not going to change. He's been here for thirty years. He's not going to change now."

At least now you *know* you are on your own. Make clear with your boss what you intend to do.

MANAGER: Look, I just can't sit there and accept this behavior. I have people earning one third what Gordy earns, and they produce five times the work he does. It just is unacceptable.

BOSS: Well, the reason for the high salary is because he was a manager once. He had to be moved out of the management job, and no one wanted to cut his salary.

MANAGER: Whatever the reason for the salary, we have the right to demand a fair day's work for it. The guy is doing nothing.

BOSS: No one knows what he earns.

MANAGER: *I* do. You'll have to back me up. I'll put everything in writing and let you review the write-up before I talk to Gordy.

And this is the way you will have to proceed. Write down exactly what the poor performance is. Be specific, and relate only to the performance. Use statistics. Some samples:

The average customer-service engineer spends 60 percent of the time working on technical problems with customers. Gordy is only making himself available 10 percent of the time.

The average customer-service engineer resolves about four problems per day. Gordy resolves about four problems per week.

Focus on specific performance goals that are not being met:

Gordy, within 90 days, I expect that you must be performing at the minimum departmental averages for performance. Specifically, you must be doing (list).

Take the write-up to your boss for review. He or she won't want to read all this, but the boss can't stop you from running the department, either. Just say something like:

I wanted you to review this before I had a meeting with Gordy on this subject. Let me know if you have any suggestions. This is your copy. During my discussion with Gordy, I am going to tell him that you are available if he wants to complain about me and discuss all of this with you.

This helps your reluctant supervisor with decision making. You are not asking for permission. You are only telling him or her how to support you, which is what he or she will have to do.

Gordy is in a protected group, so I am also going to advise Human Resources that this discussion is going to happen. I will give them a copy of this write-up as well.

Here again, you are not asking for permission. You are only keeping your boss informed. Let the Human Resources officer read the write-up; ask for any input as well. Also advise that you are going to allow Gordy to come to Human Resources if he wishes. Again, don't ask their permission to proceed. Just keep them informed and advise them on how they can help. Saying it another way, you are going through the steps available to correct a problem, even if the people who are supposed to help don't want you to go through the steps.

How should you handle the meeting with good old Gordy? This will not be a pleasant experience. Gordy has been talked to many times before. He's an old pro at getting out of work. Be upbeat, direct, explain your position, and end this discussion:

MANAGER: Gordy, we need to talk about your performance. As you know, we have been through many counseling sessions over the past months. You are my highest-paid employee, and I am going to have to ask for a much higher performance level.

Here, let's review this write-up together. I wrote everything down, so that there would be no misunderstanding. This is what I need for you to do. (Review the list.) This is the minimum acceptable performance, Gordy. For now, as I have written here, your performance is unacceptable. I will have to release you from the payroll unless I have a dramatic improvement within the next three months.

GORDY: I just do not know how to do these things. I have not been trained on these systems yet. I need more support. The job has changed since I was assigned here. I did not know I would have to do these things.

Be prepared for comments of this type. These folks always need additional training. They are always persecuted by events around them.

MANAGER: Jobs change all the time. This is your job now, and there are no others. All of us have the responsibility to keep up with the technical requirements of our respective jobs. The laboratory equipment is available to you, as it is to everyone else in the department. The technical manuals are all available as well. You have more tenure and experience than anyone in the department. You are also in my highest salary bracket. You must perform at these minimum standards, as we have discussed and as I have put forth in writing. I have no choice but to insist on this level of performance. If you need additional developmental hours, you will have to find them during your work day. We are all responsible for keeping up with the technical developments of our jobs, and with continuous change.

GORDY: No one has ever said this about my performance before. No one has every complained about anything I have done before.

Gordy will likely try to impugn your integrity. Let him.

MANAGER: I can't speak for others, only for myself and what I see. I can only follow my responsibilities to the best of my ability. My boss has a copy of this write-up. I also have placed one in your personnel folder downstairs. You can feel free to discuss this with my boss, if you wish. But for me, I must have the performance standards as described. You can keep this write-up for your own records.

At minimum, good old Gordy will go to your boss. He may also go to personnel to complain about you. Let him; it does not matter. You have already informed all these folks and have drawn your line in the sand. The die is cast. Your boss and personnel have no choice but to support your actions. You are focused totally on performance, and you are following all of the rules. No one can ask for more.

Don't expect miracles, however. You will likely have many talks with Gordy. He's been around, knows how to get out of work, and has his own agenda. Stay on him. You have already made your position known; keep pouring it on. Keep everything in writing, and discuss only his performance. Never mention his personality. Be specific with all the details. Use measurable terms to discuss his performance, such as:

> The departmental average for (activity) is ten units per day. After extensive training, coaching and counseling, Gordy is only averaging two units per day. His performance is below the minimum level of acceptable performance. The performance must be improved immediately, and the improvement must be permanent. Gordy must, at minimum, improve his performance until it is at least on the departmental average.

Your many write-ups should be variations on this basic theme. State specifically that Gordy will be removed from the payroll. Always be certain your boss and personnel get copies of the write-ups in advance. Just ask them if they have any additional suggestions. Don't ask for their approval of the direction you are taking.

Maintaining steady and consistent pressure will likely turn Gordy into a modest, somewhat below-average performer, and you should be satisfied with this. He is never going to be a star. He is a long-tenured employee, who has been a poor performer his entire working career. His poor performance has been acceptable forever. It is unrealistic for you to expect a total rebirth.

PEER MANAGERS WON'T COOPERATE: HOW TO PROMOTE PEOPLE FROM THEIR DEPARTMENTS

Your company does not have job posting. Before interviewing Ellen from another department for a promotional position in your department, the rules require you to go through Ellen's current manager. Unfortunately, Ellen's manager is not much of a team player and will not grant the promotional interview. Ellen's manager is finding all sorts of excuses to delay the interview. How can you get access to Ellen without breaking any rules or creating major political problems?

The natural tendency in these situations is to cry foul and go screaming to personnel. You can do this, and probably win. Ellen's manager is being selfish and not playing by the rules.

But things are seldom simple. Ellen's manager is probably a sly old fox who knows the system well him- or herself, and has likely used all the loopholes. There are many barriers that could be tossed up. He or she could claim the workload is currently too heavy to release Ellen, or plan a promotion for Ellen within the department. Ellen's manager could also dream up other tactics, all of which would serve to stop your frontal attack.

The best thing to do is to back off for a while and let things cool down. Frontal attacks do not go over well in corporate politicking, or any kind of politicking, for that matter. While some time goes by, arrange to talk with Ellen. Find a problem or two she can help with. The lunch room and coffee machine are great places for meetings, and for sending messages.

And what message should you send? Do not tell Ellen you want to interview her; that would be a direct violation of the rules. However, be sure Ellen and everyone anywhere near her knows you are growing your organization. Advertise your vision and goals. Let the rumor mill know how you are going to fulfill your mission. Turn some of your most trusted confidants loose to help you spread the word. Be sure everyone knows the qualifications you're looking for. Be doubly sure that the qualifications you need are exactly *Ellen's* qualifications.

Your goal here is to plant a thought, an idea. Your goal is to get Ellen interested in your operation and some of the people currently on your staff. The rules stop you from directly asking her to join you. However, the rules do not stop her from seeking an interview with you. If she comes to you, or goes to her supervisor seeking permission to talk to you, the tables have turned in your favor. That's exactly what your are trying to do.

SAVING THE GOOD GUY WHEN YOU DON'T HAVE AN AVAILABLE JOB

A sister department is being disbanded. Andy is a great guy working in this sister department. You would like to save him for the company and, perhaps, for a future position in your department. But you cannot get a requisition allowing you to increase your payroll. What other leadership strategy is available to you?

The first thing to do is to fight as hard as you possibly can for an emergency requisition. Your argument would be that Andy is a "Superman," a great find for the company, and should be kept. You will need him next year when the business picks up.

Your boss will probably support this logic, but his or her bosses will likely not support him. It's a fact of life. The business must be saved today. Tomorrow's problem created today is another matter. Emergency or temporary requisitions are seldom supported, as all other managers are screaming too. All managers have a superman they are trying to save.

A more subtle approach can sometimes work. Even when things are in chaos, and some operation is being disbanded, someone usually needs help somewhere. Find this person. Find someone with an open requisition. Get a message to this individual that they should go after your superman, Andy. Explain all of Andy's merits to this individual, and explain why Andy would be great for his or her position. Convince this person that he or she should save your superman today and that you will take Andy tomorrow.

Andy, however, may not be a perfect fit for this other job. Or, may not even be interested in this other department. It's okay. Get a message to Andy. Talk to him informally, or send a messenger to talk with him. Not everyone understands office politics. Let him know you have long-term interests in him, but current business constraints temporarily block your maneuverability. Make the message clear that you want him to compromise in the short term and take the available job. He can be a candidate for your operation in the long term. This scenario can frequently be used to save some of the best people.

MINIMIZING BAD NEWS TO THE BOSS

How can you present bad news to the boss so that the impact is minimized? Above all, don't procrastinate. This seems to be the biggest problem many of us have in dealing with error. We avoid communicating with the boss, somehow hoping the mistake will magically go away. It won't. If anything, mistakes get worse as time passes. In business, available options and timing are always important. Procrastinating can seriously distort the timing. Even more importantly, procrastinating can also serve to limit both the number and range of options available. These are undesirable circumstances and will make the error worse and more difficult to deal with.

What's the boss going to do? If the bad news occurred because you made a mistake, well, how bad is the mistake? A very serious mistake costing tons of money means you lose your job. If you don't tell the boss, you will lose your job anyway. These big things can never be covered up for long.

Certain other types of mistakes, such as having an affair with a subordinate, or stealing company money, will likely cost you your job as well. And they should. Such mistakes are clearly errors in judgment and reveal poor integrity.

By and large though, a mistake, even a bad mistake, will probably not cost you much at all. Handled correctly, it may not even cost you a promotion or merit increase. Most bosses and organizations are quite tolerant. Further, we are all aware that people make errors. There are many organizational checks and balances to help control the scope and magnitude of the error. It is unlikely that one mistake will totally overwhelm the structure. Usually, when a structure totally falls apart, it is because of many mistakes. Each new mistake builds upon its predecessors. All the mistakes compound together, creating the ultimate organizational crash. Remember Watergate?

The best way to deal with bad news is just to toss it out there as soon as you become aware of it. Walk into the boss's office and throw it on the desk. Saying something like "I really messed this up, and felt that you needed to know" should be sufficient. Then describe in plain terms what went wrong. Don't offer excuses or explanations as to why the mistake occurred, unless you are asked to do so. Offering excuses suggests a coverup. You describe what went wrong. Let the boss decide if he or she wants an explanation.

Being asked by the boss why something went wrong is usually a plus because it suggests that the boss doesn't plan an execution. More likely, he or she is trying to learn and is trying to decide if any systemic modifications are necessary.

The best way to minimize the impact of the error is to put it in some sort of context. Create a list. Start with the several positive steps you have taken toward the goal you are pursuing. Then list the mistake, describe its impact on the goal, and then discuss the corrective action you have taken to reverse the mistake. Continue to list additional positive steps you have taken toward the goal:

I wanted to briefly summarize where we are on the project. To date, we have completed seven steps toward the ultimate goal. We have three more to complete. The first four steps in our plan went perfectly. We proceeded without a hitch and were right on schedule. Step five was tough, really tough. I just miscalculated what we had to do and ended up with a real problem. You should know about it, just in case you hear something. Specifically, we had a problem with the (description of the problem). I have taken corrective action. I went on overtime with the team, consumed some of our contingency budget, and completed (list). This recovery strategy worked well, but did put us behind schedule. With steps six and seven, I was able to make up some additional lateness, but we're still two weeks late. I don't think we are going to recover the two weeks. I wanted you to know this before I talked to the customer about the lateness. It's going to be tough telling the customer about the lateness, but, it's better to tell him now.

MAKING DECISIONS WHEN THE BOSS WON'T

The belief that only competent people get promoted to leadership positions is one of the most common misconceptions in business. The fact is that many in leadership positions do not know how to lead. Organizations, however, are always in motion, and the incompetent may not lead for long. But he or she is leading now. If you are working for this person, you have a problem. It is frustrating to work with a poor leader.

Good leadership requires making decisions, and many incompetent bosses simply don't know how to do it. They don't know how to rationalize the step-by-step analysis of situations, or take constructive steps toward any kind of decision. Thousands of productive hours are wasted every day as employees sit around waiting for bosses to make decisions they do not know how to make.

Your boss may have difficulty making decisions for lots of reasons, and not all reasons are skill related. For example, some company owners hate to approve layoffs or concur with the decision to release surplus employees. They may very well recognize that business planning is less than perfect, and that reductions in the workforce are necessary to save the business. But for political reasons, they just don't want their names associated with workforce reductions. They don't want their image in the community tainted. They will let you release people, but they won't join in the final decision. At the monthly Rotary meeting they want be in position to say, "the operational people must have decided they had surplus productive hours available."

Some don't know how to evaluate risks associated with decision making. Others fear the decision-making process, while still others are too weak to decide anything. Sometimes emotions get in the way. For example, suppose the owner's son works in your operation, can't do the job, and must be fired. It is unrealistic for you to expect the owner to support, concur with, or in any way endorse this decision. However, the owner can and probably will accept and live with your decision if you choose to make it. He or she can accept the fact that you have determined his or her son can't do the job, but just can't concur with your position. There is a big difference between agreement and acceptance.

Whatever the reason, you are the one stuck when the boss can't decide between reasonable options. And all jobs are more difficult when you must make decisions without a support structure.

How do you work with a boss who cannot make decisions? The simple answer is you must make decisions for him or her. You can decide for the boss, either verbally or in writing. I recommend that you do both. Make all the decisions, explain the decisions you have made, what you are going to do, and then back up your decisions in writing. The written memos are necessary to create a paper record of the decision process. The memos will serve as the boss's approval and endorsement, should anyone ask questions about the decision later.

Don't give this boss options. Remember, he or she can't decide. Giving options will only slow things down and lead to more questions or other issues you will have to consider. If you give several good options, he or she will always suggest just a few more things that should be evaluated before the decision can be made. Of course, you are the one who will have to evaluate all the superfluous and redundant issues.

In dealing with this person, always explain the options you have considered, the course of action you are going to pursue, and when you are going to pursue this particular action. Use language like this:

> We're going to evaluate systems A, B, C and D. I will let you know what direction we will take just as soon as I complete our evaluation of these options.

> To accomplish the (goal), we will need to spend $20,000. The money is in the budget, and I am planning to authorize the expenditure on September 15.

> Paul is simply not working out. I have tried repeated coaching and counseling sessions. I don't think he is going to make it. I am going to have one additional session with him next Thursday. At that time I am going to give him a written memo describing exactly what must occur over the next three weeks. I am also going to tell him in writing that I am planning to release him from the payroll in three weeks if all of the goals are not met.

All these decisions must be backed up with memos. The memo should state the decision specifically and give the boss an opportunity to respond. Do not, however, ask him to respond or approve the decision. The memos should be informative, not requests for approval.

Memorandum

To: Boss

From: Director, Customer Service

Our plan to reduce the number of quality problems is taking hold. The number of incoming problems is reduced. Business projections suggest we should discontinue our plans to increase the staff. Accordingly, I have instructed Human Resources to stop the hiring process.

The Production department is shorthanded because of its quality-improvement efforts and it has an interest in some of our people. I am planning to transfer three people next month after we complete the current quality-improvement projects.

Memorandum

To: Boss

From: Director, Customer Service

We have completed our studies for new call-tracking software. We have evaluated five vendors and have determined that the Alpha system would best suit our current needs. The Alpha system can also grow as we expand servicing operations over the next five years. This software is a vital link in our continuing effort to improve response time. The Alpha system is twenty percent higher in price. However, it affords us additional reporting capability which we feel justifies the higher price.

Purchase orders have been completed for Alpha. I will release the $20,000 in purchase requests to Alpha on September 15.

Memorandum

To: Boss

From: Director, Customer Service

The attached write-up was shared with Paul today. It specifically defines the performance standards he must maintain in order to remain employed with us.

I have advised Paul that he will be released from the payroll on October 15 if all of the standards outlined in my memo are not met.

I will let you know how things work out on October 16.

POSITIONING YOUR DEPARTMENT: GAINING VISIBILITY FOR CUSTOMER SUPPORT

Look for the type of good performance you want and reinforce that behavior publicly. Start with those outside your immediate operation who offer support to your department (give credit to others before giving credit to yourself). Find a person who did the right thing for some customer. Do not reinforce something ordinary, but don't limit your search to the outlandish moon shot that happens once in a lifetime, either. Find good performance that is a tad above the norm. Make sure that it, or something similar, could be reproduced by others. Of course, make sure it is something you want others to replicate.

Send this individual a memo. Be sure to describe specifically what happened and why the behavior was important to the customer and the company. State how the performance impacts the company's goals and objectives. Send copies of the memo to his boss, the company president, and to personnel. Post the memo on the bulletin board in the cafeteria.

Memorandum

To: Gary Larson

From: Director of Customer Service

I really appreciate the extra effort in getting the number 23654 replacement pump shipped overnight to Apex. Our plant was already shutting down for the night when we learned about the problem, and I know you really had to scramble to make this shipment happen.

Gary, this you should know: Our quick response saved Apex 15,000 gallons of product, which would have spoiled without the replacement circulation pump. Apex says the product your special effort saved has a market value of about $60,000. Count on it: They will remember you for a long time.

Performance like yours is what gives life to our Customer First campaign. Thanks again, Gary. Great job.

cc: President, Personnel, Cafeteria Bulletin Board

Letter campaigns can be continuous and will have value as long as they reinforce specific behavior such as the sample suggests. Avoid reinforcing "general-goodness." Letters will create positive attention for the individuals identified in the memos, the overall customer-service message, and your department. You do not need to catch everything that happens, but you do need to catch most above-average things that happen. Start a campaign, look for these above-average things, and build on them to enhance your overall operation as well as your department.

Look at the company newsletter, too. These instruments offer a great opportunity to sell yourself, your department, and the customer-first messages you are pushing. Get to the editor, and you will likely find him or her cooperative. These type of company instruments are underused and are all too often filled with nothing more significant than recent births, deaths, or bowling scores. Help channel the content to hard business news. You will be offering a valuable service to the newsletter, yourself, and your mission. I know of one individual, one of five top paid executives of a billion-plus-in-sales company, who successfully delivered attention to his early achievements with the use of the company newsletter. One cannot get promoted without first being noticed by someone at a higher level.

Publish the following ideas in your company newsletter:

Customer Service Operation Reports Our Complaint Level Is Down by 25% This Year

"Everyone in the organization should be congratulated," said Customer-Service Director, Helen Jansen. "One year ago we identified selected key problem areas. We have been working with production and engineering through the year on eight key issues. The results are incredible. Working together, we have eliminated four major problems, which were producing most of our problems in the field."

Just what are those results? Consider this: Every complaint costs the company ($ amount) just to process the paper and get some answer to the customer. Our total market is very small. Our customers know each other well. In addition to hurting current business, we were also hurting our reputation in the field and therefore our future business . . .

Engineering Comes Up a Winner

Everyone was having a fine day two months ago when the phone rang on Ron Jackson's desk. The (product) launch was going well. Customers loved it; positive accolades and piles of orders were coming from everywhere.

We thought it couldn't happen. But then it did. "I was the one who ruined Ron's day," said Ted Smith, Director of Customer Service.

Over the past two years, the new product team had pumped endless hours into thinking of every contingency on every possible application for the new (product).

"Everyone was working closely together, and we had this one in the bag," said Smith. "But then it hit from nowhere. The customer called. She wanted to make a very large purchase of (product) and needed for it to perform with (application). We just never dreamed of this application," noted Smith. "But, then again, that's what our Customer First campaign is all about. It's about what we do when the unexpected happens. Ron and his people made it happen."

And how did Ron Jackson and his troops rise to the occasion? First a swat team was formed. With only two weeks to study the application, it was able to recommend . . .

On-Time Shipping Goals Reached: Customer Service Sends Special Thank-You Card to Sales Department

(Photo caption) The group photo includes everyone in customer service and manufacturing standing under the large "Thank You" banner.

Everyone knows it: Shipping what we promise to ship is a major part of keeping our total corporate promise and is critical for maintaining our reputation in the marketplace. "We wanted to ship products on the promised date 100 percent of the time," noted Michele King, Customer-Service Vice President. Customer Service established the goal two years ago and assigned a task force the responsibility for generating a road map which would ensure achievement of the goal.

"By the second meeting," noted King, "it was obvious that the goal was completely impossible to achieve without support from the sales force. We had to get salespeople talking with us about our basic values as an organization."

The task force had quickly concluded that creating the promise in the first place really occurred in two parts: first, internal processes needed to be sufficiently controlled so that we can do what we say we are going to do, and second, we should only promise to do what we can do. "Sales needed to be involved in the second part," commented King, "as it held the lead position in controlling the customer's expectation."

Sales jumped into the objective, and a cooperative relationship was established from the beginning. Sales wanted to be in the task force, too. The task force came up with six operational guidelines . . .

Use your trade press to build a following behind your department and your mission. Trade press is always looking for high-quality copy and industry expertise. With some effort, you can create both. Stories for the trade press are similar to those developed for the company newsletter, with some significant exceptions:

☎ Never sell your own company or yourself. The sure way to guarantee your story is not printed is to turn it into a sales pitch for your company. The article in the trade press is to inform the reader on critical things happening in the trade. Advertising in that magazine is for those trying to sell their respective companies.

☎ Always give something away. Give something to your customer through the article. Make it an educational "how to" piece. How should the customer do this or do that? How can the customer get more value, more good, more something? How can the reader get some additional gain from the industry?

☎ Make the article between 500 and 1,000 words. Keep the story line tight. If the topic is broad, discuss only one sliver. You can discuss other slivers in other articles.

☎ Sign your name with title and send a photo. Make one closing statement about your credentials: "Jane Smith is Customer Service Director at Apex company. The company is the world's largest supplier of wonder software." There is no guarantee your photo will be published. However, it might be. In sending the photo, you have nothing to lose and the possibility of something to gain.

You will need to sell your first few articles to the trade press. Call the editors, follow up with them, explain why they must print your articles, write them letters, go visit them, find out what they are featuring in which particular month. In short, keep pushing until you get four or five articles published. After you become known, they will start calling you, asking your opinion, quoting you in stories, and asking you to develop articles.

GETTING OFFICE SPACE WHEN NONE IS AVAILABLE

Office space and equipment is easier to get than you think. the simple answer is to not worry about it. If you need the people, and you have authorization to hire, bring them on the payroll. Be sure to notify the facilities allocation people that you are out of space. Tell them in writing what your needs are. List desks, computers, and so forth. Tell them when you will need the equipment. Be sure also to tell them that there is no space available within the existing walls of your office suite.

Facilities-planning folks may come back to you and simply state that there is no additional space available for your expansion plans. Be sure to notify your supervision if this occurs. Other than keeping people such as your boss informed, you can, essentially, ignore the protestations of the facilities-planning people. Leave them to solve their problems; you have your own to solve. Continue with your recruiting and hiring plans. Be sure to explain the space problem and your political limitations to potential recruits. It really is a good idea to give applicants this type of information and involve them in these or similar real-world issues. Watching their reaction to the information will help you judge their character. It tells you a lot if the applicant grimaces when you say his or her office will be in the swamp for the foreseeable future.

Sooner or later, you will find the person you want to hire. So hire him or her. Now there is a problem, which is fine. Problems must be solved. Judy Roy is ready to start work. Where are you going to put her? Call facilities people and tell them she will start on Monday and you want to know where she will be put temporarily while they work on the permanent solution. It makes no difference to you where she is put. The critical point is that there is a problem to solve. If she is put in the hallway temporarily, this is fine. Someone will have to put a desk, phone lines, computer, and so forth out there. She may be placed in the department next door. This, too, is fine. The issues still apply. Somehow, she will have to be tethered to your operation temporarily, all of which will cost money and efficiency. Sometimes, creating an issue is the only way to resolve an issue.

And what about that new piece of equipment you need and is approved? The same rules apply. Simply order whatever the equipment is and create a space issue, which must then be resolved. Don't be above stealing a bit of space, either. Be alert to the ever-shifting environment around you. Perhaps some department or other is moving. If so, "temporarily" borrow the vacated space for your people or needed equipment. Simply put them in the space. If someone complains, just tell them it is a temporary placement to alleviate a space problem and that you will move out just as soon as permanent space is found.

If your boss is the bottleneck, refusing to allocate needed space, be sure to let him or her know how much the decision is costing. You need this space for a reason. Somehow that needed space helps to increase sales, or reduce costs. Relate your need back to these two issues. For example, suppose you need the space for a simulator to train customers on operation of your new wonder product. If you train customers effectively, they will stop breaking your equipment, and your warranty expense will decrease. This would be exactly the argument you should make.

WHEN/HOW TO SOCIALIZE WITH SUBORDINATES

Socializing with your subordinates is a great idea. It is great for team building and morale. The general who can take the time to visit the first-line troops in the barracks will have a better fighting force on the battlefield.

Be sure not to play favorites. If someone on your staff calls a party for supervisors, be sure all supervisors are invited before attending yourself. If the party is for the entire department, be sure everyone has been invited before accepting an invitation yourself.

If you are having a party, invite everyone who works for you, or no one. Include spouses, and significant others. If you are only inviting office friends, make sure none of the office friends you invite is a direct subordinate.

Always migrate with the largest group as the party ebbs and flows. Mingle throughout the group. Don't allow yourself to get isolated and parked in a corner with one or two individuals. This might signal that you are cozying up to favorites. Be especially careful around those of the opposite sex. Rumors are always floating around and desperately trying to hook themselves to anything, either real or imagined. Do not discuss shop.

Consider a night on the town. Or sponsor an evening at a football game, or dinner at a favorite local restaurant. These events can all be "pay your own way" again, invite spouses, and do not discuss shop.

Picnics work well, too. Make the managers and supervisors run the grills for everyone else. Maybe you can find the dollars to cover these events in the departmental budget.

The etiquette is the same for all these events. The simple rules are:

☎ don't play favorites

☎ invite all or none

☎ don't isolate yourself with one or two folks

☎ don't talk shop

☎ invite spouses and significant others

Tip: Try a contest. Organize a baseball game. Challenge a sister department. But avoid contests that may be controversial; for example, don't organize an evening at the local gambling casino.

YOUR BOSS AND SUBORDINATE, MARRIED TO OTHERS, ARE HAVING AN AFFAIR: NOW WHAT?

Only the two people in the affair believe it is a secret from everyone else around them; it is not. Signals have been sent, and they were picked up on the office radar. The secret rendezvous was not secret. Everyone knows what is going on, some are already gossiping about it, but most are staying mum. Usually there is no real proof the affair is happening. The evidence is simply those signals we all understand so well. And everyone is well aware of the pickle you're in.

Your position is quite difficult; stay focused. In my training and consulting practice, I run into grumbling about these situations more often than you might think. From a theoretical perspective, the affair is not relevant, because it has nothing to do with the business. From a practical point of view, however, you have a management mess on your hands. Sooner or later, this situation is going to hurt productivity and people. The best you can do is prepare for the inevitable.

Pretend that you know nothing about it. Do not say anything about the affair to anyone, including your most trusted confidant. Why? Because you don't have a trusted confidant. They don't exist when these scenarios flair up. You cannot trust anyone within the company, or anyone outside the company who may speak to anyone within the company. The situation is just too juicy, and people love to talk. Be assured your long-term trusted confidant will speak to his or her long-term trusted confidant. Shortly, office radar will be targeted to your every move and all your thoughts. And everyone already knows your position is impossible. So stand above the fray. Let others oil the gossip mill, while you emerge as the leader.

Maintain a business-as-usual posture while watching your amorous subordinate very carefully. Keep him or her involved in meetings and other routine low-risk business activities. Cut him or her out of all sensitive or controversial discussions. Assume your subordinate takes everything you say directly to your boss.

This is a great time to do that much-needed cross-training you have been planning. No one knows what is going to happen when the affair boils over. Either one or both of these folks may be fired or might, because of all the embarrassment and commotion, leave willingly. Either your boss or his or her lover may go on extended sick leave or on unpaid absence. You can't, and shouldn't, worry about the boss, but be sure your amorous subordinate is backed up all the time. Train others in the department to cover for him or her.

Be careful around your boss as well. Avoid sensitive and controversial topics. Avoid anything you do not want your staff to know about. Assume everything said to the boss flows directly to the staff through his or her partner in the affair. Treat your boss as if everything were normal, and in no way should you discuss his or her partner. Certainly, don't criticize. If your boss asks about this particular subordinate, make sure you use general nondescriptive language to discuss performance. Comment only on work, not personality.

Get a little closer to your boss's boss. Don't mention the affair, but try to get closer. He or she may already know about the affair anyway and may be taking actions that cannot be shared with you. Your relationship with this person is going to be critical when the lid blows off the affair. Make sure he or she knows about the good job you are doing. Find ways to keep him or her informed of events in your department and the key issues you face.

It would be a good idea to get your subordinate transferred, if you can. Do some discreet inquiries, but be careful of messages that may flow back to the other half of this mess, your boss. Obviously, do not suggest to your boss that his or her lover should be transferred, but it certainly would be to your advantage if you can get some other manager to come after this person. Sell him or her to others, if you can.

After all is done to manage the department, just sit tight, act ignorant, ignore all gossip, conversations, or other inquiries on this subject. Remember, you need to stand above the crowd now to pick up the pieces later. If your boss's boss comes to you in private, just follow his or her lead.

This is about all you can do. When the pot boils over, don't participate in all the snickering and gossiping, even though there will be plenty of opportunity. Keep things moving; get the job done. Either your boss, subordinate or both will go. No matter who quits, is transferred, or is fired, you are in the best position to pick up the pieces if you stand above the mess and keep everyone else focused on work-related issues. You want to be remembered as the one who did not get involved in all the gossiping.

SUBORDINATES ARE HAVING AN AFFAIR

In the theoretical world, just as in the scenario above, this private relationship between consenting adults is technically none of anybody's business unless it affects job performance directly. However, there is a difference between the theoretical business-book world and the practical world of real work, productivity, customer service, and leadership. In the practical world, this relationship matters and will impact the department's productivity negatively. If it were possible for this affair to have no impact, you would not be aware of its existence in the first place. If you know about the affair, it is a problem, and you should take action.

Even if specific performance issues cannot be directly linked to the private liaison between these two, there will still be an impact on the organization. People working in the same department who also have a private relationship together will behave differently than people who interact only in the professional work environment. Even if these two try to hide the relationship, there will be noticeable differences. Others will become aware of the relationship. Rumors will start.

Do not discuss your observations with anyone. Your departmental confidants are especially off limits in this situation. Do not criticize the individuals in the relationship for having the affair. Remember, this is none of your business and has nothing to do with the work issues. Say nothing to anyone about it.

Create job-responsibility changes. Move both individuals to other jobs. Arrange for them to work in departments that are not closely related, preferably jobs in two different buildings. Arrange new responsibilities that do not require them to interact professionally. Be sure the affair can only continue during nonwork hours. Create some business reason for making these changes, and do allow either party a choice in the decision. Do not create punitive moves.

I recall one situation where a sales manager and an office secretary started a relationship. Both were single at the time and ultimately married one another. However, the courtship period was definitely noticeable and disruptive to the office. Everyone knew the relationship was growing. (Let's call the sales manager Tom and the secretary Pat.)

Tom was told his skills were needed in another division to help with planned sales growth. He interviewed for the job, evaluated its potential for his career, and turned it down. Some time later, the board chairman, an individual four or five levels above Tom, caught up with him for a quick hallway meeting. He got eyeball to eyeball with Tom and said something like: "Look, we really need for you to take that job. We need you there now, and I want you to take that job." Tom accepted the position.

Another job was ultimately found for Pat, too. The new jobs were in different buildings. No one was hurt, and the growing relationship could no longer interfere with company business.

What happens if you are in a smaller company and don't have the flexibility of moving people around? Or perhaps there are no other jobs available. This makes things much harder, but if no changes are made, the situation will ultimately hurt your operation. Even if these two divorce their existing mates and marry each other, your authority as manager will still be undermined. (Even when spouses share ownership of the same business, more frequently than not, management difficulties arise if they are both employed by that business.) It is to your advantage to end your working relationship with these individuals. Release both of them, but not at the same time. The simplest thing to do is release them from the payroll because of some real or imagined changes in the workload. Lay them off without cause and allow them to collect unemployment insurance. This action, of course, will cause your state insurance premium to rise. However, the higher rates may be the lowest-cost way out of this mess.

You could also release them for cause. But this will be a much harder thing to do. The relationship itself would not be a just cause for dismissal. To protect yourself, you will need specific work-related reasons. Waiting for performance to deteriorate could cost you more in terms of damage to the business than the higher unemployment insurance premium.

The worst of all actions would be to do nothing and hope the affair will simply go away. There is no simple way out of this situation.

DEALING WITH A SEXUAL MISSTEP

Work is over, and the holiday break starts tonight. Business is booming, and the team has been running flat out for months. Everyone is giddy. The day ends, and an impromptu party cranks up at the local pub. It's right across from the office, and all are in attendance.

The night is wild, the music is loud, the drinks are flowing. People are crowded in together, and it's just too intimate. That gorgeous one you hired last year is right there, all over you. It starts with a simple touch or two. It's not that big of a deal, but it happens. Then there is eye contact, the booze starts to talk, and, clearly, you both want more to happen. Given different circumstances, maybe something more would have happened, but, in the end, nothing does. Somehow, the brakes are applied, clothes stay on, you both cool down, and the night ends. Everyone goes home.

The holiday vacation goes by, and it's time for work again. The incident has been on your mind throughout the break. What are you going to say when you see him or her at work on Monday?

Go to the office, and go through your normal rituals. Don't bring the incident up to the subordinate involved or to anyone else. Don't apologize to him or her, or make any other personal overures. Don't do anything that could suggest to your subordinate that you are even aware the incident had occurred.

Maintain this posture from here on, manage your operation, and let time go by. The incident will fade, and life will go on. Next time, have one less drink.

But the subordinate may be uncomfortable. He or she may be worried about the image created and may come to you to apologize or to say something. What should you do then?

SUBORDINATE: Uh, look, I wanted to apologize for what happened during the party.

BOSS: Nothing happened. No reason to apologize for anything.

SUBORDINATE: Well, uh. But I was embarrassed by . . .

BOSS: I don't remember a thing. You have no reason to be embarrassed.

SUBORDINATE: (After a long pause.) Thanks.

BOSS: I need for you to look at the Richards account for us. What is happening with that . . . ?

The subordinate may also come to you and try to build on the incident. Here's a suggested response:

SUBORDINATE: I, uh, really enjoyed the party just before the holiday break.

BOSS: It was a lot of fun.

SUBORDINATE: Yeah. I especially liked the direction you and I started to take.

BOSS: Oh, gosh. Sometimes everyone just goes nuts. I need for you to look at the Richards account for us. What is happening with that . . . ?"

Maintain this position. Assuming he or she is a reasonably mature person, your subordinate will get the hint.

SOMEONE IS GETTING "TOO CLOSE" TO A SUBORDINATE

Not all of us share the same skills or perceptual processes. Management needs considerable style in dealing with the many individuals with diverse backgrounds who share modern work spaces. Someone will be working with the customers in the office. Someone else has the job of keeping the shop floor clean. Both individuals are needed to create a viable organization, and both need to earn a living. They need to work together, but it is unlikely that they will have other common interests. However, miscues can flair up quickly and can come from humble beginnings. Consider this possibility: Your young, attractive, well-spoken customer-service representative needs to be in the shop laboratories and product demonstration areas. She regularly escorts customers into the shop and spends time demonstrating equipment and processes. She also performs customer training in these shop areas. The shop laborer is performing his assigned tasks in the surrounding areas. (We'll call him Jerry.) Being the well-mannered person your customer-service representative is, she regularly offers a friendly greeting to Jerry when she sees him strolling about. Jerry is approximately her age, or perhaps a few years older, and totally misreads her casual greetings and intent.

And therein the problem starts. Jerry starts to say more than just hello. He starts hanging around the demonstration area, just watching and spending a lot of time around her. He stares. Jerry is fabricating issues, finding reasons to talk. Things are getting creepy.

Her sensors light up. She realizes her error, but it is too late. She was only being friendly, but Jerry has picked up the wrong message. Nervously, she comes to you for help.

You have a problem. She must continue working in the shop. This guy has not really done anything wrong. He has not violated any company policies. But still, you don't want anything to go wrong, either. You can go to Personnel and discuss the issue. This direct action, though, depends upon the competence of your personnel department. If it is good, it will appreciate the sensitivity of this thing and help you with strategy. If weak, Personnel may try a direct approach, which might make things worse. For example, they may elect to counsel Jerry directly about his behavior around your service representative. Using this direct approach could be a disaster. Jerry will surely know that your customer-service representative talked to someone. You can protect her reasonably well on company premises, but how can you protect her in the parking lots or on the way home from work? A more subtle approach may be better.

Let's keep things complex and assume your Personnel department is relatively weak. You must find some other communications channel.

To resolve this situation, a discreet approach is necessary. First, advise the rep to say nothing to Jerry, to ignore him as much as possible. If she sees him, she should, to the degree possible, walk away from him. She should not directly confront him in any way. If possible, keep her out of the shop area altogether for a week or so until you have time to sort out some action.

Information is power. Find out who this guy is. You can get his name from the customer-service representative. Get his department identification and employee number from Personnel. As a manager, you can finesse this. Go to Personnel and find a low-level records clerk in the back room. Do this personally; do not send a delegate. You don't want information to start spreading. Be authoritative. State that you need some departmental numbers. Give this clerk the laborer's name and ask for his record. You don't need anything in writing, just Jerry's clock number and department number. Find out who is responsible for his department. Get the information and then leave quickly. Don't raise any policy or procedure debates.

Now you need to select someone who has the ultimate responsibility for Jerry. Be careful who you select to help you. Do not go to Jerry's immediate supervisor. Jerry will probably be relatively low in the organization and his immediate supervisor will not be much help. Look three or four levels above Jerry's immediate supervisor. You want a fairly sophisticated manager to help you with this. Be careful who you select, as you are going to only get one shot at this. The person you select had better be pretty slick. If you select the wrong ally, you could make a mess.

"Cold call" the one you select. Walk into his or her office, close the door, and try something like this:

MANAGER: Jack, got a minute or two?

JACK: Just a few.

MANAGER: Do you know a fellow named Jerry? He's a laborer here in manufacturing and works over in department 123. He works for Dan Cortez. I've got his clock and department number. Here it is.

Drop the note with the name and numbers on Jack's desk. This demonstrates you can get information when it is necessary to do so, and that this is an important matter to you. Jack probably won't touch the note. Neither will he ask how you got this information or who else you have talked to. He knows the note is on his desk and what it says. Just leave it.

JACK: Yeah, I know him. He's mostly okay, only about a half-quart low. He does a little work for us, cleans up a bit. We pay him, and get something out of him. It's better than having him on welfare.

MANAGER: It's fine with me. But we seem to have a bit of a problem. Do you know that young woman, Betty, who works with us in Customer Service? She's been here about a year or so.

JACK: I've seen her around. Seems all right.

MANAGER: Jerry hangs around the training and demonstration area sometimes. I guess he's cleaning up around there and so on. Betty needs to spend time in that area.

Anyway, he says "hi" to Betty. She wants to be nice and returns the greeting. She greets him regularly; she doesn't want to ignore him just because he's a laborer. Things have been going on for a while, everybody just working and so on. Seems like Jerry is over at the demonstration area just about every time Betty is there now. Maybe Jerry's getting the wrong idea. Seems like he is spending a bit too much time around her. Seems he's trying to get too close.

JACK: Yeah, you have to watch these guys. I'll talk to his supervision. We'll have to get him back in line.

MANAGER: I don't want to go after him. Nothing is going to happen around here, we both know that. I'm worried about everywhere else, though. What about the parking lot? Maybe Jerry might stop by Betty's car just to say hello. Maybe he might follow her home to ask her out or something. He might get upset. I don't want to stir the pot. We've got to resolve this and keep Betty out of it. I don't want his supervision to know we're discussing this.

JACK: I'll go after his supervision. Jerry's out of his work area. It's his supervisor's responsibility to keep him in his work area and to make sure the job is done. He can't get the job done if he's not in his work area.

MANAGER: We've got to shield Betty.

JACK: He's out of his work area. Anybody can see that; I can see that just by walking around. I will have some people discuss the policies with his supervisor. Jerry's not allowed to wander all around the shop. It's policy that he stay in his work area. Something might happen, some emergency or something, and we may need his help quickly. We can't be running all over creation to find him. He must stay in his work area and support his own operation. That is what he is paid for. Besides, how can he get the job done if he is not in his work area?

Just sit there for a few moments and look at him. He won't move either. He will wait for your move. After a long pause, just get up and walk away. Leave the note. If you have been successful and you picked the right guy, he will also rise, grab the note, and shove it in his pocket. He, too, will likely walk out of his office. There is no reason to follow up with Jack further on this matter. Then speak to Betty. Later in the day try this:

MANAGER: Betty, tomorrow you can go back in the demonstration areas. It will be business as usual, and I don't think you will see much of Jerry. If you do, please let me know. Thanks for sharing your concerns with me.

There is no reason to share much more than this. She most likely won't ask for more, either.

Index

A

Abusive customer, 156-57
Action
  decisive action in response to call,
    26-28
  making promises to customers, 27-28
Additional charges, and customer-
  requested changes, 105-7
Advance payment, explanation about,
  76-78
Appearance, 232-35
  cleanliness factor, 233, 234
  and customer impressions, 234-35
  uniforms, 233-34
Automated Response Unit (ARU), 16-19
  design of system, 17-18
  educating customers about, 18
  and type of business, 18
  voice used for, 19
Automatic Call Distributor (ACD), reasons
    for use, 15

B

Bad news, presenting to boss, 384-85
Billing errors, incorrect customer bill,
  166-67
Bounced check, 178
Burn in of products, 59
Buying influences, and on-site service
    calls, 235

C

Call-management software, 24-25
Certification, and customer training,
    226-29

Closing call, 28
Coaching service representatives confi-
    dence building, 321-23
  in correct use of product, 318-19
  in customer involvement with
    progress reports, 327-30
  on improving technical performance,
    319-21
  to investigate problems, 325-27
  in research/learning, 323-25
  termination of poor performers,
    331-34
Collections
  for account fifteen days overdue,
    172-73
  for account sixty days after invoice
    date, 179-81
  for account thirty days overdue, 173,
    175-76
  aggressive tactics, 174-75
  bounced check, 178
  credit suspension, 185-87
  legal action, 190-91
  marginally late payments, 173-74
  missed installment payment, 177-78
  payment problems reported by
    customer, 176-77
  prevention of problems, 171-72
  repeated late payments, 185
  seriously delinquent account, 181-84
  stopping service, 187-89
Complaints
  bad replacement part, 140-41
  customer challenges to technician,
    147-48
  damaged product, 117-18
  defective product, 118-22
  disappointing performance of product,
    128-31